Access to Education for the Disabled

ACCESS TO EDUCATION FOR THE DISABLED

A Guide to Compliance
with Section 504 of the
Rehabilitation Act of 1973

by
Salome M. Heyward

McFarland & Company, Inc., Publishers
Jefferson, North Carolina, and London

British Library Cataloguing-in-Publication data are available

Library of Congress Cataloguing-in-Publication Data

Heyward, Salome M., 1953–
    Access to education for the disabled : a guide to compliance with
section 504 of the Rehabilitation Act of 1973 / by Salome M.
Heyward.
      p. cm.
    Includes bibliographical references and index.
    ISBN 0-89950-732-8 (sewn softcover: 50# alk. paper) ∞
    1. Handicapped children–Education–Law and legislation–United
States.   2. Architecture and the physically handicapped–Law and
legislation–United States. I. Title.
KF4210.H49 1992
344.73'07911–dc20
[347.3047911]   92-54090
                                                   CIP

Manufactured in the United States of America

McFarland & Company, Inc., Publishers
 Box 611, Jefferson, North Carolina 28640

Acknowledgments

I wish to express my appreciation and special thanks to the following individuals without whom this book would not have been completed:

Marianna, for invaluable assistance.

Lauren, Katie, and Mallie, for unwavering emotional support in the face of trying circumstances.

Paula, for editing, beyond the call of duty.

Jackie, for keeping my life in order . . . barely.

Emily, Audrey, and Madeline, for helping me to be four.

Julie, for psychological support.

Tara—*because* . . . I can.

Paul, for assisting in "Bubba building."

Doug, for aggravation.

Mom and Dad and all my friends, for putting up with me during the writing/birthing process.

Contents

Introduction

No otherwise qualified handicapped individual . . . shall, solely by reason of her or his handicap, be excluded from participation in, be denied the benefits of, or be subjected to discrimination. (Section 504 of the Rehabilitation Act of 1973, 29 U.S.C.A. § 794.)

How does one fashion effective compliance strategies in the educational arena? This is a concern of many of the individuals, agencies, and institutions that must comply with Section 504. One of the most difficult questions facing educators today is how to provide services to handicapped individuals in a manner that is both appropriate to their needs and responsive to financial realities. These realities often require educators to make decisions on the basis of the economic burdens involved, rather than on what is in the best interest of their students. Anyone who doubts the validity of this statement needs only to consider the rising number of complaints of discrimination being filed with federal agencies, the costly legal settlements that educational agencies and institutions are having to agree to, and the growing dissatisfaction regarding the delivery of services expressed by parents, educators, students, and handicapped individuals.

Section 504 is the mystery civil rights statute. Everyone seems to understand it in theory, but the practical application of its compliance standards continues to generate a great deal of confusion. This confusion is easy to appreciate when one considers the unique compliance problems the Rehabilitation Act (hereinafter, "the Act") presents. For example:

1. Compliance standards under the Act and the implementing regulation are not limited to mandates against discrimination, but also include a positive duty to make reasonable accommodations to meet the needs of "qualified" handicapped persons. Thus, unlike other civil rights statutes where the primary concern is eliminating consideration of personal characteristics—such as race, sex, or age, which are not legitimate eligibility criteria for participation in programs or services offered—under Section 504 there are circumstances under which personal characteristics—a particular person's handicap/disability—*must* be considered.

2. On the elementary and secondary school levels, recipients of federal funds are asked to serve two masters—Section 504 and the EHA[1]— two statutes so similar in scope and focus that it is difficult to place them in the proper perspective regarding enforcement responsibilities. The somewhat fuzzy relationship between the two has been a source of consternation for school districts and state agencies and the distinctions between them have eluded even the Supreme Court on several occasions.

3. The federal enforcement agency involved (the Office for Civil Rights) has not been particularly adept at presenting its policy interpretations and rulings on a national level.[2] As a result, since not all interested parties are privy to the same information regarding pertinent compliance issues, the perception has arisen that the agency is not properly performing its duty with respect to providing technical assistance, and is inconsistent in interpreting and enforcing the regulations.

Factors such as the ones described above have coalesced to produce confusion and conflicts that make compliance with Section 504 a difficult task at best, and, at worst, a nightmare of staggering proportions for all concerned.

This book presents an analytical approach to the field of disability discrimination law. It begins by focusing on the concept of civil rights compliance in general, and proceeds to a detailed examination of the unique compliance issues presented by Section 504 and its implementing regulations. We have discussed the pertinent provisions of the regulation from the perspective of participants in the field of education.[3] My purpose is to identify for the reader (a) the legal principles that form the basic compliance standards under the statute and regulations; (b) the controversies the resolution of which will dictate future development of the law; and (c) compliance strategies that are both consistent with legal principles and responsive to the legitimate concerns of educators and administrators. My goal was to present the information in a practical, usable fashion. To that end, I have attempted to keep the legal jargon to a minimum and to avoid indulging in purely theological legalistic discourse. The legal principles are discussed through the use of court cases and hypotheticals that reflect the issues and concerns faced daily in the educational arena.

A brief word about the Americans with Disabilities Act (ADA). For those of you who are attempting to reconcile your compliance responsibilities under Section 504 and those imposed by the ADA, the best place to start is to review the policies, practices and procedures which you adopted pursuant to Section 504. Since the ADA, in large measure, mirrors Section 504, if you are in compliance with Section 504, you are arguably in compliance with the ADA. However, the ADA's emphasis on employment and physical accessibility will require you to sharpen your existing compliance strategies.

In this text, we have limited our discussion to those few instances where it is clear that the ADA imposes different standards. Further, while the ADA uses the terms *disabled* and *disability,* in conformity with the language of Section 504 and its implementing regulations, the term *handicap* is used in this text.

Part I: The Evolution of Compliance Standards Under Section 504 of the Rehabilitation Act of 1973

Indeed, attempting to fit the problem of discrimination against the handicapped into the model remedy for race discrimination is akin to fitting a square peg in a round hole.
—*Garrity v. Gallen*, 522 F. Supp 171, 206
(D. New Hamp. 1981)

The history of compliance under Section 504 reflects a lack of understanding regarding the nature of civil rights statutes in general, and the mandates of Section 504 in particular. This part examines three important characteristics of civil rights statutes, as well as the factors that make Section 504 unique, and outlines the basic principles that form the foundation of compliance responsibilities under the Act and its implementing regulations.

1

Civil Rights Compliance Standards: Trying to Stand on Shifting Sand

Achieving compliance with civil rights statutes and regulations is a difficult, frequently confusing, and sometimes overwhelming task. One needs only to review the history of compliance under the Rehabilitation Act of 1973 to verify this fact.[1] A full 19 years after its passage, those responsible for complying with Section 504 of the Act are still vehemently arguing over basic issues.[2] Such issues include:

1. Who are "qualified handicapped persons"?
2. What are "reasonable accommodations"?
3. How does the enforcement agency exercise its rights to investigate charges of discrimination?
4. What does the responsibility to provide program access entail for the recipient of federal financial assistance?

Indeed, when one reviews most of the recent controversies regarding compliance with Section 504 and its implementing regulations, one begins to wonder whether any of the parties understand the plain meaning of the words used in those documents. Further, it is clear that there is general confusion regarding the basic principles that form the foundation of the legal mandates involved. What causes this confusion and the resulting conflicts? Who or what is responsible for the creation of this "compliance nightmare"? As with many problems, it is easier to identify those at fault than to isolate causes and find solutions. In this instance, all the parties must share the blame: (a) an enforcement agency (the OCR), which is unwilling or unable to provide clear and consistent guidance regarding the enforcement of the Act and its regulations; (b) educators and administrators who have used the issues of affirmative action and academic freedom to avoid fully complying with the Act; and (c) parents and advocacy groups who have attempted to turn the proscriptions of an antidiscrimination statute into a legal responsibility to provide preferential treatment. In order to understand fully this compliance nightmare, we must begin by analyzing the unique compliance problems that civil rights statutes and regulations pose.

Civil Rights Laws Are Imperfect

Statutes that seek to regulate actions that are taken because of discriminatory attitudes are troublesome in the extreme. They are by nature overly broad and, therefore, given to a considerable amount of subjective interpretation. There is a vast difference between a statute that prohibits driving faster than 55 miles per hour and one that prohibits discrimination on the basis of handicap or disability. In the first instance, one has an objective standard, a framework, whereby compliance is easily measured. Either a motorist did or did not exceed the allowable speed limit; the question is straightforward. On the other hand, determining whether one has violated a law that precludes discrimination is more complicated. The law states generally that discrimination on the basis of handicap is prohibited and provides examples of unlawful discriminatory acts. But, except for those examples, there are no clear-cut objective standards. It is virtually impossible to devise objective standards by which to assess actions or behavior that is the product of subjective emotional bias. Those who insist on such objectivity are destined to be disappointed and frustrated by the Act.

Civil Rights Compliance Standards Are "Fluid"

Compliance standards for civil rights laws must possess a certain degree of elasticity because of the inherent subjective nature of discrimination. The drafters of the regulations are not concerned with one or two impermissible acts, but rather with an infinite range of actions and decisions. They are, in essence, trying to devise standards that will reach all actions or decisions that can conceivably be influenced by unlawful discrimination. For example, the regulations provide that

> (a) (1) No qualified handicapped person shall, on the basis of handicap, be subjected to discrimination in employment.

and that

> (b) The provisions of this subpart apply to:
> (1) Recruitment, advertising, and the processing of applications for employment;
> (2) Hiring, upgrading, promotion, award of tenure, demotion, transfer, layoff, termination, right of return from layoff and rehiring;

(3) Rates of pay or any other form of compensation and changes in compensation;

(4) Job assignments, job classifications, organizational structures, position descriptions, lines of progression, and seniority lists;

(5) Leaves of absence, sick leave or any other leave;

(6) Fringe benefits . . .

(7) Selection and financial support for training . . .

(8) Employer-sponsored activities, including social or recreational programs; and

(9) Any other term, condition, or privilege of employment.[3]

Every policy/procedure in the employment arena appears to be covered. It is simply not possible, however, to outline specifically every single circumstance in which the question of discrimination might be an issue. Therefore, because an indefinite number of possibilities must be considered, the compliance standards used must provide for a significant degree of flexibility regarding interpretation. As a result, the mandates of the Act are couched in a maze of gray-area terms, e.g., "undue hardship," "substantially limits," "reasonable accommodation," and "readily accessible." These are phrases that lend themselves to a variety of interpretations when applied to real-world situations, and that people can argue about vehemently. They mean little or nothing in a vacuum.

The question of whether actions are based upon unlawful discrimination or are legitimate and nondiscriminatory can be answered only by analyzing the facts of each individual case. Overall, it is a "reasonable person" compliance standard. Would a reasonable person, after reviewing the facts of the case, conclude that discrimination occurred? What would a reasonable person conclude that the terms "undue hardship," "substantially limits," "reasonable accommodation," etc., mean under the circumstances in question? That there are no concrete definitions to hang a hat on is a source of enormous frustration for those who want the law to state specifically and succinctly what is and is not unlawful discrimination. The Court in *Dexler v. Tisch* aptly described the problem by noting that "no standard for determining the reasonableness of an accommodation has been formulated."[4] Further, the drafters of the regulations concluded that it was not "possible" to define the term "substantially limits."[5] The question of what is reasonable "must be decided on a case-by-case basis."[6]

Successful Compliance Requires Compromise

Successful compliance can rarely be achieved through a rigid adherence to the *written* word of the statute and the regulations. Issues generally cannot be reduced to a choice between black and white, and the answer to what is lawful or unlawful often falls in a disturbingly wide gray area. Therefore, one must adhere to the spirit as well as the letter of the law. As noted by the Supreme Court, a balance must be struck between "the rights of handicapped individuals to be integrated into society and the legitimate interest of [service providers and employers] in preserving the integrity of their programs."[7] One must be willing to compromise to strike this balance. When faced with questions of compliance, it is a mistake to begin an inquiry by asking whether the law requires a particular action. When one begins by asking whether the law mandates that a particular action be taken, one has already assumed an adversarial posture. The issue has been reduced to "Do we have to do it?" This is an oversimplification of the problem and often leads to arguments regarding competing interpretations of gray-area words and phrases found in the regulations.

A more fruitful approach to conflict resolution is to ask whether there is a way of providing meaningful access to the handicapped while at the same time protecting the integrity of the program. Asking this question allows one to see both sides of the issues and be open to alternatives that will address the needs of all parties. With one approach one is saying to the opponent, "Let's try to work it out"; with the other one is saying, "Let's fight."

Consider the following hypothetical as an illustration.

> Kathy falls and injures her back while at work. She is unable to work for over two months. Upon her return, she provides her employer with a statement from her doctor which says she can no longer sit for long periods of time or climb stairs. Kathy requests a meeting with her supervisor to discuss restructuring her job.
>
> **Scenario One:** The company attorney starts the meeting by stating that in his review of the law he did not find any regulatory provision or court decision that required the company to restructure Kathy's job if she can no longer perform her duties. A heated discussion follows between the company's attorney and Kathy's representative regarding this interpretation of the requirements of the Act and regarding general concepts such as "essential functions" of the job, "reasonable accommodations," etc. Very little time is spent trying to fashion a workable solution to Kathy's problem.
>
> **Scenario Two:** The attorney starts the meeting by asking Kathy what she has in mind regarding job restructuring. She states that she needs a straight-back chair and to be allowed to use the building elevator. She also needs to be permitted to take regular breaks. Kathy's supervisor has no problem with her use of the chair and the elevator, and, after some discussion, it is agreed that Kathy will be permitted to take two fifteen-minute breaks in addition to those provided all employees, and shorter breaks, as needed, so long as she completes her assignments in a timely fashion.

As one can see, the opening question (or statement) is vitally important. Often it will mean the difference between successful resolution and protracted litigation.

Individuals have trouble complying with civil rights statutes because they fail to fully comprehend the importance of the factors discussed above. They approach compliance with a rigid, follow-the-letter-of-the-law posture and often fall into what I have labeled a "minimalist approach to compliance," coupled with a "floodgate mentality." For example:

> Susan, a hearing-impaired student, is a graduate student in engineering. She is of the opinion that the interpreters normally provided are not acceptable because they are not familiar with the technical language used, and, as a result, she would not be able to fully participate in her classes. She requests an interpreter who is familiar with engineering terminology and concepts. Such an individual would cost $10 an hour more. The director of Handicapped Student Services is concerned about the impact the additional expense will have on his budget, and the Section 504 coordinator is unsure of the college's legal responsibilities. The president calls in the university attorney, who spends most of her time dealing with property and employment issues and who, in the past, has depended upon the 504 coordinator for guidance regarding Section 504 issues. The attorney advises the president to consider the matter very carefully, because if he gives in to Susan's request it will open the floodgates and other students will request the same service; once he says "yes" to one student, he can't say "no" to others. She reminds the president of the tremendous cost involved if "all those students" request the service. Suddenly, the president is not concerned with providing Susan an interpreter; he's concerned about all those other students and the hundreds of thousands of dollars it will cost to provide them interpreters. Of course, he must protect his institution from this group of marauding students who are seeking to bring it to the brink of financial doom. He announces that there will be no interpreter for Susan.

The difficulty with this approach is that it is not conducive to negotiation and compromise and frequently turns a small problem into a major controversy. Thus, those faced with the responsibility of complying with civil rights statutes, such as Section 504, should approach their task with the following points in mind:

1. There are very few concrete principles. The question is whether a reasonable person would conclude that unlawful discrimination has occurred.
2. Compromise must be uppermost in one's mind. The rights of the individual must be balanced against the duty to preserve the integrity of the program/service.
3. The spirit of the law must be adhered to, as well as the letter of the law.

2
Nondiscrimination Versus Affirmative Action

Section 504 is not a particularly lengthy or complicated piece of legislation. It provides in pertinent part:

> No otherwise qualified handicapped individual in the United States, as defined in section 706(7) of this title, shall, solely by reason of his handicap, be excluded from participation in, be denied the benefits of, or be subjected to discrimination under any program or activity receiving federal financial assistance.[1]

It is an antidiscrimination statute. Succinctly put, it prohibits recipients of federal financial assistance from discriminating against "otherwise qualified" handicapped individuals. But what does this mean in plain English? How does one determine which actions are discriminatory when, clearly, there are circumstances under which a person's disability may preclude that person from meeting "legitimate" program requirements?[2] To answer these questions, one must understand the proper connection between the concepts of an "otherwise qualified" handicapped individual and illegal discrimination. The Supreme Court has stated that "the question of who is 'otherwise qualified' and what actions constitute 'discrimination' under the Section would seem to be two sides of a single coin."[3] Thus, when analyzing a recipient's decision not to provide access to a handicapped person, the issue can be framed as follows:

> *Was the denial a discriminatory act?*
> *Or was the denial based upon the fact that the individual was not "otherwise qualified"?*

The Supreme Court has defined the issue as unlawful discrimination versus affirmative action; that is, recipients are prohibited from discriminating but not required to take affirmative action. The Court has further held that one distinguishes between these two legal mandates by conducting an individualized inquiry which balances the rights of the handicapped against

7

the legitimate interests of recipients.[4] Since a significant number of the controversies that arise under Section 504 and its implementing regulations involve a failure to understand this distinction, it is imperative to have at least a nodding acquaintance with all the issues involved.

The Court introduced the affirmative action–unlawful discrimination dichotomy in *Southeastern Community College v. Davis*, its initial ruling under Section 504 and its implementing regulations. In *Davis* the Court sought to answer the question of

> Whether § 504 of the Rehabilitation Act of 1973, which prohibits discrimination against an "otherwise qualified handicapped individual" in federally funded programs "solely by reason of his handicap," forbids professional schools from imposing physical qualifications for admission to their clinical training programs.[5]

In ruling that the school was not required either to admit a student whose physical limitations prevented her from safely participating in the program, or to modify its program by providing the student with individual supervision or eliminating clinical coursework, the Court stated, regarding the compliance standard under Section 504, that

> Section 504 by its terms does not compel educational institutions to disregard the disabilities of handicapped individuals or to make substantial modifications in their programs.
>
> [N]either the language, purpose, nor history of § 504 reveals an intent to impose an affirmative-action obligation. (*Id.* at 405, 411.)
>
> It is possible to envision situations where an insistence on continuing past requirements and practices might arbitrarily deprive genuinely qualified handicapped persons of the opportunity to participate in a covered program. . . . Thus, situations may arise where a refusal to modify an existing program might become unreasonable and discriminatory. (*Id.* at 411–13.)

Thus, the test after the *Davis* decision for determining whether access should be provided was

> If substantial modification or fundamental alteration of the program is required or an undue financial and administrative burden was involved, it represents an impermissible attempt to impose an affirmative action obligation.
>
> If, however, the modification did not rise to those levels, *i.e.,* "substantial," "fundamental," or "undue burden," a refusal to provide access would be considered unreasonable and discriminatory.

The problem with this compliance standard is that if strictly applied, it would make it nearly impossible to accomplish the congressional goal of fully integrating handicapped individuals into American society.[6] This congressional mandate would certainly place demands on recipients which could arguably be classified as "affirmative." Where does the duty to remove obstacles to the full participation of handicapped individuals fit in this dichotomy?[7] It is interesting that even the Court acknowledged that the task of distinguishing between the two would be a difficult one.

> We do not suggest that the line between a lawful refusal to extend affirmative action and illegal discrimination against handicapped persons always will be clear. (*Id.* at 412.)

This is something of an understatement given the number of vague words and phrases that were used, e.g., "substantial," "fundamental," "undue burden," and "unreasonable." The Court responded to the confusion created by its *Davis* ruling by seeking to clarify the matter in *Alexander v. Choate*:

> In *Davis,* we stated that § 504 does not impose an "affirmative-action obligation on all recipients of federal funds" . . . Our use of the term "affirmative action" in this context has been severely criticized for failing to appreciate the difference between affirmative action and reasonable accommodation . . . [R]egardless of the aptness of our choice of words in *Davis,* it is clear from the context of *Davis* that the term "affirmative action" referred to those "changes," "adjustments," or "modifications" to existing programs that would be "substantial" . . . or that would constitute "fundamental alteration[s]" in the nature of a program . . . rather than to those charges that would be reasonable accommodations. (*Id.* at 300–301 n.20.)

The Court restated the *Davis* standard as follows:

> *Davis* thus struck a balance between the statutory rights of the handicapped to be integrated into the society and the legitimate interests of federal grantees in preserving the integrity of their programs: while a grantee need not be required to make "fundamental or substantial" modifications to accommodate the handicapped, it may be required to make "reasonable" ones. . . . The balance struck in *Davis* requires that an otherwise qualified handicapped individual must be provided with meaningful access to the benefit that the grantee offers.
> [T]o assure meaningful access, reasonable accommodations in the grantee's program or benefit may have to be made. (*Id.* at 300–301.)

So after *Alexander,* we retain our "limiting adjectives" (substantial, fundamental, undue and unreasonable) and add the following clarification:

> Recipients must make reasonable accommodations if they are necessary to provide meaningful access to the programs, services or benefits offered.

With *Alexander* and *Davis,* the Court established

[A] continuum in which some modest modifications may be necessary to avoid discrimination but other more substantial modifications are not required by section 504.[8]

The Court further refined the standard, in the *School Board of Nassau County v. Arline,* by stating that the question of whether a person is otherwise qualified required "an individualized inquiry."[9] *One must balance the competing interests involved to properly characterize an action as either affirmative action or illegal discrimination.*

As our analysis of the pertinent Supreme Court decisions reflects, this question of whether a proposed action represents affirmative action or discrimination is not an easy one to resolve. "There is no bright line separating those who are 'qualified' and those who are not."[10] The compliance standard outlined by the Court has five important components:

1. The Act does not impose an affirmative-action obligation.
2. Recipients need not make accommodations which would require fundamental or substantial modifications of the program or result in undue financial and administrative burdens.
3. Refusal to provide reasonable accommodation is discriminatory.
4. "Otherwise qualified" handicapped individuals must be provided meaningful access, and to ensure such, reasonable accommodations may have to be made.

AND

5. an individualized inquiry which balances the rights of the handicapped individual to be provided access against the interest of the recipient in protecting the integrity of its program must be conducted.

As noted by the Court in *Alexander,* "the ultimate question is the extent to which a grantee is required to make reasonable modifications in its programs for the needs of the handicapped."[11] What the Court has created, in essence, is a system of checks and balances. It is a recognition of the fact that what is involved is not a matter of absolute rights and responsibilities, but rather of legitimate interests on both sides. It requires, with respect to each case, that a determination be made regarding whose interest is most in need of protection. It is clear that the fifth component is the most important part of the five compliance standards. One cannot resolve the discrimination vs. affirmative action dilemma unless one performs the individual inquiry described in component five.

Unfortunately, the fifth component is the compliance standard that is most often ignored in the face of conflict. Generally a handicapped individual is on one side—insisting upon being accommodated and yelling about discrimination, and a recipient is on the other side—refusing the accommodation and yelling about affirmative action. It is the legal equivalent of, "Is it live or is it Memorex?" The real problem is that the parties are arguing about *absolute* rights and responsibilities where there *are* no absolutes. The necessary balance of interests is reduced to little more than a knee-jerk argument in the never-ending battle between handicapped individuals and recipients. It is an oversimplification of the compliance standard that distorts the legal requirements.

As a result of this distortion, some rather imaginative arguments have been made to limit the authority of Section 504 and its implementing regulations. Specifically:

1. The implementing regulations are invalid in whole or in part because they require affirmative action.[12]
2. The recipient need not come forward with the necessary evidence to support the denial of a requested accommodation until the handicapped individual clearly establishes that he or she is an "otherwise qualified" individual.[13]
3. The decisions of administrators and educators are entitled to absolute judicial deference. Recipients must be free to make purely academic decisions without judicial interference.[14]

These arguments constitute a rather broad attempt to relieve recipients of responsibility under the Act and implementing regulations, and, as such, have led to troublesome compliance problems for recipients who utilize them. Each of these arguments ignores important pronouncements by the Supreme Court regarding the compliance standards under Section 504.

"The Regulations Are Invalid"

While the Court in *Davis* did acknowledge that an interpretation of the regulations that required affirmative action "would raise grave doubts about their validity,"[15] it has consistently maintained that the regulations and the interpretations of the enforcement agency are entitled to great deference:

> Identification of those instances where a refusal to accommodate the needs of a disabled person amounts to discrimination against the handicapped continues to be an important responsibility of HEW.[16]
>
> This Court generally has deferred to contemporaneous regulations issued by the agency responsible for implementing a congressional enactment. . . . The regulations particularly merit deference in the present case: the responsible congressional committees participated in their formulation, and both these committees and Congress itself endorsed the regulations in their final form.[17]

> We have previously recognized these regulations as an important source
> of guidance on the meaning of § 504.[18]

Thus, the Court has repeatedly upheld the validity of the regulations and the
importance of the enforcement agency's interpretation. Therefore, to have
any hope of success, an attack on the validity of the regulations must be a
narrowly focused attack which questions specific agency actions or interpretations regarding a specific issue(s) rather than a general attack on the
validity of the regulations as a whole.

"Otherwise Qualified"

The argument that the recipient need not take any action until the individual
establishes that he/she is "otherwise qualified" ignores the connection between the otherwise-qualified question and the discrimination question. As
noted by the court in *Alexander,* one question cannot be answered without
answering the other as well:

> *Davis* addressed that portion of § 504 which requires that a handicapped
> individual be "otherwise qualified" before the nondiscrimination principle
> of § 504 becomes relevant. However, the question of who is "otherwise
> qualified" and what actions constitute "discrimination" under the section
> would seem to be two sides of a single coin; the ultimate question is the ex-
> tent to which a grantee is required to make reasonable modifications in its
> programs for the needs of the handicapped. (*Id.* at 299.)

In *Wynne v. Tufts University School of Medicine,* the Court of Appeals held
that the university had an obligation to provide reasonable accommodations
and rejected its claim that it was entitled to judgment because the complainant had failed to establish that he was an "otherwise qualified" handicapped individual.[19] Further, as noted by the Court in *Brennan v. Stewart,*
the question of whether an individual meets the "otherwise qualified" requirement of Section 504 does not end if the individual cannot initially meet
the program requirements.[20] The question of whether there is a reasonable
accommodation which will allow the individual to participate is "part of the
'otherwise qualified' inquiry."[21] Thus, recipients will not be permitted to
avoid their responsibility to determine whether a reasonable accommodation exists.[22]

"Judicial Deference"

The Court has recognized that the decisions of educators are entitled to
deference.[23] However, the deference afforded is not absolute.[24] The Supreme

Court specifically endorsed the following standard regarding proper judicial deference in *Arline:*[25]

> A handicapped individual who cannot meet all of a program's requirements is not otherwise qualified if there is a *factual basis in the record reasonably demonstrating* that accommodating that individual would require either a modification of the essential nature of the program, or impose an undue burden. (emphasis added)[26]

Assertions of academic freedom and the right to deference will not be honored in the absence of evidence that supports the recipient's decision. The Court in *Wynne v. Tufts University* made the point quite eloquently when concluding that the mere statement of the dean of the medical school was insufficient to support the denial of accommodation to a student:

> [T]here is a real obligation on the academic institution to seek suitable means of reasonably accommodating a handicapped person and to submit a factual record indicating that it conscientiously carried out this statutory obligation. (*Wynne v. Tufts University, supra* at 16.)

Regarding the Dean's affidavit, the Court noted:

> There is no mention of any consideration of possible alternatives, nor reference to any discussion of the unique qualities of multiple-choice examinations. There is no indication of who took part in the decision or when it was made. Were the simple conclusory averment of the head of an institution to suffice, there would be no way of ascertaining whether the institution had made a professional effort to evaluate possible ways of accommodating a handicapped student. (*Id.* at 21.)

Recipients must provide compelling evidence to support decisions which result in a denial of access to handicapped individuals. As the preceding discussion reflects, the distinction between affirmative action and illegal discrimination is a fuzzy one at best. Examples of circumstances where the courts have declined to require recipients to take affirmative action include residential placements for handicapped students, admission of profoundly retarded students to a state school for which they did not meet the admissions requirements, elimination of graduation criteria, and modifications to provide access to public transportation.[27] Courts have rejected the affirmative action argument and maintained that Section 504 required that affirmative steps be taken regarding the following issues: the enforcement agency's authority to conduct investigations, residential placement for a handicapped student, the need to provide reasonable accommodations, and the validity of the auxiliary aid provision (§ 104.44[d]).[28]

3
The Recipient's Obligation

The uncertainty which recipients express regarding their obligations under Section 504 and its implementing regulations is to some degree justified. Although Section 504 is patterned after and similar to other nondiscrimination statutes and regulations,[1] there are interesting twists that make compliance under the statute and regulations a little more difficult to conceptualize. Under other antidiscrimination statutes the primary purpose is to eliminate differential treatment on the basis of race, sex, national origin, age, etc. The recipient is admonished to create a homogenous environment, and under few circumstances is it permissible to treat members of the protected class differently. However, under Section 504 there are two distinct responsibilities: the recipient must (a) treat handicapped individuals the same as similarly situated nonhandicapped individuals and (b) consider and address the unique needs of "otherwise qualified" handicapped individuals. Furthermore, while the statute "forbids discrimination based on stereotypes about a handicap," it does not "forbid decisions based on the actual attributes of the handicap."[2]

Recipients are no longer functioning in the color-blind/gender-free "uniform" environment they are familiar with, but rather in a hybrid environment where they can consider a person's handicap in determining eligibility, cannot discriminate against otherwise qualified handicapped individuals, and must accommodate the unique needs of handicapped individuals if that is necessary to provide "effective" benefits or services.[3] Suddenly the prohibition against discrimination on the basis of handicap begins to take on a foreboding air. The Court in *Garrity v. Gallen* accurately described the problem of trying to reconcile the mandates of Section 504 with other antidiscrimination statutes.

> [T]he Title VI [race] and Title IX [sex] models were not automatically adaptable to the problem of discrimination against the handicapped, but involved a very different analytical undertaking. Indeed, attempting to fit the problem of discrimination against the handicapped into the model remedy for race discrimination is akin to fitting a square peg into a round hole, as revealed by the regulation's numerous exceptions and exemptions to the sweeping nondiscrimination statute.[4]

14

This chapter attempts to isolate the basic principles which form the foundation of compliance responsibilities under Section 504 and its implementing regulations. Hopefully, it will assist one in understanding those "numerous exceptions and exemptions."

There are two primary compliance responsibilities under the Act: the duty not to discriminate against qualified handicapped persons, and the duty to provide meaningful access to the programs, services, or benefits offered. The nondiscrimination mandate requires that handicapped individuals be treated in the same manner as similarly situated nonhandicapped persons.[5] Thus, it would be unlawful discrimination to deny enrollment in a program to a student who has excellent credentials and meets established admission requirements solely because he has multiple sclerosis.[6]

Remember: it is not unlawful discrimination to consider an individual's handicap in determining his or her eligibility if it is relevant to participation in the program or activity in question. Recipients are not precluded from requiring that a handicapped individual meets "legitimate physical qualifications," nor are they required to ignore the "limitations which result from the handicap."[7] Mere consideration of an individual's handicap does not automatically trigger a finding of a violation under the implementing regulations. "The pivotal issue is not whether the handicap was considered, but whether under all of the circumstances it provides a reasonable basis for finding the plaintiff not to be qualified."[8]

Meaningful access has been provided if handicapped individuals are placed in the position to use, enjoy, and participate in programs or services to the same extent or degree as nonhandicapped individuals. An institution has not provided meaningful access if it makes its library accessible to students in wheelchairs by ramping the entrance, but fails to provide a way for them to utilize library materials housed on the second floor, or provides access to the materials for only one hour a day, whereas nondisabled students have access to them for eight to ten hours daily.[9]

Although most people understand the legal obligations described above as separate compliance standards, they often fail to understand how they are interrelated. It is impermissible to treat qualified handicapped individuals differently—nondiscrimination mandate—*except* insofar as it is necessary in order to provide them with meaningful access.[10] For example:

> A company has a summer job training program in which any employee who has worked for the company for six months or more is permitted to participate. Those who complete the program make up the applicant pool for promotions within the company. Jim, a dyslexic who has worked for the company for two years, applies for the summer program. Jim's supervisor, while noting that he is a good, conscientious employee, feels that he is slow

in learning new tasks and, therefore, recommends that he be given a test to measure his aptitude for promotion. Further, he recommends that if the test indicates deficiencies, a special course be developed that Jim would be required to complete before being permitted to participate in the summer program.

A school district has a policy of not providing transportation services for after-school activities. Is it permissible for the district to refuse to provide transportation services to a handicapped student who must stay after school to receive physical therapy services which the district has identified as being a necessary part of her educational program?

As noted, the recipient is warranted in providing different or separate service only when it is necessary for the provision of equal access to the services, programs, or benefits offered. The student who needs transportation services after school is entitled to them, because the district has determined that physical therapy services are necessary for her to benefit from her educational program. If she is denied transportation, she is denied full educational services. She should not be penalized because the district is unable to provide complete educational services to her during the regular school day. In Jim's case, separate services are not necessary to provide access. The only requirement for participation in the program is six months of continuous service. Jim meets that criteria. Jim's supervisor may have good intentions in seeking to provide him with additional training, but it has not been demonstrated that Jim is any less qualified to participate in the program than other employees. *Remember*: the need to provide "meaningful access" to a "qualified handicapped/disabled individual" is the only thing that justifies differential treatment.

One of the questions most commonly asked regarding the enforcement of Section 504 is: Isn't it unfair to nonhandicapped persons? This question more than any other indicates a lack of understanding regarding the concepts of nondiscrimination and preferential treatment. The Act does not require preferential treatment. As noted by the Court in *P.C. v. McLaughlin*

> The "clearly established law" concerning § 504 indicates that its central purpose is to assure that handicapped individuals receive "evenhanded treatment" in relation to the nonhandicapped.... The Act does not require all handicapped persons to be provided with identical benefits.... Rather, it seeks to ensure that handicapped individuals have an opportunity to participate in and benefit from programs receiving federal assistance.[11]

What one must do under the Act is strike a balance between "the rights of handicapped individuals to be integrated into society and the legitimate interests of [service providers, employers, etc.] in preserving the integrity of their programs."[12] The goal is to place handicapped individuals in an equitable position as compared to the nonhandicapped.[13] The parameters of the legal mandates can best be understood by using a rather simple illustration. Visualize a group of individuals competing in a one hundred-meter race. The only criterion for participating in the race is to be at least 18 years old. One of the competitors is at a disadvantage because he or she has no shoes. How does one ensure that each competitor has an equal opportunity to compete? Certainly the answer is not to punish the disadvantaged competitor by refusing to allow him or her to compete (discrimination), nor is it to give him or her a ten-meter head start (preferential treatment). The solution is to lend the competitor a pair of shoes so that he or she has an equal opportunity to compete (meaningful access). This is the balance that must always be struck. Do not change the rules of the game or guarantee results; just make sure everyone who is qualified has the opporunity to play.

The principles listed below are also important components of the compliance standards of Section 504.

1. Recipients of federal financial assistance are required to comply with Section 504 and its implementing regulations. The "program or activity that receives or benefits from such assistance" refers to all operations of the recipient, not just the specific program which receives the assistance. *De Vargas v. Mason & Hanger-Silas Mason Co.,* 911 F.2d 1377 (10th Cir. 1990).
2. Blanket policies and procedures that are applied to handicapped individuals as a class are suspect. The regulations require individualized consideration of the skills, abilities and needs of each handicapped person. *Arline, supra.*
3. The compliance standard under Section 504 is "reasonableness." "What is considered to be 'reasonable' must be decided on a case-by-case basis." *Nathanson, supra* at 1385.
4. Recipients are required to address or accommodate only handicapped conditions of which they have knowledge, or of which they could reasonably be expected to have knowledge. *Nathanson, supra* at 1381.
5. Neither the courts nor the enforcement agency will interject themselves into controversies that are purely matters of educational methodology. *Regents of University of Michigan v. Ewing, supra.*
6. "Actions challenged as discriminatory must be given rigorous scrutiny." *Jacobson v. Delta Airlines,* 742 F.2d 1202, 1205 (9th Cir. 1984).
7. Section 504 does not prohibit the consideration of an individual's handicap if it is relevant to legitimate program requirements or eligibility standards. *Davis, supra* at 407.
8. "[T]he ultimate question is the extent to which a grantee is required to make reasonable modifications in its programs for the needs of the handicapped." *Alexander v. Choate, supra* at 299, n. 19.

9. Only "otherwise qualified" handicapped individuals are entitled to protection under the Act and the implementing regulations.
10. The decisions of recipients regarding the provision of services to handicapped persons are entitled to deference if there is a "factual basis in the record" that reasonably supports them. *Strathie v. Department of Transportation, supra* at 231.

Part II: An Overview of Section 504 of the Rehabilitation Act

Congress passed § 504 to encourage treatment of the handicapped on the basis of individualized assessment of ability; ironically, however, the legislation has had the effect of forcing federal courts . . . to draw broad and imprecise classifications of handicaps.
—Garrity v. Gallen, 522 F. Supp. 171, 206
(D. New Hamp. 1981)

This part discusses the pertinent provision of Subpart A of the regulations. Subpart A includes definitions of such terms as "handicap" and "qualified handicapped person," as well as a listing of the specific acts of discrimination prohibited by the Act. Many of the words and phrases defined are those "gray area" words or "limiting adjectives" discussed in Chapter 1. Examples are presented of how these words and phrases have been interpreted by courts and the enforcement agency. *Remember:* the compliance standard is "reasonableness," and as a result case-by-case determinations are required.

4

Who Must Comply:
The Meaning of "Recipient"
and "Federal Financial Assistance"

Section 104.1 provides that the purpose of the regulations is

> [T]o effectuate section 504 of the Rehabilitation Act of 1973, which is de-
> signed to eliminate discrimination on the basis of handicap in any program
> or activity receiving federal financial assistance.

In order to trigger the obligation to comply with the Act and the regulations,
the person or entity must be a recipient of federal financial assistance.[1] In
this chapter we will look at the meaning of the terms "recipient" and "federal
financial assistance" and the nature of the obligation imposed upon
recipients.

Recipients

How does one identify a recipient? Is the term limited to those who receive
federal assistance directly or does it apply to all persons or entities who
benefit from the use of said federal financial assistance? To answer these
questions, one must understand how the following phrases have been interpreted by the courts: (a) "any program or activity receiving federal financial
assistance"; (b) "benefits from such assistance"; and (c) "assistance . . . extended directly or through another recipient." These phrases define the
jurisdictional authority of the enforcement agency. Does a literal application
of the phrase "program or activity receiving federal financial assistance" too
severely limit the ability of the agency to address discriminatory practices
and procedures? Do the phrases "benefits from" and "extended directly or
through another recipient" permit the enforcement agency to assert jurisdiction once any person or entity comes in contact with federal financial
assistance, no matter how tenuous the connection? These questions concern

the degree to which the enforcement agency may become involved in both the internal and external operations of entities that are in some way connected with the flow of federal financial assistance.

"Program or Activity"

> A teachers college operates a weekend program for school-age children. The program is used to train student teachers. While some programs at the college are recipients of federal financial assistance, the weekend program does not receive federal funds. The college refuses to accept handicapped students in the weekend program because it feels the extra expense of serving handicapped children is prohibitive. The college argues that the weekend program is not subject to the requirements of Section 504, because the program is self-supporting and not a recipient. Is the college's position correct?

This case would have raised considerable debate over the issue of whether the weekend program was a "program or activity receiving federal financial assistance" in light of the Supreme Court's rulings in *Grove City College v. Bell* and *Consolidated Rail Corporation v. Darrone*.[2] In those cases the Court held that the Title IX and Section 504 prohibition against discrimination in any program or activity receiving federal financial assistance "only addressed discrimination . . . in the particular program or activity specifically supported by federal funds." (*Id.* at 570–76). The Court interpreted the regulations as imposing a program-specific requirement with respect to discriminatory policies and procedures.[3] Under these holdings, it would have been insufficient to establish merely that a program operated by a college receiving federal financial assistance had a discriminatory admission policy; it would have also been necessary to show that the specific program was a recipient of federal financial assistance.[4]

This intolerable and often impossible burden was removed by the passage of the Civil Rights Restoration Act of 1987, Pub. L. 100-259, 102 Stat. 28 (1988). It provides, in pertinent part, that "the term 'program or activity' means *all of the operations of*" the entity in question [emphasis added].[5] The Restoration Act provides for institution-wide coverage if any component of the entity receives assistance, thus eliminating the need to trace federal financial assistance to a specific program or activity. Therefore, the enforcement agency would have jurisdiction over the admissions practices in the weekend program. Further, the OCR has determined that such a program

> [I]s an integral part of the postsecondary education program operated by the recipient. Even though the program is self-supporting, the college provides the teachers and facilities for the program, and its students teach in the program as part of the graduation requirements.[6]

However, an issue that remains open regarding the program-specific requirements of *Grove City* and *Darrone* is whether the institution-wide standard set forth in the Restoration Act should be applied retroactively to cases initiated prior to its passage. The courts of appeal are split on this issue, with the Tenth Circuit holding that the Act should not be retroactively applied, and the Second and Fifth Circuits ruling that it should.[7] Clearly this is an issue which must be resolved by either the Congress or the Supreme Court.[8]

"Benefits From" and "Extended Directly or Through"

How far does the enforcement agency's authority extend? Is it permissible to trace the flow of federal aid beyond the recipient directly provided assistance to other persons or entities to whom benefits derived from the assistance can arguably be said to accrue? If one were to trace the federal financial assistance provided a university or a state's department of education, noting how many persons or entities came in contact with the aid or benefitted from its use in some way, the list would be long indeed. Furthermore "tying the scope of § 504 to economic benefit derived from . . . expenditures . . . would give § 504 almost limitless coverage."[9] It was not the intent of Congress to draw all those individuals or entities in the enforcement net of the Department of Education. Unquestionably, it takes more than casual contact or secondary benefit to make one a "recipient of federal financial assistance."

The first step in identifying a recipient is to look to the purpose for which the assistance is provided, and to those who are identified by the grantor as recipients or intended recipients. The duty to comply with Section 504 is part of a contract between the federal government and the grantees of federal financial assistance. This duty to comply is the "*quid pro quo* for the receipt of federal funds."[10] Assumption of these obligations is a voluntary undertaking on the part of the grantees; therefore, recipients are "those who are in a position to accept or reject those obligations as a part of the decision whether or not to 'receive' federal funds."[11]

U.S. Department of Transportation v. Paralyzed Veterans of America, supra, provides a clear distinction between recipients and those that merely receive some economic benefits from federal financial asisstance. The question before the Court was whether the receipt of federal financial assistance by airport operators conferred authority, under Section 504, to the Civil Aeronautics Board to regulate all airline carriers, including those that did not directly receive federal financial assistance, "by virtue of the extensive program of federal financial assistance to airports" from which the commercial airlines derived significant benefit.[12] The Court ruled that the federal funds in question were provided exclusively to the airport operators, and that commercial airlines merely derived collateral economic benefit from the use of the airports. To find otherwise, said the Court, would require one to take the rather dubious position that "airport operators convert the cash into runways and give the federal assistance — now in the form of a runway — to the airlines."[13]

Which entities in the following examples are recipients?

> A school district permits students from a private academy to participate in the district's Chapter I program, a federally funded program.
>
> The district uses federal funds to construct ramps and modify bathrooms so that a private academy will be accessible to mobility-impaired students.
>
> A state's department of education receives a general grant for Chapter II programs from the U.S. Department of Education. It then allocates those funds among the individual school districts that actually implement the programs. The state has no direct involvement in delivery of services under the Chapter II programs; it merely assumes oversight responsibility.
>
> A college that receives no direct federal financial assistance enrolls students who receive federal monies under the Basic Educational Opportunity Grant Program (BEOG). The college argues that it is not a recipient because the students are the direct recipients; the assistance to it comes indirectly. (*Grove City College v. Bell.*)

In the examples involving the private academy, the school district is the direct recipient of federal financial assistance, *i.e.*, Chapter I funds. The private academy becomes a recipient in the second example, when federal funds are used for modifications to its facilities. The improvements to the facility represent federal financial assistance. Appendix A clearly provides that nonpublic schools do not become recipients solely "by virtue of the fact that their students participate in . . . federally funded programs."[14]

In the third example, the state department of education, as well as the entities to which the funds are dispersed, are recipients. States are not permitted to insulate themselves from responsibility merely because the direct delivery of services is performed by local school districts.[15] In addition, indirect recipients such as the individual school districts and Grove City College will also not be permitted to avoid responsibility under the Act. Further, the college's argument in *Grove City* confuses "intended *beneficiaries* with intended *recipients*."[16] In that case, the Court concluded that the students were merely the beneficiaries and conduits through which the aid was passed to the intended recipient — the college. The Court specifically rejected any "distinction between direct and indirect aid."[17]

> A secretary alleges that she was fired from her job because of her handicap. She was employed by the State Bar Association. The Association does not receive federal financial assistance directly. However, two entities associated with it do receive such funds. The first entity uses a portion of the federal funds received to pay back a loan to the Association. No funds flow

from the second entity to the Association, but its secretary does bookkeeping for the Association.

In *Niehaus v. Kansas Bar Association, supra,* the Court held that the loan repayment could not be classified as receipt of federal funds. Further, the limited involvement with the second entity did not establish that the Association "benefitted directly" from the receipt of federal funds. Using the principles outlined in *Paralyzed Veterans,* the Association was not the intended recipient of the federal financial assistance provided and was not the party with authority to choose to assume the obligation to comply with Section 504 by virtue of the receipt of the assistance.

Federal Financial Assistance

The regulations list numerous services, monies, and property that are considered federal financial assistance, e.g. funds, facilities, loans, grants, transfer or lease of property for less than fair market value, proceeds from the transfer or lease of real or personal property, etc.[18] Conversely, the regulation provides that contracts of insurance or guaranty and procurement contracts are not federal financial assistance. However, the Court in *Moore v. Sun Bank of North Florida,* 923 F.2d 1423 (11th Cir. 1991) has held that Section 104.3(h) of the regulation is invalid with respect to the portion which excludes programs receiving federal financial assistance in the form of contracts of insurance of guaranty. The simple test for determining whether something is federal financial assistance is, "Does it constitute a subsidy or is it compensation for services rendered?"[19] This test works quite well when what is at issue are grants to entities that involve little or no consideration passing to the grantor from the grantee. However, it becomes a little more difficult when a party has negotiated a contract with the government that is extremely favorable. For example, a university purchases property from the government for $250,000; the fair market value of the property is $750,000. Is the university a recipient of federal financial assistance? Clearly, the property was acquired for far less than it would have been if the agreement had been with a private entity. If a party contracting with the government benefits in its dealing with the government "to a greater extent than if it were dealing with another party," it is legitimate to argue that it is receiving federal financial assistance;[20] however, the conclusion should not be based solely on market value. As noted by the Court in *Jacobsen v. Delta Airlines:*

> [F]air market value by its very nature is constantly changing. . . . [U]nder Delta's test anyone who has negotiated a favorable procurement contract with the government would find himself subject to the Act. . . . We think that

in determining which programs are subject to the civil rights laws, courts should focus not on market value but on the intention of the government. Courts should determine whether the government intended to provide assistance or merely to compensate.[21]

The Nature of the Obligation

Applicants for federal financial assistance are required to sign an assurance that they will operate their programs and activities in compliance with the regulation implementing Section 504.[22] Only persons or entities that elect to participate in federal financial assistance programs must execute the assurance. The only option for those who do not wish to sign an assurance is to not participate in such programs. In *Grove City*, the Court upheld the Department's right to terminate assistance for refusal to execute an Assurance of Compliance without a finding that actual discrimination has occurred. "Congress is free to attach reasonable and unambiguous conditions to federal financial assistance that educational institutions are not obligated to accept."[23]

Section 104.5 also provides the time period during which the assurance will obligate the recipient. Section 104.5(b) provides, in pertinent part:

> [Real property]— . . . the period during which the real property or structures are used for the purpose for which federal financial assistance is extended or for another purpose involving the provision of similar services or benefits.[24]
>
> [Personal property]— . . . the period during which it retains ownership or possession of the property.
>
> [All other cases]— . . . the period during which federal financial assistance is extended.
>
> Clark University is awarded a federal building and property. The university converts the building into a gymnasium. After using the building for 25 years as a gym, the university sells it to a textile company, which plans to demolish the building and build a laboratory on the property. How long does Clark University retain its recipient status? What about the proceeds of the sale? Is this federal financial assistance? If so, under what circumstances would the proceeds not be federal financial assistance?

This example illustrates the covenants that attach to federal financial assistance provided in the form of property. Clark University remains a recipient as long as it benefits from the federal financial assistance. Thus, Clark is a recipient for the 25 years it uses the building and remains a recipient if it receives the proceeds from the sale of the building. However, if Clark turns over the proceeds to the federal government, its recipient status ends at that point.

A school district is awarded monies under the Federal School Construction Assistance Program for construction of facilities. It last received such funds in 1970. In 1988, a majority of the facilities built with the funds are still in use. The district argues that its obligation does not extend beyond the year of construction unless it continues to receive additional federal funds for maintenance and operating expenses for the facilities. What is the duration of the contractual obligations associated with the funds?

The obligation extends as long as the facilities are in use for the purpose for which the funds are expended.[25]

5
Determining Who Is Handicapped

To assert a claim of discrimination under the Act, one must first establish that he or she is a handicapped person.[1] The regulation defines "handicapped person" as being:

> [A]ny person who (i) has a physical or mental impairment which substantially limits one or more major life activities, (ii) has a record of such an impairment, or (iii) is regarded as having such an impairment. § 104.3(j)(1).

This definition, perhaps, has more troublesome gray areas, or nebulous words and phrases, than any other provision of the regulations. It is difficult, if not impossible, to read only § 104.3(j)(1) and have a clear understanding of what constitutes a "handicap" under the Act. Section 104.3(j)(1) does, however, contain two important elements. First, it establishes a two-part test for determining whether an individual is a handicapped person. The person not only must have a physical or mental impairment, but the impairment must also "substantially limit . . . major life activities." Second, protection is provided for individuals who may not, in fact, be handicapped.

Physical or Mental Impairment

Section 104.3(j)(2)(i) doesn't really define a physical or mental impairment in a useful way.[2] Unless one has a medical degree, terms used, such as "genito-urinary" and "hemic and lymphatic" mean very little. So, where does one begin in an attempt to arrive at a working definition of "handicap"? Appendix A provides some clarity by offering the following list of conditions or diseases which meet the definition of "handicap" in the regulations:

> Orthopedic, visual, speech and hearing impairments, cerebral palsy, epilepsy, muscular dystrophy, multiple sclerosis, cancer, heart disease, diabetes, mental retardation, emotional illness and . . . drug addiction and alcoholism.[3]

Further, courts have found the following to be handicaps: an infant with impairments at birth, a person with one kidney, epilepsy, or a contagious disease.[4] One must keep in mind that

> [T]he definition does not set forth a list of specific diseases and conditions that constitute physical or mental impairments because of the difficulty of ensuring the comprehensiveness of any such list.[5]

The definition is, in fact, so broad that it certainly could be argued that almost any condition could be classified as a "handicap" under the Act. There is a temptation to merely perform a cursory analysis regarding the question of whether the individual has a physical or mental impairment. However, review of the qualifying statements in Appendix A, court decisions, and enforcement agency interpretations does permit one to isolate some general guidelines in the area.

a) The provision speaks only in terms of physical and mental handicaps.

> Joe, a drug addict, served a prison term for selling drugs. Once he is released from prison, he applies for a job at the local university. He is seen by an instructor while filling out an application in the personnel department. The instructor advises the personnel director of Joe's history, and on that basis Joe is denied employment.
> An individual who is 56 years of age charges that he was fired because his employer feels that older employees have increased absences because of illnesses associated with advanced age.

"Environmental, cultural, and economic disadvantage are not . . . covered; nor are prison records, age or homosexuality."[6] Thus, if Joe is denied employment because of his prison record, he is not protected. Similarly, the 56-year-old may have a claim regarding age discrimination, but he is not a handicapped person.

b) The definition of "handicap" is not limited to traditional disabilities.

Thus the Court held in *Doe v. Postal Service* that a transsexual denied employment based upon his intention to undergo "gender reassignment" could bring a case under Section 504.[7] The court specifically held that coverage under Section 504 was not limited to "traditionally recognized disabilities." Further, the Court in *Blackwell v. Department of Treasury*, held that

[W]hile homosexuals are not handicapped, it is clear that transvestites are because many experience strong social rejection in the workplace as a result of their mental ailment made blatantly apparent by their cross-dressing lifestyle.[8]

While the regulation was subsequently amended to exclude conditions such as transsexualism from the definition, attention deficit disorders, atmospheric allergies and stress-related disorders such as Chronic Fatigue Syndrome have been held to be handicaps. See *Walders v. Garrett,* 765 F. Supp. 303 (E.D. Va. 1991) and the Department of Education's 9/16/91 memorandum regarding attention deficit disorders.

c) Physiological, transitory, and voluntary conditions are not considered handicaps.

Therefore, a left-handed individual who is forced to use his right hand by his employer, a body builder who cannot meet the airlines' weight requirement, an individual who claims to have unsubstantiated impairment that prevents him from going to work, and an individual with myopia corrected to 20/20 vision through the use of corrective lenses are not "handicapped persons."[9]

d) Temporary conditions may qualify as handicaps.

Joe breaks his leg in a football game and, as a result, he must use a wheelchair for two months. He requests special accommodations during the period, *i.e.,* permission to park in parking spaces designated for handicapped persons, and movement of his classes from the second floor to the first. Joe is issued the requested parking permit, but the school decides to have Joe do his classwork alone in the office rather than move the classes for two months. The school justifies its decision on the basis that Joe's impairment is a temporary condition.

The determination of whether a handicap is permanent or temporary does not resolve the issue of whether an individual is handicapped under the regulations.[10] The OCR found a school district in violation for implementing a policy that illegally penalized students with temporary disabilities. The district's policy denied credit for course work to students with more than 14 absences (excused or unexcused). The student in question was injured in an accident, exceeded the acceptable number of absences, and was consequently denied credit for her course work. The OCR found that the policy had "the potential effect of denying students with temporary disabilities . . . the educational benefits to which they might be entitled."[11]

e) Contagious diseases are considered handicaps.

> Susan is a teacher who contracted tuberculosis as a child. The condition was in remission when she was hired as a teacher. She has worked for the school district for thirteen years. She is an above-average employee. After thirteen years, she experiences three relapses of tuberculosis. After her third relapse, she is fired by the district. Is she a "handicapped person" under Section 504?

The Supreme Court faced this question in *School Board of Nassau County v. Arline*. The Court, in finding that Gene Arline was a "handicapped person," articulated the following important principles:

> [T]he fact that a person with a record of a physical impairment is also contagious does not suffice to remove that person from coverage under Section 504. Arline's contagiousness and her physical impairment each resulted from the same underlying condition, tuberculosis. It would be unfair to allow an employer to seize upon the distinction between the effects of a disease on a patient and use that distinction to justify discriminatory treatment. (*School Board of Nassau County v. Arline, supra* at pp. 282 and 285.)

The subject of impairment from AIDS (and the [legal] treatment of persons with AIDS [PWA's]) is both controversial and legally unsettled. Court decisions have recently begun to provide a framework of how AIDS should be viewed with respect to Section 504:

1. The Court of Appeals for the Ninth Circuit in *Chalk v. U.S. District Court* held that a teacher with AIDS was handicapped within the meaning of Section 504.[12]
2. The U.S. Attorney General's Office in October 1988, as a result of the Supreme Court's decision in *School Board of Nassau County v. Arline*, issued a legal opinion "extend[ing] the protection of Federal anti-discrimination laws" to persons infected with the Human Immunodeficiency Virus (HIV).[13]
3. The Court, in *Martinez v. School Board of Hillsborough County* (1988), concluded that a school-aged child with AIDS, denied the opportunity to attend school without significant restriction, *i.e.*, being taught in a glass enclosure separated from her classmates, had a physical or mental impairment which substantially limited one or more major life activities and was, thus, a "handicapped person."[14]

Thus, contagious diseases are not excluded from the definition of handicapping conditions. While the Civil Rights Restoration Act discusses persons with contagious diseases within the employment context, it does not appear to alter judicial interpretation of the regulations regarding these conditions; *i.e.*, the issue of contagiousness is an issue to be considered when determining whether an individual is "qualified." *Remember*—while issues such as the behavioral manifestation of the individual's impairment and the health risk to others may be relevant to the question of whether the individual is "qualified," they are not relevant with respect to the question of whether he/she is "handicapped."

f) Persons who are alcoholics or drug abusers are entitled to coverage under the Act.[15]

Drug addicts and alcoholics are . . . handicapped . . . if their impairment substantially limits one of their major life activities."[16] The Department has acknowledged the problems with providing protection to these individuals. Specifically,

> The Secretary wishes to reassure recipients that inclusion of addicts and alcoholics within the scope of the regulation will not lead to the consequences feared by many commenters. . . . The fact that drug addiction and alcoholism may be handicaps does not mean that these conditions will be ignored. . . . In other words, while an alcoholic or drug addict may not be denied services or disqualified . . . solely because of his or her condition, the behavioral manifestations of the condition may be taken into account.[17]

Further, both Congress, in amending Section 504, and the courts have stated that the Act provides protection only to "rehabilitated or rehabilitating" abusers.[18] However, the troublesome part of this limitation is that minimal guidance has been provided regarding the standard which the recipient should use to determine if someone is "rehabilitated." In addition, how many chances should a recipient give an individual to be "rehabilitated"?

> **Caveat:** The drafters of the regulation made a distinction between the terms "impairment" and "handicap." As noted in Appendix A, "it should be emphasized that a physical or mental impairment does not constitute a *handicap* for purposes of Section 504 unless its severity is such that it results in a substantial limitation of one or more major life activities."[19] While this distinction is helpful in understanding the principles underlying the regulations' explanation of what constitutes a "handicapped person," the courts and OCR have *not* maintained such a distinction in their rulings and have used the terms interchangeably. Thus, it is important to remember when reading any OCR or court documents that the terms are treated, often, as synonymous, and one must look to the context in which the words are used to determine their meaning.

Substantially Limits Major Life Activities

This phrase is the essence of the definition of a handicapped person. "It should be emphasized that a physical or mental impairment does not constitute a handicap for purposes of Section 504 unless its severity i such that it results in a substantial limitation of one or more major life activities."[20]

> Donna is pregnant. Her company has a policy which precludes the use of extended sick leave during pregnancy. She contests the policy as a violation of Section 504. Is the company's treatment of pregnant women discrimination against handicapped individuals? What if Donna experiences complications which limit physical exertion during the final three months of her pregnancy? What if this condition requires her to remain in bed for the final three weeks of her pregnancy, which would increase her absences beyond the company's acceptable limit?

A normal pregnancy is not considered a handicap because it does not substantially limit one or more major life activities. Clearly, the drafters of the regulations did not consider the ability to see one's feet and rise from a chair without assistance to be major life activities. However, if as a result of being pregnant one also suffers from a physiological condition that does result in a substantial limitation, that condition would qualify as a handicap under the regulation.[21] In the example, the three months where physical exertion is limited for Donna still raises questions regarding whether she is handicapped. Specifically, to what extent does it preclude her from performing major life activities, such as her normal job functions? The three weeks' confinement to bed, however, clearly represents a substantial limitation. This hypothetical reflects the difficulty in attempting to "nail down" a working definition of the phrase "substantially limits." Just what exactly does it mean? The drafters of the regulations readily admitted that "the Department does not believe that a definition of this term is possible at this time."[22] It is clear that the impairment cannot be insignificant, or have a negligible or merely speculative impact on the individual.[23] Conversely, it is equally clear that an impairment that is totally debilitating would be characterized as "substantially limiting." Still, on this continuum from trivial/negligible to debilitating, where does one draw the line of demarcation for impairments that qualify as "handicaps" under the regulation? The answer is that one cannot approach the problem in this manner. There are no absolute general rules or simple formulas that can be used to easily identify such impairments. As stated previously, this is a gray area phrase; therefore, one must determine what "substantially limits" means on a case-by-case basis.[24]

What about the term "major life activities"? The regulations provide examples of such activities, e.g., "caring for one's self, performing manual tasks, walking, seeing, hearing, speaking, breathing, learning and working."[25] The regulations do not provide any further edification. As will be shown in the discussion that follows, the question of whether one is a handicapped person within the meaning of § 104.3(j)(1) involves trying to quantify the degree of restriction that a physical or mental condition imposes on an individual's abilities. In other words, using the "reasonable person" compliance standard, given the facts of the particular case, would a reasonable person conclude that the impairment substantially limits one or more major life activities?

To answer this question, one's analysis should involve reviewing certain pertinent information.

1) The nature of the impairment

Generally there are no arguments regarding traditional impairments or those listed in Appendix A as being handicaps.[26] However, there is a tendency to discount impairments that are more difficult to see or understand. For example, in *Perez v. Philadelphia Housing Authority*, the employer charged that Ms. Perez's back and leg impairment was not a handicap because "she suffered from transitory back pain and not from a commonly recognized handicap."[27] The Court concluded that such a "generalized approach" was unacceptable. *Remember* — the definition of handicap is not limited to traditional impairments. Furthermore, a combination of impairments can also result in an individual being classified as a "handicapped person." The impairments may be considered together.

2) The manifestations of the impairment for this particular individual

The determination must be made on an individualized basis. One is not concerned with just the general characteristics of the impairment. "The determination of who is a handicapped person under the Act is best suited to a 'case-by-case determination'."[28] Further, "It is the impaired individual that must be examined, and not just the impairment in the abstract."[29]

3) The major life activity in question and the extent of the limitation imposed by the impairment

Once again, it is an individualized inquiry into "whether the particular impairment constitutes, for the particular person, a significant barrier to employment."[30] Analyzing the question in this way will provide a framework for "quantifying" the degree of limitation the impairment imposes. For example,

> A student who has been diagnosed as having a learning disability is denied special education services because he or she has a 3.5 grade point average. Another student who has a hearing impairment and a chronic ear condition

and whose academic work is above average is also denied such services. Are these students handicapped persons?

In both these cases, the OCR found that the school district did not violate the regulations by failing to define the students as handicapped. The fact that these students were adequately performing in class indicated that their impairments did not substantially limit one or more major life activities, in this instance, functioning in the educational arena.[31] The OCR specifically endorsed the proposition that a student "succeeding in regular education does not have a disability which substantially limits the ability to learn."[32]

> **Caveat:** The above cases must not be read as standing for the proposition that students who are performing adequately in class will never be classified as "handicapped." For example, if the learning-disabled student was unable to interpret directional signs, and the hearing-impaired student could not hear fire alarms, both would need special assitance in an emergency situation, and the recipient would need to review, and possibly modify, its evacuation plan to be sure these students' handicaps were accommodated. The key thing to remember, again, is that each situation should be reviewed to determine whether the impairment substantially limits a major life activity in that context.

The examples discussed above are fairly clear-cut. However, difficult situations always pose the problem of just how broadly or narrowly the phrase should be interpreted. Consider the case of an individual with a mild case of strabismus—commonly known as cross-eye—who was hired to sort letters. His job required him to operate a mail-sorting machine, as a result of which he suffered eyestrain, headaches, and excessive tearing. His physician confirmed that the symptoms were produced by the use of the machine, combined with his strabismus. Before the difficulties he experienced as a sorter, the individual's health and vision were unaffected by his condition. He was fired because of his inability to use the mail-sorting machine. The Court, in *Jasany v. U. S. Postal Service, supra,* relying on the fact that the individual's condition heretofore had no impact on any of his activities, particularly his work, concluded that he was not a handicapped person. Courts have held that an individual's inability to perform a particular job or job function as a result of an impairment that does not have a negative impact on the individual's ability to obtain other employment is either not a substantial limitation or does not involve a major life activity.[33] The Court, in *E. E. Black, Ltd. v. Marshall,* using employability as a guideline, provided a broad framework for interpreting the phrase "substantially limits." The Court noted that the phrase should not be interpreted so broadly as to provide coverage under the Act to "any individual who is capable of performing a particular job, and is rejected for that particular job because of a[n] . . . impairment," nor so narrowly as to deny coverage to an individual who, because of an impairment, is "disqualified from employment in his chosen field." The Court provided the following examples of individuals in each category:

> [A]n individual with acrophobia who was offered 10 deputy assistant accountant jobs with a particular company, but was disqualified from one job because it was on the 37th floor.
>
> A person, for example, who has obtained a graduate degree in chemistry and is then turned down for a chemistry job because of an impairment is not likely to be heartened by the news that he could still be a streetcar conductor, an attorney or a forest ranger. A person who is disqualified from employment in his chosen field . . . is substantially limited in one of his major life activities.

Thus, it is the impact on the ability to work, not the ability to perform a particular job, that is important. Mere inability to perform in a specific context, or failure to meet a particular criterion or requirement, does not make the individual a "handicapped person."

In addition to being mindful of the guidelines described above, it is also helpful to review specific court decisions to ascertain what the courts have determined to be a person with a "handicap." These include:

A receptionist-clerk with back and neck pain.[34]

A custodian with asthma.[35]

An individual with limited mobility in her left arm and shoulder.[36]

A person with an anxiety disorder that was exacerbated by driving to work in heavy traffic and by working the late night shift.[37]

An individual with paranoid schizophrenia who demonstrated a threatening and belligerent attitude.[38]

An individual with achondroplastic dwarfism.[39]

A person who exhibited symptoms characteristic of multiple sclerosis and viral myelitis whom physicians could not conclusively diagnose.[40]

It is also important to remember that, in addition to the usual documentary evidence used to support the existence and severity of an impairment, courts will also depend on the statements of the individual regarding the nature and severity of the impairment. For example, the courts in *Forrisi* and *Jasany* based their conclusions, in part, on the fact that the individuals admitted that their impairments had not substantially limited their lives or their employability.[41]

"Has a Record of/Is Regarded As"

The protection provided to "handicapped persons" is not limited to individuals who actually have an impairment.[42] "Congress was as concerned about the effect of an impairment on others as it was about its effect on the individual."[43] Therefore, it was important to provide protection to those who are substantially limited not by an impairment but "as a result of the negative reactions of others to the impairment."[44]

> Joe, Bill, and Sam apply for jobs at the same company, and all are initially offered a job pending the outcome of a company-related physical examination. They are examined on the same day by Dr. Jones. Sam reports a history of epilepsy that is controlled by medication, while Bill reports a history of emotional illnesses. Bill's medical history, however, indicates that he no longer has an emotional impairment. Joe is in perfect physical condition; no physical abnormalities were noted. In his haste to rush the physical reports to personnel, Dr. Jones inadvertently notes on Joe's report, instead of Sam's, the information regarding the epileptic condition. The hiring official, upon seeing the information on Bill's and Joe's reports, rescinds the offers of employment. He fears that an individual who might have seizures would be a danger to others and a potential embarrassment. Likewise, he feels the job would be too stressful for an individual with a history of emotional illness. Can Joe and Bill bring a claim of handicap discrimination?

The regulations provide protection to individuals who have a history of, or have been misclassified as having, a mental or physical impairment. Joe clearly fits the category of someone who has been misclassified. Regarding Bill, the regulations have been interpreted to mean that the physical manifestations of the disease are not relevant. No distinction is made between whether the condition is active or no longer present. (*Arline v. School Board of Nassau County, supra*). The Supreme Court noted in *Southeastern Community College v. Davis* that protection under the Act is afforded to those who "may at present have no actual incapacity at all."[45]

> Alice weighs approximately 350 pounds. She is an excellent typist and is amazingly agile for her size. She has worked for the SLIM Corporation for 15 years. She has always been rated as above average in her job performance, and her weight has placed no discernible limitations on her work. She applies for the job of secretary to the president, which would be a significant promotion for her. Although, with respect to technical skills, she is the most qualified applicant, she is denied the job. The president depends on his secretary a great deal, and it is felt that Alice would have a high rate of absenteeism because of the physiological problems and illnesses associated with obesity. Also it is felt that a person of her size would not be able to run errands and perform all the nonsedentary activities that are required. In the 15 years that Alice has worked for the company, her attendance record has been above average, and she has performed all the tasks that would be required in the new position. Does the company's action make Alice a "handicapped person"?

Normally obesity alone is not considered a handicapping condition. Certainly, in this case, Alice's condition does not substantially limit one or more major life activities. She is able to perform her job with no difficulty. However, the treatment received by Alice and the assumptions made regarding her physical limitations produce a substantial limit to a major life activity, *i.e.,* performance of a job for which she is most qualified. An individual who is not handicapped will be classified as a "handicapped person" under the Act if the individual is treated as if he or she were a handicapped person.[46] As noted in Appendix A, this part of the definition of handicapped person provides coverage to individuals who might not normally be considered handicapped, "such as persons with disfiguring scars, as well as persons who have no physical or mental impairment but are treated by a recipient as if they were handicapped."[47] The key is the perceptions and attitudes of those imposing the restrictions or limitations. In *Larry P. v. Riles,* black students who were placed in classes for the educable mentally retarded were held to be "handicapped" despite the assertion that the students were, in fact, not retarded. The recipient's act of placing them in such classes indicated they were "regarded as handicapped."[48]

6
"Qualified Handicapped Person"

Is the individual a "qualified handicapped person"?[1] This is not an easy question to answer. "There is no bright line separating those who are 'qualified' and those who are not."[2] Any definition of qualified status must begin with the Supreme Court's decision in *Southeastern Community College v. Davis.* In *Davis* the Court held that an "otherwise qualified handicapped person is one who meets *all* of a program's requirements in spite of his handicap."[3] In *Alexander v. Choate,* the Court further refined the definition:

> The balance struck in *Davis* requires that an otherwise qualified handicapped individual must be provided with meaningful access to the benefit that the grantee offers. . . . [T]o assure meaningful access reasonable accommodation in the grantee's program or benefit may have to be made.[4]

Thus, a qualified handicapped person is one who can meet all of the program requirements with reasonable accommodation.[5] As noted by the Court in *Brennan v. Stewart*:

> [I]t is clear that the phrase "otherwise qualified" has a paradoxical quality; on the one hand, it refers to a person who has the abilities or characteristics sought by the grantee; but on the other, it cannot refer only to those already capable of meeting *all* the requirements—or else no reasonable requirement could ever violate § 504, no matter how easy it would be to accommodate handicapped individuals who cannot fulfill it. This means we can no longer take literally the assertion of *Davis* that "an otherwise qualified person is one who is able to meet *all* of a program's requirements." The question after *Alexander* is the rather mushy one of whether some "reasonable accommodation" is available to satisfy the legitimate interests of both the grantee and the handicapped person.[6]

Is the individual a qualified handicapped person? The recipient's responsibility to provide "meaningful access" is triggered by an affirmative answer to this question. There is a tendency to minimize the importance of this question and move right to the issue of whether discrimination has occurred.

Joe has multiple sclerosis and uses a wheelchair. He is a salesman and applies for a regional sales manager's position at XYZ corporation. The job
specifications require ten years of sales experience, membership in the state
professional sales association and training in management. While Joe has 15
years of sales experience, he has not had any management training and is
not a member of the state association. Although no other applicant exceeds
Joe's years of sales experience, they all have some management training and
are also members of the association. Joe charges that he did not get the job
because of the reaction to his condition. He believes that he was not hired
because it was felt that his appearance was not acceptable to clients. Is Joe
a qualified handicapped person?

The question of possible discrimination does not arise until it has been determined that the handicapped individual is qualified. Joe's failure to meet the
minimum specifications for the job precludes him from being considered for
the position. *Remember*—protection is not provided under the Act and its
regulations unless the person is qualified.[7] Simply determining that one is
handicapped is not sufficient. The person must be both handicapped and
qualified before an obligation arises under the Act. Further, qualified status
is not eternal.

A student in his third year of residency in medical school begins to have
seizures associated with his diabetes. His condition, which had been adequately controlled up to that point, is uncontrollable and results in extensive
absences. The school recommends that the student take a leave-of-absence
until his health improves. School officials argue that his absences resulted
in his missing valuable clinical experience and his uncontrolled and un-
predictable seizures placed patients in danger. The student refuses and
argues that his above-average performance entitles him to continue in the
program. Is the student a qualified handicapped person?

As noted by the Court in *Doe v. Region 13 Mental Health–Mental Retardation Commission, supra,* an individual that had once been considered
"otherwise qualified" can lose that status. The worsening of the student's
condition prevents him from performing adequately, and, therefore, he is no
longer qualified.

There are three basic questions to be answered in determining whether
an individual is a qualified handicapped person: has an individual inquiry
been conducted; are the criteria, standards, or requirements legitimate; and
is there a reasonable accommodation.

"Individualized Inquiry": The inquiry must be an assessment of the skills
and abilities of the handicapped individual in conjunction with the criteria,
standards and requirements.[8]

Mary Ann is a graduate student who is denied admission to a research project that is necessary for the completion of her degree program. Mary Ann

is an above-average student and has completed all the course prerequisites for participation in the project. The project requires working with radio-active material. Mary Ann has epilepsy that is adequately controlled by medication. The professor in charge of the program rejects Mary Ann because he feels it is too dangerous to have persons with epilepsy working with radioactive material.

While a recipient is not required to ignore the "limitations which result from the handicapped . . . mere possession of a handicap is not a permissible ground for assuming an inability to function in a particular context."[9] It is impermissible to exclude an entire group of handicapped individuals on the basis of a general perception of the limitations of individuals with a particular impairment.[10] The individual abilities of each handicapped person must be considered. While an individual with epilepsy whose condition was not controlled by medication might pose a significant danger in handling radioactive material, Mary Ann's condition, which is adequately controlled by medication, does not warrant such a categorical exclusion.

> **Caveat:** Courts have approved categorized disqualification without requiring "individualized consideration" where the handicapping condition poses a significant risk to the safety of the handicapped person as well as others. See *Davis v. Meese* (insulin-dependent diabetics precluded from position of special agent and investigative specialist for the FBI).[11] It is important to remember that the risk must be significant, not merely speculative. It should also be noted that this case involved an FBI policy, and questions of national security were raised.

Criteria, Standards, and Requirements: The criteria, standards, and requirements used to screen out handicapped individuals must be legitimate, reasonable, necessary, and rational related to the program's goals and purposes.[12]

> A student with excellent academic credentials applied and was admitted to medical school on the basis of false information she provided regarding her mental health. She has an extensive history of mental illness. Over a period of nearly three years, which included her medical school enrollment, she exhibited a psychiatric disorder that was manifested in over 20 instances of self-inflicted bodily harm and suicide attempts, as well as serious physical attacks on her doctors and others. Also, she continually refused to submit to recommended medical treatment. She was forced to withdraw from medical school as a result of her impairment. In the five years subsequent to her withdrawal, she obtains a Master of Science degree in Health and Policy Management and performs successfully as a research assistant for the federal government. Despite the fact that she had not received the extensive therapy recommended, during the five-year period there is no recurrence of the previous violent and self-destructive behavior. Her request to be reinstated in medical school is rejected on the basis of the evaluations of

several psychiatrists who state that she continues to suffer from a serious psychiatric problem, and that the stress of medical school would cause her previous destructive behavior to recur. The student asserts that her previous medical history should not have been used to disqualify her.[13]

"Section 504 does not compel [recipients] to disregard the disabilities of handicapped individuals.[14] Thus, clearly, recipients do not have to ignore the impact a handicap will have, if it is important to the individual's participation or performance.

> [T]he plaintiff's handicap may be a permissible factor to be taken into account in determining whether he is qualified. The pivotal issue is not whether the handicap was considered but whether under all of the circumstances it provides a reasonable basis for finding the plaintiff not to be qualified.[15]

However, "where an individual's handicap is unrelated to reasonable requirements for participation in the activity, [S]ection 504 prohibits denying the individual's participation on the sole basis of his or her handicap."[16] Thus, recipients may not refuse:

> to provide interpreters for deaf parents and thereby deny them the opportunity to participate in conferences initiated by the school district;[17]
>
> to admit an individual into a graduate program solely on the basis of his having multiple sclerosis;[18]
>
> to permit mobility-impaired students to enroll in business education classes because the program is not accessible;[19]
>
> to hire a handicapped individual as a teacher because he did not have a bus driver's permit;[20]
>
> to permit an individual to return to work as Director of Nursing because her impairment precluded her from standing or walking for prolonged periods of time.[21]

Reasonable Accommodation: The individualized inquiry which must be conducted requires that a balance be struck "between the statutory rights of the handicapped to be integrated . . . and the legitimate interest of [recipients] in preserving the integrity of their programs."[22] This balancing process is an integral part of the determination of whether an individual is a qualified handicapped person.[23] Once it is established that the handicap prevents meaningful access, the inquiry continues, and an assessment must be made as to the availability of reasonable accommodations.[24] *Remember*—an accommodation is not reasonable if it requires substantial modifications, fundamental alterations, or undue administrative or financial burdens.[25]

The real question becomes the "reasonableness of a refusal to accommodate a handicapped individual."[26]

> Joe applies for a job as a research assistant at a major university. There are positions available on several projects for which Joe is qualified. The project which Joe would most like to work on is a two-million-dollar federal grant project involving studying the effects of radiation. The job that Joe seeks requires the preliminary testing of radioactive matter with an instrument that he is unable to use. Joe has a muscle impairment that does not interfere with his gross-motor skills but limits fine-motor movements that require a great deal of dexterity. While the most important work of the research assistants involves analyzing data and developing new experiments based upon the analysis—tasks which the university feels Joe is uniquely qualified for—approximately 40 percent of the work requires the use of the instrument. Because of Joe's impressive credentials, the university investigates the possibility of acquiring an alternative instrument that would permit him to work on the project. The university advises Joe that there is no alternative instrument capable of performing all the necessary tests. Therefore, the university declines to offer him a job on the project. Joe recommends that the university either modify one of its four machines at a cost of $5,000 or hire a college work-study student to perform the tests for him. The university refuses to modify the instrument because the modified machine could only be used by Joe which would require the other 11 research assistants to share the remaining three machines, thus increasing the time needed to complete the project. Hiring a work-study student is not cost efficient, because the work is so specialized that the individual hired would have to have the qualifications of a research assistant. Therefore, the university would be hiring two research assistants instead of one. Is the university justified in rejecting Joe's recommendations?

The denial of the position was not an act of discrimination, because Joe's impairment prevented him from performing "an essential function of the job in question."[27] Joe's recommendations clearly were not reasonable under the circumstances. The answer would be different if the modification to the instrument Joe recommended cost only one hundred dollars and had a removable attachment that would not prevent the other assistants' use of the instrument. Those modifications would be minimal, and should the university continue to refuse to hire Joe, one could certainly argue that the refusal was arbitrary, unreasonable, and discriminatory.[28]

Generally, the choices regarding the provision of accommodations are not so clear-cut as those presented in the example above. A review of actual cases reveals that there are few objective guidelines and once again it is a "reasonable person" compliance standard. For example:

1. In *Rothschild,* the school district was required to provide interpreters for deaf parents to provide them access to meetings, conferences, etc.,

directly related to their child's academic or disciplinary status, but the district was not required to provide the services for extracurricular activities, including graduation. The Court concluded that it would be an undue financial and administrative burden to require the district to "subsidize parental involvement in extracurricular activities."[29]

2. The University of Alabama was required to provide transportation services equivalent to those provided nonhandicapped students. The Court noted that "in light of the [university's] annual transportation budget of $1.2 million, an expenditure of $15,000 . . . is not likely to cause an undue financial burden."[30]

3. The federal government was not required to provide a blind individual a voice synthesized computer, since it ultimately accommodated him by providing him with readers of his choice.[31]

4. The state department of education was not required to admit profoundly retarded visually impaired children to the school for the blind, because they did not meet the criteria of being "in the trainable mentally handicapped range and above." The Court stated that the students were not qualified. It concluded that there was no reasonable accommodation, because the school did not employ teachers with the necessary expertise, and its mission would have to be changed.[32]

These examples reflect the balancing process the Supreme Court outlined in *Alexander*. The question that must be answered is, when all pertinent factors are considered—cost, hardship, the duty to include handicapped individuals, etc.—how substantial is the burden the recipient must assume.

Section 104.3(k) provides definitions for the term "qualified handicapped person" with respect to employment; preschool, elementary and secondary services; postsecondary services; and "other services." While the two-part test discussed above for determining "qualified" status applies to all these categories, each has unique features that must be considered.

Employment

According to Section 104.3(k)(1) a qualified handicapped person is a handicapped person who, with reasonable accommodation, can perform the essential functions of the job in question. But what are essential functions?

> A blind individual applies for a job as superintendent of a school district. The job qualifications include a Ph.D. in education administration and seven years' experience as an administrator. One of the responsibilities of the superintendent is visiting all the district's schools. Members of the hiring committee express concern that a blind individual would have difficulty fulfilling that responsibility because of the logistics of arranging for someone

to assist with transportation. The blind applicant meets the job qualifications. Is providing one's own transportation an essential function of the job?

A nursing aide has back surgery. As a result of the operation, she is unable to lift more than ten pounds. The hospital refuses to reemploy her because it is felt that the duties of a nursing aide, which require extensive lifting and bending, would result in a reinjury to her back. Her principal duty had been caring for profoundly mentally handicapped children. Aides are required to lift and carry the children, some of whom weigh over 50 pounds. Is lifting over ten pounds an essential function of the job?

Mary, who has osteoarthritis that precludes her from standing for extended periods of time and from walking up stairs, works in a college admissions office as a data entry clerk. The primary duty of the clerks is to work with computers and word processors. Although such duties are not listed in the job description, occasionally, during class registration, the clerks are asked to assist students in the registration process. This usually requires more standing and physical activity than Mary can tolerate. Is assisting in registration an essential function of the job?

Those things identified as essential functions must be job-related, and must reflect the important aspects of the job. They must be legitimate and necessary requirements for the job.[33] While it certainly can be argued that lifting is an essential function of the job of the nursing aide, such is not the case with respect to providing one's own transportation in the case of the superintendent's position. The school superintendent is being hired to manage and direct the day-to-day activities of the district. Clearly, the manner in which he is transported to and from meetings in performance of those duties is of little consequence. Further, as noted in Appendix A, "difficulty in performing tasks that bear only a marginal relationship to a particular job" should not be used to disqualify handicapped individuals.[34] Thus, Mary, in the third example, should not be penalized for her inability to perform additional tasks which are not related to her primary job responsibilities.[35]

A postal worker is rendered unable to perform her duties as a letter carrier because of a work-related injury. She requests reassignment as a distribution clerk. The job description states that the position requires lifting packages weighing up to 70 pounds and continuous kneeling and bending. Both the worker's personal physician and the employer's examining physician state that she could not perform a job requiring excessive bending and strenuous lifting. Therefore, she is denied the job. The worker had occasionally worked as a distribution clerk before her injury; she states that she could perform the job without difficulty and that there was only minimal lifting involved. She also states that she has not noticed other clerks doing heavy lifting. The employer does not dispute her statements but instead maintains that lifting is an essential function of the job. Does the employer's statement that lifting is an essential function resolve the matter?

The mere fact that the employer says that an activity is an essential function, or that the job description lists it as such, does not resolve the issue. The employer must present sufficient evidence establishing that it is, in fact, an essential function. Further, generalizations are not sufficient; they must be based upon "individualized" assessments of the situation at issue. In this instance, the following questions must be answered by the employer:[36]

a. Is there any significant difference between the clerk job that the worker performed previously and the one for which she is presently applying?
b. Are all distribution clerks required to do such lifting on a regular basis?

> An employee who has diabetes and hypertension has an unacceptable number of absences. She advises her employer that her absences are the result of her impairments. Her employer accommodates her by changing her to part-time status, but she continues to have numerous absences. She is ultimately fired. Is her claim that the employer discriminated against a qualified handicapped person valid?

The employee is not a qualified handicapped person. "It is elemental that one who does not come to work cannot perform any of his job functions, essential or otherwise."[37]

> A physical education instructor suffers from progressive osteoarthritis. It restricts his ability to participate in strenuous physical activity, and, as a result, he is reassigned to a position as health instructor. The following school year, although he is satisfactorily performing his job as a health instructor, he is terminated because of budget constraints. The school can afford to employ only two health instructors. In determining whether the instructor is a qualified handicapped person, which is the "position in question" for which he must be capable of performing the essential functions?

The position in question is the one the individual is "denied" as a result of an adverse employment decision.[38] In this case, the position in question is the job from which the individual was dismissed.

Preschool, Elementary, and Secondary

Section 104.3(k) states that "qualified handicapped person" means

> (2) [A person] (i) of an age during which nonhandicapped persons are provided such services, (ii) of any age during which it is mandatory under state law to provide such services to handicapped persons, or (iii) to whom a state is required to provide a free appropriate public education under Section 612 of the Education of the Handicapped Act.[39]
>
> A school district offers an after-school program for first through sixth grades and students aged 5 to 13 years old. Information given to parents regarding the program provides that all students who meet the grade and age

requirements are eligible for enrollment in the program. When the parents of two handicapped students seek enrollment in the program, the district advises the parents that it has insufficient funds to hire an aide to assist in caring for the students and refuses to enroll them in the program. The students are ages 8 and 15. Are these students "qualified handicapped persons"?

If a district chooses to provide extra services to nonhandicapped students in a particular age group, it must also offer those services to handicapped students. Thus, the eight-year-old student is a qualified handicapped person. If, in the above example, the district had adopted other eligibility criteria for its program, such as course prerequisites or a level of performance on a standardized test, then the handicapped students would also have to meet those criteria to be qualified.[40] The criteria must also be rationally related to the program or services offered.[41]

A school district, in compliance with EHA, offers educational services to handicapped students until they attain the age of 22. Nonhandicapped students are provided educational services until age 20. No student in the district has received services beyond age 22. A handicapped student reaches age 22 during the school year, and the district terminates services prior to the end of the school year. Is the action of the district appropriate?

The OCR, in a letter of findings for Williamson County School District, found that the district had not violated Section 504 and its implementing regulations, because the student was no longer a qualified handicapped person once she reached age 22, and evidence revealed that the district had consistently applied its termination policy to all students.[42]

Postsecondary

Section 104.3(k)(3) states that a "qualified handicapped person" is "a handicapped person who meets the academic and technical standards requisite to admission or participation."

The term "technical standards" refers to all nonacademic admissions criteria that are essential to participation in the program in question.[43] For example,

June, an out-of-state student with dyslexia, applies to XYZ University. Her academic qualifications include being in the top third of her class, a 3.0 grade point average, and a 975 on the SAT. The university's minimum admission criteria are a 2.5 grade point average and a minimum of 850 on the SAT. In addition, the university permits out-of-state students to fill only 20 percent of the available slots. Out-of-state students compete with other out-of-state stuents for admission to the freshman class. June charges that she is discriminated against on the basis of her handicap, because she is denied admission to a freshman class that has an average grade point average of 2.6 and an SAT score of 900. However, the average performance of out-of-state students is a 3.3 grade point average and an SAT of 1100. While June clearly meets the academic standards of the university, she does not meet the technical standard of being an in-state student. She does meet the standard of an out-of-state student and is judged fairly against other out-of-state students.

Other Services

Section 104.3(k)(4) states that "qualified handicapped persons" means a handicapped person who meets the essential eligibility requirements for the receipt of such services.

> Parents who are hearing impaired request that a school district provide a sign language interpreter to assist them in participating in school meetings and conferences. The district refuses, arguing that the parents are not "qualified handicapped persons." (*Rothschild v. Grottenthaler, supra.*)

The Court in *Rothschild* concluded that the parents were entitled to the services because they were "qualified . . . with respect to other services" under section 104.3(k)(4). The Court cited several OCR decisions regarding parent participation in school functions and specifically stated, in noting that such meetings and conferences were "other services":

> The school district and Superintendent Grottenthaler contend that the Rothschilds are not "otherwise qualified" because they are not eligible to receive educational services. . . . However, the school district's proposed interpretation of regulation 104.3(k) is inconsistent with its plain language. Regulation 104.3(k) does not define "qualified handicapped person" with regard to the category of institution . . . but rather the category of service offered by the recipient institution.
>
> Thus, while the school district is subject to section 504 in providing educational services, that is not the only area in which it must refrain from discrimination on the basis of handicap. . . . "Other services" . . . in this case, include parent-teacher conferences, meetings with school district personnel, and other parent-oriented services related to the education of its students.[44]

Special Concerns

Alcoholism/Drug Addiction

A university rejects an applicant for admission because, despite the applicant's outstanding academic record, a history of alcoholism is discovered.

> The applicant presents evidence that he has received treatment and is no longer an active alcoholic. Is the university's summary rejection permissible? Is an alcoholic who is currently receiving treatment entitled to be considered a qualified handicapped individual? What about a drug user who has completed a treatment program and whose physician states that he can return to work and who applies for a job in a pharmacy?

While persons cannot be excluded solely on the basis that they are an alcoholic or drug abuser or have a history of such, recipients need not ignore their condition when determining whether they are "qualified."[45] Their condition must be considered in terms of whether it precludes them from meeting the performance criteria and or eligibility standards in question. Appendix A provides a clear outline of the factors which must be considered:

> With respect to the employment of a drug addict or alcoholic, if it can be shown that the addiction or alcoholism prevents successful performance of the job, the person need not be provided the employment opportunity in question. For example, in making employment decisions, a recipient may judge addicts and alcoholics on the same basis it judges all other applicants and employees. Thus, a recipient may consider . . . past personnel records, absenteeism, disruptive, abusive or dangerous behavior, violations of rules or unsatisfactory work performance.
>
> A college may not exclude an addict or alcoholic as a student, on the basis of addiction or alcoholism, if the person can successfully participate in the education program and complies with the rules of the college and if his or her behavior does not impede the performance of other students. (Appendix A at 484.)

Further, courts have held those who are active drug addicts or alcoholics are not entitled to protection under the Act.[46]

Contagious Diseases

> Susan is a teacher who has Hepatitis B. She has had several relapses, but at present the disease is in remission. John is a teacher of special education students. He was hospitalized with pneumonia and was subsequently diagnosed as having AIDS. After his hospitalization, he was determined to be fit to return to work. Mary, an office worker, has tuberculosis. The condition has been in remission for years, but she has had a relapse and the disease is now active and can be transmitted to others. Are any of these individuals with contagious diseases qualified within the meaning of Section 504?

As noted by the Court in *Chalk v. U. S. District Court, Central District of California* — a case in which a teacher diagnosed as having AIDS had been reassigned from his teaching position despite the fact that the medical evidence established that he presented no risk to his students — the principal question is, under what circumstances can an individual with a contagious disease be considered otherwise qualified?[47] The Supreme Court, in *School Board of Nassau County v. Arline, supra* at 287, noted that the interest of "protecting handicapped individuals from deprivation based on prejudice, stereotypes, or unfounded fear" must be balanced against "such legitimate concerns . . . as avoiding exposing others to significant health and safety risks." The Court further noted that:

> A person who poses a significant risk of communicating an infectious disease to others in the work place will not be otherwise qualified for his or her job if reasonable accommodation will not eliminate the risk. The Act would not require a school board to place a teacher with active, contagious tuberculosis in a classroom with elementary school children. (*Id.* at 287 n.1.)

The next question, of course, is what does "significant risk" mean? The Supreme Court also outlined the factors which must be considered:

> (a) the nature of the risk (how the disease is transmitted); (b) the duration of the risk (how long is the carrier infectious); (c) the severity of the risk (what is the potential harm to third parties); and (d) the probabilities the disease will be transmitted and will cause varying degrees of harm. (*Id.* at 288.)

Applying the above factors, a qualified individual cannot be excluded on the basis of speculation and unreasonable fear. In *Chalk v. U. S. District Court, Central District of California, supra* at 707–8, the appellate court specifically noted that fact when reversing the district court's decision. On the district court level, the judge had rejected the consensus of medical evidence (which reflected that the individual was not a significant risk) and denied him status as a qualified handicapped person on the basis of a speculation that there might be a "small risk" that the medical profession as yet had not discovered. The court of appeals held that excluding an individual on the basis of such speculation violated the *Arline* standard.

> Fred is a kindergarten-age student with AIDS. He is involved in an altercation with another student in which he bites the student's pants leg. The other student suffers no injury as the skin is not broken. Fred had previously exhibited, and continues to exhibit, aggressive behavior in the classroom. Does the possibility that Fred might bite other students justify his exclusion from school since there is a remote possibility that the HIV might be transmitted to his classmates or teachers?

When faced with this situation in *Thomas v. Atascadero Unified School District,* the Court held that the preponderance of medical and scientific evidence revealed that the student did not pose a significant risk.[48] The Court specifically noted that "any theoretical risk of transmission of the AIDS virus . . . is so remote that it cannot become the basis for any exclusionary action." (See also *Martinez v. School Board of Hillsborough County*.)[49]

Thus, the courts have established that the significant risk can be neither speculative, remote, nor "a mere theoretical possibility." *Kohl v. Woodhaven Learning Center* presents a case in which the risk was determined to be significant. The individual was an active carrier of the most infectious form of Hepatitis B. Further, he was mentally impaired, bilaterally blind, and frequently exhibited maladaptive behavior such as scratching, biting, and self-abuse. The Court, in determining that the individual was not a qualified handicapped person, held that a 10 to 15 percent chance of infection was an "unacceptable risk."[50] See also *Doe v. Washington University* (E.D. Mo., October 2, 1991), a case in which the district court upheld a dental school's dismissal of a student who was HIV-positive "even though the risk of transmission . . . was not capable of precise measure."

Congress addressed the issue of contagious diseases in the Civil Rights Restoration Act of 1987. The Act redefines handicap in the employment context as follows:

> For the purpose of Sections 503 and 504, as such sections relate to employment, such term does not include an individual who has a currently contagious disease or infection and who, by reason of such disease or infection, would constitute a direct threat to the health or safety of other individuals or who, by reason of the currently contagious disease or infection, is unable to perform the duties of the job.

Since the above language merely mirrors the judicial definition of individuals who are not qualified handicapped persons, *i.e.*, those who present a significant risk, it appears that this new language will not result in the exclusion of individuals who were previously afforded protection under Section 504. The most important question raised by this new provision is whether courts will interpret the phrase "would constitute a direct threat to the health or safety of other individuals" as a less stringent standard than the "significant risk" standard and, thus, exclude a greater number of individuals from protection.

7
Discriminatory Actions Prohibited

> *No qualified handicapped person shall, on the basis of handicap, be excluded from participation in, be denied the benefits of, or otherwise be subjected to discrimination under any program or activity which receives or benefits from federal financial assistance.*[1]

Section 104.4 provides the general prohibitions against discrimination. They are, in pertinent part, prohibitions against (a) denying qualified handicapped persons the opportunity to participate; (b) providing aids, benefits or services that are not "equal to" or not "as effective as" those provided others; (c) providing different or separate aids, services or benefits which are not necessary for providing meaningful access; and (d) providing significant assistance to third parties that discriminate against qualified handicapped persons.[2] Courts have succinctly summarized these prohibitions as follows: Section 504 prohibits denying qualified handicapped individuals opportunities and benefits solely on the basis of their handicaps.[3] This antidiscrimination mandate addresses discrimination "stemming . . . from simple prejudice" as well as discrimination that results from refusing to provide reasonable accommodations.[4] In the preceding sections of this text, we have discussed in great detail the legal theories that form the foundation of this antidiscrimination mandate. In this chapter both hypotheticals and actual cases are used to demonstrate how the enforcement agency and the courts have interpreted and applied the general prohibitions of § 104.4.

"Discriminatory Actions Prohibited"[5]

Examples of discriminatory actions that are prohibited include:

> a. An adult vocational education class with an open admissions policy for those 18 years old or older denies admission to all

51

individuals with mental impairments because it is believed the level of work is too advanced for individuals with such impairments.

b. A student who uses a wheelchair is denied the opportunity to try out for the university's track and field team as a javelin thrower. Despite the fact that he had competed in the event in high school, the university denies his request for safety reasons.

c. A woman is employed as an attendant on a bus for handicapped persons. Her duties include assisting them on and off the bus and providing any assistance they might need while they are on the bus. She has been employed in this capacity for three years and has received high ratings regarding her job performances from her immediate supervisor, the bus driver. The personnel manager for the transportation department discovers that she is being treated for a heart impairment. In the two years since she was diagnosed as having the condition, she has performed the job without mishap. The manager concludes, however, that it is too dangerous to have an individual with a heart impairment performing the strenuous task of assisting individuals in wheelchairs on and off the bus.

d. Mary is a student with a learning disability. She is 20 years old. State law requires that handicapped students be provided education services until they reach age 20. State law also permits students to continue attending until they graduate. Thus, students who fail grades can repeat them and ultimately may receive more than 12 years of education. Mary's parents seek to extend her education by noting that she is classified as being in the 10th grade. The school district refuses to continue to provide Mary services, noting that handicapped students' education does not follow the same progression as nonhandicapped students who have a goal to graduate. It is also noted that no handicapped student has ever been provided more than 14 years of education.

e. A school district offers an after-school program for its students. It is an open-admissions program, and each student is charged $30 per week. When faced with the prospect of admitting handicapped students, the district offers the parents of those students the choice of either paying $50 per week to cover the cost of an aide to assist the teacher in providing services to the students, providing an aide themselves, or reducing their children's participation in the program to one hour a day instead of the three hours provided to other students.

f. A school offers three educational tracks to its students: basic, advanced, and vocational. Students are permitted to select their educational tracks in the ninth grade. Special education students who are taking regular education courses are also permitted to select their educational tracks. However, the special education director, based upon his educational beliefs and background, feels that all special education students should be exposed to some vocational course work. Therefore, those students are required to either enroll in a minimum of two vocational courses or have a 2.5 grade point average before they are permitted to select the college preparatory track.

These examples reflect that decisions, criteria, or procedures that exclude qualified handicapped persons on the basis of fear, speculation or stereotypical attitudes regarding their skills and abilities are impermissible. Each individual's attributes, abilities, and limitations must be measured against the criteria in question. Furthermore, handicapped persons cannot be required to meet higher standards or assume greater costs than non-handicapped persons in order to gain access to the services or benefits provided. Recipients also may not condition the participation of the handicapped persons on their acceptance of lesser services or benefits.[6]

Can a balance be struck between the rights of handicapped persons and the recipient's need to maintain the integrity of its program and services? Consider the following examples:

a. The parents of a deaf student reject the educational program offered by the local school district. The district offers a cued speech program for hearing-impaired students at a centralized location. While the parents concede that their son has excelled in the program, they demand that the district duplicate the program at his neighborhood school. Can the district refuse to duplicate the program and insist that the student participate in the centralized program? (*Barnett v. Fairfax County School Board*.)[7]

b. A learning-disabled student enrolls in a community college, advises the admissions officer of her impairment, and requests the following auxiliary aids and academic adjustments: use of a tape recorder in class, extended time on tests, and tutors for all her classes. The college agrees to her request for extended time and use of a tape recorder, but denies her request for tutors. She is advised that the college does not provide tutoring assistance for its students. The student maintains that her prior school experience supports the need for tutors. Can the college refuse to provide such services?

c. The university's policy regarding the provision of auxiliary aids results in the denial of such aids to students who fail to demonstrate a need for financial assistance. Deaf students, therefore, are denied interpreter services. Does the university's policy violate the regulation? (*U.S. v. Board of Trustees of the University of Alabama, supra.*)

These cases provide some insight regarding this tension between the rights of handicapped individuals and the responsibilities of recipients. The recipient's responsibilities extend only to those things which are necessary for providing meaningful access to the program or services which it offers. To answer the questions raised in the examples, one must determine whether the accommodations requested will provide the handicapped individuals the opportunity to participate in the programs or services on an equal footing with nonhandicapped individuals. In the *Barnett* case, it is clear that the school district had fulfilled its responsibility under the Act and the regulation by providing the student access to a program which his parents admitted he excelled in. To require the recipient to go beyond this provision of meaningful access and provide hearing-impaired students individualized programs at their neighborhood schools would be the type of "substantial modification" or "undue administrative and financial burden," or both, that the Supreme Court held recipients were not required to make.[8] The same is true for the student who requested tutoring. Her impairment limited access to the information being provided in class and delayed her response time when being tested. She was at a disadvantage compared to nonhandicapped students whose ability to assimilate and feed back information was not so hampered. The use of the tape recorder and the extra time on tests addressed her limitations and provided her the opportunity to participate equally. Tutorial services, however, do not provide access to information, but rather are additional instructional services to enable the student to understand the content of the information that is being imparted.[9] Nonhandicapped students, as well as handicapped students, could benefit from such additional instruction. The fact that one is handicapped does not entitle one to such an additional benefit. While the Act and the implementing regulations do not permit recipients to provide handicapped persons with lesser services or benefits, they also do *not* require that recipients provide handicapped persons with greater services or benefits. The key is equivalence. Conversely, the University of Alabama case is an example of a recipient failing to provide meaningful access to qualified handicapped persons. As noted by the Court, in rejecting the university's assertion that requiring it to provide interpreters exceeded the scope of Section 504:

> [I]n some instances the lack of an auxiliary aid effectively denies a handicapped student equal access to his or her opportunity to learn. . . . In the context of a discussion class held on the third floor of a building without elevators, a deaf student with no interpreter is as effectively denied meaningful access to the class as is a wheelchair-bound student. (*U. S. v. Board of Trustees of the University of Alabama, supra* at 746.)

Consider the following examples:

> a. A company has a summer job training program in which any employee who has worked for the company for six months or more is permitted to participate. Those who complete the program make up the applicant pool for promotions within the company. Jim, who has dyslexia, has worked for the company

for two years and applies for the summer program. Jim's supervisor, while noting that he is a good, conscientious employee, feels that he is slow in learning new tasks and, therefore, recommends that he be given a test to measure his aptitude for promotion. Further, he recommends that, if the test indicates deficiencies, a special course should be developed for Jim, which he would be required to complete before he is permitted to participate in the summer program.
b. A school district has a policy of not providing transportation services for after-school activities. Is it permissible for the district to refuse to provide transportation services to a handicapped student who must stay after school to receive physical therapy services that the district has identified as being a necessary part of her educational program?

A recipient is warranted in furnishing different or separate services only when it is necessary for the provision of equal access to the services, programs, or benefits offered. The student who needs transportation services after school is entitled to such because the recipient has determined that physical therapy services are necessary for her to benefit from her educational program. If she is denied transportation, she is denied full educational services. She should not be penalized because the district is unable to provide complete educational services to her during the regular school day. However, in Jim's case, separate services are not necessary to provide access. The only requirement for participation in the program is six months of continuous service. Jim meets that criterion. While Jim's supervisor may have good intentions of providing him with the additional training, it has not been demonstrated that Jim is any less qualified to participate in the program than other employees.

a. A vocational education program contracts with local businesses to provide on-the-job training for its students. One of the employers refuses to hire a handicapped student although the student is qualified for the position in question. Therefore, the student is assigned to another employer, and a nonhandicapped student is referred to the first employer.
b. A school district permits the local YMCA to use its gymnasium for the Y's basketball games. Fred's team participates in the league. When league officials discover that Fred is deaf, they advise his coach that he cannot play. They state that the participation of handicapped individuals would increase the potential for injuries and, thus, result in their insurance premiums increasing.
c. The Flimflam Corporation, a recipient of federal financing assistance, formed a nonprofit service organization, the Training Center, which provides adult vocational training. The Training Center is a separate entity that does not itself receive federal financial assistance. Employees of Flimflam work at the Center

as trainers; Flimflam assigns all new employees to the Center for training, and it has purchased training equipment for the Center. The director of the Training Center asserts that it is not a recipient of federal financial assistance when refusing to provide accommodations to qualified handicapped persons.

The regulation clearly provides that a recipient may not provide support to an "entity or person that subjects participants or employees in the recipient's program to discrimination.[10] The first two examples illustrate the principle that the support need not be financial. The use of a facility or a student which provides tangible benefits to the entity is sufficient. The key is whether the recipient provides "significant assistance" to the nonrecipient.

Significant assistance, according to H.E.W., can be of two forms: tangible support or intangible support. Tangible support includes direct financial assistance, the provision of facilities, equipment, or real property, secretarial and management services. Intangible support includes actions which identify the recipient with the discriminatory organization or bestow recognition upon the organization, such as provision of a faculty sponsor or advisor.[11] Moreover, the nature of the relationship between the recipient and the other entity must also be considered. How substantial is the relationship? The financial support provided by the recipient should be considered. Do the entity's activities relate so closely to the recipient's program or activity that they should be considered activities of the recipient itself? In the case of Flimflam, it would be legitimate to argue that the Training Center was merely an alter-ego of the corporation and find Flimflam in violation of Section 504.[12] Keep in mind that the recipients in the above examples, *i.e.*, the vocational education program, the district, and the Flimflam Corporation, would be held in violation of the Act, *not* the employer, the YMCA, or the Training Center.

"Equally Effective"[13]

Appendix A provides the following definition of the term "equally effective":

[E]qually effective . . . is intended to encompass the concept of equivalent, as opposed to identical, services and to acknowledge the fact that in order to meet the individual needs of handicapped persons to the same extent that the corresponding needs of nonhandicapped persons are met, adjustments to regular programs or the provision of different programs may sometimes be necessary.[14]

a. The university's library, which was built in 1950, is inaccessible to mobility impaired students. The university plans to make library services accessible by either using a bookmobile or establishing a library annex. The students object to the book-mobile, noting that they will not have effective access to the library materials. They state it would be extremely difficult to complete research projects without personal access to all services.

b. Doug, a visually impaired student, alleges that the university denied his admission to its law school based upon the use of a criterion, the LSAT, which discriminates against handicapped students. He notes that handicapped students traditionally score below the norm on the test. When Doug took the test he was provided a reader and extended time. Further, the university's admissions decisions are also based on the students' grade point averages, past academic records and personal references.

c. A university housing department offers the following options to students: air-conditioned, double rooms with common bathrooms; single rooms with private bathrooms; and air-conditioned, double rooms with private bathrooms. However, the only rooms which are accessible to mobility-impaired students are the double rooms with common bathrooms and the single rooms with private bathrooms. The single rooms cost more.

Are the recipients providing equal access to handicapped persons in these examples? The question to be answered is whether the steps which were taken by the recipient provide full benefits or access to the program or services. As noted previously, the recipient need only place handicapped persons on equal footing with those who are not handicapped.[15] In our examples this would mean that handicapped individuals would be afforded an equal opportunity to utilize the library, gain admission to law school, and benefit from on-campus housing. Each of our examples presents a principle which is important to one's understanding of the term "equally effective." Specifically:

1. The choice or options provided handicapped persons do not have to be identical. When one applies this standard to the housing situation, it is clear that the university is not in violation solely because the double rooms with private bathrooms are not accessible. The important factor is that, when viewed as a whole, the same range of choices is available to handicapped students. As long as the choices are comparable, they need not be the same. The university would be in violation if it only provided single rooms to handicapped students or if handicapped students whose conditions necessitated special accommodations (such as living in a double room alone) are charged more for their rooms.[16]

2. Recipients are not obligated to make exceptions to their standards and, as a result, serve persons who are not qualified. With respect to the LSAT, the university's responsibility is to ensure that handicapped applicants are afforded an equal opportunity to meet its academic standards.

The student was not only accommodated with respect to the test itself, but other admission criteria were considered as well. Ultimately, handicapped individuals must be as qualified as the successful applicants.[17] The recipient is not required to produce the identical result or level of achievement. The OCR has taken the position that so long as such decisions considered other factors, it ". . . will not find an institution out of compliance if that institution requires the submission of test scores by applicants, even though there is a possibility that the tests do not reflect the individuals' aptitude as accurately as they do for nonhandicapped applicants."[18]

3. While recipients are allowed flexibility in determining the methods which will be used to provide access, they are "required to give priority to methods that offer handicapped and nonhandicapped persons programs and activities in the same setting."[19] [T]he provision of unnecessarily separate or different services is discriminatory."[20] This principle would lead to the conclusion that the most appropriate solution to the library accessibility problem would be establishing an annex. Further, one could also argue that the students are correct in asserting that the other method would not provide comparable access. However, the recipient could also provide access by making the entire catalog system available to handicapped students and then employing work study students to retrieve the books and materials.

"Separate or Different Programs"[21]

A school district hosts an annual Olympic festival for its students. In conjunction with this festival, a special Olympic section for handicapped students is also offered. Jim, a student classified as emotionally conflicted, registers for track and field events and is advised that he has to compete in the special Olympic section. Jim insists he is qualified to compete in the festival events with nonhandicapped students.

A university provides a special college program for learning-disabled students for their freshman year. This program is geared to assisting students in negotiating the college environment in conjunction with meeting their special education needs. The program is one quarter in length, and the students take only ten hours instead of the standard 12 to 14 credit hours. Three of their ten hours are a special study skills orientation course. All learning-disabled students are enrolled in the program for the first quarter without regard to the nature and extent of their impairment.

Handicapped individuals cannot be denied the opportunity to participate in programs or activities for which they are qualified. As noted in Appendix A, handicapped persons have the "option of participating in regular programs despite the existence of permissibly separate or different programs."[22] Thus, if Jim and the learning-disabled students are qualified, they must be permitted to participate in the regular programs.

"Methods of Administration"[23]

a. A school policy provides that no students may be transferred to a new school without board approval. However, the district constructs a new facility and notifies all parents of handicapped students that they will be transferred at the beginning of the next school term. The proposed transfers are not submitted for board approval. When the removal of the students from their neighborhood schools is contested by the parents, the board rules that its transfer policy does not apply to the assignment of handicapped students.

b. Severely handicapped children who are wards of the state are placed in local school districts as well as private institutions. The state relinquishes responsibility for development of the educational programs to the entities where the students are placed. As a consequence, some of the students are not provided appropriate educational services. While the state assumes responsibility for its failure regarding the private nonrecipients, it maintains that the recipient school districts are solely responsible for the violations regarding the other students.

c. University officials are advised through student complaints that the College of Business is refusing to provide effective auxiliary aids and academic adjustments to handicapped students. The officials decline to take direct action regarding the matter noting that the university's practice is to respect autonomy of administration within the individual colleges.

d. A company has a policy of not hiring individuals with epilepsy for its machinery division. A hospital has a policy of not permitting guide dogs in the hospital. Both employers justify these policies on the basis of safety.

The examples above all reflect violations of Section 504 and its implementing regulations. They illustrate that recipients should neither adopt formal policies nor implement informal procedures which result in discriminatory treatment of qualified handicapped persons. Such policies and procedures are generally an attempt to exclude entire groups of individuals based upon perceptions of the abilities or limitations of the group as a whole.[24] Further, recipients such as the university and the state, who have oversight responsibility with respect to subrecipients, can neither ignore nor tacitly approve actions of subrecipients that violate the regulations.

"Site or Location of a Facility"[25]

Does the construction of the following facilities violate the regulations?

> The state proposes to construct a new vocational education center on a lot where the terrain is such that it would be virtually impossible to make the facility accessible to mobility-impaired individuals.
>
> A school district wishes to add a new art center to its existing facility. The hilly terrain presents serious accessibility problems.

While the regulations clearly prohibit the construction of a new facility that would exclude an entire group of handicapped persons, Appendix A expressly provides an exemption with respect to the second example. It notes that the regulations were not intended "to apply to construction of additional buildings at an existing site."[26]

8
Procedural Requirements

Subpart A includes mandates regarding appropriate remedial action, requirements regarding notice and grievance procedures, and the impacct of other laws and requirements on the obligation to comply with Section 504.[1]

Remedial Action[2]

Generally § 104.6 requires recipients to take remedial action if they are found to be in violation of the regulation. Recipients may also take voluntary action to relieve or address "conditions that led to limited participation by handicapped persons whether or not the limited participation was caused by any discriminatory action."[3] However, if the recipient chooses to take voluntary action, it should ensure that the action does not violate the Act and the regulations. For example, if a college were seeking to increase the graduation rate of learning-disabled students, it would violate the regulations to require all learning-disabled students without regard to their individual skills and abilities to take developmental courses during their first semester. Learning-disabled students who met the criteria for participation in regular classes should be permitted to enroll in such classes.

Which of the following are appropriate remedial actions?

    a. A student is not provided requested accommodations, *i.e.*, a reader and extended time, for a college placement test. Consequently, his score on the test indicates that he should be placed in developmental courses. He charges the college with discrimination, and the college is found in violation of Section 504. The student objects to taking the test a second time and asks that he be placed in advanced courses based upon his high school grades.

    b. A 20-year-old student, seeking to transfer from a private school to a public school, is denied appropriate educational services for a year and a half. State law requires that handicapped students receive educational services up to the age of 22. The student requests one-and-a-half years of compensatory services beyond his twenty-second birthday as a remedy for the district's violation.[4]

    c. A university is found in violation of Section 504 for denying handicapped employees tenure. The university is required to award tenure and to reimburse them for any financial losses, including offering tenure to individuals who have left the institution's employ as a result of being denied tenure. Additionally, the university is required to develop a training program for its managers and administrators to instruct them regarding the requirement of the Act and its implementing regulations.

    d. A district is found in violation for refusing to provide three handicapped students summer school services. Although state law requires that handicapped students who would regress without extended school year services be provided such services, the district has a policy of providing summer school services only to seniors who need credits for graduation. The district is required to evaluate the three students to determine whether they meet the criteria for extended school year services. An advocacy group for handicapped students charges that all of the district's handicapped students (289) should be reevaluated to assess their need for summer school services.

Appendix A provides the following examples of appropriate remedial action: provision of services to persons previously discriminated against, reinstatement of employees, and development of a remedial action plan.[5] The remedial action should eliminate the discriminatory practices and compensate those who have suffered the effects of the past discrimination (as example "b" illustrates).[6] Individuals who are compensated may include those no longer affiliated with the recipient as well as those who would would have been a part of the recipient's program were it not for the discrimination (example "c"). However, remedial action may not be used to require a recipient to provide services to handicapped persons who are not qualified. Thus, in example "a," the appropriate remedial action is to provide the requested accommodations for the student to take the test. The student is not entitled to enroll in advanced courses unless he meets the criterion, *i.e.,* the necessary score on the placement test. Similarly, with respect to example "d," the district is required only to consider students for summer school services who meet the criteria, *i.e.,* those who might suffer regression without such services and those who are seniors needing credits for graduation.

       A school district fails to provide a full school day to handicapped students because it employs a certified special education teacher only on a part-time basis. Parents file complaints with the state department of education. The state verifies that services are not being provided to the students but takes no action to ensure that the students are provided services. Which entity should be required to remedy the violation of the regulations?

The regulations expressly provide that the OCR may find more than one recipient in violation and, consequently, require all to implement remedial action. Since the state department of education "exercises control over" the school district, which is guilty of discrimination, both the state and the district can properly be required to take action to obtain a full-time certified teacher for the students. *Remember*—"Should a recipient fail to take required remedial action, the ultimate sanctions of court action or termination of federal financial assistance may be imposed."[7]

Section 104.6(c) requires recipients to conduct self-evaluations to identify policies and procedures which discriminate and to take steps to eliminate them, and recipients were required to conduct such evaluations within the first year of the effective date of the regulations. Therefore, since the time for completing the self-evaluation and implementing the changes has long since passed, unless a recipient admits to having never complied with § 104.6(c), this provision of the regulations generally is not at issue.

"Responsible Employee," Grievance Procedures, and Notice

The primary purpose of §§ 104.7 and 104.8 is to advise handicapped individuals of their rights and provide them with avenues to raise concerns regarding possible violations of those rights. To that end, a recipient is required to designate a person to coordinate its efforts to comply with the regulations;[8] to adopt grievance procedures for resolution of complaints;[9] and to provide initial and continuing notice of its obligation not to discriminate.[10]

> Susan, an employee of Corn University, files a complaint with the OCR because her supervisor refuses to accommodate her handicap. The university's attorney challenges the OCR's right to investigate, asserting that Susan is required to file an internal grievance prior to seeking redress from the OCR.

While the OCR encourages individuals to use the grievance procedures available prior to filing a complaint, there is no requirement that they do so. "The regulation does not require that grievance procedures be exhausted before recourse is sought from the Department."[11] Further, the use of the grievance procedure cannot be limited to students.[12]

Which of the following nondiscrimination statements are acceptable?

    a. Dunn College does not discriminate on the basis of race, color, national origin, sex, or handicap.
    b. Dunn College does not discriminate on the basis of handicap in any of its programs.
    c. Dunn College is an equal access/equal opportunity institution.

The first two statements are appropriate. The recipient need not specifically reference Section 504 nor state specifically that it does not discriminate with respect to employment or admissions. Additionally, a single statement may be used to meet the notice requirements of both Section 504 and other civil rights statutes. The phrase "equal access/equal opportunity" does not comply with the regulatory requirement that the notification advise that the recipient "does not discriminate on the basis of handicap."[13]

> The university's notification statement identifies the Vice President for Student Affairs as the individual responsible for compliance with the regulations. Neither the name of the individual nor any other information is provided. Is this an appropriate notification?

It is not necessary to identify the coordinator by name. It is sufficient to identify the individual by position. However, the OCR has taken the position that a notice that fails to provide information on how to contact the individual is not "an effective notice."[14]

Other Laws or Requirements

Recipients will not be permitted to avoid their obligations under the Act and the regulations by asserting that state or local laws take precedence.[15] Further, recipients should not assume responsibility for the future employability of qualified handicapped persons by denying them the opportunity to pursue the occupation or profession of their choice. Often instructors actively discourage or, in some instances, refuse to allow qualified handicapped persons to pursue programs or courses of study, because they feel that the individual would not be able to obtain gainful employment at some future date.

> Marka Medical School averages 1,500 applications for the 175 slots available for its first-year class. Since standardized test scores and college grade point averages alone are inadequate criteria for reducing the applicant pool, the school's admissions committee uses other factors which are felt indicative of potential success or failure in the medical profession. The factors considered include: family background, affiliation with successful medical professionals or organizations, and evidence of a successful work history. The committee also looks for indications that the applicant would be able to withstand the stress and rigors of medical school and the medical profession. An otherwise qualified student who is being treated for a mental disability is denied admission. The committee questions whether the student can withstand the stress; ultimately it bases its decision on the fact that, historically, the state licensing board has been disinclined to license an individual with a history of serious mental illness. It is felt that it would be a mistake to give a valuable slot in the freshman class to someone whose

chances, it feels, of graduating are below average, and whose chances of getting licensed are even worse. Does the school violate the regulations in denying the student admission?

The school's actions are in violation of the regulations. The decision to exclude the student is based upon a perception that individuals with mental impairments cannot withstand the stress of attending medical school, and that the student's employment options would be limited once graduated. There is no evidence that this student's impairment contraindicates stressful situations such as medical school. Furthermore, the regulations expressly prohibit excluding handicapped persons based upon the perception that employment opportunities will be limited for them in a particular occupation or profession. The student in question may choose to practice in a state that does not have such restrictive licensing history or may have no interest in private practice. "The presence of limited employment opportunities in a particular profession does not excuse a recipient from complying with the regulation."[16]

A recipient constructing a new facility follows the state building code for providing accessibility for the facility. The building code standards are not equivalent to the regulatory accessibility requirements. Is it permissible for the recipient to deviate from the regulatory standards?

The regulations do not prohibit compliance with all laws that are inconsistent. The key question is whether the law imposes limitations on the "eligibility of qualified handicapped persons." Thus, if the state building code provides equivalent or greater accessibility than the regulatory standards, the recipient may follow the state standards.[17]

Part III: Access to Facilities

The goal of providing accessible programs is to foster in-
dependence and avoid humiliation.
—*Hindsdale* (NY) Central School District
EHLR 401:349 (1989)

The primary compliance problem that recipients have under Subpart C is differentiating between the compliance standards for existing facilities and those for new facilities.

9
The Duty to Provide
Access to Facilities

The mandate to provide program access requires that recipients ensure that qualified handicapped persons are not excluded from programs or activities simply because the recipients' "facilities are inaccessible or unusable."[1] Subpart C, which addresses program access, while arguably the most straightforward subpart of the regulations, presents some interesting problems for recipients. Consider *The United States of America v. The Board of Trustees of the University of Alabama.*[2] This case illustrates many of the significant issues that recipients face under Subpart C. The pertinent facts of the case are as follows:

> The University of Alabama's business education laboratory is housed on the second floor of a building that is inaccessible to physically handicapped students. Classes held in the building cannot be relocated to provide access to handicapped students because the equipment cannot be moved. Handicapped students seeking enrollment in business education either (a) defer enrollment hoping the lab will be relocated, (b) are taught alone in an isolated setting where the laboratory experience cannot be duplicated, or (c) are given the choice to take courses on an ungraded basis. The university declines to take additional steps to make the laboratory accessible. The university's swimming pool used for instruction and recreation is also inaccessible. In addition, while the university provides transportation services for its employees and students 12 hours a day, services for handicapped students needing a wheelchair lift are limited to four hours a day. There is only one accessible bus available, and this bus is sometimes rescheduled, without notice, to accommodate a student making a special request. Further, when the bus is used for off-campus trips, there are no transportation services available to handicapped persons.

The Court found the university in violation, noting that the arrangements for the business education courses "did not fully replicate the laboratory experience provided to [other] students" and did not provide "the opportunity to work with other students cooperatively."[3] With respect to the transportation services, the Court held that the university was not offering handicapped persons "equally effective" services.[4] The Court also ruled that the university had to make its swimming pool accessible. Careful review of this case reveals the origin of most of the compliance problems that arise under Subpart C. Those problems can generally be traced to a failure to understand or acknowledge two very important facts regarding the mandate to provide program access.

1) Each recommended action regarding program access should reflect the goal of Subpart C.

The goal of providing accessible programs is to permit handicapped individuals to participate freely and independently in the programs, benefits, and services offered. Actions that segregate them and deny them the opportunity either to interact with their peers or participate in the programs of their choice violate the regulations.[5] Nor should the recipient select methods of providing access that serve only to humiliate handicapped individuals.[6] Recipients must make the same variety and scope of programs or activities available to handicapped students as are provided to nonhandicapped students. The opportunities available to them cannot be limited solely on the basis of their handicapping condition.[7] The ultimate goal is to make all programs and facilities "readily accessible."

2) Subpart C provides two compliance standards: program access for existing facilities and facility access for new construction and alterations.

The program access standard is less stringent. It is an acknowledgment on the part of the drafters of the regulations that it would be too expensive, if not impossible, to make many facilities built before the effective date of the regulations fully accessible. Therefore, recipients need only devise methods to make the programs offered in such facilities accessible. However, new facilities (those constructed after the effective date of the regulations) are to be "readily accessible and usable by handicapped persons."[8] This language has been interpreted to require complete accessibility.[9] The key is that it is the *facility* which must be usable by and accessible to handicapped persons.

Recipients, most notably postsecondary institutions, frequently attempt to apply the program accessibility standard to new construction. For example, can a university building new housing for its students make only rooms on the first floor accessible to its mobility-impaired students? What about the students' rights to move about freely and interact with their peers on the second floor and above? Can it be argued that the university is in effect impermissibly segregating the students? These are certainly legitimate questions.

Given the fact that the "readily accessible" standard, if applied literally, appears to be an absolute standard, it would seem that the university's only avenue under the regulations would be to argue that to require it to make the facility totally accessible would be an undue financial and administrative burden.[10] However, this claim, except in extraordinary circumstances, would be somewhat difficult to prove, since the cost of making a facility accessible would generally be a small fraction of the total cost of the project. There is clearly a need for a policy interpretation regarding this issue. Unfortunately this is an area in which the enforcement agency, to date, has failed to articulate its policy on a national level.

The key to complying with Subpart C is to incorporate the goal of the mandate to provide program access in one's decision-making and to ensure that one is applying the correct compliance standard.

> The Superintendent of Flamdoodle School District is puzzled by a complaint filed against the district for failure to make its programs accessible. In response to the complaint, he provides extensive evidence that all the school buildings in the district have been renovated to provide total accessibility. The complaint states, in pertinent part, that a mobility-impaired student was prevented from participating in a field trip because the off-campus facility was not accessible, and that school board meetings are held in a state building to which individuals in wheelchairs cannot gain access. The superintendent is unsure of what his responsibilities are regarding facilities which are not within his control.

It is important to remember that an educational program may include activities that occur away from the school campus, e.g., field trips, athletic events, theater productions, and vocational-technical programs. A determination of accessibility for the program, then, must include a review of the methods used to ensure all activities and programs are accessible, not simply a determination of accessibility on the campus. The superintendent also needs to keep in mind that access must be provided to those activities that are part of the district but not related to a particular educational program, such as administration office visits, board meetings, and other activities in which participation by parents and students is required or encouraged. The recipient's responsibility is not limited to actual delivery of educational services.[11] It is also important to remember that the duty to provide access includes ensuring appropriate means of communication and interaction for participants that are, for example, hearing impaired or visually impaired.[12]

> A student in a wheelchair is provided access to a building through the back door. She must travel down a poorly lit walkway where the maintenance department stores discarded equipment and materials, and, then, has to use the service entrance. Often the door is locked, and she must wait for a building employee to open it for her.

A program or activity is readily accessible when "it is conducted in a building and room that mobility-impaired persons can enter or leave without assistance from others."[13] Thus, the access provided cannot be illusionary, and the methods used must be effective. The building is not readily accessible if the student must negotiate a dangerous walkway and wait for someone to open the door for her. The passageway should be safe, and either the door should be unlocked or the student provided a key. The OCR has also ruled that it is unacceptable to require a handicapped person to travel a great distance to reach an accessible facility.[14]

> Drake School District is found in violation by the OCR following a compliance review. District officials acknowledge accessibility problems but assert that they have insufficient funds to make the necessary changes. The OCR is asked to delay compliance proceedings until the district acquires the necessary funds from the state. After attempting for three months to acquire funds from the state, district officials ask that the accessibility standards be waived until such time as the state legislature provides funds for the necessary alterations.

Waivers are not permitted, because it was determined that the regulations provide sufficient flexibility to allow program accessibility to be provided "short of extremely expensive or impractical physical changes."[15]

Existing Facilities

The recipient's *program or activity,* when viewed "in its entirety," must be "readily accessible to handicapped persons."[16] It is the program as a whole that must be made accessible, not all of the recipient's facilities.[17] Methods that may be used include reassignment of classes or services, providing aides, use of alternate sites, and making alterations to the facilities.[18] *Remember*—recipients need not make structural changes to existing facilities unless there is no other way to provide program access.

> Breakly School District operates 12 schools. Six of the schools were built in the 1980s and are accessible, while only three of the six schools built prior to 1977 are accessible. Mr. and Mrs. Kirt's daughter is mobility impaired and is assigned to one of the accessible elementary schools. The Kirts are upset because she is not permitted to attend her neighborhood school along with all the other children in her subdivision. District officials advise the Kirts that the neighborhood school is not accessible. Mr. and Mrs. Kirt argue that Section 504 requires that all of the district's schools be made accessible.
> Cheapskate College decides to resolve the issue of program accessibility by assigning all handicapped students to its newest branch campus, which can be made accessible at minimum expense. It is asserted that this is an acceptable approach because all three of its campuses offer the same programs,

and it would relieve the other two campuses of the economic and administrative problems of addressing program accessibility.

The hypotheticals illustrate two important principles concerning program accessibility. First, not all of a recipient's facilities must be made accessible; second, the programs or activities offered to handicapped persons must be offered in the most integrated setting appropriate. Therefore, Mr. and Mrs. Kirt's objection to their daughter's placement solely on the basis of the fact that every facility is not accessible does not entitle them to relief pursuant to Section 504.[19] Cheapskate College's approach is not acceptable. The drafters of the regulations specifically rejected actions that segregate handicapped individuals. It was noted that, "[W]hile a public school district need not make each of its buildings completely accessible, it may not make only one facility or part of a facility accessible if the result is to segregate handicapped students in a single setting." Similarly, the suggestion made by postsecondary institutions that colleges and universities could establish educational consortia solely for handicapped students was not approved. It was stated that such consortia "would discriminate against qualified handicapped persons by restricting their choice in selecting institutions of higher education and would, therefore, be inconsistent with the basic objectives of the statute."[20] Therefore, Cheapskate College cannot limit the attendance opportunities of qualified individuals to just one of its branch campuses. When deciding to make only some facilities accessible, recipients must maintain maximum integration for handicapped individuals.[21]

> Joseph, an orthopedically impaired high school senior, objects to the school he is assigned to because his transportation time, 45 minutes, is 15 minutes longer than that of nonhandicapped students, and because the school does not offer some of the advanced and honors courses that are offered at the other high schools in the district. District officials maintain that the assignment is appropriate because the school is the most accessible in the district.
>
> Susan, who attends Lier's Law School, is upset that the commercial law course she wants to take is offered in an accessible location only in the afternoons and evenings. The 9 A.M. class, which she prefers to take because she works for a law firm in the afternoon, is offered in an inaccessible facility. The school attempts to accommodate Susan's need for a morning class but is unable to provide an accessible classroom for a 9 A.M. session, and the professor is unable to rearrange his schedule to teach the class at another time. Susan insists that the school must provide her access to the 9 A.M. class.

What does the phrase, "the program, when viewed in its entirety, is ready accessible" mean? The OCR has stated that if a public school is operating facilities that are not accessible, it must ensure that:

1. all programs offered in any inaccessible buildings are offered at other accessible locations;

2. handicapped students are able to participate in all school activities;
3. the amount of time handicapped students spend in travel is comparable to the amount spent by nonhandicapped students; and
4. handicapped students receive equivalent or equally effective services.
        See OCR Response to Inquiry, EHLR 305:41 (1987).

Therefore, Joseph has a legitimate argument regarding his placement, because his transportation time is significantly longer than that of non-handicapped students and he is unable to take courses offered only at inaccessible schools.[22] Susan, however, will not be successful in challenging the college's actions. Appendix A specifically provides that "a university may not exclude a handicapped student from a specifically required course offering because it is not offered in an accessible location, but it need not make every section of that course accessible."[23]

Which of the following are acceptable methods of providing program accessibility?

> Mrs. Murray, the music instructor, prefers to conduct her class in the school auditorium on the stage. When a student in a wheelchair is assigned to her class, the principal instructs Mrs. Murray to relocate the class to an accessible room.
>
> The top two floors of the college's library are inaccessible. Access is provided to handicapped students by placing card catalogues in an accessible area and providing student aides to retrieve books and search for materials identified by the students. A group of handicapped students insists that the college make structural alterations to allow them to get to the upper floors. The second floor houses periodicals, while the third floor is used merely for storage of discarded equipment.
>
> The East Pahokee School District, East Pahokee, Montana (population 10,000), has a student population of less than 1,000. Its facilities consist of an elementary school (grades K–8) and a high school (grades 9–12). Both facilities are multi-storied buildings built during the 1920s; neither is accessible to mobility-impaired students. A parent advocate from Helena makes a presentation at East Pahokee and notices the inaccessible facilities. She tells the district that it needs to make its facilities accessible. The district responds that it hasn't had any mobility-impaired students, and does not, now, have any mobility-impaired students living in East Pahokee, so there is no need to make its program accessible.

Recipients are not required to make structural alterations to existing facilities if other effective methods of providing accessibility are available.[24] Those methods may include "redesign of equipment, reassignment of classes or other services to accessible buildings and making aides available."[25] Therefore, the methods chosen by the recipients in the first two examples are acceptable. *Remember*—structural modifications are not required unless that is the only means of providing access. Further, when determining what steps are necessary to make a program accessible, one must keep in mind that the extent of the revisions or modifications is tied to the need for handicapped individuals to have access. Therefore, in the library example, the recipient would not have to implement procedures to make the third floor accessible, because no research material is housed on that floor. Regarding Pahokee's policy, the absence of handicapped students does not relieve a recipient of the responsibility to make its programs or activities accessible. The OCR has noted that such a policy:

> [I]gnores the needs of those persons living in the area who temporarily become disabled and other persons who do not live in the community, but who are otherwise eligible to participate in the services provided by the recipient. . . . Finally, mobility-impaired persons may decide not to participate or enroll in the . . . program because its services presently are inaccessible.[26]

> The university offers a nationally recognized doctoral program in oceanography. An integral part of the doctoral program is research conducted on the university's oceanographic ship. A mobility-impaired student has been accepted into the program and is anticipating participating in the research. The university has already determined that it is impossible either to provide the research in another location or to make alterations to the ship that would make it accessible. What can the university do? Is physically carrying the student an acceptable means of providing access?

Carrying has been determined to be an unacceptable method of providing access to mobility-impaired individuals. However, carrying may be used (a) where it is "expedient" until construction is completed, or (b) in "manifestly exceptional" cases.[27] While the fact situation above presents a clear example of a "manifestly exceptional" situation, we note that the failure of the OCR to provide guidance regarding the meaning of the phrase "manifestly exceptional" may prove difficult in cases that are not so clear cut. Further, if carrying is utilized, the aides must be instructed in the safest and least humiliating manner of carrying, and the service must be reliably provided.[28]

New Construction

Facilities must be constructed "in such a manner that the facility or part of the facility is readily accessible or usable by handicapped persons."[29]

> Recalcitrant State University is involved in a full-scale fight with the Militant Handicapped Student Association (MHSA) regarding the building plans for several new facilities that the university expects to construct in the spring.

MHSA is threatening to sue because the plans, as presently drawn, reveal that there will be a number of accessibility problems, *e.g.*, the swimming pool for the student center will not be equipped with a lift, the medical administration building and the faculty center have a number of areas that can be reached only by climbing several flights of stairs, and many restrooms in the new facilities are not accessible. University officials respond to MHSA's concerns as follows:

a. The swimming pool in the existing athletic facility has a lift, so mobility-impaired students can continue to swim there.
b. The new buildings are designed to conform to the 1950s architectural style of the other campus buildings, and the planning committee has made sure that the first floor of all buildings will be accessible, so programs or activities may be relocated as necessary.
c. While not all restrooms are accessible, there are a sufficient number of accessible restrooms.

Is the university in violation of Section 504 as MHSA claims? The university is seeking to apply the program accessibility standard to new construction. As noted previously, the standard for new construction requires that such facilities be designed and constructed in a manner to make them readily accessible to and usable by handicapped persons. Recipients are not permitted to apply the lesser standard of program accessibility to new construction as Recalcitrant University is attempting to do.[30]

> Karsten University's gymnasium suffered extensive damage during a winter storm. The university is planning major renovations for the 75-year-old building and requests the OCR's guidance regarding the proper standard to use for program accessibility. The planned renovations entail totally replacing the main floor facilities and repairing the stairs leading to the second and third floor. The cost of the project is projected to be $375,000. The president questions whether the renovation project has to include plans to make the racquetball courts on the third floor of the building totally accessible. The planning committee states that every proposal to make the floor accessible would increase the cost of the project by a minimum of $250,000, and would require eliminating one court and replacing one support wall to make room for an elevator. It is noted that the construction of the stairways makes a chairlift impractical as well as dangerous.

In general, if alterations are made to a portion of a building in which accessibility could be improved, the alterations must be made in the manner that will provide maximum accessibility. Thus, if a part of the renovation to the gymnasium involved replacing the stage and previously the stage was inaccessible, the newly designed stage should include a ramp to provide access. Conversely, this provision would not apply to changes such as repairing light fixtures or the ceiling since accessibility would not be at issue.[31] However, the regulatory provision does state that such alterations should be made "to the maximum extent feasible," which implies that there are no limits to a recipient's responsibilities. Appendix A states that the limiting phrase was included

> [T]o allow for the occasional case in which the nature of an existing facility is such as to make it impractical or prohibitively expensive to renovate the building in a manner that results in its being entirely barrier-free.[32]

Neither the regulatory provision nor the Appendix provides any further guidance regarding the meaning of "impractical" and "prohibitively expensive." Further, OCR's letters of findings and policy statements are not informative. Therefore, these questions must be answered on a case-by-case basis. Clearly, Karsten University could persuasively argue that increasing the cost of the project by $250,000 and replacing a support wall on a 75-year-old building is both "impractical" and "prohibitively expensive."

Part IV: Elementary and Secondary Education

The most sensitive nerve in the human body is the parental nerve.

—*Eva N. v. Brock*
741 F. Supp. 626, 627 (E.D.K., 1990)

Subpart D applies to recipients that operate preschool, elementary, secondary and adult education programs and activities. While the recipients in question are primarily state and local educational agencies (LEA's), this subsection of the regulations also applies to some private education programs (see § 104.39). The author recognizes that there are a substantial number of court decisions in which the applicability of Section 504 has been held to be strictly limited to questions of nondiscrimination. It has, in fact, been asserted that specific provisions of the regulations are invalid because they go beyond requiring nondiscrimination and, instead, mandate affirmative action. Furthermore, courts have ruled that Section 504 does not guarantee a right to free appropriate public education to handicapped individuals.

Chapters 10 through 18 focus on how the enforcement agency has interpreted and applied the Act and the implementing regulations. The majority of the court decisions cited involve interpretations of the EHA. When these cases are reviewed in conjunction with OCR Letters of Findings, which are also cited, it becomes clear that the OCR has, in large measure, used EHA case law as a yardstick in its enforcement of Section 504. Chapter 19 is an in-depth look at the controversy regarding the enforcement of Subpart D and the impact of both Section 504 and the EHA on the elementary and secondary education arena.

10
Entities Responsible
for Providing Services

When one thinks of the entity responsible for providing educational services to a handicapped child, or any child for that matter, one normally envisions the child attending a public school in his or her neighborhood. In this case, the responsibility for providing services would fall to the local education agency (LEA). However, school districts and states use numerous methods to serve disabled students that result in their receiving services in a variety of nontraditional manners. For example:

> LEA (1) refers the student to LEA (2)
>
> LEA (1) refers the student to a private institution
>
> LEA (1) refers the student to a state-operated facility
>
> LEA (1) refers the student to a state-operated facility that then refers the student to LEA (2)

These examples reflect how confusing the question can be of what entity, or entities, are responsible for providing educational services to an individual child. When considering this question, there are three important issues that must be addressed.[1] They are:

A. The LEA's responsibility to students "in its jurisdiction" [§ 104.33(a)].
B. The LEA's responsibility to students referred to programs "other than the one it operates" [§ 104.33(b)(3)].
C. The state's oversight responsibility.

"In" the Recipient's Jurisdiction

> Marcia's parents, who make their home in Maine, send her to live with her grandparents in Seattle. When her grandparents present their guardianship papers and seek to enroll her in school in Seattle, they are informed by

school officials that she cannot be served unless tuition is paid. It is the district's position that Marcia is not entitled to a free public education because, despite her temporary residence in Seattle, the domicile of her parents and, therefore, her own, is in the state of Maine. Marcia's grandparents are advised to either pay tuition or request financial assistance from the school district that had previously provided her educational services in Maine. Does the word "in" refer to Marcia's domicile or residence?

What exactly does the phrase "in the recipient's jurisdiction" mean in terms of establishing which recipient has primary responsibility for providing educational services?

Legal textbooks are filled with long-winded discussions regarding the meaning of the terms "domicile" and "residence" in various contexts, and the importance of differentiating between them in establishing legal rights and responsibilities.

> *Domicile*—A person's legal home. The permanent residence of a person or the place to which he intends to return even though he may actually reside elsewhere. A person may have more than one residence but only one domicile.

> *Residence*—Place where one actually lives or has his home; residence implies something more than mere physical presence and something less than domicile.[2]

Is this distinction really relevant to the question of which agency is responsible for providing educational services? Fortunately, the drafters of the regulations answered this question with an unequivocal NO. They anticipated the nature of the disagreements that would arise in interpreting the phrase "in the recipient's jurisdiction" and avoided the legal nitpicking by specifically providing in Appendix A that "the word 'in' encompasses the concepts of both domicile and actual residence."[3] Thus, recipients are not permitted to deny services to handicapped students on the basis of the legal distinction between one's "domicile" and "residence," and Marcia is entitled to receive educational services during the time she resides with her grandparents.

In *Sonya C. By and Through Olivar v. Arizona Department of Education*, the Court succinctly disposed of the "domicile" versus "residence" argument, as follows:

> [A] child's domicile may determine which State pays for the education, but the child's presence determines who must provide the services.[4]

The Court further stated, quoting *Rabinowitz v. New Jersey State Board of Education*, 550 F. Supp. 481, 486 (D. New Jersey 1982), that

[t]he court can discern no congressional intent to allow a participating State to refuse to educate a handicapped child clearly within its borders for bona fide reasons. (*Id.* at 711.)

Thus, the child's lawful presence within the district or the state determines responsibility regarding the delivery of services. Questions regarding the legality of the child's presence arise when the child is residing with persons other than his or her parents. This is an area where one must look to state law concerning the delivery of services to such children. The OCR's rulings in this area are instructive. In Normal Community Unit School District (EHLR 352:434:, 1987), the OCR found a district in violation for failure to provide educational services to a student whose mother had moved to another state, leaving the child in the custody of a caretaker. The OCR concluded that the district's claim that evidence of legal guardianship must be shown was not supported by state law, and that the child as a resident of the district was entitled to educational services. The key in such cases appears to be the requirements under state law, because the OCR has also found that a district was not in violation for requiring evidence of legal guardianship where state law required it. (See Greenville County School District, LOF 12/8/89.) Thus, it is legitimate for a state to condition entitlement to free educational services upon evidence of properly executed legal guardianship.

Students Referred to Other Programs

Following the maxim espoused by the courts in *Sonya* and *Rabinowitz,* one would assume that assigning responsibility for providing educational services is a simple matter of ascertaining the child's lawful "presence."[5] However, it is not quite that simple. Consider the following cases:

> Burwicke and Lyons are adjoining counties. The Lyons County School District operates a special school for deaf students. Burwicke has contracted with Lyons to provide services to hearing impaired students who cannot be appropriately served in Burwicke. The contract provides that Burwicke will reimburse Lyons for all expenses incurred. The 12 Burwicke students served in the Lyons school reside in the school's dormitory during the week and travel home only on the weekends. As a result of financial difficulties, Burwicke ceases reimbursing Lyons in the middle of the 1985-6 academic year. Lyons County terminates services to the students, claiming that they are the responsibility of Burwicke. The students are without services because Burwicke cannot provide an appropriate educational program for them. Which recipient is responsible for serving the students?
>
> Jim is referred to a residential placement by his local school district. After two months, Jim's parents complain to officials of the local school

district that the residential facility has not fully implemented Jim's IEP. Jim's parents are advised to raise their concerns with either the residential facility or the state department of education. The officials argue that the local school district cannot exercise authority over a private facility that is not in its jurisdiction.

Under state law, special educational units are formed which provide educational services to handicapped students. The special units are provided EHA funds through the state. The units provide all services necessary for educating handicapped students, e.g., hire staff and provide instructional services, classroom space, and facilities. Bartow School District, a member of such a unit, has referred students to the unit and refuses to address complaints made by the parents of handicapped students regarding the delivery of services. The district's attorney advises the parents that the units, which are recipients of federal financial assistance, have been assigned full responsibility to provide educational services to handicapped students under state law, and, therefore, Bartow is not responsible for providing a free appropriate public education to the students.

As the above cases reflect, although the rule seems fairly simple, the water gets muddy pretty quickly. The regulations at 104.33(b)(3) provide:

> A recipient may place a handicapped person in or refer such person to a program other than the one that it operates as its means of carrying out the requirements of this subpart. If so, the recipient remains responsible for ensuring that the requirements of this subpart are met with respect to any handicapped person so placed or referred.

And paragraph 23 in Appendix A provides in pertinent part:

> If a recipient places a child in a program other than its own, it remains financially responsible for the child, whether or not the other program is operated by another recipient or educational agency.

Thus, in all the above cases, the recipients that refer the students are primarily responsible for ensuring that the students receive appropriate educational services. This is true even in instances where other recipients have assumed responsibility for the *actual* delivery of services. The regulations provide no conditions under which the referring recipient may legitimately shift that responsibility.[6] This mandate, however, does not preclude states from implementing programs that provide for the transfer of that responsibility. The OCR has ruled that a state program that transfers the responsibility for providing a free appropriate public education from the school district may be permissible under Section 504. Specifically, the state of Nebraska implemented a parent-choice enrollment program, a provision of which stated that the resident district would delegate its responsibility to provide educational services to the non-resident choice district. The OCR ruled that this provision did not violate Section 504 and concluded:

> [T]he Office for Civil Rights would treat children participating in a choice program as being in the jurisdiction of the choice district. The choice district would, therefore, be responsible for compliance with Section 504, and the district of residence would not be responsible under Section 504 for actions or inactions occurring after the delegation took effect for the particular child.
>
> [I]t is not inconsistent with the EHA-B or Section 504 for a state that has adopted an interdistrict choice program to require the district of residence to transfer responsibility for providing FAPE to the district of choice.[7]

This ruling by the OCR does not appear to alter the mandate that the referring district remains primarily responsible for insuring that appropriate educational services are provided because, under the Nebraska program, the transfer of the student to another district is based upon parental choice rather than a referral by the resident district.

There are instances where more than one recipient may be held responsible for the delivery of services to students. When a student is referred to an entity that is also a recipient (as in the first and third examples above), both the sending and the receiving agency or district must comply with Section 504. Thus, while Burwicke and Bartow are primarily responsible, Lyons and the special education unit would also be held accountable under the Act. To understand the competing and concurrent responsibilities that might arise, it is helpful to view recipients as having two distinct duties: *The duty to actually provide appropriate educational services*—§ 104.33(a):

> A recipient that operates a public elementary or secondary education program shall provide a free appropriate public education to each qualified handicapped person who is in the recipient's jurisdiction.

And the duty to provide sufficient funds to implement the educational program—Paragraph 23 of Appendix A and § 104.33(c):

> If a recipient places a child in a program other than its own, it remains financially responsible for the child, whether or not the other program is operated by another recipient or educational agency.

While normally these two duties are lodged in one recipient, when more than one recipient is involved, the responsibilities are often shared. Disagreements regarding the extent to which these responsibilities are shared frequently result in recipients inadvertently violating the regulations. The above-described regulatory mandates are somewhat difficult to reconcile in situations where students are referred from one recipient to another. Specifically, how can the receiving recipient be responsible for providing services to referred students in its jurisdiction while at the same time the referring recipient is primarily responsible for delivery of services to students it refers? If the students are not properly serviced, which recipient is at fault—

the receiving or the referring recipient? The Burwicke/Lyons case is an excellent example of this problem. Clearly, in failing to provide financial support for the students, Burwicke has not fulfilled its responsibility, but since the students are in Lyons' jurisdiction, can Lyons legitimately terminate services? Appendix A clearly addresses circumstances such as this. It provides, in pertinent part, that

> in no case may a recipient refuse to provide services to a handicapped child in its jurisdiction because of another person's or entity's failure to assume financial responsibility.[8]

This mandate makes it clear that the primary concern of the federal enforcement agency is the *actual* delivery of services to students. Recipients may disagree regarding who must assume financial responsibility for serving students, but these disagreements must not result in students being denied services.[9] Lyons County certainly has a legitimate claim against Burwicke County for its refusal to honor the contract, but the students cannot be made the victims of the dispute. Federal enforcement agencies have little or no interest in how recipients resolve financial disagreements if there is no negative impact on the delivery of services to students. For example, the OCR ruled that it did not violate Section 504 for a state to limit reimbursements to local school districts for out-of-state placements since the practice did not have a negative impact on the services provided students, *i.e.*, they were appropriately placed and the local school districts were providing sufficient funds to cover the cost of the out-of-state placements.[10] As noted by the OCR in its March 5, 1990, letter to the Nebraska Department of Education, "Federal law does not dictate the funding mechanisms that states may employ to ensure that responsible school districts can pay for necessary services for children with handicaps."[11]

There are circumstances, however, where the school district in which the child is located is not responsible for the provision of educational services. Presence of the child is not the key to determining which recipient should provide services in the following instances:

> Ricky, a 14-year-old student with serious emotional problems, has been picked up by the police on four occasions for violent destructive behavior. On the last occasion, the juvenile court removes him from his parents' home and places him in the state mental health facility for evaluation. State officials advise his parents that Ricky will be at the institute for a minimum of three months and that educational services will be provided at the institute. Ricky's mother expresses concern that the institute staff is not qualified to provide appropriate educational services and requests that the local school district provide for Ricky's educational needs. The district tells Ricky's mother that since it neither placed nor referred Ricky to the state facility it is not responsible for providing services to him. She is advised to

resolve the matter with state officials since the court order made the state responsible.

Bill's local school district concludes that an appropriate education cannot be provided for him in the district. Bill is referred to a private residential program in another school district. Does the school district in which the private residential program is located have a respnsibility to ensure that the services provided him are appropriate?

Local school districts are not responsible for serving students who have appropriately been placed under the state's jurisdiction. The OCR has consistently held that the state has exclusive responsibility for such students. "A state assumes the primary responsibility for providing FAPE [free appropriate public education] to those children who have been appropriately placed in its custody, for example, children who have been placed by court order in a state institution. By virtue of their placement, these children no longer are under the jurisdiction of a particular LEA, but rather are 'in the jurisdiction' of the state."[12] Thus, the school district in which the child is *present* is relieved of financial responsibility. Unlike the situations above in which two school districts are involved, school districts under such circumstances are not responsible, even if the state fails in its responsibility to serve the child. The state has been held to be exclusively responsible.[13]

The same principle appears to apply to students referred by one school district to private institutions in another school district, although the OCR's rulings have been somewhat confusing in this area. The referring school district has exclusive responsibility for ensuring that the private institution complies with Section 504 and its implementing regulations. The important factor is that the district in which the private institution is located had no involvement in the referral and placement of the students.

Are there any circumstances under which a local school district would be obligated to serve a student who was properly placed in a state's program or facility? For example, in the hypothetical above, if the state institute determined, after an evaluation of Ricky, that he should attend school in the local school district, can the district refuse to serve Ricky on the basis that provision of educational services is the exclusive responsibility of the state? No. If the responsible state agency determines that the appropriate educational placement is the local school district, the district cannot refuse to serve the student if it can properly provide the necessary services.[14] Of course, recipients will not be held responsible if the parents reject a proffered appropriate placement and place the child themselves.[15] (See Chapter 12 for a detailed discussion of this issue.)

The State's Oversight Responsibility

In some instances, states have sought to limit their responsibility to comply with Subpart D since, with the exception of special purpose schools, they do not directly operate educational programs or provide educational services to students. Under the grant provisions of the EHA, states are basically the conduit for federal funds provided to local school districts to serve handicapped students. The fact that the states receive the funds makes them recipients pursuant to § 104.3(f) of the regulations. Further, § 104.4(b)(4) provides that recipients may not "directly . . . or through other arrangements" take actions that result in discrimination against qualified handicapped individuals.[16] In other words, states *must* exercise oversight responsibility over those to whom they provide federal funds and ensure that LEAs comply with Section 504 and the implementing regulations.[17] Further, courts have been unsympathetic to the attempts of state officials to limit their responsibility by asserting that they are not in the business of direct delivery of educational services:

> Finally, the State's stiff-necked, obstinate adherence to the premise that education is the responsibility of the local school districts within the State, pursuant to State law and regulations, is a fiction which I find totally unpersuasive. . . . The State may not be technically required to monitor compliance with Section 504. Its failure to ensure compliance by the local school districts, however, implicates it under Section 504 insofar as the State's status as the recipient of federal financial assistance obligates it not to permit, directly or indirectly, programs benefitting from federal financial assistance received by the State, to discriminate against handicapped persons.[18]
>
> The State is a recipient under Section 504 and is therefore prohibited from discriminating on the basis of handicap, whether directly or through subrecipients . . . . The state department is an appropriate subject for suit in an action under Section 504.[19]

The duty to ensure that LEAs comply with Section 504 requires more than passive observation by the state. For example, in a California case, the OCR ruled that the state's oversight responsibility would require it to cease funding the LEA or necessitate it to obtain a court order to force compliance.[20]

Beyond the fact that the state, as the entity which channels federal funds to local school districts, cannot abdicate its responsibility to monitor districts and ensure compliance, the extent of its involvement in direct delivery of services remains in question. Consider the following scenario:

> Mary, a student with a speech impairment, is not provided necessary speech services by her local school district because the district has been unable for two years to hire a speech therapist. Mary's parents contact the state

department of education and insist that the state provide the necessary services for their daughter. The state refuses to take action asserting that the provision of services to Mary is the responsibility of her local school district, not the state.

Does the obligation not to discriminate through subrecipients require the state to take the affirmative step of providing the educational services if the LEA refuses to do so? Can the state's oversight responsibility be expanded to include direct delivery of services? The Ninth Circuit Court of Appeals has held that states can be required to actually provide services to students not properly served by local school districts. The Court specifically held that § 1414(d) of the regulation implementing the EHA "requires direct action when a local education agency has one or more handicapped children who can best be served by a regional or state center designed to meet the needs of such children."[21] The Court further stated that where the local district's failure is "significant," the state must assume responsibility for assuring that appropriate services are provided.[22] The Supreme Court affirmed the position of the Court of Appeals, noting that the justices were "equally divided on the question of whether a court may order a state to provide services directly to a disabled child where the local agency has failed to do so.[23]

It is not clear that the state would have the same responsibility to provide direct educational services under Section 504. While § 1414(d)(3) of the regulation implementing the EHA speaks specifically regarding the state's responsibility to provide educational services, there is no regulatory provision under Section 504 which could be unquestionably interpreted as requiring the state to step into the shoes of the LEA regarding direct delivery of services. The Act does not impose the same level of specific involvement on the part of the states as is required pursuant to the EHA. This appears to be the type of "affirmative action" which courts have ruled that Section 504 does not mandate.[24] Whether one concludes that such a responsibility exists under Section 504 is ultimately based upon how the question of whether Section 504 *guarantees* a right to an appropriate education is answered. (See Chapter 19 for a detailed discussion of this issue.) At present, it would appear that such an obligation would not be imposed upon the states pursuant to Section 504.

Location and Notification

Section 104.32 of the regulation imposes an obligation on recipients to locate and identify "qualified handicapped persons residing in the recipient's jurisdiction."[25] Does the duty to locate and notify require that school officials gain access to every home in the district's jurisdiction to ascertain whether a handicapped child who is eligible for services resides therein, or is it sufficient for district officials to wait to identify the children when they seek to enroll and provide information to parents and guardians regarding their programs and responsibilities at that time? While we know that acceptable performance on the part of school districts lies somewhere between these two extremes, it is often difficult to pinpoint that elusive middle ground. Let us consider Mrs. Clark's case, as an example:

> Mrs. Clark has three children, one of whom, Doug, is visually impaired and has a learning disability. The Clarks presently reside in Bevell County where Doug attends Wildwood, a private school. Bevell County does not have a special program for learning-disabled students who are visually impaired, and Mrs. Clark feels such a program is essential in order for Doug to maximize his educational experience. Mr. Clark's company has just transferred him to Davita County. In anticipation of the move, Mrs. Clark calls the superintendent's office in Davita County to gather information regarding the services provided handicapped students. She is hopeful that the county will offer a program comparable to the one Doug is enrolled in at Wildwood. Mrs. Clark talks to the Special Education Director, and they debate the advantages of programs such as the one offered at Wildwood. The director expresses the opinion that the programs at Davita for visually impaired students are just as effective as those at Wildwood. While Mrs. Clark makes it clear that she has a handicapped child, she does not offer any specific information regarding Doug's condition and his educational needs. The director mails Mrs. Clark the district's brochure, which outlines the services and programs offered to handicapped students. Based upon the information they gather about Davita, the Clarks decide that it is best that Doug remain at Wildwood.
>
> Doug accompanies Mrs. Clark when she goes to Davita to enroll her other children. When she is asked whether Doug will also be attending, she states that he is enrolled at Wildwood. There is no further discussion of Doug and his educational needs, but Mrs. Clark is again given the district's brochure which describes the services offered handicapped students. Doug attends Wildwood for four years, and during that time there is no further contact between the Clarks and school officials regarding Doug's educational needs. During the four years, the district's program for visually impaired students improves substantially and, in fact, is very similar to the program Doug is enrolled in at Wildwood.
>
> Mrs. Clark is furious when she hears about the district's improved program in casual conversation with other parents. She demands that the district reimburse them for the Wildwood tuition for the period of time during which the district could have been serving Doug in a similar program. Mrs. Clark argues that the district had notice of Doug's existence and his needs because of her discussions with the Special Education Director and their visit to the district office. She reasons that the director was aware of her preference from their discussion and when the district's program was altered in a way that made it comparable to Wildwood's, she should have been notified.
>
> District officials argue that the identification and notification procedures which they utilize are sufficient. These procedures primarily consist of visiting

and providing information to private schools in its jurisdiction, mailing brochures to parents of handicapped children as well as sending them home with all enrolled students, public announcements on two television and radio stations, newspaper ads, speeches to parents and advocacy groups and placing brochures in the offices of pediatricians, as well as other public places throughout the district. They argue that there were at least three ways the Clarks could have learned of the existence of the new program: (a) the brochure sent home with all students, including Mrs. Clark's children; (b) information packets provided Wildwood; and (c) the presentation given to community groups, several of which the Clarks were members of. District officials adamantly insist that they had no responsibility to personally call Mrs. Clark and invite her to enroll her son in the new program.

This case raises some very important questions. Specifically,

1. How extensive does a district's outreach activities have to be?
2. How does one measure the "effectiveness" of these activities?
3. What responsibility, if any, does a district have to handicapped persons who are receiving educational services from other agencies or entities, such as a private school?

In order to answer these questions, one must begin by focusing on the purpose of § 104.32. The goal of the provision is to ensure that qualified handicapped individuals are advised of the recipient's responsibility to provide a free appropriate public education and the availability of such. It is "information-giving so that parents and the handicapped may choose whether they desire to participate in the public program."[26] The obligations imposed by the regulations are not insignificant. Districts *must* develop procedures to identify, locate, and notify handicapped persons and their parents on an annual basis. Further, it is not acceptable for a recipient to adopt procedures but fail to fully implement them.[27]

> After two or three weeks of class work in kindergarten, Sarah's teacher notices that Sarah is having trouble with exercises that involve fine-motor skills and spatial relationships. Sarah is referred for evaluation and is found to have a severe learning disability. After she agrees to Sarah's placement in a special education program, her mother finds out that Sarah could have received services the previous year that would have helped to prepare her for kindergarten.

What if there are unserved handicapped children, like Sarah, found in the district who were not identified by the district? The effectiveness of a recipient's procedures is often questioned when such procedures fail to reach a particular child or group of children. However, the mere fact that there are qualified handicapped individuals who are not reached is not a proper criterion to use to measure the successfulness of a recipient's outreach activities.[28]

The regulatory mandate is not absolute. Recipients are instructed to "undertake to identify" and "to take appropriate steps to notify."[29] This language indicates that one must look to the quality of the recipient's actions rather than bottomline results to assess performance. In *David H. v. Spring Branch Independent School District, supra* at 1339, the court emphasized that a school district would be held accountable for the thoroughness and extensiveness of its efforts to identify unserved handicapped persons in its jurisdiction. The court rejected the claim that the district was at fault for failing to identify a particular child and stated, "It may be that defendants did not identify every unserved student. But this is not what the provision requires." The key is that the procedures adopted and implemented by the recipient should reflect a "good faith" effort to identify, locate, and notify unserved qualified handicapped persons and their parents.

Questions may also arise regarding the actual methods the recipient uses to identify and notify persons.

> Balsam Unified School District performs its annual "Child Find" effort in May of every year. Its efforts consist of surveying day care centers (both public and private), church kindergartens, and private schools. On June 1st, Balsam announces how many handicapped students are being served in programs other than the district's.
> Dunne School District annually provides notice of the services it provides by sending letters to parents of handicapped students enrolled in the district.

The procedures utilized must permit the district to reach those not presently served. Therefore, procedures that merely provide notice to those already served by the district (Dunne School District's procedures) are inadequate.[30] It is also not sufficient to merely determine the number of individuals who are not being served as Balsam has done. Furthermore, while recipients will not be penalized for failing to reach every child, if school officials have knowledge of particular handicapped students and their educational needs who are not being served, they must not only inform the parents of their responsibility and the availability of educational services in general, but must also provide information regarding the *specific* programs that are offered to children with the impairment(s) in question.[31] Thus, if Mrs. Clark had contacted the district and provided specific information regarding her son and his needs, it would have violated § 104.32 of the regulations if district officials had failed to provide her information regarding the programs which were available for learning-disabled students with visual impairments.

As to the question of the district's responsibility to students served by other agencies or entities, § 104.32 defines "unserved individuals" as those who are not presently receiving a *public* education. Therefore, recipients may not ignore students attending private schools in their outreach activities.[32]

However, students placed in state-operated educational programs are viewed as receiving a "public education" within the meaning of the regulations and, therefore, districts are not obligated to identify and locate children in such programs.[33]

It is also important to remember that notification efforts must take into consideration the need for various forms, formats, and languages to reach parents with sensory impairments or native languages other than English.[34]

Handicapped Individuals Who Must Be Served

§ 104.33(a) of the regulations provides that:

> A recipient that operates a public elementary or secondary education program shall provide a free appropriate public education to each qualified handicapped person who is in the recipient's jurisdiction, regardless of the nature or severity of the person's handicap.

The three most important phases in this regulatory provision are (a) "qualified handicapped person," (b) "in the recipient's jurisdiction,"[35] and (c) "regardless of the nature or severity of the person's handicaps."

Qualified Handicapped Persons

With respect to public preschool, elementary, secondary, or adult education services, the regulations define qualified status in terms of age.[36] The regulatory mandate is straightforward. Any handicapped individual meeting one of the three criteria outlined in § 104.3(k) is "qualified." Thus, if a school district offers an after-school program for students between the ages of six and 13, it would violate the regulations to refuse to permit handicapped children in that age group to participate in the program.[37]

> [T]he consideration is whether the recipient, either under state law, court order or simply as a matter of practice is providing services to nonhandicapped individuals in a given age group. If so, qualified handicapped persons—that is, handicapped persons in the age group—also must be served.[38]

Pursuant to the EHA, states generally provide educational services to handicapped students between the ages of three and 21. However, it is important to remember that eligibility under the EHA is "but one of three categories of handicapped children qualified . . ." under the regulations implementing Section 504.[39] The majority of the controversies that arise regarding qualified status in elementary and secondary education involve the termination of services to handicapped students who cease to meet eligibility criteria, and the denial of services to handicapped persons in special programs and special purpose schools.

> Kathy is being provided educational services, but she reaches age 22 during the middle of the academic year. The school district maintains that services may be terminated on her birthday, while Kathy's parents contend that she should be permitted to complete the academic year.
> Warren is a visually impaired and severely mentally retarded child. His parents seek to enroll him in the State School for the Blind. He is denied enrollment because the school's admission standards limit enrollment to those who are, at a minimum, trainable mentally retarded. Warren meets the age criteria for enrollment in the school.

Are Kathy and Warren entitled to the services their parents request?

The OCR has held that once handicapped individuals reach age 22, the age at which the state is no longer required to provide educational services, they are no longer qualified within the meaning of § 104.3(k)(2), and recipients may therefore cease delivery of services. Thus, while the district's action of terminating services to Kathy during the academic year may be injudicious, it is not a violation of the regulations.[40]

Regarding Warren, handicapped individuals must meet all legitimate eligibility criteria. In this instance, in addition to an age requirement, the school also requires that, to be eligible, those enrolled must be minimally "trainable." Warren does not meet this criterion and is, therefore, not qualified.[41] A recipient may choose to limit participation in its program(s) so long as "no child is barred from the program solely on the basis of handicap," and the selection criteria are "rationally related to the special educational needs of individuals in the categories served."[42]

Regardless of the Nature or Severity

Upon a first reading of the mandate that qualified handicapped individuals be provided a free appropriate public education "regardless of the nature or severity of the person's handicap,"[43] most would assume that the language of this provision would not be applied literally. Surely, the realities of financially overextended school systems, as well as the considerable burdens that would be imposed by serving individuals with serious impairments, would warrant, if not demand, that exceptions be made to this absolute statement. What, for example, is the recipient's responsibility to the handicapped students, described in the cases below, and how should the recipient balance their needs against the rights of the other individuals involved, *i.e.*, teachers and classmates?

Sally is a 15-year-old student who has an emotional impairment. Her record at Smelt High School reflects a long series of suspensions and lesser disciplinary actions reflecting unsuccessful attempts to modify her behavior. Sally's behavioral problems continue to escalate until she begins to physically threaten her classmates and teachers. When she bites a teacher, the principal recommends and the Board approves her expulsion. Despite the protestations of Sally's parents, the Board refuses to reinstate her based upon the opinion of medical experts that Sally will continue to exhibit inappropriate aggressive behavior.[44]

Mary, a student with extensive physical impairments, requires constant attendant care. The care provided includes suctioning her lungs and occasional cardiopulmonary resuscitation.[45]

Earl has severe spasticity, brain damage, joint contractures, dislocated hips, and scoliosis. He is nonambulatory, quadriplegic, and cortically blind. Educational experts hired by the district assert that Earl cannot "learn" in the traditional sense of the word and, therefore, would not benefit from formal educational services.[46]

Carte School District refuses to provide educational services to Bill, a child who is trainably handicapped and has been diagnosed as having AIDS, unless his parents agree to his being taught in a glass enclosure that separates him from his classmates.[47]

While these examples are extreme and would certainly lead some to argue that recipients should be relieved of the responsibility of providing educational services to the students in question, compliance with § 104.33(a) of the regulations requires that these students be served.

The meaning of the phrase "regardless of the severity of the handicap" was unequivocally answered in *Timothy W. v. Rochester School District, supra,* a case involving the meaning of the phrase in the EHA.[48] In that case, the district court reached the startling conclusion that if a child does not possess an ability to learn or "benefit from" educational services, as defined by the Supreme Court in *Hendrick Hudson Central School District v. Rowley,* a district need not provide services.[49] The Court specifically concluded that "a handicapped child who does not have learning capacity was not intended to receive special education." This decision defied what had long been presumed to be an absolute responsibility to provide educational services to handicapped students. The district court sought to introduce an exception to the literal meaning of the phrase "regardless of the severity of the handicap" and open a new battlefield regarding services which should be provided to profoundly and severely handicapped children. However, the court of appeals expressly rejected the district court's finding, noting that the "district court erred in requiring a benefit/eligibility test as a prerequisite," and stating that "a school district has a duty to provide an educational program for every handicapped child in the district, regardless of the severity of the handicap." *Timothy W., supra* at 962, 973. The Court outlined the state's responsibility under the Act as follows:

The Statute is permeated with the words "all handicapped children" whenever it refers to the target population. . . . There is nothing in the Act's language which even remotely supports the district court's conclusion that "under [the Act], an initial determination as to a child's ability to benefit from special education, must be made in order for a handicapped child to qualify for education under the Act." The language of the Act is directly to the contrary. . . . The language of the Act in its entirety makes clear that a "zero-reject" policy is at the core of the Act, and that no child, regardless of the severity of his or her handicap, is to ever again be subjected to the deplorable state of affairs which existed at the time of the Act's passage, in which millions of handicapped children received inadequate education or none at all. In summary, the Act mandates an appropriate public education for all handicapped children, regardless of the level of achievement that such children might obtain. (*Id.*, at 960–62.)

Despite the fact that this case interprets the language of the EHA, there is no reason to believe that the identical mandate under Section 504 would be interpreted differently by the courts. In fact, the drafters of the regulations implementing Section 504 describe the responsibility of recipients in similar terms as those used by the Court in *Timothy W.*, in stating that the "requirements are designed to ensure that no handicapped child is excluded from school on the basis of handicap." It also noted that Subpart D "conforms to the standards established in . . . the EHA" regarding basic requirements such as the duty to provide a free appropriate public education regardless of the nature or severity of the handicap.[50]

Therefore, when recipients are faced with the task of providing services to handicapped persons with serious impairments, the question is never whether the services must be provided, but rather how a program or service be provided that addresses their individual educational needs. The severity of the impairment is simply one of the factors to be considered in deciding upon the type of program that must be developed. This principle helps resolve our earlier question of what services, if any, are the students in our examples entitled to.

Earl's handicap is identical to that of the child in *Timothy W.* He is entitled to receive educational services. Remember, educational services cannot be assessed solely on an academic level, particularly for students with severe handicapping conditions. "Where basic self-help and social skills such as toilet training, dressing, feeding and communication are lacking, formal education begins at that point."[51]

How does the district balance Sally's right to receive services against the obvious physical threat which she poses to her peers and teachers? In *Honig v. Doe, supra* at 700, 707, a case in which the Court considered the appropriateness of a school district indefinitely expelling emotionally handicapped children for "violent and disruptive conduct related to their disabilities," the Supreme Court rejected the argument that there exists a "danger exception" that gives schools the right permanently and unilaterally to exclude students, particularly emotionally disturbed students, from school. The Court stated that Congress, in enacting legislation regarding the education of the handicapped, rejected such exclusionary practices and required that states educate handicapped students "regardless of the severity of their disabilities." The Supreme Court held that the removal of handicapped students from school must be with the permission of the parents or as a result of the completion of proper review proceedings. Thus, the school district's solution with respect to Sally is unacceptable. (See also, Edcouch-Elsa Independent School District, EHLR 352:393 [1987].)

This does not mean, however, that recipients are handcuffed with respect to dealing with students that pose an immediate threat. The Court specifically endorsed the OCR's policy that permits districts to suspend handicapped students for up to ten days. Such short-term suspensions should be used to protect the safety of others. They would also allow the recipient time to consider the need for alternative placement for the student. See Honig v. Doe, supra at 708.[52]

Regarding Mary's needs, recipients are not required to provide medical services that "might well prove unduly expensive or beyond the range of their competence."[53] Courts have not required recipients to assume the role of primary health care providers. In such cases the question becomes whether members of the district staff could perform the services with a minimum of training and difficulty.[54] If not, the student should not be denied services; instead, solutions such as the parents assuming the cost of employing the attendant, or the provision of homebound services should be considered. (See Chapter 11 for a complete discussion.)

Despite the emotionally volatile nature of the AIDS controversy, it is settled law that the mere presence of the disease is not sufficient to deprive an individual of protection under the Act. It was held in Martinez v. School Board of Hillsborough County, 861 F.2d 1502 (11th Cir. 1988) that individuals with communicable diseases are entitled to protection if either the threat of transmission does not rise to the level of "significant," or, if the threat is "significant," reasonable accommodations are available to reduce the risk of transmission. Only individuals who are not "otherwise qualified," i.e., the possibility of transmission is "significant," may be excluded.[55] However, it is important to keep in mind that, even if the risk level of Bill's illness did rise to the level of being "significant," he would still be entitled to services in an alternative setting, e.g., homebound services.

11
Appropriate Education

What is an appropriate education? Section 104.33(b) defines it as:

> (1) [T]he provision of an appropriate education is the provision of regular or special education and related aids and services that (i) are designed to meet individual educational needs of handicapped persons as adequately as the needs of nonhandicapped persons are met, and (ii) are based upon adherence to procedures that satisfy the requirements of §§ 104.34, 104.35, and 104.36.

> (2) Implementation of an individualized education program developed in accordance with the Education of the Handicapped Act is one means of meeting the standard established in paragraph (b)(1)(i) of this section.

However, reading this definition provides little insight into what the educational services provided disabled students must be. What standards does one use to determine whether the educational needs of handicapped students are met "as adequately as those of the nonhandicapped"? The analysis section of the regulations is also not particularly informative. It merely restates the regulatory provision and gives examples of what special education services might include, *i.e.*, specifically designed instruction in classrooms, at home, or in private or public institutions and may be accompanied by such related services as developmental, corrective and other supportive services (including psychological, counseling, and medical diagnostic services).[1]

Unfortunately, "appropriate education" is a concept that we are more comfortable describing by saying what it is not, rather than what it is. For example, recipients have been found in violation of § 104.33(b)(1) for failing to:

provide handicapped students with certified teachers,[2]

properly evaluate students,[3]

consider the individual educational needs of students,[4]

implement the IEPs of students,[5]

provide transportation services,[6] and

provide placement in a timely fashion.[7]

This chapter discusses the elements that are the essence of an appropriate education, *i.e.*, individualization, meaningful access, and educational benefit. Also addressed are the difficult questions that the requirement to provide an appropriate education poses for recipients. Specifically,

1. How does one assess the appropriateness of an educational program?
2. Do recipients have to design and implement educational programs that will allow handicapped students to reach their maximum potential?
3. Is it realistic to compare the educational services provided handicapped students with those provided to nonhandicapped persons to ensure that the educational needs of the handicapped are met "as adequately as the needs of [the] nonhandicapped"?
4. To what extent should federal agencies and courts—noneducators—become involved in the business of assessing the adequacy of educational programs?

Educational Benefits

> Bob, a student with serious behavioral problems, is provided the following services as a part of his educational program: weekly counseling sessions and assignments to a BD resource class when his behavior warrants it. In addition, a behavior modification plan is developed. It provides that whereas he will not be subject to suspension, all disciplinary infractions will result in specific punishments. Bob's parents request that he be exempt from all forms of punitive disciplinary action. They believe that the plan should emphasize good behavior and provide rewards for acceptable behavior. The district agrees to include a reward system in the plan, but refuses to eliminate the punitive measures. School officials advise Bob's parents that the specialists and staff members that work with Bob feel that his problems would be exacerbated by such an approach. Bob's parents argue that he is being denied an appropriate education because the punitive measures employed would deprive him of valuable class time.
>
> Sam is failing fourth grade for the second time. He has been evaluated by the school and the test results indicate that he has some difficulty assimilating information. Sam is placed in the Chapter 1 program for remedial assistance, provided tutoring, and summer school is recommended to his parents. Sam's mother provides the results of an independent examination in which he is diagnosed as having an attention deficit disorder and insists that he be placed in the school's learning-disabled program. The special education director advises Sam's mother that the learning-disabled program is not an appropriate placement for him.

The hypotheticals above reflect the ongoing conflicts between parents and educators regarding the appropriateness of educational services. They call to mind a battlefield with parents on one side demanding the best services for their children, and recipients on the other, arguing that many of the parental requests are not the responsibility of the educational system, and the innocent students in the middle. One begins a quest for a working definition of "appropriate education" by considering the pertinent parts of the definition provided in § 104.33(b)(1): "An appropriate education is one which meets the individual educational needs of the handicapped as adequately as the needs of the nonhandicapped are met." However, this doesn't indicate the types of educational programs that recipients must offer. Clearly the recipient's responsibility is significantly greater than merely opening the school door and permitting handicapped individuals to enter. The courts have recognized that it would be a futile exercise to limit the recipient's responsibility to merely providing the same educational services to the handicapped as are traditionally provided to nonhandicapped students. The mandate under Section 504 has been likened to that under Title VI to provide non–English-speaking children bilingual instruction. The court made such a comparison in *David H. v. Spring Branch Independent School District,* by noting that Section 504 required something more than "equal access to education."[8] The court, in holding that states and local education agencies have the responsibility to provide meaningful education, quoted the Supreme Court's decision in *Lau v. Nichol,* as providing the definitive standard regarding the provision of educational services to students with special needs:

> [T]here is no equality of treatment merely by providing students with the same facilities, textbooks, teachers, and curriculum; for students who do not understand English are effectively foreclosed from any meaningful education. The statute, then, does not merely prohibit the denial of access to federally funded programs, but also gives handicapped persons an equal opportunity to enjoy the benefits of such programs.[9]

Thus, recognizing the right of handicapped students to receive special treatment and services, proper assessment under the regulations depends on the results achieved from participation in the programs offered, *i.e.,* receipt of educational benefits.

The Supreme Court in *Hendrick Hudson District Board of Education v. Rowley* defined the meaning of access to a free appropriate public education.[10] In that case, a conflict developed between the parents of a student with a hearing impairment and school officials, because the parents felt her educational program should emphasize cued speech, while school officials favored a total communication approach relying on sign language. The parents insisted that their program was the only one that would allow the student to benefit from the services offered to the maximum extent possible. School officials conceded that many experts felt that the program recommended by the parents allowed individuals with hearing impairments to reach their maximum potential but maintained that their approach would permit the student to benefit from the services offered and function successfully in school. The Court rejected the conclusion of the lower courts that the mandate to provide an appropriate education under the EHA required states to "maximize the potential of each handicapped child."[11] The Court, in defining an appropriate education, said: "the 'basic floor of opportunity' . . . consists of access to specialized instruction and related services which are individually designed to provide educational benefit to the handicapped child." Thus, the responsibility is to provide "educational benefit." The Court specifically stated that it is not correct to "speak in terms of 'equal' services" when discussing the appropriate education standard. The Court noted that "the requirement that states provide 'equal' educational opportunities would . . . present an entirely unworkable standard" that would require either "furnishing handicapped children with only such services as are available to nonhandicapped children" or "the furnishing of every special service necessary to maximize each handicapped child's potential."[12] The Court found both of these approaches to be unacceptable.

Perhaps the most important pronouncement made by the Supreme Court is that access to educational services means "to confer some educational benefit," not to "maximize the potential of each handicapped child." Therefore, while it may be true that the program proposed by the student's parents would maximize her educational experience, the school district is not required to provide such a program. School officials must be permitted to make decisions regarding the delivery of services that are within their area of expertise. As noted by the Court in *Kerkam v. McKenzie,* "proof that loving parents can craft a better program than a state offers does not alone entitle them to prevail."[13] Thus, the operative question is not whether the best educational program has been developed, but whether the proposed program will "confer some educational benefit."[14] See also *Daniel RR v. State Board of Education* ("States need not provide every conceivable supplementary aid or service").[15]

The next puzzling question that must be addressed is how does one assess educational benefit. The success or failure of nonhandicapped students is measured in terms of grade levels culminating in graduation. The educational programs of handicapped students, in most instances, do not conform to such an orderly progression. Often handicapped students perform under IEPs that reflect similar goals year after year, with the termination of their educational careers being marked by their reaching the legal age limit for the provision of public educational services. Therefore, on the continuum between the provision of minimum or no services and services which maximize potential, it is very difficult to determine where those services that "confer some educational benefit" fall. Consider the educational programs of Thomas and Andrew described below. Do they fail "to confer some educational benefit"?

Thomas is severely retarded, has a mental age of a three-year-old, and is nonverbal. He also has physical impairments that restrict his ability to walk and limit his fine-motor skills. Thomas was placed in a private residential program until he reached school age and his parents enrolled him in public school. Thomas is properly evaluated and a day program is recommended. Although his parents feel that a residential program is more appropriate, they are persuaded to let Thomas try the day program. After three months, Thomas' parents advise school officials that they feel he is not progressing and request a residential placement. They argue that, without the constant reinforcement that such a program provides, he regresses and is constantly having to relearn the same things. The school denies the parents' request. They feel that Thomas' ability to learn is severely limited and the day-to-day living skills he is being taught could be very easily reinforced at home. Further, it is felt that he is benefitting from his placement and a residential program would provide marginal improvement at best.

Andrew, a child with severe behavioral problems and numerous discipline referrals, is evaluated and placed in a special education class. Despite the existence of a behavior modification plan and an IEP developed to address his needs, his record continues to reflect numerous disciplinary referrals and sanctions. Both Andrew's parents and his teachers express concern that his bouts of inappropriate behavior are increasing rather than decreasing under the new program. The special education director refuses a request for a placement meeting because Andrew was given a complete battery of tests only eight months previously, and the plan and the IEP were developed based upon those test results.

The Supreme Court in *Rowley* acknowledged the difficulty of determining whether educational benefit has been conferred:

> The determination of when handicapped children are receiving sufficient educational benefits to satisfy the requirements of the Act presents a more difficult problem. The Act requires participating states to educate wide spectrums of handicapped children, from the marginally hearing-impaired to the profoundly retarded and palsied. It is clear that the benefits obtainable by children at one end of the spectrum will differ dramatically from those obtainable by children at the other end, with infinite variations in between. One child may have little difficulty competing successfully in an academic setting with nonhandicapped children, while another child may encounter great difficulty in acquiring even the most basic of self-maintenance skills. We do not attempt today to establish any one test for determining the adequacy of educational benefits conferred upon all children covered by the Act.[16]

The only general rule the Court provided is that, for those handicapped students served in the regular education setting, the program provided "should be reasonably calculated to enable the child to achieve passing marks and advance from grade to grade."[17] For all other handicapped students, we are left with the rather imprecise yardstick of "personalized instruction with sufficient support services to permit the child to benefit educationally from that instruction."[18] The Court indicated that the determi-nation of whether benefit had been conferred should be made on a case-by-case basis and, in fact, specifically stated that it was confining its analysis of the issues to the facts of the case before it. However, it did outline the basic inquiries that must be made in order to determine whether recipients have met their obligations to provide an appropriate education. The two questions that must be answered are:

a)   whether procedural requirements under the Act have been complied with, and
b)   is the educational plan developed for the child reasonably calculated to enable the child to receive educational benefits?

The most important part of this standard is whether recipients have com-plied with procedural mandates. Courts have taken the position that if the procedural requirements have been followed, there is a great presumption that the proposed program is appropriate.[19]

The OCR has essentially applied the same standard pursuant to Section 504. The regulations at section 104.33(b)(1)(ii) provide that the procedural requirements of sections 104.34, 104.35 and 104.36 must be satisfied. Fur-ther, Appendix A provides:

> It is not the intention of the Department except in extraordinary cir-cumstances to review the results of individual placements and other educa-tional decisions, so long as the school district complies with the "process" requirements of this subpart (concerning identification and location, evalua-tion, and due process procedures).[20]

While the above statement would seem to comply with the judicial deci-sions we discussed earlier and would strictly limit the OCR's review of substantive educational decisions, we note that the OCR has liberally ap-plied the "extraordinary circumstances" exception, i.e., cases that may in-volve exclusion of a child from the education system or a pattern or practice of discriminatory placements or education. Therefore, it is best not to base one's treatment or review of a case on the presumption that the OCR will limit its review to "process" requirements. However, recipients are still ad-vised to strictly adhere to the "process" requirements because, while the OCR conducts more substantive reviews than would seem appropriate, the agency does afford great deference to the educational decisions of recipients if those requirements have been followed. The vast majority of the agency's violation findings are those in which procedural errors have been made.[21]

If the evidence establishes that the procedural requirements have been complied with, one is again back to the question of how to determine whether the program "fails to confer some educational benefit." Beyond the blatant refusal of a recipient to provide any educational services whatsoever or the provision of services which are totally at odds with the weight of professional evidence,[22] noneducators are left grasping at straws in their attempt to assess the relative worth of individual educational programs. Judges have, in fact, acknowledged the incongruity of courts passing judgment on educational matters.[23] Indeed, the Supreme Court in *Rowley, supra* at 208, admonished courts "to avoid imposing their view of preferable educational methods upon the states." Thus, if there are no procedural deficiencies, the educational placement is presumed to be correct in the absence of *powerful* evidence to the contrary. Courts will respect the purely academic decisions of educators unless they are arbitrary or capricious.[24] Using this standard, one's analysis should center on whether the recipient has made a "good faith" effort to provide educational services. Recipients will not be permitted to provide educational programs that confer only "*de minimis*" or "trivial advancement," nor will they be permitted to ignore overwhelming evidence indicating that the program(s) being offered is unsuccessful.[25]

The disagreements regarding Thomas's and Andrew's educational programs, discussed above, clearly reflect the difference between educational judgments that should be respected and those that may be questioned. In Thomas's case, the argument is really a philosophical one regarding educational approaches for instructing profoundly and severely retarded children. This is not a proper arena for noneducators such as the OCR to interject themselves regarding the substantive issues. The problem with Andrew's program is somewhat different. It raises the question of whether it is reasonably calculated to enable the child to receive educational benefit. While it may not be proper to second-guess educators regarding whether an educational approach is the correct one without evidence to the contrary, it is legitimate to question a program such as Andrew's in which there is ample evidence that it is not successful. The important point to remember is recipients will not be permitted to ignore evidence that the prescribed educational program is not benefitting the student. If a reasonable person would raise questions about the propriety of the program, the recipient would be well-advised to review the placement to assure itself of the program's appropriateness.

Individual Needs

The regulatory mandate that the educational program be "designed to meet the individual needs" of handicapped students is also an important component of an appropriate education. The touchstone for determining whether appropriate educational services are provided to a handicapped student is "individualization."[26] While recipients seem to have no difficulty treating handicapped students as individuals for evaluation and assessment purposes, they are often guilty of ignoring this mandate with respect to the actual delivery of services.

> Wrong Way School District places all multihandicapped high school students in the same class regardless of the nature of their handicapping conditions. The parents of the 15 students involved question the appropriateness of the placement. They also complain that their children are being denied the right to take vocational education classes because related aids and services are not provided for vocational education classes.
>
> The IEPs of a group of students who need speech services reflect that 11 of the students are receiving identical services, *i.e.,* two 45-minute sessions per week. The evaluation data for the students reflect that the students have varying needs and skill levels. The speech pathologist that serves the district states that, while some students could benefit from more sessions, she is unable to provide them because her time is limited. She serves all of the schools in the district.
>
> Brian and his parents have just moved to Alcorn County School District. They provide his evaluation data and IEP from his previous school to Alcorn officials. The officials advise Brian's parents that all the services listed on his IEP can be provided except extended school-year services. The officials state that it was the district's policy not to provide summer school services to any students except those needing credits for graduation. Alcorn disputes the charge that such a policy discriminates against handicapped students. It is noted that handicapped students who need credits to graduate are also permitted to take summer school classes.

These hypotheticals are examples of some of the most hotly contested issues regarding the recipient's duty to address the individual needs of handicapped students: special purpose facilities, extended school-year services, and limited resources. The cases involving extended school-year services are instructive regarding the failure of states and school districts to assign proper importance to the mandate that educational programs and services meet the individual needs of handicapped students. In those cases, state laws that restricted the provisions of educational services to handicapped students to 180 days were held to violate Section 504 or the EHA or both, because they imposed a program restriction that did not take into consideration the needs of the students.[27] As noted by the Court in *Crawford, et al. v. Pittman, et al.,* 708 F.2d 1028 (5th Cir. 1983):

> Mississippi's policy of refusing to consider or provide special education programs of a duration longer than 180 days is inconsistent with its obligations under the Act. Rigid rules like the 180-day limitation violate not only the Act's procedural command that each child receive individual consideration, but also its substantive requirements that each child receive some benefit and that lack of funds not bear more heavily on handicapped than nonhandicapped children.

The argument that such judicial decisions fail to pay proper deference to the decisions of educators is not valid, because school districts are not being told that they must provide extended school-year services to a particular student or a particular group of students; rather, they are advised that their policies and procedures must provide the freedom to consider such as an option should a student's unique needs warrant it.

The same principle applies with respect to special-purpose schools. States and districts certainly have the right to provide such schools for particular classes of handicapped students. However, they must be able to establish that the placement of *each* child in the school is based upon his or her individual needs.[28]

Further, external factors such as economic or administrative expediencies cannot be used to dictate the nature or degree of services a student receives.[29] In addition, the fact that students with different needs receive identical services creates a presumption that individual needs are not being addressed. Any policy or practice that either "inhibits considerations of the individual needs of handicapped children" or that results in a delivery of services that does not address their individual needs violates the Act and its implementing regulations.[30]

However, there is one area in which the OCR's interpretation of the regulations appears to create confusion regarding the concept of providing services that address the students' individual needs. It involves the grouping of students by age. For example, a school district provides educational services to students between the ages of 4 and 16 in the same classroom setting. The mental ages of all the students are within the same range, e.g., between 6 and 18 months, and they all receive essentially the same type of educational instruction.

Is this an appropriate placement for all of the students? The OCR has found school districts in violation because they failed to comply with state requirements that the age range of students grouped together not exceed four years.[31]

The theory apparently is that it is beneficial for students to be placed with other students close to their chronological ages. The OCR's position is confusing! If the educational program adequately meets the individual needs of the students given their similar mental ages, why are their chronological ages relevant? Why is the OCR assuming the responsibility of enforcing state law if the district has arguably complied with the federal mandate? It is important to note that at least one administrative law judge has rejected the OCR's use of state laws as support for its violation findings.[32] There certainly may be instances where failure to place students with their peers may deprive them of an appropriate education, but surely such a finding should be supported by more than a requirement under state law.[33]

"As Adequately as the Needs of Nonhandicapped Persons Are Met"

The phrase "as adequately as the needs of nonhandicapped persons are met" requires that the educational programs for handicapped students compare favorably to those that are offered nonhandicapped students. The question that immediately comes to mind is whether such a comparison is a useful endeavor, since it is clear that the vast majority of handicapped students require different services and programs than those provided nonhandicapped students.[34] How does a recipient fulfill the commitment to provide special and unique services on the one hand and make sure those services are comparable to its traditional program on the other?

> Parents of profoundly and severely retarded students complain that while nonhandicapped students receive five and a half hours of instruction a day, their children receive an average of only four hours of instruction. The school district admits that the students are only receiving four and half hours of education a day but asserts that this is unavoidable, because there are only three busses to transport the students and their transportation time is, on average, 45 to 60 minutes longer than that of nonhandicapped students. The parents challenge the four-and-a-half-hour figure by noting that the district is including the lunch period as instructional time.
>
> A teacher of a TMR class takes a three-month leave of absence. Rather than employing a certified substitute teacher, the school decides that the aide can adequately serve the students because she has worked with the teacher and most of the students for two years. A complaint is filed because the students will not be served by a certified teacher.

There is no real conflict between the requirement that the individual educational needs of handicapped persons be met, and the requirement that their needs be met as "adequately as the needs of nonhandicapped students are met." The key is that the services provided each group must be comparable unless the individual needs of the handicapped students demand otherwise. If services provided are not comparable, the burden is on the recipient to establish that the individual needs of each handicapped student are addressed by the different or separate aid, benefit, or service. Thus, the school district must provide evidence that four and a half hours of educational instruction meets the needs of *each* of the students. It is not appropriate to reduce instruction time because of the inadequacy of the transportation program. Similarly, the school district will have difficulty producing convincing evidence that the TMR students have educational needs that can be appropriately met by an aide rather than a certified teacher. As noted by the administrative law judge in *Missouri State Department of Education v. United States Department of Education*—a case in which the state was charged with discriminating against handicapped students as a class by providing them with only a five-hour school day while nonhandicapped students were provided a six-hour day—"To establish a violation of Section 504, it is necessary only to establish that there exists a class of handicapped children who are limited to a school day of five hours by a policy that is not based on an individualized educational program for each child as required by the Act."[35]

An additional concern is how does one quantify the degree to which the needs of handicapped students are met versus those of nonhandicapped students. The only meaningful way to make such a comparison is in terms of the "quality" of the services offered. Appendix A of the regulations describes the compliance standard as follows:

> The quality of the educational services provided to handicapped students must equal that of the services provided to nonhandicapped students; thus, handicapped students' teachers must be trained in the instruction of persons with the handicap in question and appropriate materials and equipment must be available.[36]

The cases in which states and school districts have been found in violation for providing services and programs to handicapped students that are "inadequate" are numerous. For example:

Shorter school days[37]

Improperly trained or uncertified teachers[38]

Failure to hire teachers and therapists[39]

Failure to provide related aids and services[40]

Provision of inadequate materials and classroom space[41]

Failure to provide sufficient educational choices[42]

Hardy County School District has unsuccessfully attempted to hire a physical therapist for two years. As a consequence, students needing these services have received them from unsupervised teachers and aides. Does the fact that the district has attempted to hire a therapist protect it from charges that it fails to provide the students with an appropriate education? While it was acknowledged that there might be a shortage of trained professionals to meet the needs of recipients (see Appendix A, p. 493), a district is not thereby permitted to avoid its responsibilities. The district must make every effort to provide the services, which may include contracting with a local professional to provide the services.[43] The OCR, however, has made allowances when, despite extensive efforts, a district has been unable to hire the necessary professionals.[44]

The regulations provide that implementation of an IEP developed in accordance with the EHA meets the standard of providing appropriate education.[45] However, it is important to keep in mind that complying with the EHA is only one means of complying with § 104.33(b)(1). The fact that the IEP does not strictly comply with the EHA requirements does not violate Section 504. In fact, Section 504 does not even require the development of an IEP. Section 504 requires that an appropriate education be provided; therefore, one must determine whether the deficiencies in the student's IEP prevents the provision of an appropriate education. The district's actions should be scrutinized in terms of whether the procedural requirements of sections 104.34, 104.35, and 104.36 have been adhered to, and whether an education that meets the individual needs of the handicapped student has been provided. If the answer to both questions is yes, the omission of items required under the EHA is not a violation of the regulations implementing Section 504. (See OCR Response to Inquiry, EHLR 305:18 [1982].)

Related Aids and Services

> Alice, a student with a history of behavioral problems, is provided special education services in the form of a behavior modification plan utilized by all of her teachers and referral to the school counselor when necessary. Alice's emotional outbursts and anti-social behavior begin to escalate, and she begins threatening her teachers. Alice's parents have her evaluated, and weekly counseling sessions are recommended to replace the sporadic referrals to the school counselor. The school district refuses to pay for the counseling because, it is argued, the services are medical rather than educational.
>
> The school district offers appropriate counseling services, but Alice's parents feel they are insufficient and place her in a private residential hospital. The hospital does not employ any individuals who are qualified to provide educational services. Although the private hospital does not provide educational services, Alice's parents assert that she needs the psychological services provided at the hospital and, therefore, the district should pay for Alice's hospitalization as a "related service."

Does the district have to provide the counseling and the psychological services? Are they related aids and services that are necessary to provide Alice an appropriate education?[46] "Related aids and services" is another one of those phrases used in the regulations for which no clear definition is provided. Beyond a brief set of examples of related services—"developmental, corrective and other supportive services (including psychological, counseling, and medical diagnostic,"—no other explanation of the term is given.[47] Therefore, the OCR has used the definition of related aids and services found in the EHA to fashion the compliance standards under Section 504.[48] Under the EHA, related aids and services are defined, at § 1401 (17) as:

[T]ransportation, and such developmental, corrective, and other supportive services (including speech pathology and audiology, psychological services, physical and occupational therapy, recreation and medical and counseling services, except that such medical services shall be for diagnostic and evaluation purposes only) as may be required to assist a handicapped child to benefit from special education.

How does one determine whether the requested services are "supportive services necessary for the student to benefit from educational instruction"?[49] The Supreme Court in *Irving Independent School District v. Tatro,* a case in which it held that intermittent catheterization was a related aid or service, stated that two questions must be answered: whether the service is "required to assist a handicapped child to benefit from special education" and whether the service is "excluded from this definition as a medical service serving purposes other than diagnosis or evaluation."[50] Thus, the key is whether provision of the services would permit the student to benefit from the educational services offered without converting the school district's primary function from a provider of educational services to one of medical practitioner. Merely determining that the student cannot attend school without the services does not end the inquiry. There is a "medical services exclusion."[51] While the service may provide meaningful access to education, it may be excluded as an essentially medical service. For example, services of a physician beyond those for diagnostic or evaluative purposes are excluded. Recipients are not obligated "to provide a service that might well prove unduly expensive and beyond the range of their competence." While schools are required to hire experts such as "occupational therapists, speech therapists, psychologists, social workers," they are not required to provide "the services of a physician or hospital."[52]

A handicapped student with significant physical impairments requires the following related aids and services: speech and language therapy, adaptive physical education, and appropriate school health services. The health services referred to require a full-time attendant. The attendant is responsible for administering medication and suctioning the student's lungs. In addition, the attendant must be prepared to perform cardiopulmonary resuscitation. Further, physicians state that the attendant would have to be either a registered nurse or a licensed practical nurse. It is felt that a school nurse would not be qualified to provide the necessary assistance. See *Detsel v. Board of Education of Auburn, supra.*

The parents of a student with cystic fibrosis and tracheomalacia request that the school district provide her with necessary medication, suction her lungs two or three times a day, and reinsert her tracheostomy tube if it becomes dislodged. It is proposed that the school staff could be trained to perform the tasks. The child's parents, who had no medical training, have performed the services. See *Department of Education, State of Hawaii v. Katherine D., supra.*

In *Irving Independent School District v. Tatro,* at 675, the Court stated that nursing services that "can be performed by a nurse or other qualified person" must be provided. The Court was persuaded by the fact that catheterization could be performed by a layperson with minimal training. Are the nursing services described above in the *Detsel* and *Katherine D.* cases the type contemplated by the Supreme Court in *Tatro*? The Court in *Detsel* said no, while the court in *Katherine D.* said yes. What distinguishes these two cases is the extensiveness of the services which were required. Specifically, in *Detsel,* the nursing services required were "beyond the competence" of school personnel, and "constant, in-school nursing care" was required. Moreover, the school would "be subjected to excessive costs and the burden of health care."[53] In *Katherine D.,* it was noted that school staff could be trained to provide the services. The Court was also persuaded by the fact that other courts had determined that "maintenance of a tracheostomy tube" was a related aid and service.[54]

The question of whether requested services are "medical" in nature, and thus need not be provided by the school district, does not turn on "the status of the health professional who provides the service."[55] An assessment of the nature and scope of the services is more relevant than a determination of whether a physician must provide them. The standard is one of reasonableness.[56] One must balance the interests involved by considering the cost, the time required, and the capacity of school health professionals to provide the service. In *Bevin,* the court distinguished cases in which intermittent catheterization and simple tracheostomy care had been held to be related aids and services by noting that they involved "intermittent care which could be provided by the school district at relatively little expense in both time and money."[57] The *Bevin* case involved a child that needed constant supervision from a nursing professional. The nurse was responsible for caring for a tracheostomy and gastrostomy tube, providing physical and occupational therapy, administering the child's oxygen supply, and ensuring that the tracheostomy tube did not become obstructed. The Court characterized the services as "varied and intensive . . . time consuming and expensive." The Court also noted, in concluding that the school district was not obligated to provide the services, that "because of this need for constant vigilance, a school nurse or any other qualified person with responsibility for other children within the school could not safely care for Bevin."[58]

It is important to note that the courts in *Bevin, Detsel,* and *Tokarcik* all specifically stated that it is legitimate to consider cost in determining whether a school district must provide a particular service. They cited *Hendrick Hudson District Board of Education v. Rowley, supra* as supporting the proposition that school districts are not required to provide the best possible education without regard to expense. The discussion of cost in those cases was associated with a determination that the particular services were medical in nature. Once the services are determined to be necessary related aids and services, recipients have not been permitted to use factors such as cost and difficulty in obtaining services as reasons for refusing to provide the services unless it can be established that it is an undue administrative or financial burden.[59]

Recipients will not be permitted to avoid responsibility by improperly using the medical exclusion, *i.e.*, by incorrectly characterizing requested services or aids as medical, emotional, or noneducational. Courts and enforcement agencies will look beyond the labels and assess the nature and the scope of the requested services.[60] The OCR has held that services such as physical therapy, speech therapy, occupational therapy, individual counseling, family counseling, and psychotherapy are related aids and services.[61] Thus, in the first hypothetical above, since Alice needs counseling services to benefit from her educational program, the school district must provide counseling as a related aid and service. Furthermore, recipients will not be permitted to condition the provision of necessary related aids and services on extraneous factors.[62]

In addition to benefitting from the "medical services exclusion," recipients are not required to provide related aids and services that do not meet the education needs of the students. Therefore, the district in our second hypothetical above does not have to pay for the psychotherapeutic program, which is isolated and not connected to Alice's educational program.[63] The requested aid or service must be necessary to enable the child to benefit from the education offered. For example, a district would not be required to administer medication to a student as a related aid or service if the medication could be administered to the child at any time during the day, including non-school hours. The fact that the parent felt that it would be more convenient to give the child the medication at school would be insufficient to impose an obligation on the school district.[64] If the recipient is providing related aids and services that are effective, parental demands for different or more extensive aids and services need not be agreed to.[65]

12
Free Education

Many educators believe that the requirement that states and school districts assume primary financial responsibility for meeting the individual educational needs of handicapped students is too onerous.[1] They argue that the burden of addressing the unique needs of handicapped students imposes potentially crippling economic demands on an already overtaxed educational system. In addition, they assert that the mandate requires them to pay a disproportionate amount of attention to meeting the needs of handicapped students, which has an adverse impact on the delivery of services to non-handicapped students.

In this chapter we will discuss the following questions regarding the obligation to provide a "free" education:[2]

> What are the specific financial responsibilities of recipients?
>
> What limits, if any, are there on the extent of their financial obligation?
>
> Are there any circumstances where the cost of a particular service may legitimately be considered?
>
> What financial responsibilities do the parents of handicapped students have?
>
> Can districts and states be required to provide residential placements under Section 504?

One hopes that the answers will provide some insight regarding the troublesome social and economic concerns of educators described above.

"Free"

Before tackling the more difficult issues of residential placement and parental responsibility, it is important to understand the basic parameters of the recipient's responsibility. Stated simply, the recipient is responsible for all costs associated with meeting a handicapped student's educational needs and providing an appropriate education.[3]

Alice, a multihandicapped student, has an educational program which includes physical therapy three times a week. Despite the fact that the placement committee concluded that it would be preferable if the services were actually provided by a therapist, the district proposes to Alice's parents that the services either be provided to her by a teacher or aide supervised periodically by a certified therapist, or that the parents take her to a local health clinic where she would receive direct services from a therapist. They are advised that if they elect to use the clinic, they would have to assume financial responsibility for the services. The district recommends that Alice receive services at the clinic because in the past the district has had difficulty contracting with a therapist to provide supervisory services.

The district's actions are questionable in two regards: (a) offering to pay only for a therapist to periodically supervise the delivery of services—if the student requires direct services from a therapist, the district cannot elect to provide the services only through teachers or aides—and (b) shifting the financial burden—it is improper, even indirectly, to seek to persuade the parents to assume responsibility for providing the services. If providing the services poses difficulties, the district, not the parents, must resolve them. The OCR has consistently found recipients in violation for such attempts to shift the financial burden of providing a free appropriate public education. For example, a recipient may not: (a) impose a limitation on the amount it will pay for necessary services, since such blanket restrictions preclude consideration of each student's individual needs;[4] (b) condition its payments on a student's parents paying for certain services;[5] (c) refer a student for an evaluation that it deems necessary but refuse to pay;[6] or (d) limit the amount of instructional services provided handicapped students based upon the nature or severity of their impairments.[7]

Moreover, while it is permissible under § 104.33(c)(1) to require the parents of handicapped students to pay "fees that are imposed upon nonhandicapped persons or their parents" for similar services, the parents of handicapped children cannot be required to pay more solely because their children are handicapped.

Magnanimous School District offers an after-school program for first through fifth grade students. The program consists of academic enrichment classes. The program director states that they attempt to provide studies and skills that cannot be normally taught as a part of the regular school curriculum. All students are eligible to enroll in the program. The sole criterion is payment of $50 a week. When parents of profoundly and severely impaired students seek to enroll their children, they are discouraged by the director who states the children could not benefit from the program because it is beyond their abilities. When the parents insist upon enrolling their children, they are told the cost of the program is $75 a week. The additional cost is justified on the basis that an aide would have to be hired to assist the teacher in serving the students. The district argues that charging the parents of handicapped students more does not violate Section 504 because the price is based upon the actual cost of providing services, a nondiscriminatory criterion.

When faced with this situation in *Riley v. Jefferson County Board of Education,* the Court held that the district's practice of using a cost-based sliding fee system for after-school care, which resulted in certain categories of handicapped students paying more, violated Section 504. The Court specifically held that "a public school cannot pass on to the handicapped the cost of providing extra care and extra training—this is precisely the sort of thing Section 504 was designed to prevent."[8]

Does this mean that states and school districts must bear the financial cost of providing such services alone? No. "[A] recipient's financial obligations need not be met solely through its own funds. Recipients may rely on funds from any public or private source including insurers and similar third parties."[9] However, while third parties, such as insurers, may be required to contribute to the cost of services, the recipient must still ensure that the parents of handicapped students are not ultimately paying for the services. In *Seals v. Loftis,* the Court held that a recipient cannot require parents to use private medical insurance benefits if "the utilization of those benefits would cause them to incur a financial cost."[10] In *Seals,* parents sought reimbursement from the district for payments made to it by their insurance company. The Court ruled that while the parents were entitled to reimbursement of the amount that the lifetime benefits available under the policy would be reduced, they were not entitled to reimbursement of amounts for services that did not involve a benefit reduction and for which the parents did not have to pay a deductible. Generally, use of insurance is precluded if the insureds are subjected to financial losses, such as increased premiums, payment of a deductible, or a decrease in the lifetime benefits or the value of the coverage. Further, if insurance is used to cover costs, the recipient still remains responsible for costs the insurance does not cover.[11]

> Drake School District officials concede that the educational program which it has attempted to implement for Betty, a student with a learning disability, a seizure disorder, and behavioral problems, is unsuccessful. The placement committee begins searching for a suitable residential placement for her. The placements favored by committee members are an out-of-state program that is deemed to be the best program in the region, and an in-state program that, while not as good an all-around program, has had great success with students with Betty's behavioral problems. The members feel either program is acceptable, so they defer to the special education director. The director chooses the in-state program because it costs $10,000 a year as opposed to $42,000 for the out-of-state program. Betty's parents object to the decision being based upon the cost of the programs.

There are circumstances under which it is permissible to consider cost in selecting an educational program or service.[12] However, unless the recipient is asserting that providing the program or service would impose an undue administrative or financial burden "cost considerations are only relevant when choosing between several options, all of which offer an 'appropriate' education."[13] Thus, in the example above, since both programs would provide Betty an appropriate education, the director's decision did not violate Section 504.

Residential Placement

The regulations at § 104.33(c)(3) specifically state that recipients are financially responsible for public and private residential placements.[14] Further, Appendix A states "If a recipient does not itself provide handicapped persons with the requisite services, it must assume the cost of *any alternate placement*"[15] [emphasis added]. The OCR has enforced this regulatory provision and found numerous recipients in violation for failing to pay the costs associated with such placements.[16] Therefore, certainly one should feel confident in asserting that under Section 504, recipients are financially responsible for residential placements. However, courts have explicitly held that recipients cannot be required to provide residential placements under Section 504.[17]

Using the Supreme Court decision in *Southeastern Community College v. Davis, supra,* these courts maintain that Section 504, as part of a non-discrimination statute, does not require affirmative action and, therefore, does not guarantee a right to a free appropriate public education.[18] They assert that, under the Act, recipients are only required to make modifications to their programs which are not an undue burden. The Court in *Turillo* answered the question of whether residential placements must be provided as follows:

> [C]ourts must find a way to limit the reach of § 504 consistent with the holding of *Davis.*
> I believe that this can be done most effectively with a two-tier analysis. First, does the relief requested by the plaintiff require affirmative action? That is, is the defendant being asked to provide the plaintiff with a completely new service, or merely with modifications of an existing service provided to nonhandicapped persons? If the plaintiff seeks modifications of an existing program, then the analysis moves to the second tier: do the modifications place an undue financial and administrative burden on the defendant?
> While § 504 might require a school system to modify its schools to accommodate handicapped children, it never compels a school system to finance a private educational placement. (*Turillo, supra* at 587–8.)

These court decisions place the validity of § 104.33(c)(3) in question.[19] However, at least one court has specifically held that Section 504 *does* require that recipients finance residential placements.[20] This debate will no doubt continue to rage until the Supreme Court resolves it. At present, since the OCR maintains the validity of this provision of the regulations by continuing to enforce it, it seems prudent to operate under the assumption that recipients will be held financially responsible for such placements.[21] With this assumption in mind, one might consider the following cases:

> Arthur is a 12-year-old who has a history of medical, behavioral, and emotional problems. His home life reflects a long series of upheavals and a stressful living environment. As early as first grade, Arthur exhibited behavioral problems, and, despite the fact that he is intelligent, he shows little progress in the traditional learning environment. The district recommends a therapeutic day treatment program for Arthur, while his mother insists upon a residential placement. All experts who examine Arthur conclude that his home environment has a significant impact on his behavior. The district officials argue that the day program, coupled with family counseling, is appropriate for Arthur and that a 24-hour program would merely function as room and board and serve no educational purpose. (*Hall v. Freeman.*)[22]
>
> Betty is a severely retarded child who has an IQ of 11 and a mental age of 14 months. She was placed, for a period of time, in a residential program and showed some progress regarding skills such as toilet training. Upon reevaluation, Betty's teacher, her caretaker, and the special education director all express the opinion that she has reached her maximum level, and that it is unlikely that continued placement in a residential program will provide any educational services that could not be provided in a day program with minimal reinforcement at home. Betty's parents insist upon a residential program, while the district argues that such a program would merely be custodial rather than educational. (*Matthews v. Davis.*)[23]
>
> Sam is diagnosed as being schizophrenic. He has emotional outbursts, exhibits anti-social behavior, is disruptive in class, and threatens and attacks his classmates and teachers. Sam is unable to function in a traditional school setting. Attempts to place him in private programs that, while traditional in scope, specialize in students with emotional problems, also prove unsuccessful. Finally, it is recommended that Sam be placed in a highly structured residential program. The institute selected also operates a traditional high school on the grounds, and, therefore, the referring school district agrees to pay only the tuition for the high school and advises Sam's parents that they have to pay his room and board. Sam's parents object and cite the opinion of institute officials who have stated that Sam would be unable to attend the institute's high school because it does not provide the structure he needs. The district argues that it is responsible only for Sam's educational needs and that the emotional and behavioral problems that necessitate his placement in the institute are medical in scope rather than educational.[24]

These fact situations illustrate the difficult and confusing issues regarding a recipient's duty to provide residential placement. The regulations merely provide guidance regarding what must be provided if such a placement is "necessary," *i.e.,* "room and board and nonmedical care (including custodial and supervisory care)."[25] But the question of whether the placement is "necessary" is left unanswered. It is clear that the drafters of the regulations felt that this question would be best resolved by negotiations between recipients and parents without federal intervention; but, as the number of court cases and OCR complaints reflect, the OCR has not been granted the luxury of such passive observance.

The Court, in *Vander Malle v. Ambach, supra* at 1040, said the question of whether a district must provide a residential placement should be "based upon an analysis of whether full-time placement may be considered necessary for educational purposes, or whether the residential placement is a response solely to medical, social or emotional problems that are segregable from the learning process." But how does one distinguish between educational needs and medical, social, and emotional problems—and what happens when they are intertwined?

The Court in *Parks v. Pavkovic* outlined a series of hypothetical cases in an effort to answer those questions.[26] The Court stated, in pertinent part:

> In the first, a deaf and blind child, perfectly capable of living at home, is institutionalized on the basis of a judgment that he can get a better education in a more controlled environment. . . . In our second hypothetical case, the child is in a coma and is institutionalized because he cannot be cared for at home. . . . In the third case, an intermediate case . . . the child cannot be cared for at home because of some purely physical problem, but because of that problem neither can he be educated unless he is institutionalized. *Id,* 1404–1405.

The Court stated that the first and second cases were simple, *i.e.,* that living expenses should be provided for the student placed for purely educational reasons, while no such reimbursement was required for the child in the coma who was "completely uneducable in his condition." With respect to the third case, the Court rejected the argument that recipients should be excused from responsibility merely because "the child would have to be institutionalized quite apart from educational needs that also required institutionalization."[27] Thus, the prevailing principle is if the student is properly educable only in a residential setting, the recipient is responsible for the cost of such a placement despite the fact that noneducational problems may also be involved. Regarding our fact situations, only Sam would be entitled to residential placement. Betty and Arthur could be properly educated in a day program. It is also important to remember that in cases such as Arthur's Appendix A provides "when residential care is necessitated not by the student's handicap but by factors such as the student's home conditions, the recipient is not required to pay room and board."[28]

Once a district determines that a residential placement is appropriate, it cannot enforce policies which limit the costs it will assume responsibility for and shift the financial burden for services connected to the student's educational needs to the parents.[29] "If a residential placement is required, room, board and related services must be provided at no cost to the child's parents."[30] Related services include psychological and medical services necessary for diagnostic and evaluative purposes.[31] While recipients are not precluded from requiring that parents pay for services or products that are not related to the child's educational needs, they must use procedures that clearly isolate those noneducational items so that parents do not inadvertently pay for educational services.[32]

> Blake School District reimburses John's parents for his residential placement, but declines to pay for the following expenses: (a) the cost of John's food; (b) treatments by John's physician for his seizure disorder; (c) the cost of John's medication; (d) the cost of neurological evaluations that are necessary for the development of John's IEP; and (e) the cost of John's psychological services. The district also prorates the cost of room and board and pays only for the portion of the day during which John actually receives educational services. Which, if any, of the district's actions violate the regulations?

The district must pay for the entire room and board expense—not just a pro rata portion—plus the cost of John's food and psychological services; the district is also responsible for "medical services necessary for diagnostic and evaluative purposes," i.e., the neurological evaluations. However, the district does not have to provide reimbursement for the treatments provided by John's physician, nor for his medication, because these are purely medical services.

Transportation

Pursuant to § 104.33(c)(2), the recipient is responsible for providing transportation services to students that it places in or refers to a program not operated by it for purposes of providing them a free appropriate public education.[33] The important elements of this subpart are: (1) the student must be placed in or referred to the program by the district; (2) the services must be adequate; and (3) parents must incur no greater cost than if the student were placed in the recipient's program.

> Marcy and Jill, who are next-door neighbors, both attend a private school located in Dorn County School District. Marcy was referred to the private school by the district, while Jill was placed there by her parents. Both girls receive speech therapy three times a week. The services are provided after

school. While the district provides transportation services to the girls during normal school hours, it refuses to provide the services on the afternoons when the students receive therapy. The district argues that it is not economical to transport just two students. District officials justify this decision by noting that non-handicapped students are not provided transportation for after-school extracurricular activities and, therefore, Marcy and Jill are being treated equally. It is further argued that Jill is not entitled to any transportation services since she was placed in the private school by her parents.

Drake School District contracts with a private company to provide transportation for students assigned to a mental health facility for educational services. Parents of the students are charged $5.00 a week for transportation because the facility is located outside the county. A parent group complains because of the $5.00 weekly charge and because the services provided are inadequate, *i.e.,* the van is often late. As a consequence, the district offers to reimburse parents if they transport their children to school. Several parents object to this solution because they do not have the time or the vehicles to drive their children to school every morning. Those parents are advised to continue using the van provided by the private company.

The district need not provide Jill with transportation. When a recipient has offered an appropriate education and parents, nevertheless, unilaterally place their children in a private facility, the recipient is not responsible for providing transportation services.[34] Regarding Marcy, since she was placed in the private facility by the district, if the therapy sessions are a necessary part of her educational program, *i.e.,* essential to the provision of a free appropriate public education, adequate transportation services must be provided.[35] Necessary educational services cannot be equated with voluntary extracurricular activities. If the district is permitted to deny Marcy transportation services for her therapy sessions, in essence it would result in the denial of a free appropriate public education.

Drake School District will be permitted to charge the parents of handicapped students a fee for transportation services only if it does not exceed what such services would cost if the students were enrolled in Drake's program; *i.e.,* the fee that Drake charges all students, handicapped and nonhandicapped, for transportation. Further, while reimbursing parents who transport their children is acceptable, the district cannot refuse to provide adequate services to students whose parents cannot avail themselves of that option.

The OCR has also held that recipients cannot restrict the right of handicapped students placed in residential facilities outside of the district by arbitrarily limiting the number of home visits parents will be reimbursed for or restricting the students' home visitations to vacations and holidays.[36] In the Richmond County case, the OCR concluded, in pertinent part, that:

> Since the district provides transportation to all children in the District where their residence is over one and one-half miles to the educational services,

it must also provide similar transportation to handicapped children placed outside the District. We have determined that, because these students do not require educational services on weekends, they need not remain at the Academy on weekends and their residence remains in the District. The District, therefore, is responsible for these students' transportation. (EHLR 352:241.)

Placement by Parents

As a general rule, parents who reject an offer of an appropriate placement and unilaterally place their children in private facilities are not entitled to reimbursement.[37] However, recipients will lose this protection if they directly affirm or acquiesce in private placements made by parents.[38] What rights do parents have who disagree with the placement offered by the recipient and are ultimately proven right regarding their assertion that the proffered placement was inappropriate? Clearly the drafters of the regulations felt that such disputes should be resolved by due process proceedings.[39] But the question of whether the parents should be reimbursed if their chosen placement proves to be appropriate while the recipient's is judged to be inappropriate is not specifically answered by the regulations. Moreover, the OCR's pronouncements have generally focused on the right of recipients not to pay for unilateral placements, rather than on the rights of parents to receive reimbursements when recipients have failed to offer an appropriate program. Even when recipients have been found in violation, the OCR's tendency is to require them simply to comply prospectively.

The Supreme Court, in interpreting the EHA, has clearly outlined the circumstances under which parents who have unilaterally placed their children are entitled to reimbursement.[40] While noting that parents who unilaterally remove their children do so "at their own financial risk," the Court ruled that

> [W]here a court determines that a private placement desired by parents was proper under the Act and that an IEP calling for a placement in a public school was inappropriate, it seems clear beyond cavil that "appropriate" relief would include a prospective injunction directing the school officials to develop and implement at public expense an IEP placing the child in a private school.

The Court noted that the protections guaranteed to parents under the Act would not be complete if they are forced to choose between leaving their children in an inappropriate placement or paying for an appropriate placement, and are denied reimbursement when they are subsequently found to be right regarding the proper placement.[41] It is important to keep in mind that the placement selected by the parents must be found to be appropriate.

Courts have denied reimbursement where parents have placed their children in unapproved schools or in programs that did not adequately address their needs.[42]

Lower courts have expanded the Supreme Court's doctrine in *Burlington* to include a review of the conduct of the parties. It has been determined that the following factors are important: "(1) the existence of other perhaps more suitable substitute placements, (2) the parents' effort in securing alternative placements, and (3) the general cooperative or uncooperative position of the school district itself."[43] It has generally been held that to be entitled to reimbursement, the parents must show that they did not prematurely sever communication with the school district in an attempt to resolve the placement issues. Parents have been denied reimbursement because they unilaterally placed their children without (a) giving notice to the district, (b) discussing the matter with district officials, or (c) giving the district an opportunity to attempt an alternative placement.[44] The OCR has also ruled against parents in similar situations.[45]

These decisions reflect the grave importance placed upon the "participatory process" between parents and school districts in arriving at appropriate placements for handicapped students. It further reflects the opinion that such decisions are the province of those parties and not that of courts and federal agencies. Therefore, those seeking to successfully challenge the placement recommendations of school district personnel must fully cooperate with the district regarding the placement process. As noted by the court in *B.G. v. Cranford Board of Education, supra* at 1166,

> [T]he cooperative efforts of parents and school authorities are inextricably intertwined with a handicapped child's inalienable right to a "free appropriate public education." Whoever disrupts that cooperative venture, and thus interferes with the child's right—whether it be parents or school authorities, does so at his or her financial peril.

13
Educational Setting

Once one has determined what an appropriate education is, the next logical question is in what type of environment should this education be provided. Should a recipient attempt to provide these special services in a regular education setting, or should they be provided in a separate facility? The answer, of course, is that handicapped students are served in a variety of settings.

Continuum of Educational Settings

Regular → Regular w/Supplemental Aids and Services → Resource → Self-contained → Separate Facility → Homebound

The essential question is how to determine which of the available settings is the appropriate one. Section 104.34(a) provides, in pertinent part, that qualified handicapped persons should be educated with nonhandicapped persons "to the maximum extent appropriate to the needs of the handicapped person."[1] This provision raises two important priorities for recipients: (a) providing an education that is appropriate to the needs of the student, and (b) educating the student with nonhandicapped persons to the maximum extent appropriate. Often recipients fail to view the mandate to educate handicapped students with nonhandicapped students as an additional component in the definition of an appropriate education and, as a result, underestimate its importance.[2] It is a mistake to treat the setting in which services are offered as being of lesser importance than the quality of the services actually provided. The best way to conceptualize the connection between these two priorities is to view them as being indispensable to each other—the program is not appropriate if it is not offered in the proper setting.

"A handicapped student may be removed from the regular educational setting only where the recipient can show that the needs of the student would, on balance, be served by placement in another setting."[3] The only legitimate reason for removal of the student is to adequately address his or her educational needs. This is the starting point for every placement decision involving handicapped students. An understanding of how the regulatory principles of nondiscrimination and meaningful access are linked will help the recipient to balance the responsibilities involved.[4]

> *Discrimination Prohibited*—Qualified handicapped students should be treated the same as similarly situated non-handicapped students.[5] This principle supports the presumption that services should be provided in the regular education setting if at all possible.
> *Meaningful Access*—Qualified handicapped students should only be treated differently or provided separate services/benefits if it is necessary to meet their individual needs, *i.e.*, provide meaningful access.[6] This principle requires recipients to design educational programs to meet the students' individual needs.

Thus, as recipients move down the continuum, they must keep in mind that they are required to select the setting closest to the regular educational setting which will provide the student an appropriate education. The further away the placement is from the regular educational setting, the more pressure there will be on the recipient to justify the placement decision. Recipients have frequently been found in violation of the regulations for failure to provide proper documentation to support their placement decisions.[7] It is not enough that recipients simply assert that the placement is appropriate. The assertion must be accompanied by clear evidence that placement in a regular education setting with supplemental aids and other less restrictive placements was considered and found to be inappropriate.[8] Recipients should provide specific reasons why the students must be educated in a more segregated environment.[9] It is also important to remember that the principle of individualization requires that such determinations and documentation be made and provide for each handicapped student.[10]

> Efficiency Separate School District assigns all TMR students to its Center for Handicapped Services except the students in the northwest section of the district. District officials state that the students assigned to the Center are appropriately placed because the quality of services provided them is excellent. Specifically, the facility's classrooms are specially designed for meeting the needs of handicapped students, e.g., bathrooms and dining areas. Practitioners who provide related aids and services are at the Center full time and each teacher is provided with two aides to assist him or her. It is felt that this continuum of services could not be provided if students were placed in regular school settings because the district could not afford to hire the additional staff needed to serve all 17 schools. Staff members, who are providing services to students at the Center, state that TMR students who live within 25 miles of the Center are always placed there because the academic and developmental services provided students at the Center are excellent. They state that, while some of the students can interact with nonhandicapped students, the quality of their academic development would

certainly suffer in a regular school setting where their needs were not the primary focus. Although some parents request that their children be assigned to regular schools, the district refuses and notes that its responsibility is to provide the students an appropriate education and their needs are best served at the Center. The reason given for not assigning TMR students in the northwest to the Center is that the distance to the Center (30 to 40 miles) is too great. Those students are assigned to regular schools.

The area in which recipients most frequently have difficulty with the requirements of § 104.34(a) is the placement of a class of handicapped students in a special-purpose facility. As noted above, in order for the decision to remove a student from the regular education setting to be appropriate, it must be based upon a consideration of the individual needs of the student. The decision to place all TMR students in the same setting, because it is believed that such a placement is better for TMR students as a class, is not a decision based upon the individual needs of each student involved. A district can be found in violation, even if all necessary educational services are being provided and the program is "excellent," if those services are unjustifiably provided in a segregated setting. A recipient will not be permitted, as the officials in Efficiency School District are attempting to do, to argue that the duty to provide educational services that meet the individual needs of handicapped students supersedes the duty to provide them services in the regular environment "to the maximum extent appropriate." Remember—mainstreaming is one of the elements of providing an appropriate education. As noted by the court in Briggs v. Board of Education of the State of Connecticut: "[the fact] that a program was 'reasonably designed' is not sufficient under the Act when the challenge to the program is that it did not provide a mainstream setting to the maximum extent appropriate."[11] Also, the district's assertions that the Center is the appropriate placement for TMR students must be questioned in light of the fact that TMR students who live in the northwest section of the county are denied such a placement solely on the basis of where they live. The OCR has found districts in violation for such categorical placements.[12] Similarly, students cannot be so placed because it is more convenient, more cost efficient, or because the district has historically always served handicapped students in a segregated setting.[13] Further, the recipient's decision-making regarding the proper placement must also consider the issue of age appropriateness and the proximity of the setting to students' homes. Handicapped students cannot be arbitrarily separated from students in their age group or placed in a distant location if "an equally appropriate education may exist closer to home."[14]

Mainstreaming is not limited to academic courses. As provided in § 104.34(b), handicapped students must be provided nonacademic services "in as integrated a setting as possible." Therefore, a school district which isolates a class of multihandicapped students, not only for academic subjects but for the entire school day, would have to justify why each student could not participate in activities such as lunch, music, physical education, recess, and field trips with nonhandicapped students.[15] Recipients are also required to ensure that students in residential settings are permitted to interact with nonhandicapped students to the maximum extent appropriate.[16]

Despite the rather restrictive tone of the preceding discussion, there are circumstances under which recipients may properly remove handicapped students from a regular educational setting.

> Sam, a student with a behavioral disorder, is removed from his regular class because he is too disruptive. His parents contest the removal on the basis that his C grade point average indicates that he is benefiting from the program. School officials counter that the teacher is spending all of her time addressing Sam's needs to the detriment of the rest of the class. Is the district's action appropriate?
>
> Billy, who is a mentally retarded and speech-impaired six-year-old boy with a developmental age of between two and three, is receiving kindergarten services in a special education program. At the request of his mother, he is assigned half-day to a regular kindergarten program. The regular program placement is unsuccessful because the child requires the constant attention of the teacher or the aide and is unable to learn the skills that are being taught. The boy's mother objects to his being removed from the program. She argues that, with the proper supplemental aids—in this instance an aide to work exclusively with him—he could benefit from the placement. The teacher argues that in order for the boy to gain anything from the program it would have to be completely restructured to correspond to his developmental age. The school removes the boy from the program, but provides for continued interaction with nonhandicapped students during lunch and recess. The mother files a complaint alleging that her son is being denied a regular education. See *Daniel R.R. v. State Board of Education*.[17]

In the case of Billy, mainstreaming does not appear to meet his unique needs. It is important to keep in mind that for some students the least restrictive environment is a segregated placement. If placement in a regular classroom would preclude a student from benefiting from the educational program, it would violate section 104.33(a) of the regulations to leave the student in that placement because it would be a denial of appropriate education. While there is a "strong preference in favor of mainstreaming," the mandate to provide

> [A] free appropriate public education qualifies and limits [the] mandate for education in the regular classroom. . . . When education in a regular classroom cannot meet the handicapped child's unique needs, the presumption in favor of mainstreaming is overcome.[18]

The district's treatment of Billy provides the correct approach under the regulations. Specifically, the placement in regular kindergarten revealed that he could not be properly served in that setting, and the alternative placement permitted continued interaction with nonhandicapped students during nonacademic periods. Regarding Sam, although the district's decision was not based exclusively upon his individual needs, the removal from the class is appropriate. As provided in Appendix A, "[W]here a handicapped student is so disruptive in a regular classroom that the education of other students is significantly impaired, the needs of the handicapped child cannot be met in that environment."[19]

But even if provision of educational services in a separate facility is warranted, § 104.34(c) requires that the facility and the services offered be comparable "to the other facilities, services and activities of the recipient." For example:

> Dorne School District provides services for severely retarded students in a special school. Parents who have children assigned to the facility complain because it has no lunchroom, playground equipment, or library. They also note that the classrooms are smaller and are not air-conditioned. District officials and staff members assert that the facility is adequate for addressing the needs of the students.

The requirement that separate facilities be comparable is absolute. It is not sufficient to argue that the facilities are adequate. One of the basic tenets of the Act and regulations is that handicapped students receive equal benefits and services unless different services or benefits are necessary to address their individual needs. As noted by the Court in *Hendricks v. Gilhool, supra* at 1366, a case in which a district's failure to provide adequate classroom space was held to violate Section 504, recipients are prohibited from "furnishing to handicapped individuals facilities and services that are objectively inferior to those provided their nonhandicapped peers."[20] The Court, however, in stating that the district was not required to make the classroom space "precisely equivalent," noted, at 1369, that the disparities could not be "trivial or insignificant." The question of what are significant disparities must, again, be answered on a case-by-case basis. The responsibility to provide comparable services and activities also includes such things as extracurricular activities, length of school day, and toilet facilities.[21]

In addition to providing separate facilities for particular classes of handicapped students, recipients are also permitted to designate specific schools in their jurisdiction to serve students with special needs. For example, in *Barnett v. Fairfax County School Board,* a school district offers a cued speech program for hearing-impaired students at a centralized location.[22] The parents of a hearing-impaired student object to his being assigned to the school housing the program, because it is five miles farther from his home than his neighborhood school. They insist that the school district offer the cued speech program at his neighborhood school, despite the fact that he excels in the program at the centralized location and is mainstreamed for all courses. The Court ruled that neither the EHA nor Section 504 required the district to duplicate the program. With respect to Section 504, it specifically held that the student had not been excluded from the public education program and that requiring the district to provide every hearing-impaired student with an individualized program at his or her neighborhood school would be the type of "substantial modification" that the Supreme Court in *Southeastern Community College v. Davis, supra,* held that recipients are not required to make.

14
Evaluation and Placement

Preplacement Procedures

Section 104.35(a) provides, in pertinent part, that

> A recipient . . . shall conduct an evaluation . . . of any person who, because of handicap, needs or is believed to need special education or related services before taking any action with respect to the initial placement of the person in regular or special education or any subsequent significant change in placement.

A significant number of compliance problems seem to develop surrounding the interpretation of the following phrases:

> "need special education or related services"—What responsibility does the recipient have to handicapped students who are not eligible for special education placement?
>
> "before taking any action"—Just how tightly does this provision tie the hands of recipients regarding administrative decisionmaking?
>
> "any subsequent significant change in placement"—What is a "significant" change in placement?

Frequently, educators view their responsibility to handicapped students as being connected solely to their eligibility for placement in the special education program. This is in large measure due to the fact that, for delivery-of-services purposes, students are compartmentalized based upon eligibility standards under the EHA, and the broader definition of "qualified handicapped person" under Section 504, which provides protection to a larger group of individuals, is ignored.[1] In addition to special education, the regulations identify appropriate educational services for "qualified" handicapped persons as being "regular classes" and "education in regular class with the use of supplementary services."[2] Thus, protection under the regulations is not limited simply to those students in special education classes, since such placements are but one of the acceptable methods of providing a free appropriate public education to students. Recipients must properly evaluate and serve all qualified handicapped students who are believed to need services. Therefore, a school district that refuses to evaluate a student who has rheumatoid arthritis because it has a policy of not evaluating students who do not qualify for special education is in violation of § 104.35(a).[3]

The degree to which outsiders should be permitted to interfere with the administrative decisionmaking of those charged with the responsibility to provide educational services to students is an issue that can be endlessly debated. No one would dispute the fact that recipients must be free to make administrative decisions concerning the day-to-day operation of their educational systems without undue interference from federal bureaucrats. Section 104.35 seeks to influence those decisions that might result in "misclassification and misplacement" by requiring that recipients adhere to certain procedural imperatives.[4] Within this prescribed procedural framework, the actions of recipients are closely scrutinized to ensure that the demands of administrative expediency do not result in shortcuts regarding evaluation and placement that have an adverse impact on the students. Recipients, for example, are precluded from taking the following actions without conducting proper evaluations:

> placing students[5]
>
> changing the nature of the services provided students[6]
>
> removing, reassigning or dismissing students from classes/programs.[7]

It is also important to remember that the regulatory mandate regarding "any action" also "includes denials of placement."[8]

Of course, the requirement to evaluate means little without an understanding of when the duty to evaluate arises. What is the recipient's responsibility regarding these students?

> Warren, a tenth grade student, has an extensive disciplinary file. During the present academic year he has been suspended on ten occasions, totaling 73 days out of school. He is also frequently assigned to in-school suspension for his behavior. Warren is failing most of his courses. He has never been referred for special education evaluation. His teachers just attempt to cope with his disruptive behavior.
>
> Billy has failed the ninth grade twice. His parents believe he has a learning disability. They request that he be evaluated and submit psychological reports that reflect some learning deficiencies.
>
> Susan has been absent from school for 63 days. The school counselor recommends that Susan be evaluated for special education placement. The special education director disagrees.

Tad is referred for evaluation by one of his teachers. She feels that he has a learning disability because he is unable to fully comprehend things he reads. Also, his grades are borderline, and the counselor states that he is frustrated by his inability to succeed. Tad's parents, who are college professors, refuse to permit him to be evaluated because they feel placement in a special education class would ruin his academic career.

Recipients must initiate evaluation procedures for students when there is clear evidence that the students are experiencing academic problems that need to be addressed. Lack of action cannot be justified by the fact that the student was not formally referred by staff members. The responsibility imposed upon recipients regarding evaluating students believed to need services is proactive. This responsibility may require the recipient to override the wishes of a student's parents. Thus, if the recipient has evidence indicating that the student should be evaluated, and the parents refuse to cooperate, the recipient must take steps—such as initiating due process procedures—to ensure that the student has meaningful access to the educational program. It is important to remember that the wishes of parents will not excuse the denial of a free appropriate public education to the student.[9] Thus, the problems of Warren, Billy, and Tad must be addressed by the district.[10] Susan's absenteeism, however, without other evidence of academic problems, does not indicate a need for an evaluation.[11]

"The question of what constitutes a change in educational placement is, necessarily, fact specific."[12] There must be a change in the general education program, not just "mere variations in the program."[13] It cannot be a minor alteration such as replacing one qualified teacher with another equally qualified teacher. You must identify "a fundamental change in or elimination of a basic element of the educational program in order for the change to qualify as a change in educational placement."[14]

Which of the following can be classified as a "significant change of placement?"

A profoundly retarded child is placed in a state facility for the mentally retarded. He is bused to another facility where educational services are provided. He sustains a foot injury which prevents him from being transported for educational services. No alternative services are provided during the five months he is unable to travel.

A child's IEP provides that his parents will be reimbursed for taking him to school. The following year the school arranges for a private company to provide transportation services. As opposed to the door-to-door service provided by his parents, the new service would require one brief stop in the afternoon to pick up other children. Thus, while the travel time in the morning is comparable, the travel time in the afternoon is 10 to 15 minutes longer. The child's parents object to the new transportation services, and they argue the longer travel time would have a negative impact on his educational program. (See *DeLeon v. Susquehanna Community School District, supra.*)

Grant School District is experiencing financial setbacks that require it to close its special school for hearing-impaired students. The students are to be transferred to a state-operated school where their IEPs can be fully implemented. It is anticipated that the services offered to the students will be similar to those they were offered at the special school.

Bruce, a 20-year-old emotionally disabled student, is simultaneously enrolled in high school classes as well as a vocational training program. He meets all of the school's graduation requirements and is graduated with a regular high school diploma. Officials of the vocational training program inform him that he can continue in that program for another year; however, the school district denies his request to do so. The Commissioner of Education also refuses to permit him to continue in the vocational program pending his appeal of the district's decision. (See *Cronin v. Board of Education of the East Ramapo Central School District,* 689 F. Supp. 197 [S.D.N.Y. 1988].)

Courts have held that the complete failure to implement a child's IEP constitutes a significant change in placement.[15] Similarly, since graduation results in total exclusion from services, Bruce's being graduated can also be characterized as a significant change in placement. Also, § 104.35(a) has been interpreted as mandating that students be permitted to remain in their present placement during the resolution of conflicts regarding appropriate placement.[16] Thus, the commissioner's refusal to permit Bruce to continue training in the vocational program during the pendency of the administrative proceeding violated the "stay-put" doctrine.[17] As noted by the Court in *DeLeon v. Susquehanna Community School District,* minor changes in the daily transportation routine will not have a "significant effect" on the child's learning experience. The Court concluded that small increases in travel time (10 to 15 minutes) did not represent a significant change. However, there are circumstances under which a change in transportation services will have such a "significant effect." The OCR has ruled that a suspension of a handicapped student's school bus privileges, which results in a cessation of educational services, is such a circumstance.[18]

Are students denied an appropriate education because the evaluation and placement process takes too long to complete? The regulations do not include a standard regarding the amount of time a recipient can take to complete its evaluation and placement procedure. However, recipients have been found in violation for failure to conduct timely evaluations and placements.[19] The OCR generally has used "reasonableness" as the yardstick, *i.e.,* the extent to which the delay can be characterized as "unreasonable." Unreasonable delays deny handicapped students meaningful access to educational services.[20] How does one determine the point at which the delay becomes unreasonable and, therefore, discriminatory? The OCR has used the time frames established in the states' departments of education plans as a guideline and thereby found in violation school districts that failed to adhere to the time frames adopted by their own states.[21] However, this approach was expressly rejected by the administrative law judge (ALJ) in the Chicago Board of Education case. The ALJ succinctly described the problem with the OCR's approach when he compared New York state law, which provides only 30 days for evaluations, with Illinois state law, which provides 60 days, and queried, "But if incorporation of state law into Section 504 is appropriate as a matter of course, why would a 60-day period be considered 'reasonable' in the case of a city like Chicago, but not 'reasonable' with regard to New York City?"[22] Thus, given the uncertainty that presently surrounds the issue of timeliness, one is best advised to review the matter on a case-by-case basis. In the Chicago case, the ALJ found that delays of up to two years in evaluating students violate the regulations.

Evaluation Procedures

The purpose of the requirements of § 104.35(b) is "to prevent misinterpretation and similar misuse of test scores . . . to avoid undue reliance on general intelligence tests . . . and to avoid distortion of the test results."[23] What is important is that recipients have *procedures* in place that reflect their adherence to the mandates of § 104.35(b).[24] Often parties having disputes regarding a recipient's evaluation and placement practices lose sight of the fact that the regulations speak in terms of procedural imperatives, not substantive issues. Generally, those who assess a recipient's compliance under the Act have no special expertise regarding the science of testing or test methodology; therefore, they judge a recipient's actions in a somewhat narrow fashion. Specifically, can the recipent provide evidence that (a) the test was validated, (b) the evaluation instruments assessed the student's specific areas of educational need, and (c) the test measured the student's skills and abilities rather than the limitations imposed by the handicap? If the recipient can provide evidence that its evaluation procedures met these objectives, the OCR is not likely to look behind that evidence to raise specific substantive questions. For example, if there is evidence provided to show that a test has been validated for the purposes used, the OCR will not raise specific questions regarding the nature or content of the validation studies, nor will it enter into a dispute regarding which of two equally legitimate tests is more appropriate to use for a particular child. It is proper for the enforcement agency to avoid passing judgment on the legitimacy of a particular evaluation practice unless there is clear evidence that it violates the regulations.[25] However, because the compliance assessments are strictly procedural in nature, the requirements of § 104.35(b) are absolute and, should questions arise, the burden is on the recipient to provide clear and convincing evidence that it is in compliance.[26]

Most compliance questions that arise regarding the interpretation of § 104.35(b) are not just a simple matter of the recipient failing to develop procedures.

> Dunwick Separate School District has a large backlog of students to be evaluated for possible placement in its special education programs. For a student initially referred for evaluation, a referral checklist is completed by the student's teachers and members of the placement committee. The information to complete the checklist is gathered from observation of the student in class as well as a review of the student's grades and work products. Based upon the information gathered, a proposed placment, e.g., EMR, LD or BD, is recommended. Extensive testing is only recommended for students for whom the screeners cannot agree upon a proposed placement. Regarding the testing, the special education director assists the staff psychologist by administering some of the tests. This practice is only permissible under state law if the unlicensed individual is closely supervised by a psychologist. District officials assert that the director has had 20 years of experience in the field and she discusses all difficult cases with the psychologist.
>
> A school district administers a standardized basic skills test to handicapped students and refuses to offer test modifications such as extended time and readers. The district justifies its refusal by (a) noting that the test developer could not guarantee the validity of results taken under nonstandard conditions, and (b) suggesting that the results present a clear picture of handicapped students' performance versus that of nonhandicapped students. The test results are also used to determine eligibility for placement in several of the district's special education programs. (See Northport–East Northport Union Free School District, EHLR 352:635 [1988].)
>
> Mrs. Jones is concerned that her son was referred for special evaluation on the basis of his performance on an IQ test as well as his classroom behavior. He is given aptitude and achievement tests and it is recommended that he be placed in an EMR class. Mrs. Jones refuses to approve the placement, because review of the evaluation data reveals that there is considerable disagreement regarding whether he should be placed in the LD program or the EMR program. Therefore, she has the data reviewed by an independent evaluator. The independent evaluator recommends that an additional battery of aptitude tests be administered to resolve the question of EMR versus LD placement. Although district officials consider the report of the independent evaluator,· they decline to conduct additional testing because their psychometrist is unfamiliar with the tests in question and does not feel qualified to administer them. Further, they assert that there is sufficient evidence in the file to justify EMR placement. Mrs. Jones contests the refusal to conduct further tests. She also feels that the use of IQ test results to determine special education placement is inappropriate.

These examples reflect the type of "gray area" problems and issues that often arise under § 104.35(b). Dunwick's use of the checklist, a screening instrument, to place students violates the regulations. The checklist is at best a method to identify students with academic problems; it has not been validated as an assessment instrument. Evaluation instruments must be validated for the specific purpose used.[27] Similarly, the practice of allowing the special education director to conduct evaluations is impermissible unless performed under the direct supervision of the psychologist. Simply contacting the psychologist for difficult cases does not ensure that the tests are administered by trained personnel.[28] The district's procedures in the Northport case were also found to be in violation of the regulations. Section 104.35(b)(3) expressly requires recipients to administer tests to students "with impaired sensory, manual or speaking skills in whatever manner is necessary to avoid distortion of the test results by the impairment." Thus, it is inappropriate for the district to place students in programs using test results which do not accurately reflect their aptitude or achievement level.

Mrs. Jones' objection to the use of the IQ test is not legitimate in this instance. While, as noted previously, recipients are prohibited from using general intelligence tests as the sole or primary criterion for placement (*Larry P. v. Riles, supra* at 982), here the IQ test results are used as one of many criteria for placement. The other criteria assess specific deficiencies and needs, and, therefore, consideration of general intelligence data does not violate the regulations. In the fact situation above, the IQ results were used primarily as an initial screening device, not as the sole criterion for placement. Regarding the refusal to test further, the district's decision must be based upon the student's needs. It is not legitimate to limit evaluation instruments to those with which the psychometrist is familiar.[29]

One of the most volatile issues regarding testing in secondary education involves the requirement that students pass a "basic skills test" as a criterion for being awarded a diploma. It has been argued that the practice of awarding certificates of completion instead of diplomas to handicapped students who cannot pass the test violates Section 504. Both the courts and the OCR have held that such a diploma requirement does not unlawfully discriminate against handicapped students. The OCR has specifically held that so long as the test as a whole is validated for the purpose for which it is given, and there are procedures in place to ensure that handicapped students are provided with necessary modifications—such as extended time and interpreters—the practice of requiring handicapped students to take such tests does not violate the regulations.

> [I]t is clear that the state has a right to determine minimum education standards. In the instant case, the state has established certain skills reflective of a specific level of achievement which is required for a regular high school diploma. . . . Section 504 does not require that a recipient substantially modify its standards to accommodate handicapped persons by adopting a different achievement level or modifying the content of the test to reflect different skill objectives. (State Department of Education, EHLR 352:480 [1987].)

While handicapped students may not be denied, on the basis of their handicap, the opportunity to earn a regular diploma, recipients do not have to accommodate them by awarding them diplomas if they do not meet all the academic requirements. Further, handicapped students will not be permitted to assert that their placement in special education classes impermissibly deprived them of the right to earn a diploma if, in fact, the placements are appropriate.[30]

It is also important for recipients to keep in mind that, in addition to the difficult questions that arise regarding proper evaluation procedures for handicapped students, issues such as adequately addressing the needs of students whose proficiency in English is limited, and the existence of cultural biases in evaluations, cannot be ignored.[31]

Placement Procedures

Controversies involving the interpretation of § 104.35(c) also highlight the distinction between procedural mandates and substantive disagreements. Section 104.35(c) is procedural in scope. It prescribes the *procedures* which recipients should use "in interpreting evaluation data and in making placement decisions."[32] Clearly, under this provision, the appropriate inquiry is whether proper procedures have been developed and implemented. There is no language that would justify a recipient's actual placement decisions being scrutinized if such procedures have been adopted and implemented. However, most of the complaints filed under this provision do not address the correctness (or lack thereof) of the procedures used, but rather are vehement assertions regarding the incorrectness of the recipient's placement decisions. They are, in essence, requests that the federal enforcement agencies intervene in battles between complainants and recipients over the proper placement for a particular child or group of children. It is not possible to understand the implementation of § 104.35(c) unless one fully comprehends the significance of the fact that the compliance standards are procedural.

The fundamental rule under § 104.35(c) is that if the recipient has adopted proper placement procedures, and there is ample evidence to establish that (a) the procedures were followed, and (b) the placement decision is supported and properly documented, the OCR will not step into the shoes of the educators and second-guess the actual placement decision.[33] Courts and enforcement agencies are not qualified to make purely educational decisions.[34]

> The requirements of provision (c) are that: [A]ll significant factors relating to the learning process, including adaptive behavior, be considered. . . .

> Information from all sources must be documented and considered by a group of persons, and the procedures ensure that the child is placed in the most integrated setting appropriate.[35]

One of the basic tenets of the Act and the implementing regulations is that placement decisions should not result in "misclassification or misplacement" of students. Therefore, actions of recipients which restrict or interfere with the consideration of information that is necessary or relevant to the placement process are viewed with suspicion and generally will be found to violate the regulations. For example, recipients may not refuse to consider relevant evaluative data or reports, nor fail to conduct necessary evaluations, nor prohibit teachers from recommending certain services, such as extended school year services.[36] In addition, this consideration of "all significant factors relating to the learning process" must be more than a *pro forma* or cursory consideration. For example, a recipient was found in violation for rejecting an independent evaluator's recommendation, even though the evaluator's report had not been reviewed by a qualified expert and the recipient had not conducted its own evaluation.[37]

However, the duty to consider all relevant information is not a license for outsiders to seek to dictate the nature of the placement proceedings used by recipients. For instance, although adaptive behavior must be considered, the decision as to the method or tests to be used is solely the recipient's to make.[38] Furthermore, once a recipient has properly evaluated a student and considered all the relevant information and data, it will not be required to pay for additional evaluations simply because the parents disagree with the placement decision.[39] In addition, § 104.35(c) requires only that all relevant information or data be considered. The decision of whether to follow or implement particular opinions or recommendations is entirely within the purview of the placement committee.[40]

At what sort of meeting should the placement decisions be made? What individuals should constitute the group that makes the placement decisions? Consider the following hypotheticals:

> District officials implement a procedure whereby the special education teacher alone makes the determination regarding the amount of time, if any, handicapped students are permitted to interact with nonhandicapped students. A parents' advocacy group objects to the district's assertion that, because the teacher is most knowledge about the students' abilities, the practice is acceptable.
>
> Mr. Bellicose, who has been in numerous conflicts with district personnel regarding his daughter's educational program, arrives at an IEP meeeeting with three friends and a newspaper reporter. The district objects to all the individuals participating in the meeting, particularly the reporter. Mr. Bellicose argues that Section 504 gives him the right to bring whomever he wishes to the meeting. He also asks to tape the meeting, and the district refuses his request.

> Scott, a wheelchair athlete, wishes to compete with and against nonhandi-
> capped students in track and field. A placement committee meeting is held
> to determine whether Scott can safely participate in high school track and
> field events. The placement committee comprises the following individuals:
> the special education coordinator, Scott's counselor, Scott's father, Scott, a
> sociologist, district special education representatives, Scott's physical
> therapist, a nurse, the high school principal, the athletic director, and a
> psychologist. The committee determines that it is not safe for Scott to com-
> pete with nonhandicapped individuals. Scott's father challenges the ruling
> on the basis that none of the committee members are knowledgeable about
> wheelchair athletes and the safety factors involved. (*Hollenbeck v. Board of
> Education of Rochelle Township*.)[41]

Beyond the requirement that a group of persons knowledgeable about the child, the evaluation data, and that placement options participate, there is very little guidance in the regulations regarding who should be involved in making placement decisions. One can formulate some broad parameters regarding the meaning of this requirement by reviewing the OCR and judicial decisions.

The decision cannot be made by just one individual, and the recipient need not permit individuals who have no specific knowledge of or interest in the child, such as reporters, to participate.[42] There is no magical or special grouping of individuals that is necessary. The emphasis is on making sure that the individuals, whoever they may be, have *specific* knowledge regarding the student's needs, the placement options, and the evaluation data. General knowledge is not sufficient. The Court's decision in the *Hollenbeck* case is a good illustration of this point. The Court noted that all the participants were inexperienced either regarding athletes in general, or handicapped athletes in particular, or had no knowledge regarding wheelchair athletes and Scott's physical abilities and disabilities. (*Hollenbeck v. Board of Education of Rochelle Township, supra* at 667.) The Court also noted that some of the participants themselves doubted their ability to resolve the matter. In concluding that the provision of the EHA, which provides that "placement decisions be made by a group of persons . . . including persons knowledgeable [in relevant areas]" had not been complied with, the Court stated:

> None of these participants fully understand the dynamics of track and field
> events let alone wheelchair track. . . . The participants, while from diverse
> disciplines, failed to have the requisite knowledge of wheelchair athletics
> to determine if it was safe for Scott to participate with able-bodied athletes
> in track and field. (*Hollenbeck, supra* at 667–68.)

Thus, it is clear that it is not sufficient to simply have individuals on the committee who are familiar with the child and have general expertise. The knowledge must relate to the abilities and disabilities of the child with respect to the specific placement options being considered.[43]

Remember, the decision must be the result of something more than a cursory review of the data and evidence. There exists a responsibility to "thoroughly investigate, analyze, and discuss the issue."[44] Recipients must also document information and data considered during the placement process, including all placement options considered. The OCR has found recipients in violation because there was insufficient documentation that the mandates of Section 104.35 had been adhered to.[45]

The question regarding the recipient's right to prohibit tape recording at placement meetings has recently been answered by the courts. Parents of disabled children challenged, under both Section 504 and the EHA, a state Department of Education policy prohibiting tape recording in *V.W. and R.W. v. Favolise*.[46] The school district refused to hold IEP meetings if parents indicated that they planned to tape record the meetings. The Court ruled that the district's interest in maintaining "free-flowing" meetings without the "chilling" impact of tape recordings was outweighed by the interests of parents in understanding and participating in the development and evaluation of their children's educational programs. The Court further noted that neither the state nor federal regulations gave the district the authority to prohibit the taping.

Reevaluation

> Jim, a multihandicapped student, is placed in a self-contained EMH class. Jim is also provided speech therapy, counseling, and physical therapy. He has been served by the district for three and a half years. His parents request a full reevaluation. However, the special education director feels that a full reevaluation is not necessary because during the previous academic year Jim was reevaluated with respect to his speech and physical therapy needs, and his educational program was revised. She also notes that his counseling needs were reassessed two years previously. Jim's parents maintain, however, that he has a right to a reevaluation every three years.

Whereas the Education for the Handicapped Act requires that reevaluations be conducted every three years, the regulations implementing Section 504 require only periodic reevaluations. This is a nebulous standard. As succinctly noted by the administrative law judge in the Chicago Board of Education case (8/88 decision):

> If under Section 504, "every three years" is "one means [of complying]," what are the other acceptable alternatives]? We do not know. . . . [I]s Section 504 violated because the next staffing is, say, three years and one week later instead of exactly three years?

Fortunately, a lot of the uncertainty regarding the Section 504 standard has been removed, because many school districts have adopted the EHA standard as a means of complying with Section 504. However, it is important to remember that a violation of the EHA standard does not automatically equal a violation of Section 504. Once again, the OCR has applied a standard of "reasonableness." Is it legitimate to require a district to conduct a full evaluation of a student merely because three years have passed, ignoring the fact that specific reevaluations needed in individual areas have been conducted during the three-year period? Section 504 does not require rigid adherence to a specific time frame. Therefore, one must determine whether unreasonable delays have occurred.[47]

Remember—reevaluations *are* required prior to a significant change in placement. See discussion of § 104.35(a) in Chapter 14.

15
Disciplining Disabled Students

Few issues have caused as much controversy regarding the mandates of Section 504 and its implementing regulations than discipline. Under what circumstances may disabled students be disciplined, and what sanctions, if any, are permissible? These questions have produced many confusing answers and ignited many battles between school officials and parents. The primary reason the legal requirements have been so difficult to understand is that the proper sequence of events and the corresponding compliance standards have not been clearly explained. Terms such as "significant change in placement," "manifestation determination," and "pattern of exclusion" are frequently used, but they have generally been used in a vacuum without a proper discussion of how they are logically connected. Once one understands the proper sequence (see chart, page 139), those terms and their relationship to each other will no longer seem so mystifying and confusing. As will be discussed in detail below, before a handicapped student may be disciplined, two important questions must be answered. If the answers to *either* of these questions is *yes,* the student is entitled to protection under 34 C.F.R. § 104.35 of the regulations prior to the implementation of disciplinary sanctions. Conversely, if the answer to both is *no,* regular disciplinary sanctions may be imposed.

Significant Change in Placement

Whenever one is considering disciplining a handicapped student, a first question must be answered. Will the proposed disciplinary action result in a significant change in placement? As we discussed, according to § 104.35(a) of the regulations, "significant" means "a fundamental change in or elimination of a basic element of the educational program."[1] What does this mean in the discipline arena? Consider the following hypothetical:

> Blake High School refers the following disciplinary report to the school board for action:

Discipline Compliance Process

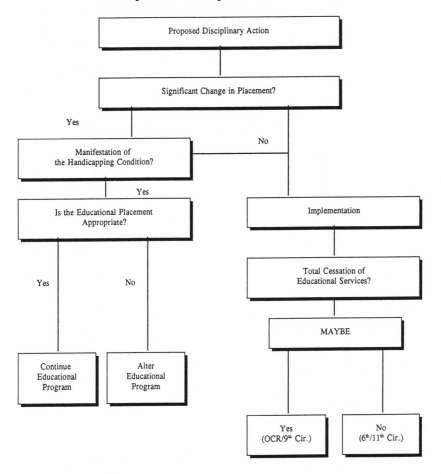

1. Male students in a learning-disabled class get into a fight with students in the BD class which results in extensive damage to the classroom and several staff members being injured. The principal recommends the following disciplinary sanctions: the two instigators of the fight should be expelled; five students should be suspended for the remainder of the term (approximately 15 days); three students should be suspended for five days; ten students should be assigned to in-school suspension for 12 days; and ten students are to be paddled.

2. The parents of Joey Franklin, an emotionally disturbed student who has been disciplined on numerous occasions, are contesting a six-day suspension. Joey's discipline file reveals that he has been suspended ten times for a total of 57 days. He has not been suspended more than eight days on any one occasion.

Which of the recommended actions, *i.e.,* expulsion, long-term suspension, short-term suspension, within-school suspension, and corporal punishment, represent a "significant change in placement"? Arguably, corporal punishment does not result in a significant alteration of the students' educational programs in this instance, but what about those sanctions which result in removal from the classroom or school?[2] A series of judicial decisions culminating with the Supreme Court decision in *Honig v. Doe, supra,* have established the legal guidelines with respect to such removals. Courts had held for many years that a total removal from the educational environment—such as expulsion or a *permanent* suspension—must be viewed as a significant change in placement.[3] However, prior to *Honig* there were no such clear-cut rulings with respect to removals that did not represent a total exclusion. For example, the OCR has stated in numerous administrative decisions that suspensions of more than ten days are a significant change in placement, whereas the Ninth Circuit Court of Appeals in *Doe v. Maher* approved a state policy that sanctioned suspensions of 20 to 30 days. The court specifically held that such suspensions did not represent a significant change of placement. The Supreme Court, in *Honig,* provided the definitive answer to this question by specifically rejecting the Ninth Circuit's decision and adopting the OCR's policy that any suspension of more than ten days constitutes a significant change in placement.[4]

The legal mandates are not as clear for short-term suspensions, *i.e.,* those of ten days or less. The OCR's policy is that a series of short-term suspensions that, in aggregate exceed ten days, may also be considered a significant change in placement if they reflect a *pattern of exclusion.*[5] The phrase "a pattern of exclusion" is sufficiently nebulous to permit subjective judgment to enter the picture, and it is here that much of the controversy regarding disciplinary procedures arises.

The best way to understand the application of the pattern-of-exclusion policy is to view it in terms of what pattern of behavior the policy is aimed at preventing. The actions the OCR is trying to reach are those that have a significant negative impact on the delivery of educational services to students. In plain terms, the OCR is after those recipients who would circumvent the restriction regarding suspensions of more than ten days simply by repeatedly suspending disabled students for nine days. The key is whether the student is losing a significant amount of instructional time. Thus, one would certainly be more concerned about Joey being suspended 57 days than about Johnny being suspended four days in September for being disrespectful and eight days in December for fighting. Moreover, one would question the legitimacy of a policy or requirement that provides greater protection to a student who is, for example, suspended for a single 11-day period, than to one who, while never suspended more than eight days on any occasion, is suspended for a total of 57 days in one school year.

The factors to consider in determining whether a pattern of exclusion exists are the length of each suspension, the proximity of the suspensions to each other, and the portion of the academic year the suspensions in aggregate represent. In light of these factors, repeated disciplinary actions against a student will necessitate a review of the delivery of education services to determine whether the student's education program is being adversely affected. Intervention on the student's behalf is necessary if, when the disciplinary actions are reviewed *in toto,* a reasonable person would conclude that the student was being deprived of educational services.

It is important to remember that no distinctions are made among the types of suspensions involved. Thus, within-school suspensions are treated the same as out-of-school suspensions.[6] In fact, the OCR has ruled that suspension of a handicapped student's bus privileges may result in a significant change in placement if the suspension prevents the student from attending school for a substantial amount of time.[7]

"Manifestation Determination"

As stated above, if one determines that the proposed disciplinary action will result in a significant change in placement, the student is entitled to protection under 34 C.F.R. § 104.35. Section 104.35(a) requires that an evaluation be conducted prior to a significant change in placement. When what is at issue is disciplinary action, the first stage of this evaluation process is called a "manifestation determination." A manifestation determination must always be conducted prior to a significant change in placement except in instances where the student poses a threat to the safety of himself or herself or that of others. (Such a student may be temporarily suspended for up to ten days, but immediate steps must be taken to evaluate the student and alter his or her placement during the suspension period.)[8]

What is a manifestation determination? What information must be considered in making such a determination, and who are the parties to be involved in making the decision? In short, what does a properly conducted manifestation determination look like?

A manifestation determination is an assessment of whether there is a relationship between the student's handicap and his or her misconduct. Bill is a handicapped student who is sent to the principal's office for fighting. Bill has narcolepsy. The principal asks Bill's teacher whether Bill was asleep when he punched Joey out. Is this a proper manifestation determination? This is an extreme example, and certainly it could be argued that no further inquiry need be made. However, one should consider the types of situations that educators are more frequently faced with. Specifically, assume that the high school in our previous hypothetical reached the following conclusions after considering the nature of the students' handicapping conditions:

1. While the special education placement committee concedes that the behavior of the students in the BD class could be related to their handicapping conditions, learning-disabled students certainly do not have handicaps that excuse such conduct. It is recommended that the disciplinary sanctions be implemented with respect to the learning-disabled students.
2. The assistant principal determines that Joey's offenses, *i.e.*, skipping school, refusing to do his assignments, and refusing to dress out for gym, are not manifestations of his handicapping condition.

Do these conclusions represent proper manifestation determinations? Answering the question of whether a student's behavior is the product of his or her handicapping condition is not simply a matter of identifying the general characteristics of the condition, or determining whether the child knows right from wrong, or both. A finding that persons afflicted with a student's particular impairment are generally passive and are, therefore, not prone to fighting is insufficient information upon which to base a conclusion as to whether the aggressive behavior in question is a characteristic of that particular student's condition. In any event, a determination that a student knows right from wrong does not resolve the matter.

The Court's decision in *S-1 v. Turlington, supra* at 346, provides excellent guidance regarding these issues. The Court specifically noted that it is not sufficient to determine that students are capable of understanding right from wrong or that their handicaps are not behavioral handicaps. The Court expressly rejected the assertion of school officials that "a handicapped student's misconduct can never be a symptom of his handicap, unless he is classified as seriously emotionally disturbed." The behavior of each student should be reviewed in conjunction with available data regarding his or her handicap to determine whether there is any relationship between the handicap and the misconduct. Thus, the high school cannot resolve the matter by concluding that learning-disabled students do not have a behavioral handicap. *Remember*—each student must be evaluated on an individual basis to determine what relationship, if any, exists between the handicap and the misconduct in question. Generalizations are unacceptable because they violate the regulatory mandate that each student's individual needs be addressed.

While we know that the inquiry must focus on the specific nature of the individual student's condition, few definitive answers have been provided by either the courts or the OCR regarding the actual form a manifestation determination should take. For example, how extensive should the evaluation be, and who should be involved in the decision making? Regarding the question of who should make the determination, the Court, in *S-1 v. Turlington, supra* at 347, held that it is inappropriate for "school officials entrusted with the expulsion decision at the disciplinary proceeding" to make the determination. The Court concluded that school board officials "who lacked the necessary expertise" were not the "specialized and knowledgeable group of persons" who should conduct evaluations and make placement decisions.

Since the assistant principal is not the appropriate person to decide Joey's fate, who are the specific parties that should be involved, and what data should they consider? Should it be the same type of evaluation process that occurs when a student is initially referred for placement? The Ninth Circuit in *Doe v. Maher, supra* at 1488, seems to recommend just such a thorough process. The court rejected a determination based upon three-year-old evaluation data and held that a "comprehensive evaluation" was necessary. Conversely, the OCR has held that something less than a "comprehensive evaluation" is necessary, but has not clearly explained just what *is* necessary.[9] Therefore, recipients would be well advised to adhere closely to the requirements of § 104.35(c)(3) with respect to considering information from a variety of sources and involving persons knowledgeable about the child, evaluation data, and placement options.

A conclusion that the student's behavior is a manifestation of his or her handicapping condition does not end the inquiry. One must continue the evaluation and make a determination as to whether the student's present placement is appropriate. This entire process would serve no useful purpose if behavior that is the result of inappropriate placements is not specifically addressed by altering the student's educational program. The goal is to ensure that students are placed in a setting that is structured both to adequately respond to the specific manifestations of their handicap(s) and to permit them to benefit from the educational program offered.

It has been argued that, even if school officials conclude that the behavior is not a manifestation of the student's handicapping condition, disciplinary sanctions may be imposed, but the student must still be provided educational services. Both the Sixth and Eleventh circuits have held that "complete cessation of educational services during an expulsion period is not permitted."[10] Thus, presumably, even if school officials properly expel a student, they would still have to provide homebound services. The Ninth Circuit and the OCR have taken the opposite view, holding that educational services may be discontinued once it is properly determined that the misconduct is not a manifestation of the handicapping condition.[11] The circuits that hold that educational services may not be discontinued have gone beyond the nondiscrimination mandate of the Act and its regulations; they have grafted on a right for handicapped students, which in essence amounts to preferential treatment. Nonhandicapped students are certainly not provided educational services during expulsions and suspensions. Why are handicapped students entitled to such? School officials must follow the decisions in their circuit or the OCR's policy until the Supreme Court resolves the matter.

Remember—The interest of school officials in maintaining their right to exercise proper disciplinary control over students is just as legitimate as the interest of the OCR and parents in ensuring that handicapped students are not excluded from their educational programs. Each disciplinary action regarding disabled students should follow the procedures outlined in the chart on page 139.[12]

16
Procedural Safeguards

Section 104.36 of the regulations ensures that parents and guardians will be active participants in the delivery of educational services to handicapped students. It is the written endorsement of the principle that the provision of appropriate educational services must be a joint venture between parents and recipients.[1] The procedural safeguards include:

Notice

An opportunity to examine relevant records

An impartial hearing with opportunity for participation and representation by counsel

A review procedure

Under what circumstances does the recipient have to provide procedural safeguards? Do the actions listed below represent such circumstances?

a. Changing the number of hours of occupational therapy.
b. Changing from direct services to indirect services.
c. Dismissing a student from occupational therapy.
d. Testing of handicapped children.
e. Referring a student for evaluation.
f. A district's refusing to evaluate a student for the purpose of determining whether he or she is handicapped.
g. Making a change in school sites that results in the transfer of handicapped students from a self-contained program to a resource program.
h. Suspending or expelling a handicapped student.

The requirement that procedural safeguards be provided applies to any action involving the identification, evaluation, and placement of students believed to need special services because of their handicaps. The key to determining when such safeguards should be provided is to consider whether the decision or action in question has a significant impact on the delivery of educational services to the student. Thus, actions which involve changes in the manner in which services are provided (direct versus indirect), substantial modification of the educational program offered (change in number of hours services are offered, or changing placement from a self-contained program to a resource program), and initiation or discontinuance of services (referral, evaluation, suspension, etc.) are subject to the requirements of § 104.36.[2] It is also important to remember that *all* disagreements between school officials and parents regarding the delivery of services to the students require the provision of procedural safeguards.[3] If, for example, the parents insist that a student be placed in a learning-disabled program, and the district refuses to either evaluate or place the student, the parents must be advised of their right to request a hearing regarding the matter.

The decisions or actions must be significant. Districts are not required to justify administrative decisions that have little or no impact on the actual delivery of educational services to students. The OCR has held that transfers of handicapped students from one facility to another or from one teacher to another, when the program and services remain the same, are not significant changes in placement, and, hence, procedural safeguards need not be provided.[4] Further, if an emergency situation arises—*i.e.*, a student poses a danger to himself or herself or others—actions such as short-term suspensions may be taken prior to the provision of procedural safeguards.[5]

Recipients are not permitted to place conditions upon, or otherwise interfere with, the provision of procedural safeguards. For example, a recipient may not refuse to permit parents to proceed to a due process hearing until the parents have participated in a mediation process. While it is certainly desirable to mediate disputes prior to initiating a hearing, parents have the right to by-pass such an administrative process and immediately file for due process.[6] Likewise, the OCR has found that parents' right to a hearing contesting their child's placement could not be restricted or limited by the fact that the state was investigating the same matter.[7]

Notice must be provided so that parents or guardians may make informed decisions regarding the services offered their children. If the proposed actions are to have a meaningful impact on the delivery of services, sufficient information must be provided to enable them to exercise fully their right to consent or disagree.[8] Therefore, the notice provided must be explicit and understandable. The OCR has found recipients in violation for:

> failing to ensure that parents whose proficiency in English was limited understood the notice provided,[9]
>
> providing information only in brochures and failing to specifically advise parents at the time special education decisions were being made,[10]

failing to provide notice in writing,[11]

failing to provide information regarding the tests that were to be used to evaluate a child,[12] and

failing to inform parents who do not attend IEP meetings of their rights.[13]

If the recipient fails to provide proper notice, it is not a defense to establish that the parents obtained the information elsewhere and fully understood their rights.[14] Conversely, if the recipient has taken all the necessary steps to provide effective notice, the recipient will not be held accountable if parents fail to understand and seek clarification.[15]

> The Lynches are not pleased with their son Jeffrey's lack of progress in first grade. They believe he might have a handicapping condition and would like to have him evaluated. The principal, after meeting with Jeffrey's teacher, feels they should try some more pre-referral interventions, so he instructs the teacher to attempt a variety of alternative teaching methods along with an increase of one-on-one assistance for Jeffrey by the teacher's aide. Six weeks later, Jeffrey still has not made any progress, and the parents again ask for an evaluation. Another parent asks the Lynches if they have filed for a due process hearing on the matter. The Lynches respond that they did not know that they could.

While recipients do not have to provide notice for pre-referral activities such as consultations between teachers regarding the academic problems a student may be having, if pre-referral intervention activities are held on a more formal basis, as in the example above, it is appropriate to provide procedural safeguards. The OCR has found recipients in violation for failing to provide procedural safeguards during formal prescreening processes.[16]

While § 104.36 does require that parents and guardians be provided the opportunity to examine relevant records, it does not preclude the recipient from imposing nondiscriminatory administrative procedures for reviewing them. For example, parents may be required to request in advance permission to review the records or be allowed to review them only during prescribed time periods. The recipient may even restrict the right of parents to obtain copies of the records. But the restrictions or limitations imposed on the parents of handicapped students must be the same as those applied to the parents of all students. The recipient's policy must clearly reflect that the parents of handicapped students are not being treated differently solely on the basis of their children being handicapped.[17] The recipient may not, however, restrict actual access to relevant records. Parents may not be required to provide justification for their need to review records, nor may the recipient make it so difficult for the parents to obtain the records that they are effectively denied access.[18]

Parents and guardians have the right to request a due process hearing and a subsequent administrative review to resolve any disagreement regarding the delivery of services. This is an absolute right, and, as noted above, the recipient may not seek to restrict it by failing to provide notice, refusing to participate, or delaying its implementation unnecessarily.[19] The importance of the right to seek due process cannot be underestimated. Without this right, the other procedural safeguards would be empty promises at best, since recipients would retain ultimate authority regarding the delivery of educational services. The mandate that parents be given "an opportunity for meaningful input in all decisions affecting their child's education" requires that a third-party review procedure be included.[20] It is also important to remember that parents are not required to resolve disputes with recipients without assistance. They are entitled to have a representative, and that representative need not be an attorney. Thus, a district cannot enforce a policy of refusing to permit advocates to represent parents in due process proceedings.[21]

Once a due process hearing is requested, the student whose placement is at issue must remain in the present placement until the controversy is resolved, unless the parties agree otherwise. The "stay put" doctrine protects handicapped students and their parents from unilateral actions on the part of recipients that would deprive them of their right to participate in the educational process.[22] While Section 504 does not include the "stay put" provision, the OCR has stated that the mandate of § 104.35(a), which requires that a reevaluation occur prior to a significant change in placement, "fulfills a similar purpose." Thus, the OCR has enforced the policy that a student's present placement must be maintained during the administrative hearing and review process.[23]

> Neil and Alice have requested that the Hawkins County Public Schools provide occupational therapy and physical therapy for their handicapped son. The district refuses, so Neil and Alice file for a due process hearing. The state administrative hearings office selects as the hearing officer the special education director for Daley County Schools, which is adjacent to Hawkins County. Neil and Alice complain, saying that an employee of an adjacent school district cannot be an unbiased and impartial hearing officer as required by the regulations. Are Neil and Alice correct?
>
> Neil and Alice find out that Hawkins County Schools and Daley County Schools have a contract to share responsibilities for serving the handicapped students in their counties. Should this affect the decision to use the Daley County special education director as a hearing officer?

These hypotheticals illustrate a complaint consistently raised by parents and their advocates regarding the impartiality of due process proceedings. They assert that recipients exercise unfair control over the administrative hearing and review process; *i.e.,* they employ the hearing officers and establish the hearing procedures, and, therefore, the deck is stacked against those who seek to contest the decisions of school officials. Certainly attempts by recipients to improperly influence the process have helped to create and reinforce this perception.[24] The OCR has held that a school district may not use its own employees, such as school board members, as hearing officers to resolve disputes between parents and officials of the school district. (Policy Interpretation No. 6, Federal Register 78022612 [1978].)

The standard used by the OCR to determine the appropriateness of the due process procedures used by a recipient is that there must be a "fundamental fairness" to the procedures as implemented. The OCR has determined that the use of an employee of another school district as a hearing officer is not, *per se,* a violation of the regulations.[25] However, if the individual has an interest in the outcome of the proceedings, such as the contractual arrangement between the districts discussed in the second example above, it violates the "fundamental fairness" standard. It is legitimate for Neil and Alice to fear that the special education director's decision might be influenced by factors such as the cost implications to his own district. While parents continually raise concerns regarding the impartiality of hearing officers, a hearing officer's decision will not be overturned without substantial evidence of misconduct. Courts have held that there must be a "substantial showing of personal bias" in order to disqualify a hearing officer or obtain a ruling that a hearing is or was unfair.[26] Further, as discussed below, the OCR affords great deference to hearing officers' decisions if the recipient has complied with the procedural standards of the implementing regulations.

> Scott and Zelda file a complaint with the OCR regarding the placement decision involving their ten-year-old emotionally disturbed son, Fitz. The Gerald County School District has recommended a self-contained classroom setting in order to deal with his emotional outbursts. The parents, relying on a private evaluation, believe Fitz is capable of participating in regular education. Scott and Zelda have already been through a due process hearing, with the hearing officer ruling that the district's placement is appropriate. Now the parents are taking up the same issue with the OCR. Can they do this?

Yes, a complaint can always be filed alleging discrimination on the basis of handicap. However, the OCR will not ignore the existence of a hearing decision in investigating the complaint. The OCR handles such complaints by first determining if the issues in the complaint are identical to the issues resolved in the due process hearing. If the issues are identical, the OCR will next determine if the procedural standards of the regulations implementing Section 504 were met. In cases where, indeed, procedural standards were met and the issues were identical, the OCR defers to the decision of the hearing officer as having resolved the issues of the complaint. This policy supports the concept that issues involving individual placement are best resolved between parents and school districts in a hearing process that allows testimony and input from all interested and knowledgeable parties. As noted previously, the OCR will not review the results of individual placement decisions absent *extraordinary circumstances*. What if Scott and Zelda had filed for a due process hearing and filed a complaint with the OCR at the same time alleging the same issues? If the issues are the same, the OCR will "toll" or delay its investigation of the complaint until after the due process procedures have been completed, including the decision of the hearing officer and any appeals proceedings. Then, as above, the OCR will determine if procedural standards were met.

While due process proceedings are generally initiated by parents, there are some circumstances under which recipients must do so. Consider the following examples:

> Mary Jane is assessed as needing speech and language therapy, physical therapy, and occupational therapy. For the past six weeks, Mary Jane's principal has sent several written requests for parental consent for placement, telephoned Mary Jane's parents, and even stopped by the home, but he has yet to get the parents to agree to the new placement.
>
> Alan has been found wandering the halls of his high school, babbling incoherently about a variety of things. After meeting with Alan, the school counselor suggests that Alan be evaluated by a psychiatrist at the county hospital. Alan's father refuses, stating that psychiatrists, themselves, are "wacky."
>
> Jim and Nancy are concerned about their son, John, whose behavior at school has become worse during the current school year. It seems that since he turned 13 the intensity of his emotional outbursts has increased. Jim and Nancy have worked closely, almost daily, with district officials, suggesting a variety of alternatives. Since John has been a resident of the local hospital's program for children and adolescents several times, his parents have received guidance from the hospital's doctors, but John cannot return to the program because he is over the age limit. John's last tantrum resulted in another three-day suspension. Since this means John has been suspended for a total of 12 days, the district is asking Jim and Nancy for permission to reevaluate John with the intent to place him in a residential program. Jim and Nancy agree to the reevaluation, but tell the district that they won't agree to a residential placement. Instead, they suggest they can work with John at home if the district will provide homebound services. District officials insist that a residential placement is the only appropriate placement for John.

The district should immediately initiate procedures for a due process hearing in each of the above situations. If the district fully believes that a proposed course of action or program is what is best for the child, but the parents or guardians disagree, then the district should initiate due process procedures and defend its decisions before a knowledgeable, disinterested third party. The OCR has taken the position that districts may not acquiesce to the wishes of parents when to do so would result in the denial of a free appropriate public education to a qualified handicapped person. If the records show the educational professionals that the child's present placement is not appropriate, they are obligated to take whatever steps necessary, including intiating a due process hearing, to provide educational services that are appropriate. Although a fundamental purpose of the regulations is to guarantee that parents have continuing, meaningful input into the educational program of their handicapped child, the ultimate responsibility for providing a free appropriate public education belongs to the recipient school district.[27]

Recipients must respond to requests for due process hearings and appeals expeditiously. Since the regulations do not address the issue of "timeliness" regarding hearing and review procedures, the OCR looks to state time frames, which are generally in compliance with the EHA, to determine whether the recipient has acted in a "timely" fashion. It is important to remember that failure to comply with state guidelines is not a violation of Section 504, *per se.*[28] The question to be answered is whether the delay was "reasonable" under the circumstances or so substantial that it resulted in the student being denied a free appropriate public education. Actions that have been found to delay impermissibly the hearing and review processes include employing insufficient staff to process requests, requiring prehearing mediation, taking 181 days to complete an appeal, treating a letter of appeal as a request for information, and requiring an administrative review of the issues.[29]

The decisions of hearing officers and reviewers are binding on all parties, and attempts by recipients to subvert this rule violate the regulations. Recipients will not be permitted to label the decisions "recommendations" and thereby make their compliance nonmandatory, nor will they be allowed to assume the role of reviewer on appeal.[30] In addition, local school districts must comply with hearing officers' decisions, and state agencies must use whatever authority is at their disposal, including withholding funding or obtaining a court order, to ensure that the districts do.[31]

Often parents and advocates attempt to utilize the procedural safeguards provided under § 104.36 to control the educational process. Parents will not be permitted to use these rights to usurp the position of local educational agencies as administrators of educational programs. The right to have meaningful input in their children's educational program is not a license for parents to step into the shoes of school officials and run the school system. Federal enforcement agencies are not interested in managing educational systems, and, therefore, § 104.36 will not be used to interfere with the administrative prerogatives of recipients. Recipients may establish nondiscriminatory procedures for the review of records, prohibit disinterested third parties from obtaining access to records, determine who will participate in IEP meetings, select reviewing officers, and refuse to provide parents with written reports of progress.[32]

17
Nonacademic Services

Recipients would have minimal difficulty complying with § 104.37 if they would view their responsibility with respect to nonacademic services as being one of providing handicapped students meaningful access. They must "afford handicapped students an *equal opportunity* for participation in such services and activities" (emphasis added).[1] The majority of the violation findings regarding this provision of the regulations involve exclusionary policies and procedures or unjustified differential treatment.[2] Qualified handicapped students must be provided comparable opportunities *unless* it is necessary to provide different services/benefits to meet their individual needs.[3]

Every year the third through fifth grades at Septem Elementary School are taken to the zoo for a field trip. The students' parents are required to provide the $1.00 admissions fee as well as $2.00 for lunch. District officials decide not to permit students in the TMR and EMR classes to participate because additional aides would have to be employed to assist the teachers.

Jill is a junior high student who uses a wheelchair. She has maintained significant upper body strength through working out at her aunt's health club, although she has permanent paralysis from her waist down. In fact, her aunt recently hired her to work part-time at the club to assist members with the free-weights program. Jill's employment experience has made a significant impact on her life. She has decided she needs to learn to drive. However, when she applies for the driver's education course, she is told the district doesn't have any cars she can drive, so she will have to go to the community college to take the course. This causes two problems for her. One, she has no way to get to the college, and two, the college course costs $50 more than the high school's course.

In response to being sued by the parents of a multihandicapped student who was treated improperly by the school nurse, the district's attorney proposes that a policy be adopted requiring the parents of all students with physical handicaps to sign a statement giving the district the authority to provide services to their children and limiting the liability of the district to situations of "extreme negligence." Parents refusing to sign the statement are to be advised that their children will not be provided health services except in life-threatening situations.

The examples above illustrate actions that impermissibly deny qualified handicapped students an equal opportunity to participate in and benefit from nonacademic services. The regulations preclude limiting benefits and requiring handicapped persons to incur expenses not imposed upon nonhandicapped persons, or to meet additional standards to receive services. Thus, the TMR and EMR students cannot be denied the right to participate in the field trip on the basis of the school's inability to employ additional aides. Also, the parents of handicapped students cannot be required to sign a permission form/waiver in order to receive health services if the same prerequisite is not imposed for nonhandicapped students. For Jill, the alternative of the community college course does not represent an equal opportunity if she must provide her own transportation to the college and pay the additional $50. Although it is not necessarily a violation, per se, to offer the community college alternative, the district must take steps to equalize the opportunity offered Jill. For example, they might choose to provide Jill with transportation to and from the community college campus. Further, since the district cannot provide the course to Jill, she cannot be charged more for the course than nonhandicapped students in the district are charged.[4]

It is important to keep in mind that § 104.37 does not preclude all differences in treatment. For example:

> Mrs. Stevens receives an invitation to the school's Holiday Pageant. The invitation states that all classes will perform in the pageant. Mrs. Stevens is distressed that her son is participating in the performance while her daughter, who is in the multihandicapped class, is not. When she questions why her daughter's class is not involved, she is informed that the teacher of her daughter's class has prepared a separate holiday celebration for the students in her class. The teacher is preparing the separate ceremony because the students in her class all have mental ages of between six and 24 months, and they would not understand or enjoy the pageant. The teacher asserts that the program she is preparing is more appropriate for the students. Mrs. Stevens argues that her daughter should be permitted to participate in the pageant.

The separate holiday program for the multihandicapped class is permissible because it addresses the individual needs of the students involved. Recipients will not be permitted to treat qualified handicapped students differently if such treatment is not related to their individual needs. Nonacademic services as a part of the educational program "must, in accordance with the provisions of Section 104.34, be provided in the most integrated setting appropriate."[5] Thus, for example, it would violate the regulations to provide full-time counselors for nonhandicapped students and limit the counseling opportunity of handicapped students to meetings with their teachers.[6]

Qualified handicapped students must be permitted to participate in regular physical education and athletics activities.[7] Separate programs for handicapped students are permitted only if the opportunity to participate in regular activities is also provided. Further, recipients cannot limit handicapped students' opportunities to participate in contact sports.[8] Policy interpretation #5 provides that the regulatory requirement that handicapped students receive an equal opportunity to participate in physical education and athletics extends to contact sports as well.[9] Specifically, recipients cannot assume that a child who is missing an organ or other body part is too much of a risk to participate in contact sports. At the same time, the Department acknowledges that the recipient can require a statement of approval from the doctor most familiar with the child's condition, usually the child's or family's personal physician.

> The parents of physically handicapped students, unable to qualify for participation in the interscholastic athletic program offered by a school district, request that the district organize an intramural program for those students. The district refuses, asserting that there are also many nonhandicapped students who are unable to meet the criteria for participation in the interscholastic program.
>
> The athletic association, of which Kertin School District is a member, does not permit students above the age of 18 to participate in association-sponsored events. Jim, a learning-disabled student who is 19 years old, wants to play baseball. Jim's parents request that he be granted an exemption. They argue that the rule is discriminatory because it fails to make allowances for students whose conditions slow their academic progress. The district refuses to grant an exemption.

One must remember that, while the regulations preclude discrimination against qualified handicapped persons, it does not require recipients to exempt handicapped persons from meeting legitimate criteria and standards.[10] The parents in the two examples above are not requesting nondiscriminatory treatment, but, rather, preferential treatment. Handicapped students will be required to meet legitimate criteria applied uniformly to all students.[11] It is not a violation of Section 504 for the district to refuse to establish an intramural program (OCR's 9/10/80 policy memorandum). Further, the association's limitation is not discriminatory on its face.[12] The only way that Jim's parents may successfully attack the policy is to establish that some discriminatory act extended Jim's high school career past his nineteenth birthday. For example, suppose the school district restricted learning-disabled students to three academic courses per semester without regard to their individual needs and abilities, which resulted in Jim's delayed graduation. In that instance, the district would not be allowed to apply the rule to Jim, because it would perpetuate discrimination against a qualified handicapped person.[13]

18
Preschool, Adult Education, and Private Education Programs

The most important thing to keep in mind when analyzing a recipient's actions with respect to these programs is that not all provisions of Subpart D are applicable to these programs. Specifically, "§§ 104.32 and 104.33 apply only to public programs, and § 104.39 applies only to private programs; §§ 104.35 and 104.36 apply both to public programs and to those private programs that include special services for handicapped students.[1]

Preschool and Adult Education[2]

Under § 104.38 recipients are prohibited from excluding qualified handicapped persons and must take their needs into consideration in making their services, benefits, and activities available.

> The Alafla School District runs a preschool program for homeless urban children. This is the only preschool program the district operates. Several deaf students are referred to the program for admission, including the daughter of Ms. Ruby. School officials refuse to serve the students because they do not have staff members with expertise in working with deaf students. Ms. Ruby insists that either the students should be served in the existing program or the district should develop a preschool program for deaf students. The district refuses Ms. Ruby's request, noting that her daughter is not a homeless urban child.

Section 104.38 does not require the establishment of a preschool program for handicapped children or classes for the handicapped simply because a recipient runs a preschool program for a special population. Moreover, the district is not required to serve students, such as Ms. Ruby's daughter, who do not meet the admissions criteria.[3] On the other hand, the recipient cannot refuse to address the needs of handicapped students who meet the eligibility requirements for participation in the program. Thus, Alafla must accommodate those homeless urban students who are hearing-impaired.[4]

Clearly the compliance standards under § 104.38 are much less stringent than those applied to public elementary and secondary programs. Recipients cannot be held to the standards of §§ 104.33–104.36 with respect to these programs. For example, it is not a violation for a recipient to charge a fee to handicapped persons in an adult education program. Adult education programs are not covered by the standards of § 104.33, which provides that students *in public elementary or secondary programs* be provided a "free . . . education." Section 104.38 "does not require recipients to provide adult programs at no cost."[5]

Private Education Programs[6]

Section 104.39 prohibits the exclusion of qualified handicapped persons and imposes the compliance standards of §§ 104.33–104.38 in some instances. However, the application of these standards is conditional:

a. An appropriate education, as defined in § 104.33(b)(1) must be provided if the recipient can do so with minor adjustments.
b. The recipient may charge more for the provision of an appropriate education if any additional charge is justified by a substantial increase in cost to the recipient.
c. Recipients that operate special education programs must comply with the provisions of §§ 104.35–104.38.

The regulations provide compliance standards for two categories of private programs. It is an acknowledgment on the part of the drafters that if recipients choose not to offer special education programs, they should not be coerced into providing such services. As explained in Appendix A:[7]

> [R]ecipients that operate private education programs and activities are not required to provide an appropriate education to handicapped students with special education needs if the recipient does not offer programs designed to meet those needs. Thus, a private school that has no program for mentally retarded persons is neither required to admit such a person into its program, nor to arrange to pay for the provision of the person's education in another program.

> Robert began playing the cello at the age of five. At eight Robert lost a significant amount of his vision as a result of a viral infection. Now 15 years old, he is an accomplished cello player and is accepted into the music performance program of a highly respected academy for the performing arts. The secondary school program for the academy is accredited, offers academic high school diplomas, and receives federal financial assistance. Thirty days before the start of classes, Robert's counselor meets with him and

his parents to review his courses, practice times, and planned academic program. At that meeting his parents request that his music, tests, and class assignments be enlarged 150 percent and that his textbooks be taped. The counselor agrees and later notifies the appropriate officials. The academy does not charge the parents for the duplicating services or the expenditures for taping the textbooks. After one semester, Robert is participating fully at the academy and is making good grades. Are the counselor's actions sufficient? Should there have been an evaluation and placement meeting with appropriate personnel present? What about notifying the parents of their due process rights? If the academy had charged Robert's parents for the duplicating services and taping expenditures, would that have been a violation of Section 504?

While private entities are not required to provide special programs for students whose needs they are not capable of meeting, they are not permitted to deny services to handicapped students who, with minor adjustments, can participate in their programs.

> A private recipient without a special program for blind students . . . would not be permitted to exclude, on the basis of blindness, a blind applicant who is able to participate in the regular program with minor adjustments in the manner in which the program is normally offered.[8]

In Robert's situation, the accommodations necessary for him to participate in the academy's program were considered minor and were fully accepted by the school. The regulations do not provide a definition of "minor adjustments." Consequently, determinations of which accommodations and adjustments are "minor" and which are "major" must be made on a case-by-case basis. Like most purely educational decisions, one should presume that the detemrination of the recipient will be respected unless it appears to be arbitrary or capricious.[9] For example, a unilateral exclusion of handicapped children or a class of handicapped children during the screening process without an individual assessment of whether each child could be accommodated with minor adjustments would violate § 104.39.[10]

Regarding the cost of adjustments, paragraph (b) of § 104.39 allows private school recipients to charge parents for the increased costs related to providing the accommodations and adjustments. Such costs, however, cannot be speculative and must be substantial. Any charge to Robert's parents must be "justified by a substantial increase in cost to the recipient."[11] If the academy simply enlarged documents on its duplicating machine and sent its textbooks to Readings for the Blind, thus incurring minimal costs at most, it would be inappropriate to charge his parents. With respect to the procedural requirements, since the program Robert was enrolled in was not a special education program, it was not necessary for the academy to follow the evaluation and placement process, nor to notify the parents of any due process guarantees. *Remember*—only private education programs that operate a special education program must comply with the provisions of §§ 104.35 and 104.36 of the regulations.

Special Purpose Schools

The OCR treats special purpose schools, *e.g.,* ones with programs for a specialized group of handicapped students such as a state school for the blind, as private education programs for purposes of assigning responsibility regarding the provision of free appropriate education services to those students. When discussing the Colorado School for the Deaf and the Blind (CSDB), the Assistant Secretary described the OCR's view of such schools as follows:

> These facilities have characteristics of both public and private educational programs: like most private schools, they are usually residential, they serve only a limited population of handicapped students, and they have restrictive admissions criteria; like public schools, they are provided funds by the state and are overseen by state agencies.
>
> CSDB is more closely analogous to a private recipient than to a public school system. For example, CSDB does not have the responsibility for providing educational services to all handicapped children in its geographic jurisdiction. It serves a specialized population of handicapped students. Generally by statute, these are children who cannot be adequately served within their local communities. Thus, while CSDB will not be found in violation of 34 C.F.R. § 104.33 for failure to provide free transportation to students who are parentally enrolled at the school, it is responsible, by analogy to private recipients, for compliance with the requirements of 34 C.F.R. § 104.39.[12]

19
Section 504 Versus the EHA

Educators have traditionally viewed their responsibility to comply with these two federal statutes as being an either-or proposition. Attempts to persuade them to treat the Acts as being complementary have been vehemently resisted. The act of treating the statutes as if they were totally at odds with each other has, in large measure, prevented school districts from developing policies and procedures that ensure compliance under both. Considerable time and attention have been devoted to the EHA because federal monies are awarded based upon compliance with its mandates, while attention to compliance under Section 504 has suffered by comparison. Further, courts have themselves fueled this controversy by minimizing the legal significance of Section 504 and its implementing regulations.[1] As a result, many districts are now ill-prepared to address the ever-increasing number of complaints alleging violations of Section 504. This chapter discusses the differences between the Acts, both real and perceived, that have often led to recipients' failing to fully comply with Section 504. The significant issues are:

1. A grant statute versus a civil rights statute
2. The guaranteed right to a free appropriate public education under Section 504
3. The EHA as the exclusive remedy
4. Coverage under Section 504
5. The EHA is but one means of complying with Section 504

Civil Rights Statute

The EHA is a grant statute whereas Section 504 is a civil rights statute.[2] If one places the regulations implementing the EHA and Section 504 side by side, the first thing one notices is that the EHA regulations are much more specific. They state exactly what one must do to serve handicapped students under the Act. This is one of the principal characteristics of a grant statute.

Courts have held that if Congress wants to condition the receipt of federal funds on performance of particular acts, it must clearly and concisely state these conditions.[3] Civil rights statutes such as Section 504, on the other hand, do not provide a monetary "carrot," but rather hold out the possibility of the punitive "stick"—that is, loss of federal financial assistance—as a means of ensuring compliance.

Civil rights statutes are by their very nature general, because they are an attempt to influence actions that are the result of discriminatory attitudes, and not every single circumstance in which the statute would be applicable can be anticipated.[4] Thus, while the regulations implementing the EHA provide a specific framework and procedural steps for compliance, Section 504 basically provides that discrimination on the basis of handicap is unlawful and merely gives general compliance guidelines. It is important to remember this distinction between the EHA and Section 504 because it explains why coverage under Section 504 is broader in some respects. One of the most common mistakes made is assuming that if an individual is not entitled to protection under the EHA, he or she is also not entitled to protection under Section 504. As noted by the Court in *Rodgers v. Bennett*:[5]

> Section 504 is much broader in scope than is the EHA, prohibiting discrimination against otherwise qualified handicapped individuals in ali federal programs and programs receiving federal funding. Thus, Section 504 regulates many activities—even within the limited field of education—that are not a primary concern of the regulations promulgated pursuant to the EHA.

Guaranteed FAPE

Appendix A of the regulations implementing Section 504 makes it clear that the intent of the drafters was to adopt the standards and principles enumerated by the courts in *Mills v. Board of Education of the District of Columbia*, 348 F. Supp. 866 (D.D.C. 1972), and *Pennsylvania Association for Retarded Children v. Commonwealth of Pennsylvania*, 344 F. Supp. 1257 (E.D. 1971), as well as those of the Education of the Handicapped Act. The compliance standards that form the foundation of recipients' responsibilities under Subpart D are:

> Regardless of the severity of the handicap, handicapped persons will receive a Free Appropriate Public Education (FAPE);
>
> Handicapped persons will be educated with nonhandicapped persons to the maximum extent appropriate to the handicapped persons' needs;
>
> Educational agencies will identify all unserved handicapped persons;

Evaluation procedures will be improved to eliminate misclassifications and inappropriate placements; and

Procedural safeguards will be implemented to allow parents to influence evaluations and placements of handicapped persons.[6]

These standards provide a rather broad framework for the provision of educational services to handicapped students. They essentially prescribe the way in which recipients must provide educational services. Like the regulations implementing the EHA, what is addressed are the essential elements of the program that must be offered. Why should Section 504, a nondiscrimination statute, have the same basic standards as the EHA, an affirmative action statute that directs states to develop appropriate educational services to meet the needs of handicapped persons? Or perhaps better, does it make sense for both of these federal acts to have the same regulatory focus? This is the question that troubles educators, judges, and attorneys in their attempts to reconcile compliance statutes under both regulations. In fact, it seems to trouble everyone except the enforcement agencies.

The EHA was enacted to address the national problem of millions of handicapped children being denied educational services. Federal monies are provided to assist states and local educational agencies in developing specialized educational programs to meet their unique needs.[7] Section 504, on the other hand, was enacted to "ensure equal opportunities for the handicapped by prohibiting needless discrimination."[8] Clearly these two acts should have a different regulatory focus. Specifically,

Section 504 and the EHA are different substantive statutes. While the EHA guarantees a right to a free appropriate public education, § 504 simply prevents discrimination on the basis of handicap.[9]

Beyond its prohibition of discrimination, however, Section 504 generally does not furnish a basis for affirmative relief to the handicapped.[10]

Unlike Section 504, the Education of the Handicapped Act, 20 U.S.C. § 1400, et seq., does impose certain affirmative duties upon recipients of federal funds. In enacting the EHA, Congress sought "to assure that all handicapped children have available to them . . . a free appropriate education which emphasizes special education and related services designed to meet their unique needs." 20 U.S.C. § 1400(c).[11]

[The EHA] confers upon disabled students an enforceable substantive right to public education, in participating states.[12]

Thus, the regulations implementing Section 504 fail to adequately reflect this distinction between the two statutes that has been clearly outlined by the Supreme Court and others on numerous occasions. Given the nondiscrimination mandate of Section 504, the drafters of the regulations should have focused less on the structure or form the educational programs for handicapped students are to take and more on the right of handicapped persons to receive these services free from discrimination. It can be argued that, by adopting the same standards as the EHA, the drafters obscured the distinction between the principles of nondiscrimination and affirmative action and, in essence, with Subpart D created a hybrid that mandates, if read and applied literally, something more than nondiscrimination. But, what is this something more? Unfortunately they did not specifically say, and this, then, is the basis of much of the controversy surrounding the enforcement of Section 504 as compared to the EHA. The degree of uncertainty regarding recipients' responsibilities under Subpart D can best be understood by reviewing significant court decisions in which the question of whether Section 504 guarantees a right to a free appropriate public education has been addressed.

As stated in Appendix A, the responsibility of those operating public education programs is to either provide educational services to handicapped individuals in the regular setting or to provide them "with an appropriate alternative education at public expense." Their duty is to "ensure that no handicapped child is excluded from school on the basis of handicap."[13] This mandate, to provide any and all necessary educational services, appears to be absolute, and, in fact, many courts have taken the position that Section 504 requires that an appropriate education be provided without exception.[14] The Office for Civil Rights' behavior certainly reflects that the regulations have been enforced in this manner. In a recent administrative proceeding, the OCR asserted that Congress intended that Section 504 should have an affirmative action requirement, and that courts, including the Supreme Court in *Davis* and *Alexander,* had acknowledged that affirmative action might be necessary to prevent discrimination against handicapped persons and provide meaningful access.[15] Under these interpretations, it appears that recipients must do whatever is necessary to provide the student with appropriate educational services, including alternatives such as private residential placements.[16]

There are other courts, however, that have read the Supreme Court's decision in *Davis* as placing limitations on the right to receive an appropriate education under Section 504. They assert that the Court's ruling that Section 504 requires nondiscrimination, not affirmative action, can only be interpreted to mean that handicapped children are *not* guaranteed a free appropriate public education under the Act.[17] They reason that if one strictly follows the Court's ruling, Section 504 cannot be used to require fundamental alterations to programs that will result in "undue financial and administrative burdens." All requests for program modifications must pass a test before recipients will be forced to implement them. The Court in *Turillo* held that requests for program modifications, pursuant to Section 504, should be analyzed as follows:

First does the relief requested by the plaintiff require affirmative action? That is, is the defendant being asked to provide the plaintiff with a completely new service or merely with modifications of an existing service provided to nonhandicapped persons? If the plaintiff seeks modifications of an existing program, then the analysis moves to the second tier: do the modifications place an undue financial and administrative burden on the defendant? If they do not, then the plaintiff is entitled to relief. (*Turillo*, at 587.)

How does one reconcile the opinion of the Court in *Turillo* with that of courts that acknowledge the Supreme Court ruling in *Davis*, but hold that "Section 504 requires affirmative action to assure that the handicapped child receives an equal opportunity to benefit from his education"?[18] An in-depth analysis of the opposing schools of thought reveals that the focus of the two sides is drastically different (see table, p. 165). For those who assert that a FAPE is guaranteed, the focus is on the needs of the handicapped student and the goal is inclusion. One starts from the premise that exclusion is to be avoided at all costs and attempts to construct a program that will confer educational benefit. The threshold for providing the requested program modification is met if it will provide meaningful access to the student. The issue of denial of services is discussed primarily in terms of those services from which the student will receive no educational benefits. The question of "undue financial or administrative burdens" is asked late in the game, if at all. Further, the distinction between a nondiscrimination mandate and an affirmative action mandate is rarely discussed.

On the other side, the focus is the recipient's rights and responsibilities. The important question is whether the requested modification would impose an "undue burden or hardship," and the nondiscrimination–affirmative action dichotomy is always discussed in great detail. It is a given that recipients will not have to provide some types of services under Section 504. Denial of some services is viewed as a necessary by-product in the balancing of the need to preserve the integrity of the recipient's program against the rights of handicapped students. The debate between these two factions will no doubt continue to rage until the Supreme Court resolves it.[19] We note with interest that when faced with the opportunity to do so in *Smith v. Robinson, supra*, the Court declined to rule on the matter. The Court stated, in pertinent part:

> [A]lthough both statutes begin with an equal protection premise that handicapped children must be given access to public education, it does not follow that the affirmative requirements imposed by the two statutes are the same. The significant difference between the two, as applied to special education claims, is that the substantive and procedural rights assumed to be guaranteed by both statutes are specifically required only by the EHA.
> In light of *Davis*, courts construing § 504 as applied to the educational needs of handicapped children have expressed confusion about the extent

Two Views of Section 504

An "Absolute" Right

Pertinent court cases: *Tatro, supra, Katherine D., supra,* and *David H., supra;* OCR also takes this position. Appendix A states that recipients must provide adequate alternative services that are necessary.

Meaningful Access (*Katherine D., supra* at 528) — If the service will enable the student to attend and participate, then it must be provided "regardless of its uniqueness...." "Under [§ 104.34], the range of alternatives ... must include private school placement."

Exclusion (*Tatro, supra* at 557, 564, 565) — If the failure to provide the service or program results in exclusion, it violates § 504 unless the requested alternative or modification would not permit the individual to realize the principal benefits of the program and/or the accommodation would result in an undue financial or administrative burden.

The Key: Whether denial of the accommodation would result in exclusion.

Affirmative Action (*David H., supra* at 1336) — "Section 504 requires affirmative action to assure that the handicapped child receives an equal opportunity to benefit from his education." There is "an affirmative duty to investigate [the child's] individual needs to determine what special or additional services would be needed and then to set about to provide those services."

No Guarantee to FAPE

Pertinent court cases: *New Mexico, supra,* and *Turillo, supra.*

Recipients are not required to make fundamental alterations which result in "undue financial and administrative burdens."

Two-Tier Test (*Turillo, supra* at 586–87) —

1) Does the relief require affirmative action (a completely new service) or is it merely a modification to the existing program. If it is a modification...
2) Does the modification result in an undue financial and administrative burden.

Private residential placements need not be provided because they go beyond mere modifications to the existing program.

Three-Part Test (*New Mexico, supra* at 853–54) —

1) The existing program precludes handicapped individuals from participating.
2) Modifications would permit the individual to achieve benefits.
3) The modifications "would not jeopardize the overall viability of the state's educational system."

The Key: Whether the service/program must be provided is tied to the number of students needing the service. The larger the number the more the benefits of providing the service would outweigh the costs.

Recipients must provide modifications if the refusal to do so will result in discrimination, but the duty to modify is not unlimited.

to which § 504 requires special services to make public education accessible to handicapped children.

We need not decide the extent of the guarantee of a free appropriate public education Congress intended to impose under § 504. We note the uncertainty regarding the reach of § 504 to emphasize that it is only in the EHA that Congress specified the rights and remedies available to a handicapped child seeking access to public education.[20]

While those who argue that there is no guarantee under Section 504 assert that the regulations exceed congressional intent,[21] it is important to remember, as noted previously, that the OCR's enforcement actions clearly reflect that the "absolute" right to an appropriate education is being enforced. To date, the OCR has not specifically acknowledged or imposed limitations such as those adopted by the *Turillo* and *Colin* courts.

An Exclusive Remedy

The second line of attack on the applicability of Section 504 in the elementary and secondary arena is the argument that the EHA is the exclusive remedy for those alleging handicap discrimination. The Supreme Court sparked this controversy in *Smith v. Robinson* when it ruled that the EHA was the "exclusive avenue through which parents may enforce the rights of their handicapped children."[22] Congress amended the Act subsequent to the *Smith* decision to specifically provide that the EHA did not preclude the assertion of rights, procedures and remedies available under Section 504 and other federal statutes.[23] However, it has been held that Congress left intact the Supreme Court's requirement that private litigants must exhaust administrative remedies under the EHA prior to bringing suit in federal court. As noted by the Court in *Mrs. W. v. Tirozzi*:

> In other words, when parents choose to file suit under another law that protects the rights of handicapped children—and the suit could have been filed under the EHA—they are first required to exhaust the EHA's remedies to the same extent as if the suit had been filed originally under the EHA's provisions.[24]

How far can this requirement to first seek redress under the EHA be extended? A Georgia school district sought to extend it beyond a limitation on the right of private litigants to file suit to a limitation on the investigative authority of the enforcement agency under Section 504. The district refused to permit the OCR to conduct investigations of alleged violations of Section 504, charging, among other things, that the EHA was the exclusive remedy for parents. The Court of Appeals declined to rule in favor of the district, noting that Congress had amended the EHA to provide clearly that the EHA was not the exclusive remedy. It was further noted that *Smith* involved private litigants, while this case involved agency enforcement procedures, *i.e.*, federal supervisory powers. The Court specifically held that the "OCR's exercise of supervisory powers over the Georgia special education programs is not *plainly* outside the agency's jurisdiction."[25] This appears to be another area where a Supreme Court decision or further congressional action may be necessary.

Coverage Under Section 504

As the discussions above indicate, Section 504 and its implementing regulations are viewed by many as having limited applicability to elementary and secondary issues. Even if one subscribes to the opposing position that the regulations implementing Section 504 are valid and applicable to elementary and secondary education *"in toto,"* there are still instances where Section 504's reach is more limited than that of the EHA. For example,

> A visually impaired, hearing-impaired, and mentally retarded child is denied admission to the Kentucky School for the Blind on the basis of his mental impairment. The school's admissions policy provides, in pertinent part, that the student's primary handicapping condition must be a visual impairment and the student's academic and learning ability must be in the "trainable mentally handicapped" range. Timothy and other profoundly mentally retarded students as a class are denied admission to the school. The school's admissions policy was challenged under both the EHA and Section 504.[26]

The Court in the above case ruled that, while the students might be entitled to relief under the EHA, they were not entitled to protection under Section 504. The Court concluded that the students were not otherwise qualified under the Act because they were not "in the trainable mentally handicapped range." Further, there was no reasonable accommodation because (a) the school would be required "to hire additional instructors who possess qualifications in training the profoundly handicapped not possessed by the usual faculty"; and (b) "the mission of the institution would have to be modified."[27] The Court ruled that such actions would be the type of fundamental modifications which the Supreme Court held institutions could not be compelled to make in *Davis*.[28] Conversely, under the EHA, the state's responsibility of providing all handicapped students a free appropriate public education as a condition of receiving federal funds would require the state to place students who did not meet the admissions criteria at the school "if such placement is the only way an appropriate IEP can be designed for them."[29] The Court ruled that the state has an absolute responsibility to serve the students under the EHA.

There are also circumstances, however, where coverage under Section 504 is broader than that under the EHA:

> Jim is a student with emotional problems, *i.e.*, he will not interact with his peers and teachers, yet is an above-average student. He makes Bs in all of his classes, and his teachers feel he would qualify for advanced placement if he would participate in class. However, he refuses to participate in group activities, answer questions, or make oral presentations. Jim's hostile reactions to his teachers and peers begins to escalate, so he is referred for special education evaluation. The evaluation reveals that Jim has above-average intelligence, is performing above grade level, and suffers from depression and antisocial tendencies. The psychologist recommends counseling for Jim and that his teachers accommodate his needs by not requiring him to participate in group activities or make oral presentations in class. The placement committee refuses to provide the recommended services because Jim is not eligible for special education placement under the categories enumerated in the Education of the Handicapped Act (EHA). The advocacy group, which Jim's parents seek assistance from, argues that, despite the fact that Jim is not covered under the EHA, he is entitled to protection under Section 504.

Recipients have mistakenly taken the position that if a student is not eligible for services under the EHA and thereby not qualified for enrollment in a special education program, he or she is not entitled to protection and services as a handicapped student. It must be understood that the definition of a handicapped person under Section 504 is much broader than that found in the EHA.[30] Section 504 defines a handicapped person as a person who has a physical or mental impairment that substantially limits one or more major life activities. Further, those who are "qualified" and, therefore, entitled to protection under the Act are defined as being:

> (i) of an age during which nonhandicapped persons are provided such services, (ii) of an age during which it is mandatory under state law to provide such services to a handicapped person, or (iii) to whom a state is required to provide a free appropriate public education under Section 612 of the Education of the Handicapped Act.

> Thus, a child eligible under EHA is but one of three categories of handicapped children qualified for [a free appropriate public education]. Under Section 504, there are two additional categories of handicapped children entitled to evaluation.[31]

Further, the definition of an appropriate education in the regulations is not restricted to special education. It also provides that "an appropriate education may consist of education in regular classes and education in regular classes with the use of supplementary services."[32] Clearly, the recommendations of Jim's psychologist qualify under this definition. Thus, the proper inquiry under Section 504 is whether Jim has an impairment which substantially limits a major life activity and is a qualified handicapped person. If the answer to both question is *yes,* he is "entitled to these services under Section 504, regardless of whether [he] is so entitled under EHA." (Mesa Unified School District, *supra*).

Compliance Under Section 504

Despite the attempts of parents to make it so, compliance standards under the two statutes are not identical. Parents often file complaints under Section 504 alleging facts that, if true, would be violations of the EHA but are not violations of Section 504, *per se.* For example, it is frequently alleged that a district failed to develop an individualized education plan (IEP) or that the IEP did not include long-term and short-term goals. Neither of those acts, alone, violate Section 504. Section 504 does not require the development of an IEP. The proper inquiry under Section 504 is (a) whether an educational progarm has been developed that meets the individual needs of the student(s), and (b) whether the district has complied with the procedural requirements of Section 504. If the answer to both these questions is *yes,* the existence of a properly developed IEP is not relevant. *Remember*—compliance with the provisions of the EHA is only *one means* of complying with Section 504.[33] The determination that should be made under Section 504 is whether the recipient's actions are discriminatory or result in the student being denied a free appropriate public education.

Part V: Postsecondary Education

> "The four essential freedoms" of a university are to deter-
> mine for itself on academic grounds: (1) who may teach; (2)
> what may be taught; (3) how it shall be taught; (4) and who
> may be admitted to study."
>
> —Sweezy v. New Hampshire,
> 354 U.S. 234, 263 (1957)

Subpart E prescribes requirements for nondiscrimination in recruitment, admission, and treatment of students in postsecondary education programs and activities, including vocational education.[1] Postsecondary institutions are at a crossroads in their delivery of services to disabled individuals. Their academic decisions are being questioned and challenged with increasing frequency. Recent cases such as *Wynne v. Tufts University School of Medicine, United States v. Board of Trustees for the University of Alabama,* and *Nathanson v. Medical College of Pennsylvania* are just introductory scrimmages in what promises to be a long and costly contest over the legitimacy of efforts to accommodate disabled students.[2] After many years of developing and refining the proper procedural responses to Section 504 and its implementing regulations, these institutions are now faced with the harsh reality of addressing some very difficult substantive issues, such as

1. dealing with the often emotional task of providing for "unique needs" in a highly structured academic environment;
2. preserving academic freedom—for both the institution and individual faculty members;
3. balancing the need to require accountability from students, on the one hand, with the responsibility to provide "meaningful access," on the other; and
4. drawing the line between "reasonable accommodations" and "fundamental alterations" of the educational program.

In their attempts to address these issues, institutions are finding that the task of plotting a safe path between overzealous paternalism and callous disregard in serving disabled individuals is perilous. There are no "quick fixes"—no easy answers to the questions these issues raise. Even the enforcement agency has failed to provide meaningful responses to many of them. Moreover, the battlelines being drawn in postsecondary education are not just the predictable ones of students, parents, and advocacy groups versus the institutions. In some instances individual faculty members oppose the policies and procedures of their own institutions. The chapters that follow will not provide neat answers to the issues outlined above, but will identify compliance miscalculations and suggest substantive solutions.

Note: The author has chosen to limit the number of agency rulings cited. My review of recent rulings revealed troubling inconsistencies among the regional offices. Therefore, I felt it best to focus on the pertinent judicial decisions.

20
Facing the Challenge:
What Is the Recipient's Responsibility?

Elementary and secondary institutions and agencies are instructed to provide a "free appropriate public education"—a clear mandate—whereas postsecondary institutions are told, in essence, not to discriminate against "qualified handicapped persons." The question of who is a qualified handicapped person, rarely a significant issue in the elementary and secondary arena, moves to the forefront in postsecondary education. Recipients under Subpart E must concern themselves with two primary issues: qualified status and the appropriateness of the services, benefits, or programs provided. Further, since there is no state-mandated right to receive postsecondary educational services, the denial of services/benefits to handicapped individuals is a real possibility with respect to most decisions that are made. Therefore, recipients must recognize and understand the importance of justifying decisions that result in denial or exclusion; postsecondary institutions often create compliance headaches for themselves by failing to remember this important fact. Consider the following hypotheticals.

> The parents of a severely handicapped child, who has received a certificate of completion from high school, wishes to enroll him at a local junior college with an open admissions policy. College officials are skeptical, but are persuaded by the parents' assertions that the student has an aptitude for vocational courses. On that basis, they permit the student to enroll for a trial period of one semester. The student is accompanied by an attendant and falls asleep in most of his classes. At the end of the quarter he has not completed any assignments and seems to have no understanding of the subject matter. The college refuses to allow him to continue. His parents argue that his attendance has some positive value because he is interacting with his peers, and they assert that he has a right to attend based upon the school's open admissions policy.
>   A student who is hearing impaired requests that the university provide interpreter services during physical education classes. The university objects to paying an interpreter to watch the student participate in activities such as fencing and swimming.
>   A student with multiple sclerosis, who wishes to be an elementary school teacher, seeks to enroll in a graduate program. He is advised to consider

another career because it is unlikely that he would be employable because of his condition. Faculty members comment to the student that he would be unable to assist a child who was choking. The student questions whether he can be denied admission in the program on this basis.

In such situations many recipients devote all their attention to defending their ultimate decision but ignore the need to articulate clearly the reasons that support that decision. When compliance questions arise, the ultimate decision is not as important as the facts and evidence that support it. Except in rare instances where there is no question that the recipient's actions violate a specific regulatory provision, the "correctness" of the decision is not the primary focus.[1]

It has long been an accepted judicial principle that well-documented educational institutions' decisions are entitled to deference. These decisions will be respected as long as they are not arbitrary, capricious, discriminatory, or constitutionally impermissible. Courts "respect the academic judgment of university faculties" and have consistently indicated their reluctance to step into the shoes of educators:

> Courts are particularly ill-equipped to evaluate academic performance.[2]
> [Courts] should show great respect for the faculty's professional judgment. Plainly, they may not override it unless it is such a substantial departure from accepted academic norms as to demonstrate that the person or committee responsible did not actually exercise professional judgment.[3]
> The administration of the university rests not with the court, but with the administrators of the institution.[4]
> [C]onsiderable judicial deference must be paid to the evaluation made by the institution itself, absent proof that its standards and its application of them serve no purpose other than to deny an education to handicapped persons.[5]

It is this "deference," then, that changes the focus from the ultimate decision to an analysis of how the recipient arrived at the decision. This analysis permits judges to perform their proper function. They are, in fact, most comfortable weighing the evidence that supports an educational decision than making educational decisions, themselves. When recipients fail to articulate clearly the reasons for their decisions, they give judges and enforcement agencies the opportunity to assume the role of educators and second-guess those recipients' decisions. The most significant threat to the academic freedom of postsecondary institutions is this tendency to allow nonexperts to "play" educator. Therefore, recipients should spend less time arguing about the "rightness" of their decisions and more time analyzing them in the way that courts and the enforcement agency will, in the event that compliance with the regulations is questioned. Recipients must be able to establish both that they performed the proper analysis in determining whether they were responsible for providing the requested benefits or services, and that their ultimate decision was based upon legitimate non-discriminatory factors.

The starting point for any analysis of a recipient's decision pursuant to Subpart E is *Southeastern Community College v. Davis*.[6] In *Davis*, a hearing-impaired student was denied admission to a nursing program because the institution concluded that her inability to understand normal speech would prevent her from safely completing the program. The court upheld the recipient's decision, noting that the modifications that were requested—full-time supervision when the student attended patients, and the elimination of clinical courses—would result in a fundamental alteration in the nature of the nursing progarm. The Court specifically held that the statute and regulations did not require affirmative action. Reasonable modifications, not "fundamental alterations," are what recipients are responsible for providing. The Court further refined its opinion regarding the scope of Section 504 when, in *Alexander v. Choate,* it stated that "meaningful access" to program services and activities must be provided under Section 504, and that this duty might require that reasonable accommodations be made. "A balance must be struck between the statutory rights of the handicapped to be integrated into society and the legitimate interests of federal grantees in preserving the integrity of their programs. . . ."[7] Further, the Court ruled that "the term affirmative action referred to those 'changes,' 'adjustments,' or 'modifications' to existing programs that would be 'substantial' or 'fundamental alteration(s)'. . . ."[8]

> *Postsecondary institutions are not required to make "fundamental or substantial" modifications, and they may protect the integrity of their programs.*

This pronouncement is often how recipients summarize the important elements of the *Davis* and *Alexander* cases, in an attempt to justify decisions not to accommodate disabled individuals. Their defense of those decisions consists merely of their loudly proclaiming that the handicapped individual's request would require affirmative action or would require a fundamental alteration of their program, or both.[9] However, this posturing ignores the fact that the decisions of the Supreme Court did not provide an absolute right to maintain one's academic integrity. There are some circumstances under which a "refusal to modify an existing program might become unreasonable and discriminatory."[10] Reasonable accommodations must be made to provide "meaingful access." Thus, the recipient's protection of its academic integrity *must* be balanced against the rights of handicapped individuals, and must not be discriminatory, arbitrary, or capricious.

Postsecondary institutions, as discussed previously, are often guilty of failing to provide clear and convincing evidence to support their decisions not to accommodate disabled individuals. These failures appear to be the result of a belief that deference will unconditionally be afforded to purely educational decisions, and that the individual who alleges discrimination has the ultimate burden of persuasion, thus relieving the institution of any need to defend its actions until that burden is carried.[11] However, case law clearly reflects that courts are reluctant to uphold the exclusion of, or denial of services to, handicapped persons in the absence of evidence that the actions of the recipient were based upon legitimate and nondiscriminatory factors.[12] Conversely, where recipients have provided such clear and convincing evidence, their decisions have been respected.[13]

The Court in *Wynne v. Tufts* specifically rejected the university's claim that it was not required to provide evidence to support its decision to refuse to accommodate a learning-disabled student. The Court held that postsecondary institutions have an *obligation* to document that the necessary balancing of the responsibility to handicapped individuals and the right to maintain program integrity had occurred. It described that *obligation* as follows:

> [T]here is a real obligation on the academic institution to seek suitable means of reasonably accommodating a handicapped person and *to submit a factual record indicating that it conscientiously carried out this statutory obligation* (emphasis added).[14]

The Court identified a properly conducted assessment of whether a reasonable accommodation could be provided as including:

> [T]he institution submits undisputed facts demonstrating that the relevant officials within the institution considered alternative means, their feasibility, cost and effect on the academic program, and came to a rationally justifiable conclusion that the available alternatives would result either in lowering academic standards or requiring substantial program alteration, ...[15]

The university offered only an unsubstantiated statement of the dean of the medical school to support its determination that altering the test format (multiple choices) would result in a fundamental alteration of the program. The Court rejected the statement as being insufficient to meet the institution's statutory obligation.

> [W]e think that on the record as made thus far Tufts had an obligation of demonstrating that its determination that no reasonable way existed to accommodate Wynne's inability to perform adequately on written multiple-choice examinations was a reasoned, professional academic judgment, not a mere *ipse dixit*. There is no mention of any consideration of possible alternatives, nor reference to any discussion of the unique qualities of multiple-choice examinations. There is no indication of who took part in the decision or when it was made. (*Wynne v. Tufts, supra* at 19–21.)

Thus, recipients are advised to ensure that their decisions regarding accommodating handicapped individuals involve the proper balancing test prescribed by the Supreme Court in *Davis* and *Alexander*. Further, they must be able to present clear and convincing evidence to support academic decisions that result in the denial of access. *Remember* — There must be "a factual basis in the record reasonably demonstrating that accommodating that individual would require either a modification of the essential nature of the program, or impose an undue burden . . . ."[16]

21
Admissions and Recruitment

The admissions and recruitment procedures of recipients frequently involve the type of categorical exclusions or denials that the Act was intended to eliminate.[1] For example:

> Karta University requires that all students with learning disabilities enroll in a special program for two quarters prior to permitting them to enroll in its regular classes. The university argues that its experience with learning-disabled students establishes that their chances of succeeding are greatly improved if their initial higher education experience is in an environment geared to their needs. University officials maintain that there is a legitimate educational basis for this procedure, and that it should therefore be respected.
>
> Buck's parents charge the junior college with discrimination when he is denied admission. They charge that the fact that the college has no students with mental disabilities enrolled is evidence of discrimination. They also note that the special students' center, a facility providing educational services to high school children with mental disabilities, is excluded from the college's recruitment programs and activities to which all other regional high schools are invited.
>
> Skinflint University limits expenditures for the provision of services to handicapped students to $150,000 annually. The special services coordinator is instructed to estimate the cost of such services, and, once the cut-off figure is reached, admitted handicapped students who request services are advised to enroll at a nearby junior college. The university and the junior college have a written agreement that provides that such students will automatically be admitted. Further, the students are promised that if they obtain a 2.0 average or better at the college, they will be permitted to transfer to the university for their final two years. The university argues that the agreement with the junior college ultimately results in handicapped students being served, and that, technically, the students are not being denied admission to the university, because the two years at the junior college are comparable, and because they are guaranteed enrollment at the university for their junior and senior years.

Section 104.42(a) specifically provides that qualified handicapped persons should not be "... denied admissions or be subjected to discrimination in admission or recruitment." All the hypotheticals set forth above reflect direct discrimination against handicapped persons. They are denied an opportunity to participate, provided with opportunities that are not equal to those afforded their nonhandicapped peers and offered different, or separate, benefits and services, which have not been shown to be necessary in order for them to obtain "meaningful access."[2] "Mere possession of a handicap is not a permissible ground for assuming an inability to function."[3] Any action or practice that would exclude handicapped persons or treat them differently as a group, solely on the basis of their handicap, is suspect; more often than not it will be found to violate the Act and its implementing regulations. The mandate that "otherwise qualified handicapped individuals must be provided with meaningful access to the benefits that the [recipient] offers" precludes policies or procedures that prevent an assessment of the "qualified" status of each handicapped person on an individual basis.[4] Thus, even the benign intentions of Karta University violate the regulations, because the decision to treat the handicapped students differently was not based upon an individualized assessment of each student's abilities in relation to legitimate admission criteria and performance standards. A proper assessment would undoubtedly establish that some of the students are entitled to enroll in the regular program immediately. Furthermore, the actions of Skinflint University violate § 104.42(b)(1), which provides that recipients "may not apply limitations upon the number or proportion of handicapped persons who may be admitted." On the other hand, while handicapped individuals must be provided the same admissions and recruitment opportunities as nonhandicapped individuals, the mere fact that an institution has no handicapped students will not be viewed as evidence of discrimination.[5]

The attempts of postsecondary institutions to maintain their academic standards while, at the same time, complying with the mandates of § 104.42 do, however, present more perplexing problems than those noted above. Specifically,

a. What are acceptable criteria and standards to use in making admission decisions?
b. Are standardized tests a legitimate means to assess the skills and abilities of disabled individuals?
c. Is it possible for institutions to preserve their academic standards without considering the impact that handicapping conditions have on an applicant's ability to perform during the admission process?

Admissions Decisions

Any discussion regarding the appropriateness of admission standards, criteria and decisions must include the Supreme Court decisions in *Davis* and *Alexander.* In those cases, the Court outlined the delicate balance between a recipient's rights and its responsibilities regarding programs, services or benefits offered handicapped individuals. As discussed in Chapter 20, the Court stated that a balance must be struck between the competing interests of recipients and handicapped individuals. The right of handicapped individuals to be protected from discrimination was described as follows:

> Requirements and practices may not arbitrarily deprive genuinely qualified handicapped persons of the opportunity to participate. (*Davis, supra* at 405.)
> [A]n otherwise qualified handicapped individual must be provided with meaningful access. . . . To assure meaningful access, reasonable accommodations . . . may have to be made. (*Alexander, supra* at 300.)

Recipients' rights were described as:

> Section 504 imposes no requirement upon an educational institution to lower or to effect substantial modifications of standards to accommodate a handicapped person. (*Davis, supra* at 410–12.)
> The recipient need not make modifications which "would compromise the essential nature of the . . . program" or that would be a "fundamental alteration in the nature of a program." (*Id.,* 410, 413–14.)

Admission decisions involve a bottom-line determination of whether handicapped individuals are "qualified" to participate in the recipient's program. These decisions must initially be scrutinized in terms of the criteria used and the actual qualifications of the handicapped individual. Both the recipient and the handicapped individual must satisfy regulatory requirements.[6] The admission standards utilized by the recipient must be legitimate and nondiscriminatory.[7] The criteria/standards must also be necessary and rationally related to the goals and objectives of the program. Further, neither the statute nor the regulations preclude the consideration of physical skills and abilities and/or the use of physical qualifications as admissions criteria. "Legitimate physical qualifications may be essential to participation in particular programs."[8] As noted by the Court in *Doe v. New York University,*

> [An individual's] handicap may be a permissible factor to be taken into account in determining whether he is qualified——. [S]uch cases cannot be framed in terms of permissible versus impermissible factors. The pivotal issue is not whether the handicap was considered, but whether under all of the circumstances it provides a reasonable basis for finding the plaintiff not to be qualified or not as well qualified as other applicants.[9]

Doe v. New York University and *Pushkin v. Regents of the University of Colorado* illustrate the contrast between proper and improper consideration of physical skills and abilities in admission decisions.

An applicant with multiple sclerosis applied for a psychiatric residency program. Although he is qualified with respect to academic credentials, he is denied admission because individuals on the admission committee, who interviewed him for approximately 15 minutes each, felt that his impairment would preclude his successful participation in the program. Specifically, they concluded that his physical condition would be difficult for his patients to accept, that the applicant would have difficulty working full-time, that he had unresolved emotional problems regarding his illness, and that he would be unable to withstand the stress of residency. There is no evidence of the problems or deficiencies the committee members feared. In fact, all concrete evidence indicated that the applicant was an excellent candidate for the program: his supervisor from an earlier residency program evaluated him as having great potential; he had treated patients appropriately and performed well in that program; his illness did not have a negative impact on his work. Moreover, the psychiatrist who had treated him for four years stated that his emotional response was normal and that there were no negative side effects associated with the medication he was taking. (*Pushkin v. Regents of the University of Colorado.*)

A student with excellent academic credentials applied and was admitted to medical school on the basis of false information she provided regarding her mental health. She had an extensive history of mental illness. Over a period of nearly three years, which included her medical school enrollment, she exhibited a psychiatric disorder that was manifested in over 20 instances of self-inflicted bodily harm and attempted suicide, as well as serious physical attacks on her doctors and others. Also, she continuously refused to submit to recommended medical treatment. She was forced to withdraw from medical school as a result of her impairment. In the five years subsequent to her withdrawal, she obtained a Master of Science degree in Health and Policy Management and performed successfully as a research assistant for the federal government. Despite the fact that she did not receive the extensive therapy recommended, during the five-year period there has been no recurrence of the previous violent and self-destructive behavior. Her request to be reinstated in medical school is rejected on the basis of the evaluations of several psychiatrists who state that she continues to suffer from a serious psychiatric problem and that the stress of medical school would cause her previous destructive behavior to recur. (*Doe v. New York University.*)

The university's rejection of the applicant in *Pushkin* violated Section 504 because it was unsupported by concrete evidence and based upon impermissible stereotypes. The reasons provided to support its decision were found illegitimate and based upon incorrect assumptions regarding the applicant's handicap.[10] The decision of New York University, on the other hand, was based upon a legitimate concern aptly supported by evidence that the manifestations of the applicant's impairment might well reappear in medical school, where they had occurred in their most extreme form in the past. "The Rehabilitation Act forbids discrimination based on stereotypes about a handicap, but it does not forbid decisions based upon actual attributes of the handicap."[11]

The handicapped individual, on the other hand, must be "otherwise qualified," that is, "able to meet all of the program's requirements in spite of his handicap."[12] The ultimate question of who is "otherwise qualified" is tied to "the extent to which a [recipient] is required to make reasonable modifications in its programs for the needs of the handicapped."[13] As noted in Chapter 20, institutions cannot use the argument of the preservation of academic standards and essential program elements as a justification for refusing to undertake *any* academic adjustments to provide handicapped students with access. For example:

> Joe seeks admission into a chemistry graduate program that is highly competitive. The applicant pool is so large that each applicant who meets the academic standards is required to conduct an assigned experiment. Applicant performance is graded by the admissions committee. One of the factors considered is the time it takes the applicant to complete the experiment. Joe has multiple sclerosis and uses a wheelchair. The laboratory that the applicants used for the experiments has a number of accessibility problems: the tables are too high for him, and wheelchair mobility is restricted by the narow spaces between tables. This places Joe at a disadvantage. Joe asserts that, under the circumstances, the experiment is not an accurate assessment of his knowledge and ability. The chemistry department contends that the experiment is a necessary part of its admission process.

It is important to remember that a failure to meet academic standards or criteria does not end the inquiry; it must also be established that there is no appropriate accommodation that will permit participation in the program. In *Brennan v. Stewart,* a case in which a blind individual was denied a temporary training permit because it was determined that his blindness precluded him from complying with the licensure rule of performing 15 hours of ear impressions and otoscopic examinations, the Court ruled that it was not sufficient to simply determine that the licensure requirements were reasonable and that the individual's impairment precluded him from meeting those requirements.[14] The handicapped individual was entitled to demonstrate the existence of "some reasonable accommodation in these requirements [that met] his special needs without sacrificing the integrity of the Board's licensing program."[15]

Thus, in the example above, it can be argued persuasively that the needs of the handicapped student could be addressed without compromising the institution's academic standards. Specifically, Joe could have been tested in a laboratory that was accessible. It is a situation where a ". . . reasonable accommodation is available to satisfy the legitimate interests of both the federal grantee and the handicapped person."[16]

However, there are some circumstances under which a recipient may properly conclude that the requested modification is unacceptable because it would require a "fundamental alteration" of the program. For example:

A student—whose vision is impaired by *retinitis pigmentosa* and who also suffers with a neurological disease that restricts his motor skills, sense of touch and manual coordination—is admitted to a college of optometry. Despite his impairments, he is judged capable of successfully completing the academic program. After his admission, the college implements a new graduation requirement. All students are required to pass a proficiency examination. The examination involves performing procedures using various instruments, several of which the handicapped student is unable to perform because of his impairments. The college denies his request for a waiver of the requirement, and, as a result, he is denied a degree. The student alleges discrimination and charges that the examination measures mechanical proficiency rather than knowledge. Do the college's actions violate Section 504?

When faced with this situation in *Doherty v. Southern College of Optometry,* the Court found that the proficiency examination was a necessary part of the program curriculum.[17] The recipient presented evidence given by experts in the field to the effect that use of the instruments in question was becoming an integral part of patient care in the profession. The decision not to waive the examination was nondiscriminatory and was based upon a need to maintain an academic standard rationally related to program objectives.

> An educational institution is not required to accommodate a handicapped individual by eliminating a course requirement which is reasonably necessary to proper use of the degree conferred at the end of a course of study.[18]

With admissions decisions, the pertinent issues for a recipient are (a) whether the standards are legitimate and necessary, and (b) whether there are any reasonable modifications that will allow the handicapped individual to participate. The recipient's decision will be respected if the evidence reflects that it "conscientiously carried out this statutory obligation."[19] Institutions are free to apply their admission criteria/standards without interference, so long as it results in a "stereotype-free assessment of the person's abilities."[20] For instance,

> Equity University is interested in having a diverse student population and, in keeping with that philosophy, it has a liberal admissions exception policy. Students who do not meet the admission criteria of a 1050 SAT score and a g.p.a. of at least 2.6 are nevertheless considered for admission under the policy. Sam, a student with a history of alcoholism, had a 925 SAT score and a grade point average of 2.8. Sam's application is rejected by the committee on the basis of poor grades in his senior year. Several students with a lower SAT score or grade point average (or both) than Sam are admitted. Committee members express the opinion that performance at the end of a high school student's academic career is a good indicator of that student's

ability and desire to succeed on the college level. Sam argues that if his first semester grades—when he was being treated for alcoholism—were not considered, his record would be as good as or better than many of the students admitted. He also argues that other factors such as his good recommendations and his extracurricular activities justify his admission.

In the absence of evidence that the committee's decision was based upon impermissible consideration of Sam's handicapped condition, there is no violation of Section 504. Therefore, despite Sam's contentions, the questions of whether his first semester grades should have been disregarded, whether his recommendations and extracurricular activities should have been given greater consideration, and whether the committee was right in using senior-year grades as a determining factor are not relevant. The Act requires only nondiscrimination; it does not require that the recipient make "a correct decision."[21]

> Perfect University is recognized as the leading institution in the country with respect to serving students with learning disabilities. Based upon its experience in serving these students, the university has developed a special program for them. The program offers services such as tutoring for all courses and classes in test-taking. It is a pilot program, and enrollment is limited to 50 students on a first come—first served basis. Participating students are charged $150 per semester. All learning-disabled students not enrolled in the special program are provided accommodations in accordance with § 104.44.

The regulations do not preclude a university from offering such a program. If all qualified handicapped persons are provided services, benefits, and opportunities in compliance with the statute, the fact that it offers special services to a particular group of students is not a violation. The recipient is not refusing to provide necessary academic adjustments; it is merely providing services beyond those mandated. As noted by the Court in *P.C. v. McLaughlin,*

> The Act does not require all handicapped persons to be provided with identical benefits. . . . Rather, it seeks to ensure that handicapped individuals have an opportunity to participate in and benefit from programs receiving federal assistance.[22]

Admission Tests

> Lier's Law School admits 250 students in each first-year class. It has 2,000 applicants for its 1990–91 class. The admissions committee considers the 826 applicants who met the academic criteria of a score of 700 or better on the LSAT, and a grade point average of 3.4 or more. Joe, a blind applicant with an LSAT score of 720 and a grade point average of 3.7, is among the 826 applicants considered. The committee also considers factors such as

recommendations, college achievements and honors, and class ranking. Joe, who was ranked in the top third of his graduating class, is placed on a waiting list and ultimately is denied admission. The profile of the 1990–91 class is an average score of 785 on the LSAT and a grade point average of 3.6. Furthermore, approximately 75 percent of those admitted were graduated in the top ten percent of their high school class. Joe alleges discrimination. He argues that the fact that handicapped students, as a class, score lower on standardized tests—such as the LSAT—means that, in essence, the school denied him admission on the basis of his handicap.

Admissions policies and procedures used by postsecondary institutions are intimately tied to standardized testing. Those testing instruments are part of the foundation of their academic standards. It is also no secret that, with respect to certain handicaps, notably learning disabilities, conventional testing instruments are woefully inadequate as a useful predictor of success. The regulatory provisions that address this problem, specifically § 104.42(b)(2), can best be described as well-meaning theoretical approaches to the issue that, in practice, create more problems than solutions. Section 104.42(b)(2) provides that recipients "may not use any test or criterion for admission that has a disproportionate adverse effect on handicapped persons." However, such tests or criteria may be used if they (1) have "been validated as a predictor of success. . ." and if (2) alternative tests having "a less disproportionately adverse effect are not shown *by the Assistant Secretary* to be available" [emphasis added]. Active enforcement of this provision, which would probably produce results meaningful for handicapped persons, but which would be extremely disruptive for the testing industry, has not been forthcoming.[23] There are two specific deficiencies in the enforcement agency's approach:

a. The question of identifying alternative tests that do not have an adverse or disproportionate impact on handicapped individuals has not been adequately addressed by the OCR. The regulation places the burden of identifying alternatives on the Assistant Secretary. Despite the fact that a panel commissioned by the OCR in 1981 to study the testing issue concluded that conventional testing instruments would preclude institutions from ensuring comparable performance by handicapped applicants and recommended that alternative test instruments and methods be developed,[24] the OCR has not assumed the leadership posture in resolving the difficult issues regarding testing that the regulations impose upon it. Arguably, the agency is not qualified to address the problem in a meaningful way.

b. The regulations require that tests be validated as predictors of success. First-year grades may be used as the criterion with only periodic studies against overall success in the educational program being used. However, there doesn't appear to be a great deal of interest in the results of such studies on the enforcement level. Further, the validation studies need not isolate handicapped students. The OCR has not required institutions to study performance by comparing handicapped versus nonhandi- capped students. It is problematic that the regulations essentially re- quire recipients to ensure that handicapped individuals are accom- modated so that their performances on tests are comparable to non- handicapped students; yet, the failure to compare the performance of the two groups on tests prevents recipients from establishing that the ac- commodations are effective.

The OCR has essentially limited its enforcement activities under § 104.42(b)(2) to (a) requiring that recipients provide evidence that a test or criterion "has been validated as a predictor of success for the educational program" if it has been shown to have a disproportionately adverse impact, and (b) to rubber-stamping the *status quo* use of standardized tests. The OCR has acknowledged the complex issues regarding the use of standardized tests by taking the position that the use of a standardized test that might have an adverse impact on handicapped individuals is permissible so long as other factors, such as "prior admissions records and personal recommenda- tions," are also considered in the decision-making process.[25]

Perhaps in response to the fact that enforcement under § 104.42(b)(2) is limited at best, the OCR has required that recipients strictly adhere to the mandates of § 104.42(b)(3). This provision of the regulation requires that testing procedures be implemented "in such a manner as is necessary to avoid unfair distortion of test results."[26] The special needs of handicapped individuals must be accommodated in the administration of tests. Appendix A provides examples of the type of accommodation that is necessary.

> Methods have been developed for testing the aptitude and achievement of persons who are not able to take written tests or even to make marks re- quired for mechanically scored objective tests; in addition, methods for testing persons with visual or hearing impairments are available. A re- cipient, under this paragraph, must assure itself that such methods are used with respect to the selection and administration of any admissions tests that it uses.[27]

Consider these hypotheticals:

> Mary has a neurological impairment that severely restricts her ability to write. She is limited to writing a few sentences at a time, her writing is barely legible, and she tires easily. Mary is given four hours to complete a two-hour GRE test. Is the time extension an effective accommodation?
> Is it permissible to refuse to permit the use during a test of a calculator by a student whose handicap prevents her from performing the necessary math calculations without one?

Tests must be administered in such a way that the results do not simply reflect the impaired sensory, manual, or speaking skills of the individual — unless those are the particular skills the test was designed to measure. For example, if the institution were testing applicants for admission into an art design program, it would be appropriate to test for manual dexterity. However, in Mary's case, since the institution is seeking to measure her academic achievement, test results that reflect her restricted ability to write by hand, instead of her academic aptitude, would discriminate against her. One question that should be asked is whether the extension of a two-hour test to four hours would, itself, be too exhausting for Mary, and thus have a negative impact on her test results. The key is to select an accommodation that will not result in an unfair distortion of the test results. Thus, an accommodation that offsets Mary's writing impairment, such as providing an amanuensis, might be more appropriate than simply giving her more time to write.

The hypothetical regarding the inability to perform math calculations presents the same issue. If one is testing knowledge of math *theories and analysis,* the use of the calculator is an acceptable accommodation. In a case that involved this issue, the OCR found that the refusal to permit a learning-disabled student to use a calculator on a nursing admissions test violated Section 504.[28]

It is also important to remember that the recipient is responsible for assuring itself that appropriate methods are used in selecting and administering admission tests. The recipient will not be allowed to shift that responsibility by asserting that it was not responsible for the actual administration of the test. The fact that another entity, such as a testing service, administers the test is not relevant.

> Dolores, who is in a wheelchair, is scheduled to take, for admission to a graduate program, an exam that is being given on the third floor of the student center. She requests that she be allowed to take the exam at an alternate location because students are not permitted to use building elevators. The chairperson of the department assures her that the test monitor will provide her with access to the elevator. When Dolores arrives to take the test, she discovers that the monitor has forgotten to obtain a key from the chairperson; attempts to obtain another key prior to the start of the exam are unsuccessful. Since there is no other way to get Dolores to the test site, the monitor suggests that they seek volunteers to carry her. Dolores declines the offer because the stairs are steep and the volunteers would be inexperienced. The monitor then suggests that she meet with the chairperson and arrange to take the exam at a special session. When Dolores seeks to schedule a time for the exam, the chairperson advises her that there are insufficient time and staff available to schedule the exam, administer it, and complete the scoring in time to consider her for admission into the next class. He suggests that she wait until the next time the exam is given and seek admission to the program in the following quarter.

The recipient must ensure that admissions tests are administered in accessible facilities. Therefore, requiring Dolores to wait three months to apply to the program because the institution failed to provide an accessible facility violates Section 504. The tests given handicapped persons must also be offered as often and in as timely a manner as are other admissions tests.

Preadmission Inquiries

Which of the following are impermissible preadmission inquiries?

1. Elitist University requests that those applicants with learning disabilities be isolated during the admissions process, and that only those handicapped individuals with a viable possibility of succeeding be admitted.
2. Mary, an individual who has minimal vision in her left eye but normal vision in her right eye, seeks admission to a dental assistant program. She meets the general admissions criteria, *i.e.*, she is 21 years old and scored above average on the school's admissions exams. However, the admissions committee reserves judgment on her admission until she submits medical documentation regarding her impairment and submits to a visual examination which indicates that her limited vision in her left eye would not hamper her ability to perform the clinical work required in the program. Is the school's request for medical proof of her condition an impermissible preadmission inquiry?
3. Alice files a complaint charging Cosby University with discrimination because the testing service notified the institution that she took the test under nonstandard conditions. She alleges that the admissions committee used this notification to gather additional information regarding her handicap, and denied her admission based on that information.
4. Charles files a complaint alleging that the university discriminated against him on the basis of his handicap, a visual impairment, by denying him admission. The chairperson of the admissions committee states that the committee members were not provided any information regarding Charles' handicap; therefore, the denial could not be discrimination. Charles maintains that the university's request that a photograph be sent with the admission application is a preadmission inquiry which violated the regulations. Is Charles correct?

Preadmission inquiries are prohibited because *general* information regarding the existence of handicapping conditions is not relevant to specific admissions determinations and could be used to discriminate against individuals solely on the basis of their being handicapped.[29] The procedures of Elitist University reflect such impermissible actions. There is no legitimate reason for the institution to treat learning-disabled students differently in the application of its admissions procedures. In fact, the very act of treating them differently is based upon the improper assumption that "mere possession of a handicap," in this instance a learning disability, is evidence of an inability to function.[30]

Recipients have charged that § 104.42(b)(4) hampers their ability to determine whether applicants are qualified handicapped persons because they are precluded from gathering necessary information regarding applicants' skills and abilities. This is not a valid argument. It is not a violation of Section 504 to require that applicants meet "reasonable physical qualifications for admission."[31] A recipient may ask specific questions regarding an applicant's physical abilities as long as the physical attributes in question are rationally related to the legitimate goals of the program. Clearly, it is legitimate and rational for the school to ensure that Mary's ability to perform as a dental assistant is not negated by her visual impairment.[32] An institution may also make preadmission inquiries where there is evidence that the applicant has a condition which presents a significant or substantial risk to others.[33] It is important to remember that there must be sufficient evidence to justify such inquiry, and the possibility of risk or danger to others cannot be merely speculative.

The recipient's right to ask questions regarding legitimate physical requirements does not justify general questions regarding the physical condition of applicants. Questions such as the following are impermissible preadmissions inquiries.

> Do you have a history of a mental disability?
>
> Do you have any health problems? Or
>
> Are you in good health?

Such general questions, which are indicative of a "fishing expedition" rather than a legitimate inquiry, violate Section 504.[34] The fact that testing services "flag" tests administered under special conditions technically constitutes a preadmission inquiry under the regulations. The institution is alerted to the fact that the student may be handicapped. But the OCR has taken the position that this practice alone will not result in institutions being found in violation of the regulations. Thus, absent evidence that the university denied admission to Alice or other handicapped students solely on the basis of their handicap, the simple act of receiving "flagged" test results is not a violation. If, for example, the university isolated the "flagged" results, obtained additional information about the students involved, and denied admission to virtually all students who had learning disabilities, then such a practice would violate the regulations. Similarly, state laws that exempt learning-disabled students from standardized tests are, in effect, preadmission inquiries. Students noting that they are exempt from such tests identify themselves as learning-disabled. It is not clear whether the OCR would view such laws as being in violation of Section 504. The OCR has, however, held that school districts may not, without the student's consent, indicate on transcripts to postsecondary institutions that a student is enrolled in special education.[35]

Regarding Charles' concern, the term "preadmission inquiry," as used in the regulations, refers to general questions regarding an individual's medical history, physical or mental condition, or handicapping condition. Since photographs submitted with admissions applications would not normally provide any evidence of an individual's handicap, such requests are not considered preadmission inquiries.[36]

The real difficulty with achieving compliance under § 104.42(b)(4) is that the provision does not address the problem of preadmission inquiries in a realistic manner. Everyone in postsecondary education admits that there are numerous ways in which admissions offices obtain information regarding an applicant's handicap or disability.[37] Therefore, a regulatory provision that simply prohibits recipients from making preadmission inquiries, while ignoring the reality that the information is available and is, in fact, being impermissibly used in many instances, is not an adequate solution to unlawful discrimination in the admissions process. It would be more meaningful if the OCR would eliminate the fiction of a *"pure"* admissions process, and would instead instruct recipients to develop procedures to ensure that the information it regularly obtains regarding applicants' handicaps is not used in a discriminatory manner.

The regulations do, however, permit confidential postadmission inquiries for purposes of determining whether students may require accommodations. Recipients may also require students to provide postadmission medical information, such as the completion of a college health form, as long as the information is not used to deny admission to qualified handicapped individuals.[38] Thus, it would violate the regulation for a recipient to revoke a student's admission simply because he notes on a health form that he is HIV positive.

> Metro Junior College has a limited staff and budget for providing academic accommodations and auxiliary aids. Therefore, it requests that handicapped students needing such services note their specific needs on the admissions applications so that the services can be provided in an efficient and economical fashion. The college argues that the practice is permissible because the information is detached from the form before it is sent to the admissions committee.

While the regulations provide exceptions to the prohibition against preadmission inquiries, the conditions under which they are permitted must be adhered to strictly. The inquiries can only be made to overcome effects of past discrimination or as a voluntary remedial action. Moreover, the respondents must be informed of the purposes for which the information will be used, that their response is voluntary, that failure to respond will not result in adverse action, and that the information will be kept confidential[39] [§ 104.42(c)]. Metro's action violated the regulation because the inquiry did not adhere to the conditions of § 104.42(c).

Remember—subsequent to admissions, recipients may make inquiries regarding handicaps that may require accommodation [See § 104.42(b)(4)]. However, information provided as a result of such inquiries must be kept confidential and the purposes for which it may be used are limited to the provision of accommodations. It is the right of the student to decide whether to make the information available to the institution and the fact that he or she does so for the purposes of accommodation does not entitle the institution to use the information for whatever it wishes thereafter.

22
Treatment of Students

The regulatory provisions that address the treatment of students (§§ 104.43, 104.45–.47) essentially apply the § 104.4 prohibitions against discrimination to the postsecondary arena.[1] In addition to its general prohibitions regarding exclusion, denial of opportunities, and discrimination, § 104.43 also mandates (a) that programs and services "as a whole" provide equal opportunities for qualified handicapped persons; (b) that recipients must assure themselves that third parties whose programs or activities they sanction also provide equal opportunities; and (c) that programs and services be offered in the most integrated setting appropriate. The concept that programs and services "as a whole" must be nondiscriminatory requires something less than across-the-board access for qualified handicapped persons. It is a recognition on the part of the drafters of the regulations that, with respect to some programs, activities and services—for example those that are beyond the direct control of recipients—to require nondiscrimination in all areas would be unduly burdensome. What is important is that qualified handicapped persons are offered the "same range and quality of choices . . . afforded nonhandicapped students."[2]

Sam is a third-year medical student who requests that his residency assignment be Blett Hospital. He requests this because Dr. Patterson, a renowned blood specialist, works at the hospital. Sam is assigned to Northside Hospital, which is a new facility that is fully accessible to handicapped persons. Sam is in a wheelchair, and it is felt that Blett is not an acceptable choice, because it is an older facility with many areas, including some of the laboratories, not fully accessible. Further, medical school officials argue that the educational programs for third-year students are essentially the same at both schools. It is argued that, in fact, placement at Northside is preferable because it is newer and has more state-of-the-art technical equipment. School officials say that third-year students have little or no contact with Dr. Patterson, although it is acknowledged that he often hires third-year residents to work on his research projects. Sam maintains that there are adjustments that could be made that would make Blett accessible. The school maintains that the expense of such adjustments is unnecessary, since Northside is a perfectly acceptable placement.

What would be the resolution of Sam's dilemma using the "as a whole" principle? First, since the medical school has entered a contractual arrangement with the hospitals to serve its students during their residency, it must ensure that qualified handicapped students, such as Sam, are provided equal opportunities.[3] The fact that there is one facility, Blett, that does not provide adequate accessibility does not dispose of the issue. The real question is whether the residency program, despite the condition of Blett, provides an equal opportunity to qualified handicapped students. Thus, the medical school must ascertain whether Northside offers the "same range and quality of choice," including the opportunity to work on the research project of a renowned physician. If the opportunity at Blett is unique, the school may not discriminate against Sam by refusing to make the program at Blett accessible.[4]

The important thing to remember is that the duty to provide access to disabled students extends to all services and activities offered by the recipient to its students. There is, however, some question as to how much of a duty is owed to other individuals. For example, does the recipient have to provide interpreter services for a student's parents who are hearing impaired during graduation ceremonies? The Court in *Rothschild, supra* at 293, held that Section 504 does not require recipients to "subsidize parental involvement in extracurricular activities."

The significant regulatory mandates regarding the treatment of students are illustrated by the hypotheticals and discussions that follow.

Most integrated setting—§ 104.43(d)

> Carter College requires its freshman class to attend a three-day orientation session at the beginning of the academic year. The director of the orientation program organizes a special session for handicapped students because he feels that there are special services and information that need to be discussed with these students that are not of interest to the general population. The session for handicapped students is entitled "Special Needs Students" and is totally separate from the orientation provided the rest of the freshman class. The same information is provided to each group, except that the handicapped students are provided an additional two-hour presentation by the Handicapped Student Services Office.

Recipients must provide services and programs in the most integrated setting appropriate. While it may be appropriate to assign all students in wheelchairs to a first-floor class, it is not appropriate to assign all handicapped students, including those with no mobility impairments, to that class.[5] Similarly, in the fact situation above, it is inappropriate to create a duplicate orientation program just for handicapped students.

Course of Study/Counseling—§§ 104.43(c) and 104.47(b)

A hearing-impaired student applies for admission to a nursing program. While the evidence establishes that the student can hear adequately through the use of a hearing aid, the members of the admissions committee express the concern that hospitals would be reluctant to hire an individual with a hearing impairment. They feel that many in the medical profession are too sensitive to medical malpractice charges to take a chance on such employees. On this basis, the student is advised to consider another career.

A blind student is interested in becoming a hearing-aid practitioner. The student is informed by his faculty advisor that he would likely have difficulty obtaining a license from the board of examiners. He describes to the student the difficulty another blind applicant recently had in obtaining approval from the board. Do the advisor's statements violate the regulations' prohibition against counseling qualified handicapped students toward more restrictive career objectives?

The presumed reluctance of potential future employers is not a permissible reason to deny a qualified handicapped student the right to pursue a particular course of study. Students should not be denied opportunities solely based upon the "assumption by the recipient that no job would be available in the area in question for a person with that handicap."[6] Similar considerations and concerns are generally not expressed to nonhandicapped students. Thus, there appear to be no legitimate reasons for treating handicapped students in such a manner. However, the fact that handicapped students may not be "counseled toward more restrictive career objectives" does not preclude the recipient from providing "factual information about licensing and certification requirements that may present obstacles to handicapped persons."[7]

Health and Insurance—§ 104.43(a)

Mary has an orthopedic impairment for which she receives physical therapy treatments twice a week. Upon her arrival at the university, her parents discuss the possibility of her receiving the treatment in the college infirmary. They are informed by the director that the staff at the infirmary is not qualified to provide such services, and they are advised to arrange the treatments with a private physician. The director further explains to Mary's parents that the infirmary merely treats students' minor impairments. Mary's parents argue that the director's refusal denies Mary services on the basis of her handicap, in violation of Section 504.

The university requires students with mental disabilities, served academically by the Disabled Student Services Office (DSS), to receive mental health services from the DSS staff instead of using the campus health services provided for all other students.

Recipients are required to provide nondiscriminatory health services comparable to those provided nonhandicapped students. The recipient cannot refuse to provide qualified handicapped persons the same quality of mental health service, such as the services of mental health professionals, that it offers the total student population. However, since the college infirmary treats only minor impairments, it is proper for the institution to refuse to provide physical therapy treatments for Mary. "Recipients are not required . . . to provide specialized services and aids to handicapped persons in health programs."[8]

Housing—§ 104.45

> A university housing department offers the following options to students: air-conditioned double rooms with common bathrooms, single rooms with private bathrooms, and air-conditioned double rooms with private bathrooms. However, the only rooms which are accessible to mobility-impaired students are double rooms with common bathrooms and the single rooms with private bathrooms. The single rooms cost more. Are handicapped students provided equal access to housing?

The options provided handicapped persons do not have to be identical to those generally available. The recipient is not guilty of discrimination solely because double rooms with private bathrooms are not "accessible." The important factor is that, viewed "as a whole," the same range of choices is available to handicapped students at the same cost. As long as the choices are comparable, they need not be the same. The university would be in violation if, for example, it provided only more expensive single rooms for handicapped students, or if handicapped students whose conditions necessitated special accommodations (such as living alone in a double room) are charged more for their rooms.[9]

> The university contracts with a local apartment complex to provide off-campus housing for some of its students. Juniors and seniors are permitted to live in apartments instead of dormitories. Students in wheelchairs are unable to live in the apartments because they are not accessible. University officials advise those students that they have been unsuccessful in persuading the owners of the complex to make the necessary alterations to the facilities.

The recipient will not be permitted to avoid its responsibilities by asserting that a third party owns or controls the facility. The regulations mandate that the recipient assure itself that off-campus housing is available to handicapped students. Thus, the university's statement that the owners could not be persuaded is not acceptable. Off-campus housing must be made available to handicapped students if it is made available to nonhandicapped students. The university's responsibility would be similar if it provided a list of off-campus housing in its housing office. There would have to be accessible housing on the list, and it would have to be identified as such. It would be inappropriate for the housing office to place the burden of finding accessible housing on the students needing it. It is also important to remember that the off-campus housing, "as a whole," must be comparable to that provided nonhandicapped students. Thus, "not every off-campus living accommodation need be made accessible to handicapped persons."[10]

Financial Assistance— § 104.46

> Blake College provides total financial aid packages to its students. These packages comprise a combination of grants, loans, and college work study (CWS) funds. A group of handicapped students allege that they are being discriminatorily denied total financial aid packages because they receive a disproportionately small amount of the available CWS money. Discussions with financial aid staff reveal that general assessments regarding the employability of handicapped students are used in determining whether students should be referred for CWS jobs, that referrals are based upon general impressions, and that handicapped students are not asked to provide evidence of their ability to perform CWS jobs.

Handicapped students who meet the criteria for financial aid awards, *i.e.,* qualified handicapped persons, should be awarded financial aid to the same degree and in the same manner as nonhandicapped students. Therefore, their eligibility for aid should not be diminished by general perceptions that are not based upon the skills and abilities of the individual student. It is inappropriate for a recipient to deny, for safety reasons, all persons with a history of epilepsy, regardless of the nature and severity of their present condition, the opportunity to work at jobs involving heavy machinery. In that instance, individuals whose conditions are adequately controlled should not be treated the same as individuals subject to frequent seizures.[11]

> Jim charges that the university administers a large number of private scholarships that provide money to students based upon athletic ability, and that this results in discrimination against most physically handicapped students, because they cannot qualify for such awards. Is the university guilty of discrimination?

First, it is possible that some handicapped students would qualify for such scholarship awards. Second, the scholarships do not directly discriminate against handicapped students, because many nonhandicapped students also do not have the athletic prowess to qualify for the awards. In addition, "It will not be considered discriminatory to deny, on the basis of a handicap, an athletic scholarship to a handicapped person if the handicap renders the person unable to qualify for the award."[12] Finally, even assuming for argument's sake that physically handicapped students are disproportionately disadvantaged by the awarding of the private scholarships, the regulations permit the awarding of financial assistance pursuant to

> [W]ills, trusts, bequests, or similar legal instruments that require awards to be made on the basis of factors that discriminate or have the effect of discriminating on the basis of handicap . . . if the overall effect of the award of scholarships, fellowships, and other forms of financial aid is not discriminatory on the basis of handicap.[13]

Thus, the financial assistance program "as a whole" must be nondiscriminatory.

Nonacademic services — § 104.47[14]

> A student who has sight in only one eye is denied the right to play intercollegiate football because the college determines that there is too great a risk of eye injury. The student has had a very successful high school football career and submits a statement from an ophthalmologist to the effect that there is no substantial risk of serious eye injury.

The recipient denied the student the right to participate in football solely on the basis of his handicap. Benign intentions notwithstanding, such actions violate Section 504 and its implementing regulations. The Court in *Wright v. Columbia University* noted that courts have consistently enjoined recipients from "preventing students with various handicaps from participating in sports programs."[15] Handicapped students must be provided an equal opportunity to participate, and their exclusion from programs must be based upon their individual skills and abilities. Policy interpretation No. 5 of the implementing regulations states that it is impermissible to exclude handicapped students from participation who have "lost an organ, limb, or an appendage," and that if insurance is provided student athletes, it must be provided without discrimination to handicapped athletes.[16] Recipients can, however, require students to obtain medical clearance to participate.[17]

> A college offers an intramural athletics program. The sports chosen are based upon student interest. Tennis is offered as a sport. A group of wheelchair athletes request that wheelchair tennis be offered as well. Must the college offer the sport? If the college does offer wheelchair tennis, can all physically handicapped students be denied the opportunity to play on the regular tennis team?

The college must offer wheelchair tennis if the criterion for offering any sport is met, *i.e.*, sufficient student interest. Further, the regulations permit recipients to offer such separate or different activities only if handicapped students capable of doing so are not denied the opportunity to participate in activities that are *not* separate or different.

> KAZ is an off-campus fraternity near Clay College. While the fraternity is financially self-supporting, it is a member of the student council, is recognized as a student organization in the college bulletin, participates in homecoming activities, and, along with other sororities and fraternities, is provided secretarial and mailing services by the college. KAZ also has a faculty sponsor. Jim's father was a member of KAZ when he attended Clay, and Jim is eager to do the same. Although Jim's status as the son of an alumnus is supposed to assure his acceptance in KAZ, the membership committee turns him down because it concludes that an individual with Jim's disease—multiple sclerosis—would not "fit in." KAZ tells Jim that the fraternity's interests and endeavors largely involve athletic activities, and that they recommend that he consider an organization with more of an intellectual focus, where he would surely be more comfortable. When Jim files a complaint with the dean of student activities, he is advised that Clay College has no control over the fraternity's membership practices.

The regulations require that recipients assure that fraternities and sororities to which they provide "significant assistance" do not utilize membership practices resulting in discrimination prohibited by Section 504. But what constitutes "significant assistance"? The Court in *Iron Arrow Honor Society v. Hufstedler* held that an organization that was allowed to use university property for membership ceremonies, was identified by plaques located throughout the campus and by logos in the university catalog, was given a charter by the university, was formally sponsored by the university president, was provided secretarial services, and was assisted in its membership activities by a faculty screening committee, was indeed receiving "significant assistance" from the university, notwithstanding the organization's claim that it received no direct financial support.[18] The Court endorsed the Department of H.E.W.'s definition of significant assistance.

> "Significant assistance," according to H.E.W., can be of two forms: tangible support or intangible support. Tangible support includes direct financial assistance, the provision of facilities, equipment, or real property, secretarial and management services. Intangible support includes actions which identify the university with the discriminatory organization or bestow recognition upon the organization, such as provision of a faculty sponsor or advisor.[19]

Therefore, Clay College must take steps to ensure that KAZ's discriminatory membership practices are eliminated or cease providing "significant assistance" to the fraternity.

23
Academic Adjustments

Section 104.44—which provides that academic adjustments be made re-garding requirements and practices that discriminate, and that recipients provide necessary auxiliary educational aids—is one of the most hotly contested provisions of Subpart E.[1] Recipients have challenged its validity and sought to limit its enforcement. For example:

1. It has been asserted that the implementation of the provision, as mandated by the OCR, would result in the type of affirmative action that the Supreme Court in the *Davis* case stated was not required. The University of Alabama's use of this argument as support for an auxiliary aid policy, which denied necessary aids to students (primarily interpreter services), was rejected by the Court of Appeals.[2]
2. The Court of Appeals in *Nathanson v. Medical College of Pennsylvania* held that the recipient's obligation to provide access was not limited to simply "making the building and physical facilities accessible."[3]
3. In *Wynne v. Tufts,* the Court rejected the university's argument that the failure of the student to clearly establish that he was an "otherwise qualified handicapped individual" relieved it of the responsibility to "demonstrate that . . . no reasonable way existed to accommodate Wynne's inability to perform."[4]

Courts have specifically held that this regulatory provision, in particular its requirements to provide auxiliary aids, is a "reasonable" codification of congressional intent. Further, it has also been held that the agency's interpretation of it is in keeping with the Supreme Court's mandates in *Davis, Alexander,* and *Arline* requiring recipients to make reasonable modifications in order to provide meaningful access to handicapped persons, and holding that refusal to do so results in "illegal discrimination." As noted by the Court in *U.S. v. Board of Trustees for the University of Alabama,*

> The Supreme Court has repeatedly noted that these types of policy choices made by HEW in promulgating the implementing regulations for Section 504 are due substantial deference because the regulations were enacted with the oversight and approval of Congress.

199

> We find, therefore, that the legislative history of Section 504, along with the
> Supreme Court interpretations of Section 504 in *Davis* and *Alexander,* in-
> dicates that HEW's auxiliary aids regulation is based upon permissible con-
> struction of the statute.[5]

It is clear that recipients must do something more than simply throw
open their doors and permit qualified handicapped persons to enter. To require otherwise, "ignores the fact that in some instances the lack of an auxiliary aid effectively denies a handicapped student access to his or her opportunity to learn."[6] Recipients have "a real obligation . . . to seek suitable
means of reasonably accommodating a handicapped person and to submit
a factual record indicating that it conscientiously carried out this statutory
obligation."[7]

Once one understands that the obligation exists, the major dilemma is
determining the extent of that obligation. What does providing reasonable
accommodations mean in this context? As discussed in previous chapters,
the question of what is "reasonable" must be determined by reviewing the
facts of each particular case.[8] As is so often the case with terms and phrases
of nebulous meaning, it is more useful to speak in terms of negatives, *i.e.,*
requests that the enforcement agency and the courts have concluded are *not*
"reasonable accommodations." They have stated the recipient's responsibility to make academic adjustments does not include:

> [Adjusting] academic requirements that the recipient can demonstrate are
> essential to the program of instruction being pursued by such student or to
> any directly related licensing requirement. . . .[9]

And they have declared that:

> Section 504 imposes no requirement upon an educational institution to
> lower or to effect substantial modifications of standards to accommodate a
> handicapped person.[10]
>   An educational institution is not required to accommodate a handicapped
> individual by eliminating a course requirement which is reasonably
> necessary to proper use of the degree conferred at the end of the course of
> study.[11]
>   Accommodations that are "reasonable" must not unduly strain financial
> resources . . . would not cause "undue financial or administrative burdens"
> or "impose an undue hardship" upon the functioning of the recipient's
> program.[12]

Unfortunately, except for the *Davis* and *Doherty* rulings regarding program
requirements, what we have is another list of nebulous words and phrases,
e.g., "substantial modifications," "[essential] requirement," and "undue financial or administrative burdens."

Perhaps it might also be helpful to look at requests that have been considered "reasonable."

Modifications may include changes in the length of time permitted for the completion of degree requirements, substitution of specific courses required for the completion of degree requirements and adaptation of the manner in which specific courses are conducted.[13]

Auxiliary aids may include taped texts, interpreters ... readers ... classroom equipment adapted for students....[14]

For example, an institution might permit an otherwise qualified handicapped student, who is deaf, to substitute an art appreciation or music history course for a required course in music or could modify the manner in which the music appreciation course is conducted for the deaf student.[15]

Courts have also considered interpreters, special seating for a student with a back impairment, and note-takers as appropriate academic adjustments.[16]

Based upon the above-discussed interpretations of § 104.44, how should a recipient respond to the following requests for academic adjustments?

A learning-disabled student enrolled in a community college advises the admissions officer of her impairment and requests the following auxiliary aids and academic adjustments: use of a tape recorder in class and tutors for all her classes. She also requests that all her tests be given on a take-home basis because it takes her considerably more time than is normally provided to complete tests. The college agrees to her request to use a tape recorder, but denies her requests for take-home tests and tutors. She is offered extended time on all tests and is advised that the college does not provide tutoring assistance for any of its students. The student expresses the fear that the extended time offered might be insufficient for her needs and maintains that her prior school experience supports the need for tutors. Can the college refuse to provide the requested services?

This fact situation provides some insight regarding the tension between the rights of handicapped individuals and the responsibilities of recipients. The recipient is not obligated to provide the student with every academic adjustment requested. The recipient's responsibilities extend only to things that are necessary for providing "meaningful access" to the programs and services it offers. The issue is whether the requested adjustments and aids would provide handicapped individuals the opportunity to utilize and participate in the programs and services on an equal footing with nonhandicapped individuals.

The academic adjustments that the college denied the student would, if granted, have gone beyond putting her on "equal footing." Her impairment limited her ability to absorb the information provided in classes and delayed her response time when being tested. She was at a disadvantage compared to nonhandicapped students whose ability to assimilate and proffer information was not so hampered. The use of the tape recorder and the extended test time provided her the opportunity to participate equally. Tutorial services, however, do not provide access to information, but rather furnish additional instruction to enable the student to understand the content of the information being imparted. Nonhandicapped students, as well as handicapped students, could benefit from such additional instruction. Similarly, allowing the student to take tests at home goes beyond addressing her actual need, *i.e.,* extended test time, and provides her with an advantage not offered nonhandicapped students.

> *Caveat concerning tutorial services:* While the recipient need not provide tutorial services for handicapped students if no such services are provided nonhandicapped students, or one-to-one tutorial services to handicapped students if it only provides group sessions to nonhandicapped students, if tutorial students are provided, the recipient must provide necessary academic adjustments to allow handicapped students to benefit from such services. For example, note-takers should be provided at tutoring sessions for a student who is unable to write.[17]

> (a) A learning-disabled student enrolled in a four-year nursing program successfully completes his first two years. While he has difficulty with reading comprehension and remembering technical information, he is able to succeed through repetition and drill. Once the clinical portion of the program begins, the student starts to experience great difficulty in performing at an acceptable level. He is unable to apply knowledge acquired in classroom sessions to the clinical setting. Additionally, he has difficulty calculating medication dosages, remembering to perform assigned tasks, and reacting appropriately in stressful situations. The student's advisor requests the following academic adjustments for his clinical training: closer supervision, simulated crisis situations, and a limiting of the assignment of complex cases. The school declines to make the adjustments, noting that important elements of the clinical program would be sacrificed, and that patient safety and the quality of patient care would be compromised.

> (b) The guide dog of a blind student is accidentally killed by another student. The blind student requests that the university locate another guide dog for him. The special services department is unable to locate a suitable replacement and advises the student that he should take full responsibility for finding another dog. The student files a complaint against the university alleging that he is unable to benefit from the services and programs offered without a guide dog.

These two examples illustrate circumstances under which recipients are not required to provide auxiliary aids and academic adjustments, *i.e.,* when the academic adjustments would alter the essential nature of the program (see *Southeastern Community College v. Davis, supra*), and when the aids requested are of a personal nature.[18] In the first example, clearly the adjustments suggested would subvert the purpose of clinical training, *i.e.,* teaching students to function competently on their own as professionals. Further, the student's inability to deal with stress as well as handle complex cases would put patients at risk in the clinical setting. Thus, the student was not a qualified handicapped person with respect to the clinical program.

Regarding the guide dog, the recipient's responsibility to make its programs and services available to and usable by the general population of handicapped individuals certainly should not require it to provide such individualized services.

> A learning-disabled student, whose impairment poses difficulties with respect to meeting the university's foreign language requirement, requests that the eight-credit-hour requirement be waived. She argues that she intends to major in computer science, and, therefore, proficiency in foreign languages is not essential to her academic future and success. The university counters that completion of the foreign language requirement is a necessary part of the educational program. It is felt that knowledge of foreign languages is an essential part of the undergraduate program. The institution offers to extend the period during which the language reuqirement must be satisfied from two years to four years. Further, special computer languages, as well as tutoring, are offered to the student. Does the university have to waive the foreign language requirement? What if the student avails herself of the special assistance offered, takes five foreign language courses and is still unable to satisfy the foreign language requirement?

The question of whether educational institutions may be required to waive academic criteria or requirements is ripe for judicial review. To date, the question of determining the appropriateness of special criteria and requirements has been considered the province of educators, and both the OCR and the courts have largely taken a hands-off approach. Waiver of a necessary or essential requirement has been held to be the type of "substantial modification" which institutions are not required to make. See *Southeastern Community College v. Davis, supra, Doherty v. Southern College of Optometry, supra,* and *Pandazides v. Virginia Board of Education,* 752 F. Supp. 696 (E.D. Va. 1990). The difficulty arises in trying to determine whether a requirement is "necessary" or "essential." It is unclear how the situation will be resolved where the student attempts all of the alternative approaches and is still unsuccessful. The problem is that there is a reluctance to approve actions that will lead to a charge that handicapped students are receiving preferential treatment. It has yet to be clearly determined under what circumstances, if any, handicapped students may be exempted from requirements or criteria that other students must meet. The same problem arises regarding course substitutions.

Beyond the understandable substitution suggested in Appendix A (music history for music appreciation to accommodate a deaf student),[19] course substitutions involving advanced degree programs or technical, scientific, or clinical courses raise difficult questions regarding the appropriateness of substitution. Generally, the courts and the OCR have deferred to the judgment of educators with respect to such issues.[20] The one question which does appear to be answered is whether it is appropriate to request a waiver or exemption where alternative approaches to meeting the criteria or requirement have neither been suggested nor attempted. Neither the OCR nor the courts have responded favorably to the requests of handicapped individuals under those circumstances. In *Crancer v. Board of Regents of the University of Michigan,* the Court rejected the argument of a doctoral candidate who had a post-traumatic stress disorder that the program should establish special admissions criteria for her.[21] Thus, handicapped individuals are advised to make a good-faith effort to utilize any and all alternative approaches that are available.

> (a) The university has a policy which limits the provision of auxiliary aids to those in degree-granting programs. (*Board of Trustees of the University of Alabama*).
> (b) Jim, a blind student, challenges the college's prohibition against guide dogs in clinical settings.
> (c) Professor Jones enforces an attendance policy for his classes. Students are only allowed four absences a semester. If they exceed that number, they fail the course. Mary is involved in a car accident and misses six classes because of her injuries. Professor Jones refuses to accommodate Mary despite the fact that she has a legitimate excuse for the absences.

Section 104.44(b) prohibits the enforcement of rules that "have the effect of limiting the participation of handicapped students." In *United States v. Board of Trustees of the University of Alabama,* the Court found that the university's policy of restricting the provision of auxiliary aids to "regular students" violated Section 504 and the implementing regulations. The university impermissibly sought to limit its responsibility by denying services to students not enrolled in degree-granting, or certificate-earning, programs. Further, § 104.44(b) specifically precludes the prohibition "of dog guides in campus buildings." The OCR has found recipients in violation that implement policies such as Professor Jones', which illegally penalized students with disabilities. In a recent case, the OCR found that a district's policy, which denied students with more than 14 absences (excused or unexcused) credit for couse work, had "the potential effect of denying students . . . with disabilities . . . the educational benefits to which they might be entitled."[22]

The problems and the difficulties in this area, however, are not limited to questions of whether academic adjustments should be provided. Many additional issues are generated by the problem of balancing the rights of faculty members, the responsibilities of students, and the role of the institution (as both the protector of the students' rights under § 104.44 and as the mediator between the two groups). Further, there are questions regarding the cost and nature of the academic adjustments provided.

Responsibilities: Recipients versus Students

When does the obligation to provide academic adjustments arise, and what is the student's involvement in the process? The goal of the statute and regulations is to eliminate the consideration of handicaps and their impact except in situations where there is a direct bearing on the delivery of services and benefits or on the right to receive such services and benefits. Thus, the recipient may not raise the issue unless it has a compelling reason to do so. In the case of a student who has been admitted and who may need academic adjustments, generally the issue must be student initiated. Once the student advises the recipient of his or her needs, the recipient "may make inquiries on a confidential basis."[23] Thus, both the student and the recipient have responsibilities. Recipients are not required, and, indeed, are not permitted, to unilaterally assess the needs of students and address them in the absence of some action or request on the part of the student. But what form must this action or request take?

Nathanson v. Medical College of Pennsylvania, supra, is a good illustration of just how complicated the business of competing responsibilities can become. In *Nathanson,* a woman with a back and neck impairment was granted admission to the Medical College of Pennsylvania (MCP). Although she denied the need for any accommodations during her preadmissions interview, she experienced serious back and neck pain once she started classes. She attributed the pain, in large part, to the seating arrangements in the classrooms. She requested and was granted a leave of absence, citing the pain she had experienced in trying to take notes for six to seven hours a day. She did not ask for accommodation at that time, but rather stated that she felt that her physical condition would improve during the year, and that she would also investigate the possible modifications that could be made to reduce the physical strain during classes. Over the course of the following year the student discussed her physical problems with school officials and advised them that she needed special seating arrangements. However, she also advised them that she, herself, was taking the responsibility of obtaining a special chair. She further stated to them that her physical problems would prevent her from attending the school unless she could be accommodated. School officials contend that the student never directly requested specific accommodations. The Court of Appeals held, in pertinent part:

> In order to be liable under the Rehabilitation Act, MCP must know or be reasonably expected to know of Nathanson's handicap. Neither the Rehabilitation Act nor the regulations specify what notification is necessary to adequately inform a recipient of a person's handicap or what constitutes awareness of a handicap.[24]

Further, the court rejected the district court's finding that the student had not made a "sufficiently direct and specific request for special accommodation" by noting that this fact would be relevant only if the school "neither knew nor had reason to know that Nathanson was handicapped."[25]

Thus, the recipient is not required to read the student's mind and make assumptions regarding his or her needs, and the student is not required to say any "specific" words or phrases to trigger the recipient's obligation. The obligation arises from the knowledge that the need for assistance exists.[26] Compliance inquiries turn on the question of whether it would be reasonable, under the circumstances, to hold the recipient accountable for failure to provide academic adjustments. For example, if a student informs only one of her professors that she needs academic adjustments, it would not be legitimate to find the university in violation if the professors in her other classes failed to accommodate her needs. A student who informs his professors of his impairment, but does not request academic adjustments, also is not entitled to academic adjustments. Similarly, if a student failed to request academic adjustments until the day a test was scheduled or a paper was due, the recipient would not be responsible for making an immediate adjustment. Further, it is not acceptable for the student to assert that the disability was so obvious that the institution should have known that he or she would require academic adjustments.

> *Caveat:* In the situation where the student waits until the day the test is given or the paper is due, while it would be permissible to deny academic adjustments at that time, such adjustments should be provided in the future, if appropriate. From that point on, the recipient has knowledge of the student's needs.

> Jane, who has been classified as a learning-disabled student throughout her high school career, enrolls in the state university and requests auxiliary aids based upon her secondary school classification. The university denies her initial request because it is felt that evidence showing merely that she has been classified as a learning-disabled student is insufficient to justify the provision of auxiliary aids. University personnel suggest that Jane provide further documentation of her impairment by obtaining an updated evaluation from her personal physician, from the university's student services department at a cost of $150.00, or from the local vocational rehabilitation agency. Must Jane provide the requested documentation?

The recipient's obligation to provide academic adjustments does not arise until the student provides adequate documentation of his or her condition. The documentation must be sufficient to permit the recipient to understand the nature of the impairment and provide enough information to allow a determination to be made regarding what academic adjustments, if any, are necessary. The recipient has the right to seek more information from the student and must be given "sufficient time and opportunity to investigate."[27]

While the OCR will not substitute its judgment for the academic judgment of educators in these matters, the recipient's actions must be reasonable. Thus, while it may be legitimate to require additional documentation from a student in Jane's situation, it may not be legitimate to ask a student with obvious mobility impairment—e.g., a student in a wheelchair who requests assignment to classes on the first floor—to provide such additional documentation. The reasonableness of the recipient's position might also be questioned if the student provides detailed updated information regarding the impairment, and the recipient continues to request additional documentation. If the student has provided documentation that adequately describes the nature of the impairment and the extent of his or her academic needs, then the recipient must assume full responsibility, including financial responsibility, for obtaining additional documentation. Furthermore, a recipient could be found in violation of the regulations if the OCR determines that the continued request for documentation, coupled with the refusal to provide requested auxiliary aids, resulted in the handicapped student being denied equal opportunities on the basis of the handicap.

If the recipient determines that it is not necessary to provide a requested auxiliary aid, the OCR will usually defer to its academic judgment. However, that judgment must be reasonable. For example, a recipient's determination that a student with a hearing impairment does not need a note-taker in an art class where the students primarily work on their own individual projects may be considered appropriate, whereas the denial of a note-taker in a content course, such as art history, would be questionable. Further, a recipient may cease to provide certain accommodations under some circumstances. If, for example, a student requested interpreter services but regularly failed to attend classes at which the services were provided, the institution would be justified in refusing to continue to provide services that the student was not using. It would be an undue hardship to require otherwise. However, the recipient should avoid terminating all services to the student, and instead provide alternative accommodations. In the example above, it might choose to provide note-takers to the student until he or she demonstrated that the interpreter services would be used appropriately. Further, it is advisable that such actions not be taken in the absence of a clear policy of which both students and staff have been apprised. The institution should also document its prior discussions with, and warnings to, the student regarding terminating the accommodations. *Remember*—actions taken may not impose additional requirements on disabled students. If, for example, the college has no attendance requirement, it cannot impose such a requirement on disabled students to address the problem of paying for interpreter services when students choose not to attend classes.

> A university's student handout book contains a statement that advises students who may need academic adjustments or auxiliary aids to contact either the Section 504 coordinator or the disabled student services office. Tom's mother calls the 504 coordinator and advises him that her son has a learning disability and requests that an individualized educational plan (IEP) be developed to accommodate his needs. The coordinator tells Tom's mother that the university does not develop IEPs for students, but that Tom should visit the disabled student services office, provide documentation regarding his impairment, and that they would assist him in acquiring the necessary academic adjustments and auxiliary aids. Tom's mother calls that office and describes his impairment and his needs. She is advised to have Tom come to the office for assistance, but Tom never contacts the office. His mother asserts that his failing grades are a result of the university's failure to accommodate his needs.

While the recipient is responsible for providing information to students regarding its duty to provide auxiliary aids and academic adjustments and regarding the persons to contact to receive such, it has no obligation to accommodate needs that have not been brought to its attention or to provide accommodations that have not been requested. Unlike the responsibilities placed upon recipients in the elementary and secondary arena, postsecondary institutions are not required to locate, identify, and unilaterally develop plans to address the educational needs of handicapped students. Therefore, postsecondary institutions do not develop IEPs for handicapped students. On the postsecondary level, the student must make a *reasonable* request for assistance before the recipient has an obligation to act. Thus, although Tom's mother informed several persons of his handicap, Tom himself, the individual for whom academic adjustments would be made, neither informed the institution nor requested assistance. Under the circumstances, it would not be reasonable to hold the university responsible for Tom's lack of success.

> Two handicapped students file a complaint with the 504 coordinator because service providers, e.g., readers, are not available at all times in the college library. Kathy, a blind student, states that she has been at the library on three occasions when readers were scheduled to be on duty, but were not available. She proposes that readers should be available at all times or the college should provide a braille library. She argues that handicapped students should not be subjected to the whims of student employees. Jim complains that there are not enough employees available to retrieve books for the physically handicapped. He reports that he often has to wait 30 to 45 minutes for assistance. The library director states that the system that is used is acceptable. She argues that the schedule for readers is generally followed, but on the three occasions in question the readers had called in sick. She says that no other blind students have complained about the system. Regarding Jim's problem, she agrees to instruct the student employees to respond more quickly, but notes that the primary problem is that there are insufficient funds to hire the additional student employees.

Recipients may choose the manner in which they accommodate the needs of handicapped students. The question of compliance with the regulations will not arise so long as the methods chosen are effective. In the fact situation described above, the college's methods were not effective; Kathy was often without a reader, and Jim had to wait an unreasonable amount of time for assistance. However, these deficiencies could be corrected by simply having readers on call on those occasions when an employee calls in sick, and by arranging job responsibilities so that there are employees whose primary duty would be to assist handicapped students. The college does not have to either provide a braille library or staff readers full time as Kathy suggsted. "As long as no handicapped person is excluded from a program because of the lack of an appropriate aid, the recipient need not have all such aids on hand at all times."[28]

> Skinflint University has a policy that limits the provision of auxiliary aids to blind and deaf students to tape recorders and transcriptions, note-takers, and student readers. For other types of assistance, such as interpreters and braille or taped texts, students are instructed to contact vocational rehabilitation agencies and charitable organizations. If those entities cannot provide the requested aids, the students are advised that they must assume financial responsibility for the aids themselves. In addition, the university applies a financial means test with respect to the auxiliary aids it does provide. Based upon a financial assessment, students are required to assume financial responsibility for a portion of the expense of the auxiliary aids provided.

The question of who must assume the ultimate responsibility for the provision of auxiliary aids has not been fully resolved. The drafters of the regulations presumed that outside agencies would relieve educational institutions of much of the financial burden.

> The Department emphasizes that recipients can usually meet this obligation by assisting students in using existing resources for auxiliary aids such as state vocational rehabilitation agencies and private charitable organizations. Indeed, the Department anticipates that the bulk of auxiliary aids will be paid for by state and private agencies, not by the college or university.[29]

This presumption left unanswered the question of what would happen if outside agencies could not provide for the auxiliary aids. The OCR has answered this question by asserting that the recipient is ultimately financially responsible for the provision of auxiliary aids.[30] While the Supreme Court has not directly addressed the issue, other federal courts have also held the recipient to be responsible.[31] Most recently, in the *United States of America v. Board of Trustees of the University of Alabama, supra,* the District Court specifically adopted the OCR's interpretation of the regulations and ruled that the university's policy of applying a "financial means

test" to the provision of auxiliary aids violated Section 504 and its implementing regulations. The present interpretation of the regulations precludes
any policy that requires students to assume direct personal financial responsibility for necessary aids absent a showing of an undue administration or
financial burden. This would include requiring students to use student loan
programs to pay for the aids.

Course Examinations

Examinations and evaluations must be administered in such a way that
qualified handicapped students are not disadvantaged. Recipients must ensure that

> [T]he results of the evaluation represent the student's achievement . . .
> rather than reflecting the student's impaired sensory, manual, or speaking
> skills (except where such skills are the factors the test purports to measure).[32]

It is important to keep in mind that § 104.44(c) is in no way intended to interfere with a recipient's right to properly evaluate students. However, as
Wynne v. Tufts University, supra, reflects, the line between effective accommodation and tampering with the academic standards and integrity of an institution is often tenuous at best. In that case, a medical student with a learning disability requested that he be given his examinations orally rather than
in the multiple-choice format that was normally used. The school denied his
request, asserting that the test format was an integral part of the instructional
program for doctors and to change it would be a fundamental alteration of
the educational program. The ultimate resolution of this case will hopefully
provide a useful yardstick in assessing a recipient's rights and responsibilities
in this area. Currently, the established rule appears to be that the recipient
must present clear and convincing evidence that there was no "reasonable
accommodation . . . which meets the [student's] special needs without
sacrificing the integrity of the . . . program."[33]

> Applicants to a vocational technical school are required to have an accep-
> table score on English and math proficiency tests in order to be admitted to
> the program of their choice. Those applicants not scoring acceptable scores
> are placed in developmental studies. Susan, a visually-impaired student, re-
> quests that alternative tests in bold print be provided. The school rejects her
> suggestion as an unnecessary expense, and, instead, assigns a secretary to
> act as a reader for Susan. Susan agrees to take the exam under those cir-
> cumstances, but subsequently charges that the secretary was a poor reader,
> and that the exam results do not adequately measure her abilities.

While, as noted above, the academic adjustments or auxiliary aids provided need not be the specific ones requested by the handicapped person,

they must provide "meaningful access." [See *Stutts v. Freeman*, 694 F.2d 666 (11th Cir. 1983).] If the exam scores are the sole criteria by which the applicants are judged, handicapped persons must have the same opportunity to excel on those exams as nonhandicapped persons. Recipients must make a good-faith effort to provide accommodations which are, in fact, effective.

> Dr. Glenn has a reputation for being a very demanding instructor. Betty, a learning-disabled student, enrolls in his advanced philosophy course. The teaching method used is primarily discussion and dialogue between the instructor and the students. The students are also required to write four one-page papers. Despite the difficulty she has with reading comprehension, Betty has a B plus going into the final exam. She requests that she be permitted to use a reader or be given two hours extra to take the test because of her problem with reading comprehension. Dr. Glenn rejects the request for a reader but agrees to provide Betty one hour extra on the test. He feels that providing her more than one hour would disadvantage the other students in the class, since philosophy involves testing students' ability to reason, and a student would gain an enormous advantage by having additional time to think about the problems presented. Betty voices her concern that the extra time provided is insufficient, but takes the test under those circumstances. She receives a C on the test because, while the answers to the question she completed were above average, she has insufficient time to answer the final two questions. Betty appeals her grade, and the grievance committee rule in her favor. Betty argues that she should be graded solely on the four questions she completed and that the remaining two should be disregarded. She feels it is unfair to make her retake the test, since her failure to complete it resulted from discrimination. The committee rules that Betty should be given an hour to complete the final two questions, her grade to be based upon the complete exam.

The circumstances under which Betty was tested did not "ensure that the results of the evaluation represented [her] achievement in the course, rather than reflecting [her] impaired sensory . . . skills." Therefore, the recipient violated § 104.44(c) of the implementing regulation. While recipients need not guarantee handicapped students results similar to those of their non-handicapped counterparts, they must provide the accommodations to put them on an equal footing. Betty was at a disadvantage because, due to her handicap, she did not have an adequate amount of time to complete the test. However, Betty's solution to the problem is equally unacceptable. Allowing her to be graded on only four of the six questions shifts the unfair advantage to her corner.

It is also important to remember that grading is not an academic adjustment. Generally, recipients will not be required to alter the method or manner in which students are graded. If a student argues that grading was unfair or discriminatory, in the absence of evidence that the evaluation process impermissibly discriminated against handicapped persons, the appropriate inquiries would be whether the student is a qualified handicapped person with respect to the program in question, and whether appropriate academic adjustments were made. The primary focus would not be on the grading method or the grade the student received.

The Rights and Responsibilities of Faculty Members

The question of the rights and responsibilities that individual faculty members have regarding the provision of accommodations to disabled students has generally not been clearly answered by postsecondary institutions. The procedures implemented at many institutions require that students identify their handicap or disability to the Disabled Student Services Office, which has the responsibility of documenting the existence of the disability and determining what accommodations are appropriate. Students are then instructed to contact their professors, and to identify their needs and request the necessary accommodations. When the request is made to the faculty member, does he or she have any choice in the provision of the accommodations? Unfortunately, under the above-described procedures faculty members are essentially relegated to a nonparticipatory role regarding matters of uppermost importance to them: the nature of how they conduct their classes, and their relationship with students. Reportedly, faculty members have indicated their displeasure with such procedures (a) by challenging the Disabled Student Services Office's assessment regarding the existence of a disability or the need for accommodations, or both; (b) by refusing to assist students in arranging the accommodations; and (c) by demanding that they be permitted to review the documentary evidence regarding the student's disability. Of course, the result of such hostile responses by faculty members is that disabled students are denied effective accommodation. The problem is further compounded when the procedures fail to identify an individual or group responsible for addressing and resolving disagreements between individual faculty members and the Disabled Student Services Office; the student is trapped between them, attempting to act as a mediator.

The case of *Campbell A. Dinsmore v. Charles C. Pugh and the Regents of the University of California* (1989)[34] is an extreme example of this unfortunate standoff. In this case, a faculty member adamantly refused to provide a dyslexic student with a requested accommodation, specifically additional time on a test. The professor contested the very existence of the disability. Despite repeated attempts by the Disabled Student Services Office, administrators, and university counsel to resolve the matter, the professor continued to refuse to provide the accommodation. The student had no alternative but to file suit against the university and the faculty member. The settlement of the case required the university to develop a policy for accommodating the needs of students with disabilities, and the faculty member was required to pay monetary damages. The experience of the University of California at Berkeley is instructive in two respects: postsecondary institutions must develop and properly implement clear policies and procedures for providing accommodations to disabled students; moreover, individual faculty members can and will be held accountable for blatant discriminatory actions that deny students their rights.

It is important that the policy developed directly address the question of faculty participation. It should clearly convey to faculty members that they do not have the right to contest the existence of disabilities that have been properly documented, nor do they have the right to refuse to provide necessary accommodations. However, faculty should be provided the opportunity to participate in the decision-making regarding the types and range of accommodations that will be provided, as they relate to classroom instruction. The message should be that accommodations must be provided for properly documented disabilities, but all parties, that is, students, representatives of the Disabled Student Services Office, and faculty members, should work together to fashion effective accommodations that provide students "meaningful access" while maintaining the academic integrity of the instructional program.

The policy developed at Berkeley is an excellent example of this. It provides, in pertinent part, that (a) faculty members and Disabled Student Services (DSS) staff work together to resolve disagreements regarding the accommodations that are recommended; (b) faculty members are obligated to provide requested accommodations until the controversy is resolved; and (c) an Academic Accommodations Policy Board, which includes faculty members, has responsibility for advising faculty and administrators regarding academic accommodations for students and assisting in resolving disagreements between DSS staff and individual faculty members.[35]

Part VI: Employment

No standard for determining the reasonableness of an accommodation has been formulated.
—Dexler v. Tisch, 660 F. Supp. 1418, 1426
(D. Conn. 1987)

To date, the compliance efforts in the educational arena have primarily focused on delivery of services to students. With the recent passage of the Americans with Disabilities Act (ADA), it is predicted that the emphasis will shift to employment issues and concerns. Therefore, recipients must begin to refamiliarize themselves with the compliance standards under Section 504 because the majority of the complaints and questions that will arise pursuant to the ADA will be more appropriately handled under Section 504.

24
Meaningful Access

What does the duty to provide "meaningful access" require with respect to a recipient's employment practices? Section 104.11 provides, in pertinent part:

> (1) No qualified handicapped person shall on the basis of handicap be subjected to discrimination in employment under any program or activity to which this part applies. . . . (3) A recipient shall make all decisions concerning employment under any program or activity to which this part applies in a manner which ensures that discrimination on the basis of handicap does not occur and may not limit, segregate, or classify applicants or employees in any way that adversely affects their opportunities or status because of handicaps.

Further, § 104.11(b) provides that all terms, conditions, or privileges of employment are covered under the regulations.[1] It is also important to note that "Section 504 covers employment discrimination even in programs that receive federal aid with a primary objective other than employment."[2] From reading the general provision of § 104.11, we can say with certainty only that all terms and conditions of employment are covered under Subpart B and only qualified handicapped persons are entitled to protection.[3]

> The director of a scientific laboratory advises the six research assistants on staff that she plans to hire a coordinator to supervise the work of the assistants. The minimum qualifications for the job include an undergraduate science degree, supervisory experience, and a minimum of three years' experience as a research assistant. Dirk, one of the research assistants, applies for the job. He has no supervisory experience, and only two years' experience as an assistant. He has cerebral palsy and advises the director that because of his physical condition he would need a secretary to assist him with the clerical tasks if hired for the position. The director tells Dirk that she had not anticipated hiring a secretary and is not sure there is sufficient money in the budget to do so. Another of the assistants, who meets the minimum qualifications, is offered the job. Dirk questions whether he was not offered the job because the director did not want to hire a secretary to assist him.

The question of whether the coordinator's actions are discriminatory does not arise, because Dirk is not a "qualified handicapped person." His failure to meet the minimum requirements of the job, supervisory experience and employment for three years as an assistant, precludes his being considered for the position.[4]

However, once we get past the "qualified handicapped person" condition, the exact parameters of the antidiscrimination prohibition are not so clear-cut. It is helpful to begin our exploration by reviewing those principles that further refine or limit the antidiscrimination mandate. They concern the right of the recipient to consider an individual's handicap in making employment decisions and the distinction between "evenhanded treatment" and "preferential treatment."[5]

> Betty has worked for the state vocational rehabilitation department for ten years. She has a mental impairment. Her symptoms include anxiety, depression, and mild hallucinations. Her job performance has been rated as excellent during the ten-year period. In her eleventh year, Betty's condition worsens. She becomes acutely depressed and suicidal. Her immediate supervisor, becoming alarmed at her inability to cope with the normal job requirements, seeks guidance from Betty's attending physician. Based upon the physician's recommendations, Betty is allowed to reduce her hours to 30 a week and is relieved of much of the detailed paperwork the job requires. Shortly after she begins working on the revised schedule, a supervisory position that Betty desires becomes available. Betty is denied the position. The hiring official admits that, but for her handicap, Betty is the applicant most qualified for the job.

Recipients are not precluded from considering an individual's handicap in making employment decisions. As noted by the Supreme Court in *Southeastern Community College v. Davis*, "Section 504 does not compel [recipients] to disregard the disabilities of handicapped individuals."[6] Since Betty's employer reached a decision by comparing the actual limitations imposed by her condition with the requirements of the job, the denial does not violate Section 504. *Remember*—"The Rehabilitation Act forbids discrimination based on stereotypes about a handicap, but it does not forbid decisions based on the actual attributes of the handicap."[7]

> Perfect Corporation has a policy which requires that all employees seeking a raise must successfully complete an in-service training course. The course is offered twice a year, in June and December. Brad is absent from work in December while in a drug treatment center. When he returns to work in January, Brad requests that he either receive his raise or that the company arrange a special training session for him. He asserts that to require him to wait until June discriminates against him solely on the basis of his handicap. The company provides evidence that no employee has been given a raise without completing the course, and that all employees who have missed

a training session are required to wait until the next time the course is given.

The existence of a handicap does not entitle one to preferential treatment. Brad is treated the same as all similarly situated nonhandicapped employees; *i.e.*, those who miss the course must wait until the next time it is given. Regarding his request for an immediate raise, one will not be permitted to use the fact of being handicapped to gain exemption from a legitimate job requirement.[8]

While the above discussed principles provide some clarification regarding the recipient's responsibilities under § 104.11, the question of what actions constitute unlawful discrimination still has not been adequately answered. Consider the plight of Wanda.

> Wanda applies for two jobs with the State Department of Education. She is a diabetic and is required to take insulin. Although her condition is poorly controlled—she has frequent bouts of hypoglycemic reactions—she does not disclose this fact. The first job she applies for is as a cafeteria worker. She makes the qualified list, but once the hiring official learns she is a diabetic, she is eliminated from consideration. He feels this action is justified because heavy and dangerous equipment is used by his staff, and he fears that she will injure herself or others if she has such a reaction.
>
> The second job she applies for is a bus driver's position. When the transportation supervisor learns of her condition, he requests further information, including a statement from her personal physician. Her physician provides the information that her condition is poorly controlled and that there is a danger of losing consciousness during a bout of hypoglycemia. On the basis of this information, it is determined that it is not safe for someone with her condition to drive a school bus. Wanda believes that the denial of both jobs is illegal discrimination on the basis of her handicap.

It is often difficult to distinguish between employment decisions that are discriminatory and those that represent a legitimate exercise of the administrative prerogatives of employers. The difficulty arises, in part, because most employment decisions are based as much upon subjective factors and considerations as they are upon objective criteria and standards. Thus, the task of discerning whether a recipient's denial of an employment opportunity to a handicapped individual is an impermissible denial of "meaningful access" becomes troublesome for all parties involved. While recipients have every right to base their employment decisions on legitimate subjective factors, the federal enforcement agency has a responsibility to more closely scrutinize decisions and actions that are not supported by objective standards or criteria and that result in a denial of employment opportunities to handicapped individuals.

Recipients can greatly reduce the possibility of outside interference with their employment practices by ensuring that all decisions and actions that might result in the denial of opportunities to handicapped persons are analyzed using the following checklist:

1. Is it legitimate to consider the individual's handicap/disability; *i.e.,* does it have an impact on the performance of the essential functions of the job?
2. Are the criteria and standards that were used to assess the individual's skills and abilities rationally related to job performance?
3. Have all relevant factors been considered in reaching the determination that no reasonable accommodation is possible?
4. Is there sufficient documentary evidence to support the decision made or the action taken?

The two cases discussed below illustrate the importance of asking and answering the above questions in reviewing employment decisions.

In *Crane v. Lewis,* a former air traffic controller, who had received a disability retirement because his hearing impairment prevented him from meeting the Federal Aviation Administration's hearing requirements, applied for a position as an aeronautical information specialist (AIS) for which there was neither a specific hearing requirement nor a hearing test mandated by the FAA.[9] There was merely a general requirement that the employees be able to hear the conversational voice, with or without a hearing aid. Mr. Crane used a hearing aid. The essential functions of the job were to receive, process, verify, and disseminate information related to federal aviation. A significant part of the job involved telephone communication. Mr. Crane was denied employment because his hearing loss had resulted in his being medically retired from his previous position as an air traffic controller. Despite the fact that he presented medical evidence that he could perform the duties of an AIS, FAA officials concluded that Mr. Crane was not medically qualified. The court rejected the agency's determination because the responsible officials

a. had no authority to impose such a medical requirement;
b. had no knowledge of the extent of Mr. Crane's hearing loss and made no inquiries regarding his ability to communicate using the telephone;
c. did not make a determination regarding whether his hearing loss would preclude him from performing the essential functions of the job in question;
d. did not consider whether there was a reasonable accommodation that would permit him to perform the essential functions; and
e. were arbitrary and capricious in their refusal to consider the medical evidence that Mr. Crane submitted.[10]

In this instance the employer simply based its decision on the existence of a hearing impairment and drew "conclusions about [Mr. Crane's] ability to do the job without ascertaining the relevant facts."[11]

The second case involves an individual with achondroplastic dwarfism who applied for a position as a distribution clerk for the U.S. Postal Service.[12] Dexler was four feet five inches tall. He had significant work experience in commercial mailrooms. The position would require him to unload mail trucks, transport mail in large carriers to various work stations, and sort mail. Despite the fact that his shortness limited his ability to perform the job, it was suggested that either the job could be restructured for Dexler, or that he could perform his duties standing on a stool. The employer concluded that Dexler was unable to perform the essential functions of the job, and that there was no accommodation possible that would not require restructuring of the entire operation, or negatively impact the productivity and efficiency of the operation, or create legitimate safety concerns. The employer presented evidence that Dexler could not assist in unloading trucks, that most of the mail carriers were too large for him to operate efficiently and safely, and that the stool would be a hazard to both Dexler and other employees because of all the movement of mail carriers around it, which those pushing the carriers would be unable to see. It was also noted that the station had to process 150,000 to 250,000 pieces of mail in four-hour periods, a task that required rapid productivity and high efficiency.[13] The Court concurred with the Postal Service's assessment of Dexler's abilities and agreed that, given the nature of the operation, accommodating him would be an undue hardship because it created a significant safety risk and would substantially lower efficiency.[14]

These two cases reflect, respectively, the improper and the proper way to make employment decisions. Applying the analytic approach used in these caes to the hypothetical involving Wanda, one concludes that the employment decision of the transportation supervisor was appropriate, while that of the cafeteria supervisor violated Section 504. The transportation supervisor's decision was based upon an assessment of the manifestations of Wanda's impairment in conjunction with the essential requirements of the job, the application of a criterion—the ability to drive a bus safely—that was rationally related to the job in question, and a consideration of all relevant information, including statements of her physician.[15] Conversely, her rejection for the cafeteria job was based upon an impermissible categorical rejection of diabetics as a class. This approach violates Section 504 because "the condition of diabetes constituted an absolute bar to the application for employment" and, thus, diabetics whose conditions are adequately controlled by medication and who are arguably qualified are disqualified along with those whose conditions preclude performance of the essential functions of the job.[16]

Examples of discriminatory actions that are prohibited:

a. Mary, a teacher with excellent credentials, applies for a position at Nicke Institute, a school for children with emotional/psychological problems. She is interviewed and receives a job offer, conditioned upon favorable references. Although Mary receives glowing recommendations, the personnel director is informed that, five years previously, Mary had suffered an emotional breakdown that required treatment. On the basis of this information the offer of employment to Mary is rescinded. Mary offers to present evidence from her physician to show that she has totally recovered. The director refuses, citing the institute's policy of not hiring individuals with a history of mental impairments. The director argues that the policy is justified because the job is stressful and that individuals with a history of mental illness are likely to be prone to health impairments associated with stress.

b. Joe requests a two-months leave of absence. The company he works for has a policy of permitting employees, such as Joe, who have a tenure of ten years or more to take an extended leave of absence. In practice, such requests have been honored unless the work load of the company makes it impossible. Joe's supervisor is aware that he wants the leave to enter an alcoholism treatment center. He denies Joe's request although it is the slow season and the work load is abnormally low.

c. A mobility-impaired college professor is denied access to the second floor of the science building. While his department has assigned him an assistant to perform tasks that necessitate going to the second floor, the professor is denied the opportunity to participate in meetings with his colleagues whose offices are located on the second floor of the building.

d. Abacus University has a policy that requires newly appointed deans to attend a 40-hour supervisory training course during their first year. The course is held at a retreat 250 miles from campus. Dean Gray, who is visually impaired, was appointed as dean of the School of Education three years ago and has never been asked to attend the training. When she asks about it, the Provost simply says it won't be necessary for her to take the course.

e. Superintendent Franks, as part of a trip to Washington, D.C., has scheduled a series of recruiting visits to the universities in the area because his school district will be needing 30 new teachers in the fall. He does not schedule a trip to Gallaudet University, the university for hearing-impaired students, because the district does not need any teachers for its hearing-impaired classes.

f. A handicapped teacher who taught as a substitute for a district for more than three years has been repeatedly denied a full-time position despite the excellent evaluations she has received for her substitute work.

When finally offered a full-time position, she is not offered a permanent contract. All other new teachers, including those with less experience than she, are offered permanent contracts. Further, despite her physical disabilities, she is given a job assignment that requires considerable lifting. In addition to assigning her to a physically demanding task, the district fails to provide her with a necessary teaching assistant. Finally, when her physical condition deteriorates to the point that she can no longer do the lifting, district officials refuse to transfer her to an assignment less physically demanding. (*Recanzone* v. *Washoe County School District*, supra.)

Employment decisions that are made solely on the basis of the presence of a handicapping condition, without regard to either the individual abilities of the handicapped person or the criteria/standards in question, are suspect. Further, discrimination against qualified handicapped individuals will not be permitted on the basis of remote possibilities, such as individuals with a history of mental illness being more prone to stress-related impairments.[17] In addition, handicapped individuals may not be required to accept lesser services or benefits, meet higher standards, or accept employment terms or conditions substantially different from those offered similarly situated nonhandicapped individuals.

Sections 104.11(a)(4) and (c) address the impact of third-party contracts, such as collective bargaining agreements and insurance contracts. A recipient may not use such third-party contracts or relationships to avoid its responsibilities under the Act and the regulations.[18] Thus, for example, if a union insists upon a contract provision requiring that no employee be forced to work with someone who is either HIV positive or has AIDS, the recipient should advise the union that it cannot be a party to contractual arrangements that result in impermissible discrimination against qualified handicapped persons. The proposed contract term would require that adverse action be taken with respect to employment without a determination, on an individual basis, that the employee's impairment posed a significant risk and, thus, rendered him not "qualified."

> *Caveat:* Courts have found, however, that provisions of collective bargaining agreements may be taken into consideration when determining what are reasonable accommodations. In *Daubert* v. *United States Postal Service,* the Court held that "an employer cannot be required to accommodate a handicapped employee by restructuring a job in a manner which would usurp the legitimate rights of other employees in a collective bargaining agreement.[19]

While Section 504 does not require affirmative action, Section 104.11(a)(2) specifically provides that "positive steps" be taken to employ qualified handicapped persons in programs assisted under the EHA.[20] Does this mandate to take positive steps "equal an affirmative action obligation"? Appendix A provides clarification of this phrase by noting, in pertinent part, that

> Congress chose the words "positive steps" instead of "affirmative action" advisedly and did not intend . . . to incorporate the types of activities required under Executive Order 11246 (affirmative action on the basis of race, color, sex, or national origin) or under Sections 501 and 503 of the Rehabilitation Act of 1973.

Appendix A also provides that the obligation to take positive steps "is similar to the nondiscrimination requirement of Section 504, but requires recipients to take additional steps to hire and promote handicapped persons.[21] However, there has been insufficient interpretation of this provision of the regulations to allow one to determine what specific actions fall between nondiscrimination and affirmative action.[22] One could argue that while a school district would not be required to actively recruit handicapped persons for vacancies, should a situation arise where a handicapped applicant is as qualified as other applicants, that individual should be hired.

25
Reasonable Accommodation

Jane falls and injures her back while at work. She is unable to return to work for more than two months. Upon her return she requests that she be allowed to use a straight-back chair and the building elevator, and that she also be permitted to take regular breaks. She submits a doctor's statement that reports that her condition is aggravated by long periods of sitting or standing and by climbing stairs. Her employer ignores her request for accommodation; she is unable to perform, and her employment is subsequently terminated. Her employer argues that he is not required to employ someone who can no longer perform the essential functions of the job.[1]

A deaf person applies for a lab technician's position in a research facility. She meets or exceeds all the qualifications for the position. The administrator recognizes, however, that in order to perform in the position, the applicant would need a highly qualified (and, therefore, expensive) interpreter well versed in the jargon of the field. The administrator concludes that it is preferable to hire an individual who would not require the additional expense of an interpreter. On that basis he decides that the deaf individual is not qualified for the position.

There are some circumstances "where a refusal to modify an existing program might become unreasonable and discriminatory . . . [and] to assure meaningful access, reasonable accommodations . . . may have to be made."[2] The recipient's responsibility does not end once a determination is made that the handicap prevents or limits an individual's abilities to perform the essential functions of the job. The recipient must also determine whether reasonable accommodations can be made. *Remember*—it is a two-part inquiry. Can the handicapped individual perform the essential functions of the job? If not, are there reasonable accommodations that would permit the individual to perform the essential functions? Recipients cannot refuse to consider whether a reasonable accommodation can be made.[3] Section 104.12(d) expressly prohibits denying employment opportunities to qualified handicapped individuals solely on the basis of the need to make reasonable accommodations.

The recipient has the duty to "make reasonable accommodation to the known physical or mental limitations of an otherwise qualified handicapped applicant or employee."[4] *Reasonable accommodation* is another "gray area" phrase. We cannot clearly define it, but we know it when we see it. "No standard for determining the reasonableness of an accommodation has been formulated."[5] While the regulations provide examples of actions that are reasonable accommodations,[6] they as well as the courts generally define the concept by stating what it is not. Specifically,

1. Recipients need not make accommodations that "would impose an undue hardship on the operation of its program."[7]
2. Reasonable accommodations are not "changes," "adjustments," or "modifications" that would be "substantial" or would ". . . constitute fundamental alteration[s]."[8]
3. The issue is whether "accommodating that individual would require either a modification of the essential nature of the program, or impose an undue burden on the recipient."[9]

While these listed "negatives" do not provide a standard for determining the reasonableness of an accommodation, the Supreme Court has provided additional guidance regarding this question. The Court stated that determining what is "reasonable" is really a matter of striking

> a balance between the statutory rights of the handicapped to be integrated into society and the legitimate interest of federal grantees [recipients] in preserving the integrity of their programs.[10]

Further, there are factors that should be considered in determining whether providing an accommodation would impose an undue hardship.[11] However, as noted in Appendix A, "The weight given to each of these factors . . . will vary depending on the facts of the particular situation." For example:

> A small day-care center might not be required to expend more than a nominal sum, such as that necessary to equip a telephone for use by a secretary with impaired hearing, but a large school district might be required to make available a teacher's aide to a blind applicant for a teaching job. Further, it might be considered reasonable to require a state welfare agency to accommodate a deaf employee by providing an interpreter, while it could constitute an undue hardship to impose that requirement on a provider of foster home care services.[12]

Therefore, a proper analysis involves balancing the competing interests and attempting to quantify the degree of hardship involved.

> Cecil, who is employed as a custodian, has an accident at work. Following surgery, his doctor restricts him to light work. Cecil informs his employer that the custodian job is too strenuous for him and requests the assistant

supervisor position in the custodial division, which requires little or no physical labor and is vacant. The employer refuses to give Cecil the assistant supervisor position and advises him to apply for the job as everyone else is required to do. The employer does, however, offer to restructure Cecil's job so that no strenuous physical labor is required. Cecil insists that he be given the assistant supervisor's job.

Brad works as a records clerk and is occasionally required to lift boxes weighing 15 to 20 pounds over his head to store them. He injures his shoulder and is no longer able to raise his left arm above his head. Brad requests that a work study student be hired to assume responsibility for file storage. Instead, his supervisor offers to lower the shelves where the files are stored and provide him with a stool.

Joe applies for a job as a research assistant at a major university. There are positions available on several projects for which Joe is qualified. The project that Joe would most like to work on is a $150,000 federal grant project involving studying the effects of radiation. The job requires preliminary testing of radioactive matter with an instrument Joe is unable to use. Joe has a muscle impairment that does not interfere with his gross motor skills, but limits fine-motor movements that require a great deal of dexterity. While the most important work of the research assistants involves analyzing data and developing new experiments based upon the analysis, tasks which the university feels Joe is uniquely qualified for, approximately 40 percent of the work requires the use of the instrument. Because of Joe's impressive credentials, the university investigates the possibility of acquiring an alternative instrument that would permit him to work on the project. The university advises Joe that there is no alternative instrument available that is capable of performing all of the necessary tests, and declines to offer him a job on the project. Joe recommends that the university modify one of its four machines at a cost of $15,000 or hire a college work study student to perform the tests for him. The university refuses to modify the instrument, because the modified machine could only be used by Joe, thus requiring the other 11 research assistants to share the remaining three machines, and increasing the time needed to complete the project. Hiring a work study student is not cost-efficient, because the work is so specialized that the individual hired would have to have the qualifications to be a research assistant. Therefore, the university would be hiring two research assistants instead of one.

The hypotheticals above present a clear picture of the balancing involved. While the offers of the employers, *i.e.,* restructuring Cecil's job functions and altering Brad's work space, are "reasonable," the requests of the employees and the applicant go beyond what Section 504 and the regulations require. Recipients are not required to reassign the handicapped individual to a new position.[13] They are also not required to hire another employee to perform essentially the same functions as the handicapped individual.[14] In addition, the university would not have to accommodate Joe, because to require it either to spend $15,000 (10 percent of the budget) on an alteration only one of its employees would be able to use, or to hire two research assistants when only one is needed, would certainly "impose an undue hardship on the operation of its program." Our position would be different if the modification to the instrument cost only $100 and involved a removable attachment, thus allowing the other assistants to use the instrument. In that instance, the university's refusal could be viewed as "arbitrary, unreasonable and discriminatory."[15]

Using the Supreme Court's decisions in *Davis* and *Alexander* as a guide, courts determine reasonableness on a case-by-case basis. Therefore, it is helpful to review judicial interpretations to arrive at a working definition.[16] Specifically in the following cases, the courts have found the accommodations to be reasonable:

> *Nelson v. Thornburgh*—providing part-time readers for blind employees by employer with a $300 million operating budget;[17]
>
> *Harrison v. Marsh*—given the overall size of the federal government, e.g., budget, number of employees and number of positions, the failure to offer a handicapped individual an alternative position with less typing violated the regulations;[18]
>
> *Prewitt v. United States Postal Service*—lowering a shelf that the employee could not reach;[19] and
>
> *Recanzone v. Washoe County School District*—transferring an employee to a less physically demanding class.[20]

The following are cases in which courts have found that the requested accommodation would impose undue hardship:

> *Santiago v. Temple University*—individual cannot be accommodated for excessive absenteeism;[21]
>
> *Treadwell v. Alexander*—agency with limited resources and only two to four employees to patrol 150,000 acres would not be required to hire an individual whose condition would necessitate other employees assuming a substantial portion of his duties;[22]
>
> *Dexler v. Tisch*—use of a platform or stool which would present a safety hazard and would have a negative impact on productivity;[23]
>
> *Bruegging v. Burke*—lowering the degree of accuracy necessary for successful performance on the job;[24] and
>
> *Copeland v. Philadelphia Police Department*—reinstatement of an illegal drug user to a police force.[25]

In addition to the recipient's right to refuse to make modifications which would impose an undue hardship, there are other limitations to the duty to accommodate. Specifically:

> An individual who is recovering from coronary bypass surgery applies for a park technician job that requires a minimum of seven hours of walking and standing per day and moderate lifting (15 to 44 pounds). The applicant admits he cannot walk more than one mile a day, and his physician expresses

the opinion that the job is too strenuous for him. When denied the job, the applicant argues that the employer failed to establish that the physical requirements, e.g., walking and standing, were essential requirements of the job. (*Treadwell v. Alexander*, supra.)

A director of nursing takes a medical leave of absence from work during which she is diagnosed as having multiple sclerosis. She is released to return to work with the proviso that she limit the amount of walking and not stand for prolonged periods of time. When she attempts to return to work, she is denied her position on the basis of her physical limitations despite the fact that all of the medical reports available state that she could return to work full time. (*Carter v. Casa Central*, supra.)

The handicapped individual must be able to perform the essential functions of the job. In *Treadwell v. Alexander*, the Court concluded that walking and standing were essential functions of the job of park technicians, and, if the complainant were hired, other employees would have to perform most of his duties. A recipient is not required to accommodate a handicapped individual by eliminating essential functions of the job.[26] It is important to remember, however, that the duties or functions in question must be an "essential" part of the job. In *Carter v. Casa Central*, the Court held that standing and walking were not essential functions of the nursing director's position. Further, an employer's determination that an employee cannot perform the essential functions of the job "must be based on more than 'reflexive reactions' about a handicapped individual's ability to do the job."[27]

Brad, an individual with a mild visual impairment, works as a senior public relations specialist. His job is to answer questions about his employer's programs and services. Often he is required to conduct research to answer the more complex inquiries. Brad's immediate supervisor is concerned because Brad's error rating is significantly higher than what is considered acceptable. The problem is discussed with Brad and he is given in-service training. When his rating does not improve, Brad requests and is provided a reader. His work load is also decreased. At the end of a three-month period when Brad's performance has still not reached a satisfactory level, his supervisor concludes that his problems are not related to his handicapping condition. Therefore, he is reassigned to a junior position where all of his work would be reviewed by a senior specialist. Brad is upset because he will no longer have a reader. Must his employer continue to provide him with a reader?

Recipients are required only to provide accommodations that "overcome the effects of a person's handicap" and permit him or her to perform the essential functions of the job.[28] In the example above, Brad's job performance did not improve with the assistance of the reader. The purpose of the regulatory mandate is to enable the handicapped person to perform the job; thus, a refusal to provide accommodations that do not contribute to the achievement of this purpose is not a violation of Section 504.

A group of handicapped faculty members meet with the Section 504 coordinator and complain that the university is not providing them with adequate accommodations. They request that the coordinator address the following concerns:

a. A professor who is deaf states that the interpreters who are provided for professional conferences are not adequately trained in his specialty, electrical engineering. He states that their lack of expertise prevents him from interacting with his colleagues because much of the technical discussion is either missed or distorted.
b. Dr. Jones requests that a reader of his choice be hired to assist him in place of the college work-study students he has been using. While he concedes that the students have performed well, he finds it disconcerting to have his assistants change every three or four months.
c. A mobility-impaired faculty member complains that his participation on a departmental research project is severely restricted because his movements are limited to the first floor. The other individuals who are working on the project, as well as the lab where the majority of the work is being done, are located on the second floor. He asserts that the hiring of an assistant to run errands for him provides insufficient contact with his colleagues and the project.
d. Professor Meyer, who is unable to do more than a minimal amount of writing because of a severe arthritic condition, states she would prefer a Wang word processor to the IBM system she was provided. She feels the Wang is technically a better system.

The recipient's primary responsibility is to provide effective accommodations. A handicapped individual need not be provided every accommodation requested. A recipient must only provide those that are necessary to enable the individual to perform the essential functions of the job.[29] Thus, while the university does not have to address the personal preferences of Professors Meyer and Jones, it must provide adequately trained interpreters and devise a method to enable the mobility-impaired faculty member to participate directly in the research project.

Mary Jane has worked as a program development specialist for ten years. She has a progressive arthritic condition. Her supervisor becomes alarmed because of her reduced productivity. Mary Jane informs her that she is not performing adequately because she is experiencing difficulty writing. While her supervisor is sympathetic, Mary Jane is advised that she must find a way to improve her performance or face termination. Although they discuss the possibility of Mary Jane using a word processor, Mary Jane does not specifically request accommodation, and her supervisor does not offer it.

Doug is receiving treatment for a mental impairment. One of the

> manifestations of his condition is that he suffers anxiety attacks if he feels any pressure or stress regarding his job performance. His physician recommends that he take a five- or ten-minute break when he starts to feel anxious. Doug does not inform anyone about his condition because he fears he would lose his job. During a three-month period, the work load of Doug's division doubles. Doug copes by taking frequent breaks and on at least four occasions has to leave work because of a severe anxiety attack. When Doug receives his annual evaluation, he is reprimanded for taking frequent breaks and absences. Doug challenges the reprimand as discrimination because his handicap made the breaks and absences necessary.

Recipients are required to make reasonable accommodation to "known physical or mental limitations." They are not required to assess unilaterally the needs of employees and address them in the absence of any action or request on the part of the employee. Both the handicapped individual and the recipient have responsibilities under the Act and the implementing regulations. Doug will not be permitted to make his employer responsible for responding to a need that the employer was not made aware of. As noted by the Court in *Dowden v. Tisch,* an employee "cannot lie in ambush with a hidden handicap and then charge failure to accommodate when he is discharged for other reasons."[30] Conversely, once Mary Jane informs her supervisor of her arthritic condition, her supervisor cannot ignore the problem and make Mary Jane solely responsible for solving it.[31] It is also important to remember that, if a recipient offers a reasonable accommodation to a handicapped individual and the individual chooses not to avail him or herself of that accommodation—or if all attempts to accommodate prove unsuccessful—the recipient has fulfilled its obligation pursuant to Section 104.12 of the regulations.[32]

Further, the mandate to make reasonable accommodations does not require the recipient to ignore the impact the individual's handicap will have on the operation of its program.

> Where a handicapped person is not qualified to perform a particular job, where reasonable accommodation does not overcome the effects of a person's handicap, or where reasonable accommodation causes undue hardship to the employer, failure to hire or promote the handicapped person will not be considered discrimination.[33]

26
Employment Criteria

> The president of a company is presented with a study of its promotion practices that reflects that handicapped employees consistently score below their nonhandicapped counterparts on tests used to rank employees for promotion purposes. A group of handicapped employees demands that the company discontinue using the tests because of the adverse impact on the handicapped employees.

This hypothetical raises the question of what responsibility, if any, does the recipient have regarding the use of tests and other selection criteria. If the criteria used have an adverse impact on handicapped individuals, is the employer prohibited from using them? Section 104.13(a) provides in pertinent part that:

> A recipient may not make use of any employment test or other selection criterion that screens out or tends to screen out handicapped persons or any class of handicapped persons *unless:* (1) The test score or other selection criterion . . . is shown to be *job-related*. . . and (2) alternative job-related tests or criteria that do not screen out or tend to screen out as many . . . are *not shown by the Director to be available* (emphasis added).

Thus, while the mere use of a screening instrument that has an adverse impact on handicapped persons does not alone violate the Act and the implementing regulations, it does trigger the obligation to establish job-relatedness and to consider the availability of alternative selection criteria.

The courts have afforded considerable deference to the employment decisions of recipients.[1] Recipients are presumed to be the most qualified to identify those skills, abilities, and qualities necessary for successful job performance. Therefore, it would appear that handicapped individuals who wish to challenge recipients' decisionmaking must show clearly that the selection criteria used were not legitimately job-related and were, in fact, "unreasonable and discriminatory."[2] The Court's decision in *Crane v. Dole, supra,* provides guidelines useful in determining whether tests or other selection criteria are job-related. In *Crane,* an employer that questioned whether an applicant's hearing impairment would prevent him from performing adequately as an aeronautical information specialist devised a test to assess his ability. The Court, in rejecting the test results used to deny the handicapped applicant a position, found the use of the criterion unacceptable because:

1. The individuals who developed the test had no experience in test development and did not seek the advice of experts.
2. The test was not validated by giving it to a control group to assure that it (a) accurately reflected those skills necessary for performance of the job, and (b) could be passed by employees who were not hearing impaired.
3. While the purpose of testing the applicant was to detemine whether his hearing impairment would adversely affect job performance, the test also tested his ability to take shorthand, which was not an essential function of the job.
4. The test was given under conditions totally unrelated to those the employee would encounter during actual performance of the job.

The selection criteria used must be rationally related to the achievement of the recipient's objectives and cannot be a pretext for discriminating against qualified handicapped individuals. For example:

> Joe applies for a job as a bus driver for a mental health facility. He successfully completes the preliminary screening process and interviews with the transportation director. During the interview, Joe informs the director that he has epilepsy but that it is adequately controlled by medication, and that he hasn't had a seizure in over five years. The director offers Joe a job contingent upon his providing a statement from his physician confirming the status of his epileptic condition. Joe is upset because no other applicant is required to submit a physician's report. He feels he is being discriminated against on the basis of his handicap.
>
> Alice has worked for Insensitive School District for ten years. When the superintendent of the district retires, Alice applies for the position. The job description for the position states that an applicant should have a Ph.D. in education administration and three years' experience as a school administrator. Alice has the necessary terminal degree and was a high school principal for seven years. While the screening committee feels that Alice is the most qualified applicant, questions are raised because she is blind. Several of the committee members wonder whether she could effectively provide the necessary hands-on supervision of the 20 schools in the district. There is concern that the logistical problems involved in traveling from school to school, as well as acclimating herself to so many new surroundings, would severely limit Alice's effectiveness. The committee's uncertainty about Alice's adaptability results in her receiving a lower rating than the nonhandicapped applicants. Alice charges that the committee, in essence, is penalizing her for failing to meet a criterion, *i.e.*, the ability to see, that is not necessary for the successful performance of the job.

These hypotheticals demonstrate that, while recipients are not precluded from requiring individuals to meet legitimate physical qualifications that are essential to the job, they must show that the physical requirements or criteria are *job-related.*[3] It certainly is appropriate for an employer to require a bus driver to provide evidence that he is seizure-free, since the question of whether he can perform the job without endangering himself and others is legitimate and pertinent. However, the screening committee cannot convincingly argue that the ability to see is a legitimate or necessary requirement for employment as a superintendent. The primary function of the superintendent is to manage the school district effectively. Therefore, criteria which are legitimate are those that reflect that primary function, *i.e.,* a relevant terminal degree and a work history showing managerial experience. There is nothing about the position that supports the committee's conclusion that sighted individuals are more qualified to do the job.

The regulations place the responsibility on the federal enforcement agency (the Assistant Secretary) to identify alternative tests that "do not screen out or tend to screen out as many handicapped persons."[4] As with the difficult testing issues raised in postsecondary education, there is very little evidence that the OCR has adequately addressed the significant questions raised by the use of testing instruments or selection criteria that are arguably not valid indicators of the skills and abilities of particular classes of handicapped individuals.[5] Clearly, the office has not assumed the leadership role in resolving these questions that the drafters of the regulations sought to impose. It is conceivable that the only way to make this provision viable is for experts in the field of testing, as it relates to handicapped individuals, to begin to work with the enforcement agency in identifying such selection criteria.

Section 104.13(b) requires that recipients ensure that in administering tests to handicapped individuals, the test results reflect their "job skills, aptitude or whatever other factor the test purports to measure, rather than reflecting impaired sensory, manual, or speaking skills (except where those skills are the factors that the test purports to measure)."

> Carl is interesting in enrolling in the training program for heavy machinery operators offered by his company. All employees interested in the program are required to pass a general aptitude test. Carl has dyslexia, a condition that severely impairs his reading comprehension. He has a history of performing poorly on standardized tests. Carl is denied the opportunity to take the test orally and performs poorly on the test, as he had anticipated. Despite the fact that an alternative test reveals that he has above average intelligence and an aptitude for the training program, Carl is denied enrollment in the program based upon his score on the aptitude test. (See *Stutts v. Freeman.*)[6]

"When an employer . . . chooses a test that discriminates against handicapped persons as its sole hiring criterion, and makes no meaningful accommodation for a handicapped applicant, it violates the Rehabilitation Act of 1973."[7] The employer must ensure that the test measures the relevant skills and abilities and not just the individual's impairment. This principle is illustrated in Appendix A as follows:

> [A] person with a speech impediment may be perfectly qualified for jobs that do not or need not, with reasonable accommodation, require ability to speak clearly. Yet, if given an oral test, the person will be unable to perform in a satisfactory manner. The test results will not, therefore, predict job performance but instead will reflect impaired speech.[8]
>
> North Maloney Consolidated School district requires each applicant for an administrative position to take a 30-minute writing test. Allen, who has a physical impairment which restricts his ability to write, requests accommodation for the writing test. He states that he can either give an oral response or take extra time so he can dictate to a transcriber. The district refuses, stating that all applicants must be evaluated on how they write and his requested alternatives would preclude that.

In order to determine whether the writing test is appropriate or whether Allen should be accommodated, it is first necessary for the school district to define the function, knowledge, or skill that is being tested. Does the district want to know whether Allen can pick up a pen and write, or do they want to know whether he can comprehend written English? The distinction is important. If a job-related function is the ability to physically write English so that it is legible and comprehensible, then a recipient can test for it by requiring a writing sample. If, instead, the recipient wants to know that an applicant can structure words into sentences and paragraphs that conform to the standards of written English, then alternatives to a writing test, such as oral responses or dictation to a transcriber, could be used.

27
Preemployment Inquiries

Consider this fact pattern:

> Combs School District requires every applicant for a teaching position to complete an employment application which includes the following question: Have you ever received psychiatric treatment or experienced a nervous breakdown or neuralgia? If so, describe your past emotional problem in detail. An applicant who answers yes to this question and reports that he was diagnosed as being schizophrenic is denied a job by the school board. See *Doe v. Syracuse School District*.[1] Do the district's actions violate Section 104.14 of the regulations?

Which of the following are appropriate preemployment inquiries?

1. To all bus driver applicants, are you visually impaired?
2. To all applicants, do you have a physical or mental impairment that would prevent you from performing this job?
3. To all applicants, do you have any of the following diseases (list of 35 diseases in alphabetical order)?
4. To maintenance worker applicants, do you have any limitations that would prevent you from lifting 25 to 50 pounds or from crawling in tight spaces?

"[A] recipient may not conduct a preemployment medical examination or may not make preemployment inquiry of an applicant as to whether the applicant is a handicapped person or as to the nature or severity of a handicap."[2] The regulations do not prohibit legitimate preemployment inquiries regarding "an applicant's ability to perform job-related tasks."[3] But those inquiries must be something more than general fishing expeditions to elicit information regarding past or present handicapping conditions. As noted in Appendix A:

> [A]n employer may not ask on an employment form if an applicant is visually impaired, but may ask if the person has a current driver's license (if that is a necessary qualification for the position in question). Similarly, employers

may make inquiries about an applicant's ability to perform a job safely. Thus, an employer may not ask if an applicant is an epileptic, but may ask whether the person can perform a particular job without endangering other employees.[4]

It is important to remember that, while handicapped individuals are not exempt from meeting legitimate physical requirements, inquiries that seek to ascertain their ability to perform must be job related. An employer may not simply ask if the applicant has a handicap. A basic rule-of-thumb is, if the questions are asked of every applicant, no matter what type of position is applied for, they are, more than likely, impermissible preemployment inquiries, and are probably so overly broad as to be useless in gathering pertinent job-related information. Therefore, only question four above is acceptable, assuming the ability to lift up to 50 pounds or crawl into tight spaces is a necessary qualification for the position in question. In *Doe v. Syracuse School District,* the Court rejected the district's assertion that questions regarding the mental health of applicants were necessary to determine the applicants' "present ability to teach." The Court held that these were exactly the types of questions the regulatory provisions prohibited. The inquiry was not job related because it did not address the applicant's ability to teach. It was specifically noted that a "history of treatment for mental or emotional problems is not an indication of [the applicant's] present fitness for a position as a teacher's assistant or substitute teacher."[5] Many individuals, including some representatives of the enforcement agency, argue that question two is acceptable because it refers specifically to the job in question. However, this type of question, while technically permissible, violates the spirit and intent of the law because it is a veiled attempt to elicit information about the existence of disabilities. Further, it is too general to elicit any meaningful information regarding an applicant's qualified status.

A group of handicapped individuals files complaints against the following two companies:

> Advocacy, Inc., which has a spotless reputation for hiring and accommodating handicapped individuals, has revised its application form. The application now includes questions that require handicapped individuals who will need accommodations to give information regarding their handicaps and their specific needs.

> Unaware, Inc., requires all applicants to fill out a form that asks them to discuss in detail their handicapping conditions, if any. The form is separate from the application and is sent directly to the affirmative action officer. It is never seen by the hiring officials.

Both companies argue that they have not violated the regulations. Advocacy, Inc., argues that it is only attempting to more effectively serve handicapped employees, and Unaware, Inc., asserts that it is merely gathering applicant flow data that have no impact on hiring decisions.

The circumstances under which preemployment inquiries are permitted are limited. Section 104.14(b) permits such inquiries *only* when the employer (a) is taking remedial action to correct past discrimination, (b) is taking voluntary action to address limited participation by handicapped individuals, or (c) is taking affirmative action pursuant to Section 503 of the Act. Neither Unaware, Inc., nor Advocacy, Inc., is gathering the information for any of these purposes, and, therefore, both are in violation of the regulations. Further, even if the employer is gathering the information for one of the reasons noted above, the specific reason the information is being requested must be clearly stated; it must be noted that the information is being requested on a voluntary basis, and that refusal to answer will not result in any adverse treatment. This is an absolute standard, and it must be strictly adhered to by employers making preemployment inquiries.

> A group of graduate students protests the hiring practices of the chemistry department because a drug test is required for all individuals applying for jobs on its research projects. Department officials justify this policy by noting that many of the experiments are funded by the Defense Department and involve dangerous materials. It is felt that a high level of safety must be maintained because any accident would have serious consequences. The students argue that the drug test represents an impermissible preemployment inquiry.

Protection for drug abusers and alcoholics under the Act is only extended to "rehabilitated or rehabilitating . . . abusers."[6] The Court in *Burka* specifically commented on the question of whether such tests are considered preemployment inquiries:

> [H]olding as we do that illegal narcotics use does not, *per se,* constitute a handicap under the Rehabilitation Act, it necessarily follows that the . . . drug-testing policy does not constitute a pre-employment screening for handicap."[7]

> Joe, Frank and Bill apply for jobs at the same company and are conditionally offered jobs pending the outcome of a physical examination. Joe and Frank are required to have examinations because it is the company's policy that all persons seeking employment as security guards must pass a physical. While the company does not require individuals in maintenance, the position that Bill applied for, to pass physicals, the hiring official requests that Bill do so, because he is moderately overweight and has hypertension. Frank refuses to take the examination because he feels that the fact that his job is contingent upon passing the examination makes it an impermissible preemployment inquiry. Joe and Bill consent to the examination. The company physician reports that Bill's hypertension is adequately controlled by

medication and that Joe has a history of emotional illness, but the report, as well as reports from Joe's personal physician, indicates that Joe no longer has an emotional impairment. The offer of employment to Joe is rescinded because the hiring official feels that the job would be too stressful for an individual with a history of emotional illness. Were the actions of the hiring official appropriate?

Employers may condition offers of employment on the results of medical examinations. Frank's objection is unfounded because, once a conditional offer is made, an employer may require individuals to provide medical information so long as the information is not used to deny employment to qualified handicapped individuals. An employer may not, however, single out handicapped individuals as the only applicants whose employment offer is contingent upon results of a medical examination. The examinations must be administered to all employees in a nondiscriminatory manner.[8] Thus, the request that Bill submit to a physical was not warranted. He met the job qualifications, and the mere fact that he had hypertension should not place in question his ability to perform the job. The same is true of Joe's situation. A history of emotional illness without more is not evidence that he cannot perform the functions of a security guard. While employers have the right to make decisions based upon the results of such examinations, their determinations must be job related and nondiscriminatory.

Remember—All information collected by recipients regarding medical conditions or history must be "accorded confidentiality as medical records." [See § 104.14(d).]

Part VII: Enforcement of the Act

The key to compliance under Section 504 is balancing.
—Salome Heyward, 1991

This part includes practical guidance regarding the development of effective compliance strategies under Section 504. Some of the topics discussed are: basic principles for ensuring compliance; how to prepare for an investigation; how to negotiate a settlement with the enforcement agency; and whether discriminatory intent must be shown to make a case under Section 504.

28
Charges of Discrimination

Parties who are either raising charges of discrimination pursuant to Section 504 or responding to them must understand the following essential issues:

1. What are the elements of a cause of action under Section 504?
2. Does the charging party have to establish that he or she is "otherwise qualified" or must the recipient prove that the individual is not "otherwise qualified"?
3. Must one prove discriminatory intent to make a case under Section 504?

Elements of a Cause of Action

> To establish a *prima facie* violation of Section 504, a plaintiff must prove: (1) he or she is a "handicapped person" as defined in the Rehabilitation Act; (2) he or she is "otherwise qualified" to participate in the offered activity or to enjoy its benefits; (3) he or she is being excluded from such participation or enjoyment solely by reason of his or her handicap; and (4) the program denying the plaintiff participation receives federal financial assistance. . . . Once a *prima facie* violation of Section 504 has been established, the defendant must present evidence to rebut the inference of illegality.[1]

It is a well-established rule of law that the individual charging discrimination must present some evidence to satisfy these four elements before the recipient has to present any evidence demonstrating the legality of its actions. However, some important facts regarding each of these elements should be remembered.

Receipt of Federal Financial Assistance

The Civil Rights Restoration Act has substantially lowered this threshold. The charging party no longer has to trace the federal financial assistance directly to the "program or activity" in which the alleged discrimination occurred, if the entity, institution or organization of which it is a part is a recipient.[2] Recipient status still is the *necessary* jurisdictional element. Since only recipients are responsible for complying with Section 504, even if the charging party has overwhelming evidence regarding the remaining three elements, it would be of no consequence under Section 504. Without recipient status, there is no case. However, a case may be made under the ADA since recipient status is not a key element under that statute.

"Handicapped Person"

The definition of "handicapped person" is broad and is not limited to traditional impairments. The statute and the regulations, on this level, are inclusive to avoid discrimination which is the product of "stereotypical attitudes and ignorance" regarding types of impairments.[3] Generally, concerns regarding the effect the impairment has on the individual's ability to perform, or its effect on others, such as health or safety risks, should be raised with respect to the question of whether the individual is "otherwise qualified."

"Otherwise Qualified"

Although the Supreme Court in *Southeastern Community College v. Davis, supra,* and *Alexander v. Choate, supra,* clearly established that an individual's handicap can be considered as one of the factors in determining whether the individual is "qualified," and provided the basic framework for assessing "qualified" status, the Court failed to address the troublesome problem of whether the handicapped individual or the recipient is responsible for answering the ultimate question regarding "qualified" status. Specifically, does the recipient have to establish that the individual does not meet the standards or criteria for participation, or does the handicapped individual have the burden of proving that, in spite of the handicap, he or she is "qualified"?

Federal courts of appeals have taken opposing views on this issue.[4] For example:

> A student is denied admission to a residency program in psychiatry because of his multiple sclerosis. The evidence clearly reflects that the decision is based upon the student's handicapping condition. There is testimony from the student's own psychiatrist and those who had worked with him professionally that he is a responsible and conscientious physician, he has treated his patients appropriately and he is emotionally stable. The rejection of the student is based largely on conjecture regarding the emotional reaction of his patients to his impairment and whether the student has resolved his own feelings regarding his illness. It is also conjectured that he might miss work because of his illness, which would cause problems for his patients.

In *Pushkin v. Regents of the University of Colorado,* the Court rejected the institution's argument that it merely had to show the student was not qualified and noted that there was no concrete evidence to support the institution's determination that the student did not meet the program standards. The Court specifically rejected the argument that the institution must merely act in a rational manner when what is at issue is an act of discrimination. However, consider *Doe v. New York University,* a case in which the Court took the opposite view. A student with excellent academic credentials applied to medical school and was admitted on the basis of false information she provided regarding her mental health. She had an extensive history of mental illness. During a period of nearly three years, which included her medical school enrollment, she exhibited a psychiatric disorder which was manifested in over 20 instances of self-inflicted bodily harm and attempted suicide, as well as serious physical attacks on her doctors and others. Also, she continuously refused to submit to recommended medical treatment. She was forced to withdraw from medical school as a result of her impairment. In the five years subsequent to her withdrawal, she obtained a Master of Science degree in Health and Policy Management and performed successfully as a research assistant for the Federal Government. Despite the fact she had not received the extensive therapy recommended, during the five-year period there was no recurrence of the previous violent and self-destructive behavior. Her request to be reinstated in medical school was rejected on the basis of the evaluations of several psychiatrists who stated that she continued to suffer from a serious psychiatric problem and that the stress of medical school would cause her previous destructive behavior to recur. The Court held that "the pivotal issue regarding the institution's responsibility was . . . whether under all of the circumstances it provides a reasonable basis for finding the plaintiff not to be qualified or not as well qualified as other applicants."[5] The Court stated that once the institution established that consideration of the individual's handicap was relevant in determining whether the individual was "qualified," the handicapped individual had the "ultimate burden" of proving that he or she was qualified in spite of the handicap.

Thus, given the somewhat unsettled nature of the law in the area, what is the best approach to take regarding this issue? Since even in *Doe v. New York University* the Court held that the recipient has a responsibility to provide evidence that it properly considered the individual's handicap in making its determination,[6] it would seem that the best approach would be for the recipient to assume that it has a responsibility to present sufficient evidence to justify its decision. The appropriateness of this approach is further supported by the recent decision of the court of appeals in *Wynne v. Tufts,* in which the Court held that when a recipient denies services or an opportunity to participate to a handicapped person, it has an obligation to "submit a *factual record*" reflecting that it had sought to make reasonable accommodations (emphasis added).[7] Further, the Supreme Court in *Alexander v. Choate* ruled that "the question of who is 'otherwise qualified' and what actions constitute 'discrimination' . . . would seem to be two sides of a single coin."[8] Therefore, there would seem to be little to gain by taking the passive approach regarding the "otherwise qualified" issue. The goal of the recipient should be to provide the most compelling evidence available to support its decisions.

Evidence of Actual Discrimination

The courts have been very consistent in requiring that the charging party present clear evidence that the recipient's actions were discriminatory.[9] Mere speculation and suspicion without more are insufficient. The adverse treatment must be based upon the individual's handicap. Inconsistent or even arbitrary decisions on the part of the recipient that are not discriminatory cannot be reached under Section 504.

Discriminatory Intent

In *Alexander v. Choate*, the Supreme Court specifically addressed the question of:

> [W]hether proof of discriminatory animus is always required to establish a violation of § 504 and its implementing regulations, or whether federal law also reaches action by a recipient of federal funding that discriminates against the handicapped by effect rather than by design.[10]

In holding that protection under the Act was not limited to "conduct fueled by discriminatory intent," the Court noted that the discriminatory conduct that Section 504 was intended to reach, *i.e.,* "thoughtlessness and indifference—of benign neglect . . . would be difficult if not impossible to reach" under a discriminatory intent standard.[11] As noted by the Court in *Pushkin*

> It would be a rare case indeed in which a hostile discriminatory purpose or subjective intent to discriminate solely on the basis of handicap could be shown. Discrimination on the basis of handicap usually results from more invidious causative elements and often occurs under the guise of extending a helping hand or a mistaken, restrictive belief as to the limitations of handicapped persons.[12]

29
Relationships with the Federal Enforcement Agency

Recipients can make their relationship with federal enforcement agencies relatively painless by understanding a few simple facts about federal investigatory procedures.

1. One must fully participate in the process—being passive almost always leads to negative results.
2. Investigators love order and precision regarding policies and procedures—it makes their job easier.
3. The agency is perfectly willing to pay deference to purely educational decisions—if given the opportunity to do so.

Deference

The agency is not in the education business, and it wishes to avoid at all costs the need to step into the shoes of educators and administrators and second-guess their decisions. The restriction placed upon the agency's behavior regarding elementary and secondary education is reflective of this desire: "It is not the intention of the Department except in extraordinary circumstances, to review the result of individual placement and other educational decisions."[1] Moreover, the courts have long recognized the need to avoid usurping, under the guise of eliminating illegal discrimination, the rightful position of administrators and educators.[2]

Recipients must understand that there is a presumption, because they are the experts, that their actions and decisions are correct. However, they lose that presumption if they cannot present evidence that (1) they complied with the procedural requirements of the regulations, and or that (2) their actions or decisions that resulted in handicapped persons being denied services, benefits, or opportunities were justified. For example:

> Confused Community College does not have a specific procedure in place for providing students with necessary academic adjustments. Requests for

adjustments are responded to in a haphazard fashion if at all. On some occasions the students work the matter out with individual faculty members while on other occasions they are referred to the handicapped students services counselor. Dick is denied academic adjustments by Professor Authoritarian. Dick asserts that he specifically requested accommodation while the professor argues that there was no direct request and they only discussed his needs in a general way.

Andrew begins to exhibit behavioral problems in his senior year. His teachers have increasing difficulty controlling him in class, and over a three-month period he is suspended for a total of 17 days. Despite the requests of his parents and his teachers that Andrew be evaluated, the special education director refuses to authorize the evaluation because Andrew has a B plus average in all of his classes.

The recipients in both hypotheticals contested the OCR's finding that they violated Section 504, asserting that their actions regarding the students were, in fact, correct because neither of the students was a "handicapped person." In both instances, the recipients are trying to address a failure to comply on a procedural level—i.e., the regulations require that they have procedures in place that must be implemented when students such as Dick and Andrew are involved—by raising a substantive issue—i.e., that even if they had complied with the regulations, the students were not entitled to protection under the Act. This type of argument is a waste of time because it is an "apples versus oranges" debate. However, this approach is symptomatic of the problems that recipients have in reconciling their responsibilities under the Act and regulations with the duties and limitations of the enforcement agency.

Recipients underrate the importance of complying with the procedural requirements of the regulations, while at the same time they place undue importance on the ultimate correctness of their decisions. This is often a fatal mistake when one is dealing with a federal enforcement agency. More often than not, the question of whether one is found in violation turns not on the "correctness" of the decision, but rather on whether procedural mandates have been met. Enforcement agencies focus on whether there are policies and procedures in place that comply with the regulations, because they are the experts on procedural issues. Conversely, as noted previously, recipients are presumed to be the experts regarding substantive issues relating to delivery of educational services. Therefore, the likely outcome of the "compliance contest" between the recipient and the enforcement agency can easily be viewed as a question of whether the issue will be resolved on a substantive level or on a procedural level. The rule of thumb for recipients is: minimize the possibility of a compliance issue being characterized as procedural, because this shifts the balance of power to the agency. If the recipient complies with the procedural requirements of the regulations and provides adequate documentation to support its decisions, the procedural trap can be avoided and the recipient's decisions will be entitled to deference under the law.[3]

Preparing for an Investigation

The most important thing for a recipient to do when faced with an investigation is to understand the process and the procedures in their entirety. All too often recipients being investigated merely acquiesce during the investigative process and, in essence, "give themselves up" to the federal agency. Recipients have the right, and indeed a responsibility, to ensure that their rights and the integrity of their programs are protected. The investigative agency asserts that it is an objective reviewer. Although this may be true with respect to ultimate fact finding, it is not so with respect to procedural case processing. In that area, the goal of the agency is to make things as easy for itself as possible. Often this works to the disadvantage of recipients or complainants.

If you are a recipient, the following techniques can be used to assure that you are in the position of informed participant during the investigative process:

1. When you are advised by the Office for Civil Rights that a complaint investigation or compliance review is imminent, gather as much information as possible concerning the issue(s) involved. Don't accept the OCR's characterization of the issue(s) in its original letter at face value. More often than not those characterizations are painted with such a broad brush that they would ultimately support an investigation of your entire program if necessary. *Ask questions!* Your goal is to clarify the issues so that there will be a minimum of surprises in the course of the complaint investigation. Once you feel comfortably aware of the issue(s) that are the subject of the investigation, confirm your understanding with the investigator. Send a letter outlining your understanding of the issue(s) that will be investigated.
2. Designate a person or persons to be responsible for familiarizing themselves with the complaint and the investigative process. This (these) individual(s) should keep responsible officers abreast of the progress of the investigation, so that any problems with the scope of the investigation can be addressed as they arise.
3. It is permissible to perform your own informal inquiry prior to the OCR's investigation to ascertain the nature of the problem. This inquiry must be "low key," however. You should avoid contacting the complainant(s), because your actions could later be construed as intimidation or retaliation. Further, in questioning others regarding the issues, you should

avoid assuming an adversarial or threatening posture. The goal is information gathering. In addition, you should never encourage employees, either directly or by implication, to withhold or distort information provided to the federal agency.

4. When the OCR submits a data request letter, review it in detail and *ask questions* regarding each item requested! Make sure you know why the data are being requested and their significance to the investigation. Don't assume a passive stance and allow the OCR to go on a general fishing expedition. You should suggest alternate data or alternate ways of providing the data. The goal should be to provide the necessary data at a minimum expense in terms of resources and staff time. You should also suggest data/persons to be interviewed that are important to the issue(s) that the OCR has omitted.

5. If the OCR gives you insufficient time to collect the data and prepare for the investigation, request an extension. Don't be inconvenienced by the agency's need to meet its internal timeframes.

6. Prior to the beginning of the actual investigation (on-site or desk review), review all requested data and make a preliminary assessment based upon the review and your informal inquiries.

7. During an on-site investigation, assume as great a role as the OCR will permit. Your role should be one of observer, not of participant. If the investigator asks for additional data, *ask questions!* You should know why the data are important to the investigation. Recognize information gaps and supply what the investigator may have missed.

8. Often the investigator will provide preliminary findings. *Ask questions!* The goal is to understand what his or her concerns are and what potential problems have been identified. Provide any additional information that you feel is necessary to address those concerns and problems.

9. When advised of the agency's findings, *ask questions!* Your understanding of the agency's characterization of its findings is more important at this juncture than your feelings regarding the correctness of the findings. If the findings go beyond the issue(s) agreed upon at the beginning of the process, ask for clarification. Why was the investigation expanded or the focus changed? You have a right to specific answers to this question.

10. If you do not agree with the findings, don't be forced into providing an assurance and agreeing to corrective action. Put your objections to the findings, in writing if necessary, to the regional office as well as the headquarters staff.

These suggestions are aimed at full participation. Too often recipients take a close-mouthed, nonvolunteering approach to investigations. This is harmful if misinformation or lack of information leads to erroneous findings. It is a lot easier to provide information that will shape the findings during the investigative process than it is to get the agency to reverse itself after formal findings have been made. *Remember*—your goal is not to hamper the agency's investigation or deny access. Your goal is to make sure your rights are protected and to eliminate or minimize unnecessary intrusion. Categorical denials to requests should be avoided at all costs.

Successful Negotiations with Federal Compliance Agencies

The hallmark of settlement negotiations with a federal agency such as the OCR is that negotiations are structured so that they are totally stacked in the agency's favor. The OCR typically negotiates by calling a recipient a short time before its internal timeframe mandates that a letter of findings be issued, and requesting the recipient to agree to provide a written assurance of compliance regarding the violations found. At that juncture, the recipient is being asked to provide an assurance before seeing the OCR's written determination and the evidence that supports the violation finding(s). Although the OCR maintains that assurances obtained under such circumstances are "voluntary," there is no ignoring the fact that considerable pressure is exerted by the OCR staff to obtain such "voluntary" compliance. Holding the threat of the issuance of a violation letter over the head of recipients is certainly a powerful negotiating tactic.

The following techniques can be used to shift the balance of power during such negotiations:

1. When you become aware of a complaint of discrimination, initiate an informal inquiry. You should endeavor to know as much or more than the investigating agency.
2. Familiarize yourself with all of the data that the OCR requests as part of its investigation.
3. When the OCR requests a written assurance, request that you first be given an unofficial copy of the letter of findings. If, as in most instances, this request is refused, request further that the pertinent parts of the letter be read to you.
4. Make sure that someone who is familiar with all of the evidence is involved in the negotiations.
5. Request a discussion of the case with the regional director if the information provided by the staff is insufficient or unclear.
6. Condition the assurance you provide on your being able to reopen negotiations and modify the agreement, should your review of the letter reveal that the OCR is in error.

7. Make a Freedom of Information Act request for the investigative report and all evidence that the OCR based its findings upon, once you receive the letter of findings and the case is officially closed.
8. Refuse to provide an assurance if you, in good faith, believe that you have not violated the regulations. The OCR's procedures allow sufficient time to negotiate after the letter of findings is issued.

Request Technical Assistance

Recipients fail to fully exercise their right to request technical assistance from the enforcement agency. In part this is due to the fact that the OCR has not been forthright, in many instances, in responding to questions raised; nevertheless, providing technical assistance is one of its responsibilities, and the agency certainly should be held accountable. Recipients, as well as others, should request clarification whenever they have questions about the proper interpretation of a regulatory provision. Such requests should be made in writing so that the agency will have to respond in some fashion. Even an inadequate response by the agency can be used, should one subsequently find oneself in a compliance battle. Therefore, there is everything to be gained, and little to be lost, by making frequent technical assistance requests.

30
Developing a Compliance Program That Works

Careful attention to the following basic principles and suggestions will assist you in developing compliance strategies that work.

1. The compliance standard under Section 504 and its implementing regulations is a "reasonable person" compliance standard. What is considered reasonable is determined on a case-by-case basis.[1] While there are very few generalizations that would hold true for all cases, recipients would do well to adhere to the principle that, if a reasonable person would qustion the propriety of their actions, they should take a closer look at their compliance under the Act and the regulations. If it looks like discrimination and feels like discrimination, it probably is.

2. Adhere to the spirit as well as the letter of the law. The Supreme Court defined compliance under the Act as requiring a balancing between the interest of the handicapped individual to be included and the interest of the recipient to protect the integrity of its programs. Recipients must ensure that this balancing occurs. All legitimate alternatives should be considered prior to denying a handicapped individual benefits, services, or opportunities.

3. Provide justification for all decisions that result in the denial of opportunities to handicapped persons. Simply asserting academic freedom or that the request is a substantial modification, or an undue administrative or financial burden, is insufficient without adequate documentation.

4. Keep your focus narrow. Answer only the questions that are properly before you. For example, if the question is whether Sue should be provided interpreter services, do not expand it to a referendum on your policies and procedures regarding the provision of academic adjustments to all students. Don't treat a flesh wound with open heart surgery!

5. Do not forget the principle of individualization. All decisions regarding handicapped persons should be based upon their individual needs and abilities, and not upon generalizations regarding handicapped individuals as a class.

6. Take the emotionalism and uncertainty out of compliance by developing clear written policies and procedures that explain the rights and responsibilities of all parties.

7. Conduct a review of your programs to ensure that you comply with all of the procedural requirements of the regulations.

8. Ensure that the persons or offices that you make responsible for complying with the Act and its regulations are fully integrated into the organization and, in fact, have the authority and resources to perform their functions.

9. Avoid the unnecessary segregation of handicapped persons. Qualified handicapped persons should be treated the same as all similarly situated nonhandicapped persons unless the need to provide meaningful access requires otherwise.

10. Develop a healthy fear of litigation. Nowhere is the adage that hard cases make bad law more true than when applied to civil rights cases. Litigation is a high-stakes game, and recipients should treat it with greater respect. The point here is not to discourage all litigation; clearly, issues that go to the heart of the integrity of the recipient's program warrant litigation.[2] However, recipients must be more pragmatic in deciding to invest valuable resources on the judicial battlefield. The following questions should be considered before litigating:

> Is the integrity of the program *really* at stake?
>
> Do you have a more substantial reason for initiating the battle than simply not wishing to set a precedent by providing services or an opportunity to a particular individual or group of individuals?
>
> Have all available alternatives to resolving the controversy been considered and attempted? Timing is important. You must not initiate litigation too soon.
>
> What are you trying to win? Is there a likelihood that you will win?
>
> Will the ultimate price tag (monetary as well as public relations) justify the fight? What is the potential for losing more than you gain?
>
> Are you initiating a battle which, in essence, contests the validity of the regulations? These are extremely difficult and costly battles to win.[3]

If, after answering these questions, you still have a desire to litigate, repeat the following phrase three times before calling your attorney: "*I am an educator, not a litigator.*"

If you forget these ten principles, you need only remember the concept of balancing and the spirit of compromise. Begin to look at each controversy with an eye toward the possibility of satisfying the interests of both the handicapped individual and the recipient.

Appendix A:
List of Cases Cited

A.W. v. Northwest R. 1 School District, 813 F.2d 158 (8th Cir. 1987)

Abney v. District of Columbia, 849 F.2d 1491 (1988)

Age v. Bullitt County School District, 673 F.2d 141 (6th Cir. 1982)

Alamo Heights Independent School District v. State Board of Education, 790 F.2d 1153 (5th Cir. 1986)

Alexander v. Choate, 469 U.S. 287, 83 L.Ed 2d 661 (1985)

Americans Disabled for Accessible Public Transportation v. Skinner, 881 F.2d 1184 (3rd Cir. 1989)

Anderson v. Banks, 520 F. Supp. 472 (S.D.Ga. 1981)

Anderson v. University of Wisconsin, 841 F.2d 737 (7th Cir. 1988)

Antkowiak v. Ambach, 838 F.2d 635 (2nd Cir. 1988)

Arline v. School Board of Nassau County, 480 U.S. 273, 94 L.Ed 2d 307 (1987)

Ayers v. Allain, 893 F.2d 732 reh'g en banc 868 F.2d 1014 (5th Cir. 1990)

B.G. v. Cranford Board of Education, 702 F. Supp. 1158 (D.N.J. 1988)

Bachman v. American Society of Clinical Pathologists, 577 F. Supp. 1257 (D.N.J. 1983)

Barnes v. Converse College, 436 F. Supp. 635 (D.S.C. 1977)

Barnett v. Fairfax County School Board, 927 F.2d 146 (4th Cir. 1991)

Battle v. Pennsylvania, 629 F.2d 269 (3rd Cir. 1980)

Bentivegna v. United States Dept. of Labor, 694 F.2d 619 (9th Cir. 1982)

Bevin v. Wright, 666 F. Supp. 71 (W.D.Pa. 1987)

Blackwell v. Department of Treasury, 656 F. Supp. 713 (D.D.C. 1986)

Board of Education v. Diamond, 808 F.2d 876 (3rd Cir. 1986)

Bowen v. American Hospital Association, 476 U.S. 610 (1986)

Brennan v. Stewart, 834 F.2d 1248 (5th Cir. 1988)

Briggs v. Board of Education of the State of Connecticut, 707 F. Supp. 623 (D.Conn. 1988)

Brookhart v. Illinois State Board of Education, 697 F.2d 179 (7th Cir. 1983)

Bruegging v. Burke, 696 F. Supp. 674 (D.C. 1987)

Burka v. New York City Transit Authority, 680 F. Supp. 590 (S.D.N.Y. 1988)

Burlington School Committee v. Department of Education, 471 U.S. 358, 105 S.Ct. 1996, 85 L.Ed 2d 385 (1985)

Burr v. Ambach, 863 F.2d 1071 (2nd Cir. 1988)

Butler v. Department of the Navy, 595 F. Supp. 1063 (D.D.Maryland, 1984)

Cain v. Hyatt, 734 F. Supp. 671 (E.D.Pa. 1990)

Carter v. Bennett, 840 F.2d 63 (D.C. Cir. 1988)

Carter v. Casa Central, 849 F.2d 1048 (7th Cir. 1988)

Carter v. Tisch, 822 F.2d 465 (4th Cir. 1987)

Cavallaro v. Ambach, 575 F. Supp. 171 (W.D.N.Y. 1983)

Frazier v. Board of Trustees of Northwest Mississippi Regional Medical Center, 765 F.2d 1278 (5th Cir. 1985)
Freeman v. Cavazas, 923 F.2d 1434 (11th Cir. 1991)
Fuqua v. Unisys, 716 F. Supp. 1201 (D.Minn. 1989)
G.C. by and through W.S. v. Coler, 673 F. Supp. 1093 (S.D.Fla. 1987)
GARC v. McDaniel, 511 F. Supp. 1263, aff'd 716 F.2d 1565 (11th Cir. 1983), cert. denied, 469 U.S. 1228 (1985)
Gallagher v. Pontiac School District, 807 F.2d 75 (6th Cir. 1986)
Garrity v. Gallen, 522 F. Supp. 171 (D.New Hamp. 1981)
Gebhardt v. Ambach, EHLR 554:341 (1982)
Granite School District v. Shannon M. 787 F. Supp. 1020 (D.Utah 1992)
Grove City College v. Bell, 465 U.S. 555, 79 L.Ed 2d 516 (1984)
Grube v. Bethlehem Area School District, 550 F. Supp. 418 (E.D.Penn. 1982)
Gwinn v. Bolger, 598 F. Supp. 196 (D.D.C. 1984)
Hall v. Freeman, 700 F. Supp. 1106 (N.D.Ga. 1987)
Hall v. U.S. Postal Service, 857 F.2d 1073 (6th Cir. 1989)
Harrison v. Marsh, 691 F. Supp. 1223 (W.D.Mo. 1988)
Hayes v. Unified School District No. 377, 877 F.2d 809 (10th Cir. 1989)
Hendrick Hudson Central School District v. Rowley, 458 U.S. 176, 73 L.Ed 2d 690 (1982)
Hendricks v. Gilhool, 709 F. Supp. 1362 (E.D.Pa. 1989)
Hingson v. Pacific Southwest Airlines, 743 F.2d 1408 (9th Cir. 1984)
Hollenbeck v. Board of Education of Rochelle Township, 699 F. Supp. 658 (N.D.Ill. 1988)
Honig v. Doe, 484 U.S. 305, 98 L.Ed 2d 686 (1988)
Indiana Dept. of Human Services v. Firth (Ind. App. April/1992)
Iron Arrow Honor Society v. Hufstedler, 499 F. Supp. 496, aff'd 652 F.2d 445, vacated on remand 458 U.S. 1102, 702 F.2d 549 (5th Cir. 1983), vacated as moot, 464 U.S. 67, 787 L.Ed 2d 58 (1983), on remand 722 F.2d 213
Irving Independent School District v. Tatro, 468 U.S. 883, 82 L.Ed 2d 664 (1984)
Jackson v. Franklin County School Board, 765 F.2d 535 (5th Cir. 1985)
Jackson v. Maine, 544 A.2d 291 (Me. 1988)
Jacobson v. Delta Airlines, 742 F.2d 1202 (9th Cir. 1984)
Jasany v. U.S. Postal Service, 755 F.2d 1244 (6th Cir. 1985)
Jones v. Illinois Department of Rehabilitation, 689 F.2d 724 (7th Cir. 1982)
Kaelin v. Grubbs, 682 F.2d 595 (6th Cir. 1982)
Kattan v. District of Columbia, EHLR 441:207 (8/88)
Kerkam v. McKenzie, 862 F.2d 884 (D.C. Cir. 1988)
Kerr Center Parents Association v. Charles, 842 F.2d 1052 (9th Cir. 1988)
Kling v. County of Los Angeles, 769 F.2d 532 (9th Cir. 1985)
Kohl v. Woodhaven Learning Center, 865 F.2d 930 (8th Cir. 1989)
Kruelle v. New Castle County School District, 642 F.2d 687 (3rd Cir. 1981)
Lachman v. Illinois State Board of Education, 852 F.2d 290 (7th Cir. 1988), cert. denied, 102 L.Ed 2d 327 (1988)
Larry P. v. Riles, 793 F.2d 969 (9th Cir. 1984)
Lau v. Nichol, 414 U.S. 563 (1974)
Leake v. Long Island Jewish Medical Center, 869 F.2d 130 (2nd Cir. 1989)
Lelsz v. Kavanagh, 673 F. Supp. 828 (N.D.Tex. 1987)
Lemere v. Burnley, 683 F. Supp. 275 (D.D.C. 1988)
Lenhoff v. Farmington Public Schools, 680 F. Supp. 921 (E.D.Mich. 1988)
Locascio v. City of St. Petersburg, 731 F. Supp. 1522 (M.D.Fla. 1990)

Lunceford v. District of Columbia Board of Education, 745 F.2d 1577 (D.C. Cir. 1984)
McKelvey v. Turnage, 485 U.S. 535, 99 L.Ed 2d 618 (1988)
McKenzie v. Smith, 771 F.2d 527 (D.C. Cir. 1985)
McNair v. Oak Hills Local School District, 872 F.2d 153 (6th Cir. 1989)
Martinez v. School Board of Hillsborough County, 861 F.2d 1502 (11th Cir. 1988)
Matthews v. Davis, 742 F.2d 825 (4th Cir. 1984)
Meyerson v. State of Arizona 740 F.2d 684 (9th Cir. 1984)
Mills v. Board of Education of the District of Columbia, 348 F. Supp. 866 (D.D.C. 1972)
Moore v. Sun Bank of North Florida, 923 F.2d 1423 (11th Cir. 1991)
NAACP v. Wilmington Medical Center, Inc., 453 F. Supp. 330 (D.Del. 1978)
Nathanson v. Medical College of Pennsylvania, 926 F.2d 1368 (3rd Cir. 1991)
Nelson v. Thornburgh, 567 F. Supp. 369 (E.D.Pa. 1983).
New Mexico Association for Retarded Citizens v. The State of New Mexico, 495 F. Supp. 391 (D.N.Mex. 1980)
New Mexico Association for Retarded Citizens v. The State of New Mexico, 678 F.2d 847 (10th Cir. 1982)
Niehaus v. Kansas Bar Association, 793 F.2d 1159 (10th Cir. 1986)
P.C. v. McLaughlin, 913 F.2d 1033 (2nd Cir. 1990)
Padilla v. City of Topeka, 708 P.2d 543 (Kansas, 1985)
Pandazides v. The Virginia Board of Education, 752 F. Supp. 696 (E.D.Va. 1990)
Parate v. Isibor, 868 F.2d 821 (6th Cir. 1989)
Parks v. Pavkovic, 733 F.2d 1397 (7th Cir. 1985)
Pendleton v. Jefferson Local School District, 754 F. Supp. 570 (S.D.Ohio 1990)
Pennhurst State School v. Halderman, 451 U.S. 1, 67 L.Ed 2d 694 (1981)
Pennsylvania Association for Retarded Children v. Commonwealth of Pennsylvania, 344 F. Supp. 1257 (E.D. 1971)
Perez v. Philadelphia Housing Authority, 677 F. Supp. 357 (E.D.Pa. 1987), aff'd 841 F.2d 1120 (3rd Cir. 1988)
Polk v. Central Susquehanna Intermediate Unit 16, 853 F.2d 171 (3rd Cir. 1988)
Prewitt v. United States Postal Service, 662 F.2d 292 (5th Cir. 1981)
Pridemore v. Rural Legal Aid Society of West Central Ohio, 625 F. Supp. 1180 (S.D.Ohio 1985)
Pushkin v. Regents of the University of Colorado, 658 F.2d 1372 (10th Cir. 1981)
Rabinowitz v. New Jersey State Board of Education, 550 F. Supp. 481 (D.N.J. 1982)
Recanzone v. Washoe County School District, 696 F. Supp. 1372 (D.Nev. 1988)
Regents of University of Michigan v. Ewing, 474 U.S. 214 (1985)
Reynolds v. Block, 815 F.2d 571 (9th Cir. 1987)
Rhone v. United States Department of Army, 665 F. Supp. 734 (E.D.Mo. 1987)
Riley v. Jefferson County Board of Education, Case No. CV-989-P-0169-S (N.D.Ala. 1989)
Robertson by Robertson v. Granite City Community Unit School District No. 9, 684 F. Supp. 1002 (S.D.Ill. 1988)
Rogers v. Bennett, 873 F.2d 1387 (11th Cir. 1989)
Roncker v. Walters, 700 F.2d 1058 (6th Cir. 1983)
Rothschild v. Grottenthaler, 907 F.2d 286 (2nd Cir. 1990)
S-1 v. Turlington, 635 F.2d 342 (5th Cir. 1981)
S-1 v. Turlington, 682 F.2d 595 (6th Cir. 1982)
Salvador v. Bell, 622 F. Supp. 438, aff'd 800 F.2d 97 (7th Cir. 1986)
Santiago v. Temple University, 739 F. Supp. 974 (E.D.Pa. 1990)
School Board of Nassau County v. Arline, 480 U.S. 273 (1987)
Schornstein v. New Jersey Division of Vocational Rehabilitation Services, 519 F. Supp. 773 (D.N.J. 1981)

Appendix B:
Agency Rulings

Alabama State Department of Education, EHLR 352:41 (1985)
Aldine Independent School District, EHLR 257:411 (1983)
Alpena (AR) Public School District, EHLR 257:565 (1984)
Anne Arundel County Public Schools, EHLR 257:639 (1985)
Arcadia (CA) Unified School District, EHLR 311:27 (1983)
Arundel County (MD) Public Schools, EHLR 257:639 (1985)
Ashwaubenon (WI) School District, EHLR 311:320 (1988)
Augusta County (VA) School Division, EHLR 352:233 (1986)
Baltimore County (MD) Public Schools, EHLR 352:352 (1987)
Basin (ID) School District No. 72, EHLR 257:390 (1983)
Berlin Brothers Valley School District, EHLR 353:124 (1988)
Bethel (CT) Board of Education, EHLR 257:55 (1979)
Boone County School District, EHLR 257:103 (1980)
Boston (MA) School District, EHLR 352:382 (1987)
Boulder Valley (CO) School District RE-2, EHLR 257:297 (1980)
Brazosport (TX) Independent School District, EHLR 352:531 (1987)
Brentwood Union Free School District, EHLR 311:50 (1985)
Bridgeport (CT) Board of Education, EHLR 257:508 (1984)
Bristol-Plymouth (MA) Regional Vocational Technical School District, EHLR 353:241
    (1989)
Brockton (MA) Public Schools, EHLR 257:452 (1983)
Brockton (MA) Public Schools, EHLR 311:114 (1987)
Brush Country (TX) Special Education Cooperative, EHLR 352:639 (1988)
Butte (MT) School District #1, EHLR 311:70 (1986)
California Department of Youth Authority, EHLR 352:307 (1986)
California School for the Deaf, EHLR 257:583 (1984)
California State Department of Education, EHLR 352:549 (1987)
Canel, Aronson and Whitted (IL), EHLR 257:427 (1983)
Capistrano (CA) Unified School District, EHLR 311:21 (1982)
Carbon-Lehigh Intermediate Unit #21, EHLR 257:551 (1984)
Carlinville Community Unit School District No. 1, EHLR 352:32 (1985)
Chesterfield County Public Schools, EHLR 257:500 (1984)
Chicago Board of Education, EHLR 257:308 (1981)
Chicago Board of Education, EHLR 257:369 (1982)
Chicago (IL) Board of Education, EHLR 257:448 (1983)
Chicago (IL) Board of Education, EHLR 257:515 (1984)
Chicago (IL) Board of Education, EHLR 257:568 (1984)
Churchill County (NV) School District, EHLR 352:543 (1987)
Clark County (NV) School District, EHLR 257:245 (1981)

Red Oak (IA) Community School District, EHLR 311:24 (1982)
Rialto (CA) Unified School District, EHLR 353:201 (1989)
Richmond (IN) Community School Corporation, EHLR 352:296 (1986)
Richmond County School District, EHLR 352:240 (1986)
Riverside (CA) Unified School District, EHLR 352:170 (1986)
Riverview School District, EHLR 311:103 (1987)
Rochester (NY) School District, EHLR 311:09 (1980)
Sachem (NY) Central School District, EHLR 352:462 (1987)
St. Clair (MO) R-XIII School District, EHLR 352:201 (1986)
Salina (KS) USD #305, EHLR 352:204 (1986)
San Antonio Independent School District, EHLR 311:40 (1984)
San Diego City (CA) School District, EHLR 353:236 (1989)
San Diego City (CA) Unified School District, EHLR 352:273 (1986)
San Francisco Unified School District, EHLR 352:362 (1986)
Sanger Unified School District, EHLR 257:02 (1978)
Santee Unified School District, EHLR 353:210 (1989)
School District No. 220 (IL), EHLR 257:200 (1981)
School District of Philadelphia (PA), EHLR 257:496 (1984)
School District of Pittsburgh, EHLR 257:492 (1984)
School District of the City of Saginaw, EHLR 352:413 (1987)
Seattle (WA) School District, EHLR 352:80 (1985)
Seattle (WA) School District No. 1, EHLR 257:424 (1983)
Sheffield (AL) City School, EHLR 352:242 (1986)
South Sioux City School District, EHLR 305:46 (1988)
Special Education District of Lake County (IL), EHLR 257:34 (1979)
Special Education District of McHenry (IL) County, EHLR 258:125 (1985)
Special School District of St. Louis, EHLR 352:156 (1986)
Special School District of St. Louis County (MO), EHLR 257:322 (1981)
Special School District of St. Louis County (MO), EHLR 311:05 (1980)
Spokane (WA) School District No. 81, EHLR 257:219 (1981)
Stafford Co. (VA) Public Schools, EHLR 352:449 (1987)
State Department of Education, EHLR 352:480 (1987)
Sumner County School District, EHLR 352:248 (1986)
Sumner (VA) School District, EHLR 352:565 (1987)
Superintendent of Northwestern Local School District, EHLR 305:19 (1983)
Tacoma (WA) School District, EHLR 257:383 (1983)
Tacoma (WA) School District No. 10, EHLR 257:420 (1983)
Texas Education Agency, EHLR 352:349 (1986)
The Greater Amsterdam (NY) School District, EHLR 257:436 (1983)
Thornton Township (IL) High School District #205, EHLR 311:85 (1986)
Timothy School, EHLR 311:76 (1986)
Township High School District #211 (IL), EHLR 352:289 (1986)
Township (IL) School District #211, EHLR 257:364 (1982)
Tucson (AZ) Unified School District, EHLR 352:547 (1987)
Tuscaloosa City School District, EHLR 352:273 (1986)
Ukiah (CA) Unified School District, EHLR 311:17 (1982)
Union Beach Public School District, EHLR 257:490 (1984)
Upper Peninsula (MI) School District, EHLR 352:538 (1987)
Van Buren (AR) Public School, EHLR 257:269 (1981)
Vashon Island (WA) School District No. 402, EHLR 257:434 (1983)
Virginia Department of Correctional Education, EHLR 352:451 (1987)

Virginia Department of Education, EHLR 257:349 (1982)
Wake County (NC) School District, EHLR 257:432 (1983)
Walker County (AL) School District, EHLR 352:10 (1985)
Wauwatosa (WI) Public School District, EHLR 257:355 (1982)
West Babylon Union Free School District, EHLR 352:305 (1986)
Westwood Community School District, EHLR 352:470 (1987)
Wetzel County School District, EHLR 353:261 (1989)
Williamson County (TN) School District, EHLR 352:514 (1988)
Winston County (AL) School District, EHLR 352:66 (1985)
Wisconsin Department of Public Instruction, EHLR 352:357 (1986)
Wyoming Public School District, EHLR 311:325 (1988)
York Community High School, EHLR 352:116 (1985)
Youngstown (OH) City School District, EHLR 257:580 (1984)

LOF Cases

Board of Education of the City of New York (Case No. 02-88-1079) 12/6/89 LOF
California State University System, LOF (1985)
Connecticut State Department of Education, 3/13/1980 LOF
DeKalb County School District and Georgia Dept. of Education, LOF 4/26/90
Greenville County School District, LOF 12/8/89
Horn v. Mitchell College, 1984 LOF
Horry County School District LOF (6/6/89)
Illinois State Board of Education, March 28, 1986 LOF
Maricopa County Community College LOF, 9/1978
Memphis State University, 4/87 LOF
Mesa Unified School District Number Four, 6/28/88 LOF
Muscogee County School District, 6/88 LOF
New Castle County School District LOF (6/81)
Ogden City School District (July 1987)
Ramapo Central School District (1989)
Tulsa Junior College-LOF 1985
University of Florida, LOF (1988)
University of Washington, LOF-April 12, 1979
University of Denver, LOF (11/23/78)
Western Illinois University (8/25/82)
Whitworth College LOF (4/80)

Appendix C:
Section 504 of the
Rehabilitation Act of 1973

29 U.S.C.A. § 794 Nondiscrimination under federal grants and programs; promulgation of rules and regulations

(a) Promulgation of rules and regulations

No otherwise qualified individual with handicaps in the United States, as defined in section 706(8) of this title, shall, solely by reason of her or his handicap, be excluded from the participation in, be denied the benefits of, or be subjected to discrimination under any program or activity receiving Federal financial assistance or under any program or activity conducted by any Executive agency or by the United States Postal Service. The head of each such agency shall promulgate such regulations as may be necessary to carry out the amendments to this section made by the Rehabilitation, Comprehensive Services, and Developmental Disabilities Act of 1978. Copies of any proposed regulation shall be submitted to appropriate authorizing committees of the Congress, and such regulation may take effect no earlier than the thirtieth day after the date on which such regulation is so submitted to such committees.

34 CFR Part 104
Subpart A — General Provisions

104.1 Purpose.

The purpose of this part is to effectuate section 504 of the Rehabilitation Act of 1973, which is designed to eliminate discrimination on the basis of handicap in any program or activity receiving Federal financial assistance.

104.2 Application.

This part applies to each recipient of Federal financial assistance from the Department of Education and to each program or activity that receives or benefits from such assistance.

104.3 Definitions.

As used in this part, the term:

(a) "The Act" means the Rehabilitation Act of 1973, Pub. L. 93-112, as amended by the Rehabilitation Act Amendments of 1974, Pub. L. 93-516, 29 U.S.C. 794.

(b) "Section 504" means section 504 of the Act.

(c) "Education of the Handicapped Act" means that statute as amended by the Education for all Handicapped Children Act of 1975, Pub. L. 94-142, 20 U.S.C. 1401 et seq.

(d) "Department" means the Department of Education.

(e) "Assistant Secretary" means the Assistant Secretary for Civil Rights of the Department of Education.

(f) "Recipient" means any state or its political subdivision, any instrumentality of a state or its political division, any public or private agency, institution, organization, or other entity, or any person to which Federal financial assistance is extended directly or through another recipient, including any successor, assignee, or transferee of a recipient, but excluding the ultimate beneficiary of the assistance.

(g) "Applicant for assistance" means one who submits an application, request, or plan required to be approved by a Department official or by a recipient as a condition to becoming a recipient.

(h) "Federal financial assistance" means any grant, loan, contract (other than a procurement contract or a contract of insurance or guaranty), or any other arrangement by which the Department provides or otherwise makes available assistance in the form of:

(1) Funds;

(2) Services of Federal personnel; or

(3) Real and personal property or any interest in or use of such property, including:

    (i) Transfers or leases of such property for less than fair market value or for reduced consideration; and

    (ii) Proceeds from a subsequent transfer or lease of such property if the Federal share of its fair market value is not returned to the Federal Government.

(i) "Facility" means all or any portion of buildings, structures, equipment, roads, walks, parking lots, or other real or personal property or interest in such property.

(j) "Handicapped person." (1) "Handicapped persons" means any person who (i) has a physical or mental impairment which substantially limits one or more major life activities, (ii) has a record of such an impairment, or (iii) is regarded as having such an impairment. (2) As used in paragraph (j)(1) of this section, the phrase:

    (i) "Physical or mental impairment" means (A) any physiological disorder or condition, cosmetic disfigurement, or anatomical loss affecting one or more of the following body systems: neurological; musculoskeletal; special sense organs; respiratory, including speech organs; cardiovascular; reproductive, digestive, genito-urinary; hemic and lymphatic; skin; and endocrine; or (B) any mental or psychological disorder, such as mental retardation, organic brain syndrome, emotional or mental Illness, and specific learning disabilities.

    (ii) "Major life activities" means functions such as caring for one's self, performing manual tasks, walking, seeing, hearing, speaking, breathing, learning, and working.

    (iii) "Has a record of such an impairment" means has a history of, or has been misclassified as having, a mental or physical impairment that substantially limits one or more major life activities.

    (iv) "Is regarded as having an impairment" means (A) has a physical or mental impairment that does not substantially limit major life activities but that is treated by a recipient as constituting such a limitation; (B) has a physical or mental impairment that substantially limits major life activities only as a result of the attitudes of others toward such impairment; or (C) has none of the impairments defined in paragraph (j)(2)(i) of this section but is treated by a recipient as having such an impairment.

(k) "Qualified handicapped person" means:

(1) With respect to employment, a handicapped person who, with reasonable accommodation, can perform the essential functions of the job in question;

(2) With respect to public preschool elementary, secondary, or adult educational services, a handicapped person (i) of an age during which nonhandicapped persons are provided such services, (ii) of any age during which it is mandatory under state law to provide such services to handicapped persons, or (iii) to whom a state is required to provide a free appropriate public education under section 612 of the Education of the Handicapped Act; and

(3) With respect to postsecondary and vocational education services, a handicapped person who meets the academic and technical standards requisite to admission or participation in the recipient's education program or activity;

(4) With respect to other services, a handicapped person who meets the essential eligibility requirements for the receipt of such services.

(l) "Handicap" means any condition or characteristic that renders a person a handicapped person as defined in paragraph (j) of this section.

104.4 Discrimination prohibited.

(a) General.

No qualified handicapped person shall, on the basis of handicap, be excluded from participation in, be denied the benefits of, or otherwise be subjected to discrimination under any program or activity which receives or benefits from Federal financial assistance,

(b) Discriminatory actions prohibited.

(1) A recipient, in providing any aid, benefit, or service, may not, directly or through contractual, license or other arrangements, on the basis of handicap: (i) Deny a qualified handicapped person the opportunity to participate in or benefit from the aid, benefit, or service; (ii) Afford a qualified handicapped person an opportunity to participate in or benefit from the aid, benefit, or service that is not equal to that afforded others; (iii) Provide a qualified handicapped person with an aid, benefit, or service that is not as effective as that provided to others; (iv) Provide different or separate aid, benefits, or services to handicapped persons or to any class of handicapped persons unless such action is necessary to provide qualified handicapped persons with aid, benefits, or services that are as effective as those provided to others; (v) Aid or perpetuate discrimination against a qualified handicapped person by providing significant assistance to an agency, organization, or person that discriminates on the basis of handicap in providing any aid, benefit, or service to beneficiaries of the recipients program; (vi) Deny a qualified handicapped person the opportunity to participate as a member of planning or advisory boards; or (vii) Otherwise limit a qualified handicapped person in the enjoyment of any right, privilege, advantage, or opportunity enjoyed by others receiving, an aid, benefit, or service.

(2) For purposes of this part, aids, benefits, and services, to be equally effective, are not required to produce the identical result or level of achievement for handicapped and nonhandicapped persons, but must afford handicapped persons equal opportunity to obtain the same result, to gain the same benefit, or to reach the same level of achievement, in the most integrated setting appropriate to the person's needs.

(3) Despite the existence of separate or different programs or activities provided in accordance with this part, a recipient may not deny a qualified handicapped person the opportunity to participate in such programs or activities that are not separate or different.

(4) A recipient may not, directly or through contractual or other arrangements, utilize criteria or methods of administration (i) that have the effect of subjecting qualified handicapped persons to discrimination on the basis of handicap, (ii) that have the purpose or effect of defeating or substantially impairing accomplishment of the objectives of the recipient's program with respect to handicapped persons, or (iii) that perpetuate the discrimination of another recipient if both recipients are subject to common administrative control or are agencies of the same State.

(5) In determining the site or location of a facility, an applicant for assistance or a recipient may not make selections (i) that have the effect of excluding handicapped persons from, denying them the benefits of, or otherwise subjecting them to discrimination under any program or activity that receives or benefits from Federal financial assistance or (ii) that have the purpose or effect of defeating or substantially impairing the accomplishment of the objectives of the program or activity with respect to handicapped persons.

(6) As used in this section, the aid, benefit, or service provided under a program or activity receiving or benefiting from Federal financial assistance includes any aid, benefit, or service provided in or through a facility that has been constructed, expanded, altered, leased or rented, or otherwise acquired, in whole or in part, with Federal financial assistance.

(c) Programs limited by Federal law.

The exclusion of nonhandicapped persons from the benefits of a program limited by Federal statute or executive order to handicapped persons or the exclusion of a specific class of handicapped persons from a program limited by Federal statute or executive order to a different class of handicapped persons is not prohibited by this part.

104.5 Assurances required.

(a) *Assurances.* An applicant for Federal financial assistance for a program or activity to which this part applies shall submit an assurance, on a form specified by the Assistant Secretary, that the program will be operated in compliance with this part. An applicant may incorporate these assurances by reference in subsequent applications to the Department.

(b) *Duration of obligation.*

(1) In the case of Federal financial assistance extended in the form of real property or to provide real property or structures on the property, the assurance will obligate the recipient or, in the case of a subsequent transfer, the transferee, for the period during which the real property or structures are used for the purpose for which the Federal financial assistance is extended or for another purpose involving the provision of similar services or benefits.

(2) In the case of Federal financial assistance extended to provide personal property, the assurance will obligate the recipient for the period during which it retains ownership or possession of the property.

(3) In all other cases the assurance will obligate the recipient for the period during which Federal financial assistance is extended.

(c) *Covenants.*

(1) Where Federal financial assistance is provided in the form of real property or interest in the property from the Department, the instrument effecting or recording this transfer shall contain a covenant running with the land to assure nondiscrimination for the period during which the real property is used for a purpose for which the Federal financial assistance is extended or for another purpose involving the provision of similar services or benefits.

(2) Where no transfer of property is involved but property is purchased or improved with Federal financial assistance, the recipient shall agree to include the covenant described in paragraph (b)(2) of this section in the instrument effecting or recording any subsequent transfer of the property.

(3) Where Federal financial assistance is provided in the form of real property or interest in the property from the Department, the covenant shall also include a condition coupled with a right to be reserved by the Department to revert title to the property in the event of a breach of the covenant. If a transferee of real property proposes to mortgage or otherwise encumber the real property as security for financing construction of new, or improvement of existing, facilities on the property for the purposes for which the property was transferred, the Assistant Secretary may, upon request of the transferee and if necessary to accomplish such financing and upon such conditions as he or she deems appropriate, agree to forbear the exercise of such right to revert title for so long as the lien of such mortgage or other encumbrance remains effective.

104.6 Remedial action, voluntary action, and self-evaluation.

(a) *Remedial action.*

(1) If the Assistant Secretary finds that recipient has discriminated against persons on the basis of handicap in violation of section 504 or this part, the recipient shall take such remedial action as the Assistant Secretary deems necessary to overcome the effects of the discrimination.

(2) Where a recipient is found to have discriminated against persons on the basis of handicap in violation of section 504 or this part and where another recipient exercises control over the recipient that has discriminated, the Assistant Secretary, where appropriate, may require either or both recipients to take remedial action.

(3) The Assistant Secretary may, where necessary to overcome the effects of discrimination in violation of section 504 or this part, require a recipient to take remedial action (i) with respect to handicapped persons who are no longer participants in the recipient's program but who were participants in the program when such discrimination occurred or (ii) with respect to handicapped persons who would have been participants in the program had the discrimination not occurred.

(b) *Voluntary action.* A recipient may take steps, in addition to any action that is required by this part, to overcome the effects of conditions that resulted in limited participation in the recipient's program or activity by qualified handicapped persons.

(c) *Self-evaluation.*

(1) A recipient shall, within one year of the effective date of this part:

(i) Evaluate, with the assistance of interested persons, including handicapped persons or organizations representing handicapped persons, its current policies and practices and the effects thereof that do not or may not meet the requirements of this part;

(ii) Modify, after consultation with interested persons, including handicapped persons or organizations representing handicapped persons, any policies and practices that do not meet the requirements of this part; and

(iii) Take, after consultation with interested persons, including handicapped persons or organizations representing handicapped persons, appropriate remedial steps to eliminate the effects of any discrimination that resulted from adherence to these policies and practices.

(2) A recipient that employs fifteen or more persons shall, for at least three years following completion of the evaluation required under paragraph (c)(1) of this section, maintain on file, make available for public inspection, and provide to the Assistant Secretary upon request:

(i) A list of the interested persons consulted

(ii) a description of areas examined and any problems identified, and

(iii) a description of any modifications made and of any remedial steps taken.

104.7 Designation of responsible employee and adoption of grievance procedures.

(a) *Designation of responsible employee.* A recipient that employs 15 or more persons shall designate at least one person to coordinate its efforts to comply with this part.

(b) *Adoption of grievance procedures.* A recipient that employs 15 or more persons shall adopt grievance procedures that incorporate appropriate due process standards and that provide for the prompt and equitable resolution of complaints alleging any action prohibited by this part. Such procedures need not be established with respect to complaints from applicants for employment or from applicants for admission to postsecondary educational institutions.

104.8 Notice.

(a) A recipient that employs fifteen or more persons shall take appropriate initial and continuing steps to notify participants, beneficiaries, applicants, and employees, including those with impaired vision or hearing, and unions or professional organizations holding collective bargaining or professional agreements with the recipient that it does not discriminate on the basis of handicap in violation of section 504 and this part. The notification shall state, where appropriate, that the recipient does not discriminate in admission or access to, or treatment or employment in, its programs and activities. The notification shall also include an identification of the responsible employee designated pursuant to 104.7(a). A recipient shall make the initial notification required by this paragraph within 90 days of the effective date of this part. Methods of initial and continuing notification may include the posting of notices, publication in newspapers and magazines, placement of notices in recipient's publication, and distribution of memoranda or other written communications.

(b) If a recipient publishes or uses recruitment materials or publications containing general information that it makes available to participants, beneficiaries, applicants, or employees, it shall include in those materials or publications a statement of the policy described in paragraph (a) of this section. A recipient may meet the requirements of this paragraph either by including appropriate inserts in existing materials and publications or by revising and reprinting the materials and publications.

104.9 Administrative requirements for small recipients.

The Assistant Secretary may require any recipient with fewer than fifteen employees, or any class of such recipients, to comply with §§ 104.7 and 104.8, in whole or in part, when the Assistant Secretary finds a violation of this part or finds that such compliance will not significantly impair the ability of the recipient or class of recipients to provide benefits or services.

104.10 Effect of state or local law or other requirements and effect of employment opportunities.

(a) The obligation to comply with this part is not obviated or alleviated by the existence of any state or local law or other requirement that, on the basis of handicap, imposes prohibitions or limits upon the eligibility of qualified handicapped persons to receive services or to practice any occupation or profession.

(b) The obligation to comply with this part is not obviated or alleviated because employment opportunities in any occupation or profession are or may be more limited for handicapped persons than for nonhandicapped persons.

Subpart B — Employment Practices

104.11 Discrimination prohibited.

(a) *General.*

(1) No qualified handicapped person shall, on the basis of handicap, be subjected to discrimination in employment under any program or activity to which this part applies.

(2) A recipient that receives assistance under the Education of the Handicapped Act shall take positive steps, to employ and advance in employment qualified handicapped persons in programs assisted under that Act.

(3) A recipient shall make all decisions concerning employment under any program or activity to which this part applies in a manner which ensures that discrimination on the basis of handicap does not occur and may not limit, segregate, or classify applicants or employees in any way that adversely affects their opportunities or status because of handicap.

(4) A recipient may not participate in a contractual or other relationship that has the effect of subjecting qualified handicapped applicants or employees to discrimination prohibited by this subpart. The relationships referred to in this paragraph include relationships with employment and referral agencies, with labor unions, with organizations providing or administering fringe benefits to employees of the recipient, and with organizations providing training and apprenticeship programs.

(b) *Specific activities.* The provisions of this subpart apply to:

(1) Recruitment, advertising, and the processing of applications for employment;

(2) Hiring, upgrading, promotion, award of tenure, demotion, transfer, layoff, termination, right of return from layoff and rehiring;

(3) Rates of pay or any other form of compensation and changes in compensation;

(4) Job assignments, job classifications, organizational structures, position descriptions, lines of progression, and seniority lists;

(5) Leaves of absence, sick leave, or any other leave;

(6) Fringe benefits available by virtue of employment, whether or not administered by the recipient;

(7) Selection and financial support for training, including apprenticeship, professional meetings, conferences, and other related activities, and selection for leaves of absence to pursue training;

(8) Employer sponsored activities, including social or recreational programs; and

(9) Any other term, condition, or privilege of employment.

(c) A recipient's obligation to comply with this subpart is not affected by any inconsistent term of any collective bargaining agreement to which it is a party.

104.12 Reasonable accommodation.

(a) A recipient shall make reasonable accommodation to the known physical or mental limitations of an otherwise qualified handicapped applicant or employee unless the recipient can demonstrate that the accommodation would impose an undue hardship on the operation of its program.

(b) Reasonable accommodation may include:

(1) Making facilities used by employees readily accessible to and usable by handicapped persons, and

(2) job restructuring, part-time or modified work schedules, acquisition or modification of equipment or devices, the provision of readers or interpreters, and other similar actions.

(c) In determining pursuant to paragraph (a) of this section whether an accommodation would impose an undue hardship on the opeation of a recipient's program, factors to be considered include:

(1) The overall size of the recipient's program with respect to number of employees, number and type of facilities, and size of budget;

(2) The type of the recipient's operation, including the composition and structure of the recipient's workforce; and

(3) The nature and cost of the accommodation needed.

(d) A recipient may not deny any employment opportunity to a qualified handicapped employee or applicant if the basis for the denial is the need to make reasonable accommodation to the physical or mental limitations of the employee or applicant.

104.13 Employment criteria.

(a) A recipient may not make use of any employment test or other selection criterion that screens out or tends to screen out handicapped persons or any class of handicapped persons unless:

(1) The test score or other selection criterion, as used by the recipient, is shown to be job-related for the position in question, and

(2) alternative job-related tests or criteria that do not screen out or tend to

screen out as many handicapped persons are not shown by the Director to be available.

(b) A recipient shall select and administer tests concerning employment so as best to ensure that, when administered to an applicant or employee who has a handicap that impairs sensory, manual, or speaking skills, the test results accurately reflect the applicant's or employee's job skills, aptitude, or whatever other factor the test purports to measure, rather than reflecting the applicant's or employee's impaired sensory, manual, or speaking skills (except where those skills are the factors that the test purports to measure).

104.14 Preemployment inquiries.

(a) Except as provided in paragraphs (b) and (c) of this section, a recipient may not conduct a preemployment medical examination or may not make preemployment inquiry of an applicant as to whether the applicant is a handicapped person or as to the nature or severity of a handicap. A recipient may, however, make preemployment inquiry into an applicant's ability to perform job-related functions.

(b) When a recipient is taking remedial action to correct the effects of past discrimination pursuant to § 104.6(a), when a recipient is taking voluntary action to overcome the effects of conditions that resulted in limited participation in its federally assisted program or activity pursuant to § 104.6(b), or when a recipient is taking affirmative action pursuant to section 503 of the Act, the recipient may invite applicants for employment to indicate whether and to what extent they are handicaped, *Provided,* That:

(1) The recipient states clearly on any written questionnaire used for this purpose or makes clear orally if no written questionnaire is used that the information requested is intended for use solely in connection with its remedial action obligations or its voluntary or affirmative action efforts; and

(2) The recipient states clearly that the information is being requested on a voluntary basis, that it will be kept confidential as provided in paragraph (d) of this section, that refusal to provide it will not subject the applicant or employee to any adverse treatment, and that it will be used only in accordance with this part.

(c) Nothing in this section shall prohibit a recipient from conditioning an offer of employment on the results of a medical examination conducted prior to the employee's entrance on duty, *Provided,* That:

(1) All entering employees are subjected to such an examination regardless of handicap, and

(2) the results of such an examination are used only in accordance with the requirements of this part.

(d) Information obtained in accordance with this section as to the medical condition or history of the applicant shall be collected and maintained on separate forms that shall be accorded confidentiality as medical records, except that:

(1) Supervisors and managers may be informed regarding restrictions on the work or duties of handicapped persons and regarding necessary accommodations;

(2) First aid and safety personnel may be informed, where appropriate, if the condition might require emergency treatment; and

(3) Government officials investigating compliance with the Act shall be provided relevant information upon request.

Subpart C—Program Accessibility

104.21 Discrimination prohibited.

No qualified handicapped person shall, because a recipient's facilities are inaccessible to or unusable by handicapped persons, be denied the benefits of, be excluded from participation in, or otherwise by subjected to discrimination under any program or activity to which this part applies.

104.22 Existing facilities.

(a) *Program accessibility.* A recipient shall operate each program or activity to which this part applies so that the program or activity, when viewed in its entirety, is readily accessible to handicapped persons. This paragraph does not require a recipient to make each of its existing facilities or every part of a facility accessible to and usable by handicapped persons.

(b) *Methods.* A recipient may comply with the requirements of paragraph (a) of this section through such means as redesign of equipment, reassignment of classes or other services to accessible buildings, assignment of aides to beneficiaries, home visits, delivery of health, welfare, or other social services at alternate accessible sites, alteration of existing facilities and construction of new facilities in conformance with the requirements of § 104.23, or any other methods that result in making its program or activity accessible to handicapped persons. A recipient is not required to make structural changes in existing facilities where other methods are effective in achieving compliance with paragraph (a) of this section. In choosing among available methods for meeting the requirement of paragraph (a) of this section, a recipient shall give priority to those methods that offer programs and activities to handicapped persons in the most integrated setting appopriate.

(c) *Small health, welfare, or other social services providers.* If a recipient with fewer than fifteen employees that provides health, welfare, or other social services finds, after consultation with a handicapped person seeking its services, that there is no method of complying with paragraph (a) of this section other than making a significant alteration in its existing facilities, the recipient may, as an alternative, refer the handicapped person to other providers of those services that are accessible.

(d) *Time period.* A recipient shall comply with the requirement of paragraph (a) of this section within 60 days of the effective date of this part except that where structural changes in facilities are necessary, such changes shall be made within three years of the effective date of this part, but in any event as expeditiously as possible.

(e) *Transition plan.* In the event that structural changes to facilities are necessary to meet the requirement of paragraph (a) of this section, a recipient shall develop, within six months of the effective date of this part, a transition plan setting forth the steps necessary to complete such changes. The plan shall be developed with the assistance of interested persons, including handicapped persons or organizations representing handicapped persons. A copy of the transitional plan shall be made available for public Inspection. The plan shall, at a minimum:

(1) Identify physical obstacles in the recipient's facilities that limit the accessibility of its program or activity to handicapped persons;

(2) Describe in detail the methods that will be used to make the facilities accessible;

(3) Specify the schedule for taking the steps necessary to achieve full program accessibility and, if the time period of the transition plan is longer than one year,

identify the steps that will be taken during each year of the transition period; and

(4) Indicate the person responsible for implementation of the plan.

(f) *Notice.* The recipient shall adopt and implement procedures to ensure that interested persons, including persons with impaired vision or hearing, can obtain information as to the existence and location of services, activities, and facilities that are accessible to and usable by handicapped persons.

104.23 New construction.

(a) *Design and construction.* Each facility or part of a facility constructed by, on behalf of, or for the use of a recipient shall be designed and constructed in such manner that the facility or part of the facility is readily accessible to and usable by handicapped persons, if the construction was commenced after the effective date of this part.

(b) *Alteration.* Each facility or part of a facility which is altered by, on behalf of, or for the use of a recipient after the effective date of this part in a manner that affects or could affect the usability of the facility or part of the facility shall, to the maximum extent feasible, be altered in such manner that the altered portion of the facility is readily accessible to and usable by handicapped persons.

(c) *American National Standards Institute accessibility standards.* Design, construction, or alteration of facilities in conformance with the "American National Standard Specifications for Making Buildings and Facilities Accessible to, and Usable by, the Physically Handicapped," published by the American National Standards Institute, Inc. (ANSI A117.1-1961 [R1971]), which is incorporated by reference in this part, shall constitute compliance with paragraphs (a) and (b) of this section. Departures from particular requirements of those standards by the use of other methods shall be permitted when it is clearly evident that equivalent access to the facility or part of the facility is thereby provided. Incorporation by reference provisions approved by the Director of the Federal Register, May 27, 1975. Incorporated documents are on file at the Office of the Federal Register. Copies of the standards are obtainable from American National Standards Institute, Inc., 1430 Broadway, New York, N.Y. 10018.

Subpart D—Preschool, Elementary, and Secondary Education

104.31 Application of this subpart.

Subpart D applies to preschool, elementary, secondary, and adult education programs and activities that receive or benefit from Federal financial assistance and to recipients that operate, or that receive or benefit from Federal financial assistance for the operation of, such programs or activities.

104.32 Location and notification.

A recipient that operates a public elementary or secondary education program shall annually:

(a) Undertake to identify and locate every qualified handicapped person residing in the recipient's jurisdiction who is not receiving a public education; and

(b) Take appropriate steps to notify handicapped persons and their parents or guardians of the recipient's duty under this subpart.

104.33 Free appropriate public education.

(a) *General.* A recipient that operates a public elementary or secondary education program shall provide a free appropriate public education to each qualified handicapped person who is in the recipient's jurisdiction, regardless of the nature or severity of the person's handicap.

(b) *Appropriate education.*

(1) For the purpose of this subpart, the provision of an appropriate education is the provision of regular or special education and related aids and services that (i) are designed to meet individual educational needs of handicapped persons as adequately as the needs of nonhandicapped persons are met and (ii) are based upon adherence to procedures that satisfy the requirements of §§ 104.34, 104.35, and 104.36.

(2) Implementation of an individualized education program developed in accordance with the Education of the Handicapped Act is one means of meeting the standard established in paragraph (b)(1)(i) of this section.

(3) A recipient may place a handicapped person in or refer such person to a program other than the one that it operates as its means of carrying out the requirements of this subpart. If so the recipient remains responsible for ensuring that the requirements of this subpart are met with respect to any handicapped person so placed or referred.

(c) *Free education.*

(1) *General.* For the purpose of this section, the provision of a free education is the provision of educational and related services without cost to the handicapped person or to his or her parents or guardian, except for those fees that are imposed on nonhandicapped persons or their parents or guardian. It may consist either of the provision of free services or, if a recipient places a handicapped person in or refers such person to a program not operated by the recipient as its means of carrying out the requirements of this subpart, of payment for the costs of the program. Funds available from any public or private agency may be used to meet the requirements of this subpart. Nothing in this section shall be construed to relieve an insurer or similar third party from an otherwise valid obligation to provide or pay for services provided to a handicapped person.

(2) *Transportation.* If a recipient places a handicapped person in or refers such person to a program not operated by the recipient as its means of carrying out the requirements of this subpart, the recipient shall ensure that adequate transportation to and from the program is provided at no greater cost than would be incurred by the person or his or her parents or guardian if the person were placed in the program operated by the recipient.

(3) *Residential placement.* If placement in a public or private residential program is necessary to provide a free appropriate public education to a handicapped person because of his or her handicap, the program, including nonmedical care and room and board, shall be provided at no cost to the person or his or her parents or guardian.

(4) *Placement of handicapped persons by parents.* If a recipient has made available, in conformance with the requirements of this section and § 104.34, a free appropriate public education to a handicapped person and the person's parents or guardian choose to place the person in a private school, the recipient is not required to pay for the person's education in the private school. Disagreements between the parent or guardian and a recipient regarding whether the recipient has made such a program available or otherwise regarding the ques-

tion of financial responsibility are subject to the due process procedures of §
104.36.

(d) *Compliance.* A recipient may not exclude any qualified handicapped person
from a public elementary or secondary education after the effective date of this part.
A recipient that is not, on the effective date of this regulation, in full compliance with
the other requirements of the preceding paragraphs of this section shall meet such
requirements at the earliest practicable time and in no event later than September
1, 1978.

104.34 Educational setting.

(a) *Academic setting.* A recipient to which this subpart applies shall educate, or
shall provide for the education of, each qualified handicapped person in its jurisdiction with persons who are not handicapped to the maximum extent appropriate to
the needs of the handicapped person. A recipient shall place a handicapped person
in the regular educational environment operated by the recipient unless it is
demonstrated by the recipient that the education of the person in the regular environment with the use of supplementary aids and services cannot be achieved satisfactorily.
Whenever a recipient places a person in a setting other than the regular educational
environment pursuant to this paragraph, it shall take into account the proximity of
the alternate setting to the person's home.

(b) *Nonacademic settings.* In providing or arranging for the provision of
nonacademic and extracurricular services and activities, including meals, recess
periods, and the services and activities set forth in § 104.37(a)(2), a recipient shall
ensure that handicapped persons participate with nonhandicapped persons in such
activities and services to the maximum extent appropriate to the needs of the handicapped person in question.

(c) *Comparable facilities.* If a recipient, in compliance with paragraph (a) of this
section, operates a facility that is identifiable as being for handicapped persons, the
recipient shall ensure that the facility and the services and activities provided therein
are comparable to the other facilities, services, and activities of the recipient.

104.35 Evaluation and placement.

(a) *Preplacement evaluation.* A recipient that operates a public elementary or
secondary education program shall conduct an evaluation in accordance with the
requirements of paragraph (b) of this section of any person who, because of handicap, needs or is believed to need special education or related services before taking
any action with respect to the initial placement of the person in a regular or special
education program and any subsequent significant change in placement.

(b) *Evaluation procedures.* A recipient to which this subpart applies shall
establish standards and procedures for the evaluation and placement of persons
who, because of handicap, need or are believed to need special education or related
services which ensure that:

(1) Tests and other evaluation materials have been validated for the specific
purpose for which they are used and are administered by trained personnel in conformance with the instructions provided by their producer;

(2) Tests and other evaluation materials include those tailored to assess
specific areas of educational need and not merely those which are designed to provide a single general intelligence quotient; and

(3) Tests are selected and administered so as best to ensure that, when a test
is administered to a student with impaired sensory, manual, or speaking skills, the

test results accurately reflect the student's aptitude or achievement level or whatever other factor the test purports to measure, rather than reflecting the student's impaired sensory, manual, or speaking skills (except where those skills are the factors that the test purports to measure).

(c) *Placement procedures.* In interpreting evaluation data and in making placement decisions, a recipient shall

(1) draw upon information from a variety of sources, including aptitude and achievement tests, teacher recommendations, physical condition, social or cultural background, and adaptive behavior,

(2) establish procedures to ensure that information obtained from all sources is documented and carefully considered,

(3) ensure that the placement decision is made by a group of persons, including persons knowledgeable about the child, the meaning of the evaluation data, and the placement options, and

(4) ensure that the placement decision is made in conformity with § 104.34.

(d) *Reevaluation.* A recipient to which this section applies shall establish procedures, in accordance with paragraph (b) of this section, for periodic reevaluation of students who have been provided special education and related services. A reevaluation procedure consistent with the Education for the Handicapped Act is one means of meeting this requirement.

104.36 Procedural safeguards.

A recipient that operates a public elementary or secondary education program shall establish and implement with respect to actions regarding the identification, evaluation, or educational placement of persons who, because of handicap, need or are believed to need special instruction or related services, a system of procedural safeguards that includes notice, an opportunity for the parents or guardian of the person to examine relevant records, an impartial hearing with opportunity for participation by the person's parents or guardian and representation by counsel, and a review procedure. Compliance with the procedural safeguards of section 615 of the Education of the Handicapped Act is one means of meeting this requirement.

104.37 Nonacademic services.

(a) *General.*

(1) A recipient to which this subpart applies shall provide nonacademic and extracurricular services and activities in such manner as is necessary to afford handicapped students an equal opportunity for participation in such services and activities.

(2) Nonacademic and extracurricular services and activities may include counseling services, physical recreational athletics, transportation, health services, recreational activities, special interest groups or clubs sponsored by the recipients, referrals to agencies which provide assistance handicapped persons, and employment of students, including both employment by the recipient and assistance in making available outside employment.

(b) *Counseling services.* A recipient to which this subpart applies that provides personal, academic, or vocational counseling, guidance, or placement services to its students shall provide these services without discrimination on the basis of handicap. The recipient shall ensure that qualified handicapped students are not counseled toward more restrictive career objectives than are nonhandicapped students with similar interests and abilities.

(c) *Physical education and athletics.*

(1) In providing physical education courses and athletics and similar programs and activities to any of its students, a recipient to which this subpart applies may not discriminate on the basis of handicap. A recipient that offers physical education courses or that operates or sponsors interscholastic, club, or intramural athletics shall provide to qualified handicapped students an equal opportunity for participation in these activities.

(2) A recipient may offer to handicapped students physical education and athletic services that are separate or different from those offered to nonhandicapped students only if separation or differentiation is consistent with the requirements of § 104.34 and only if no qualified handicapped student is denied the opportunity to compete for teams or to participate in courses that are not separate or different.

104.38 Preschool and adult education programs.

A recipient to which this subpart applies that operates a preschool education or day care program or activity or an adult education program or activity may not, on the basis of handicap, exclude qualified handicapped persons from the program or activity and shall take into account the needs of such persons in determining the aid, benefits, or services to be provided under the program or activity.

104.39 Private education programs.

(a) A recipient that operates a private elementary or secondary education program may not, on the basis of handicap, exclude a qualified handicapped person from such program if the person can, with minor adjustments, be provided an appropriate education, as defined in § 104.33(b)(1), within the recipient's program.

(b) A recipient to which this section applies may not charge more for the provision of an appropriate education to handicapped persons than to nonhandicapped persons except to the extent that any additional charge is justified by a substantial increase in cost to the recipient.

(c) A recipient to which this section applies that operates special education programs shall operate such programs in accordance with the provisions of §§ 104.35 and 104.36. Each recipient to which this section applies is subject to the provisions of §§ 104.34, 104.37, and 104.38.

Subpart E—Postsecondary Education

104.41 Application of this subpart.

Subpart E applies to postsecondary education programs and activities, including postsecondary vocational programs and activities, that receive or benefit from Federal financial assistance and to recipients that operate, or that receive or benefit from Federal financial assistance for the operation of, such programs or activities.

104.42 Admissions and recruitment.

(a) *General.* Qualified handicapped persons may not, on the basis of handicap, be denied admission or be subjected to discrimination in admission or be subjected to discrimination in admission or recruitment by a recipient to which this subpart applies.

(b) *Admissions.* In administering its admission policies, a recipient to which this subpart applies:

(1) May not apply limitations upon the number or proportion of handicapped persons who may be admitted;

(2) May not make use of any test or criterion for admission that has a disproportionate, adverse effect on handicapped persons or any class of handicapped persons unless (i) the test or criterion, as used by the recipient, has been validated as a predictor of success in the education program or activity in question and (ii) alternate tests or criteria that have a less disproportionate, adverse effect are not shown by the Assistant Secretary to be available.

(3) Shall assure itself that (i) admissions tests are selected and administered so as best to ensure that, when a test is administered to an applicant who has a handicap that impairs sensory, manual, or speaking skills, the test results accurately reflect the applicant's aptitude or achievement level or whatever other factor the test purports to measure, rather than reflecting the applicant's impaired sensory, manual, or speaking skills (except where those skills are the factors that the test purports to measure); (ii) admissions tests that are designed for persons with impaired sensory, manual, or speaking skills are offered as often and in as timely a manner as are other admissions tests; and (iii) admissions tests are administered in facilities that, on the whole, are accessible to handicapped persons; and

(4) Except as provided in paragraph (c) of this section, may not make preadmission inquiry as to whether an applicant for admission is a handicapped person but, after admission, may make inquiries on a confidential basis as to handicaps that may require accommodation.

(c) *Preadmission inquiry exception.* When a recipient is taking remedial action to correct the effects of past discrimination pursuant to § 104.6(a) or when a recipient is taking voluntary action to overcome the effects of conditions that resulted in limited participation in its federally assisted program or activity pursuant to § 104.6(b), the recipient may invite applicants for admission to indicate whether and to what extent they are handicapped, *Provided,* That:

(1) The recipient states clearly on any written questionnaire used for this purpose or makes clear orally if no written questionnaire is used that the information requested is intended for use solely in connection with its remedial action obligations or its voluntary action efforts; and

(2) The recipient states clearly that the information is being requested on a voluntary basis, that it will be kept confidential, that refusal to provide it will not subject the applicant to any adverse treatment, and that it will be used only in accordance with this part.

(d) *Validity studies.* For the purpose of paragraph (b)(2) of this section, a recipient may base prediction equations on first year grades, but shall conduct periodic validity studies against the criterion of overall success in the education program or activity in question in order to monitor the general validity of the test scores.

104.43 Treatment of students; general.

(a) No qualified handicapped student shall, on the basis of handicap, be excluded from participation in, be denied the benefits of, or otherwise be subjected to discrimination under any academic, research, occupational training, housing, health insurance, counseling, financial aid, physical education, athletics, recreation, transportation, other extracurricular, or other postsecondary education program or activity to which this subpart applies.

(b) A recipient to which this subpart applies that considers participation by students in education programs or activities not operated wholly by the recipient as part of, or equivalent to, an education program or activity operated by the recipient shall assure itself that the other education program or activity, as a whole, provides an equal opportunity for the participation of qualified handicapped persons.

(c) A recipient to which this subpart applies may not, on the basis of handicap, exclude any qualified handicapped student from any course, course of study, or other part of its education program or activity.

(d) A recipient to which this subpart applies shall operate its programs and activities in the most integrated setting appropriate.

104.44 Academic adjustments.

(a) *Academic requirements.* A recipient to which this subpart applies shall make such modifications to its academic requirements as are necessary to ensure that such requirements do not discriminate or have the effect of discriminating, on the basis of handicap, against a qualified handicapped applicant or student. Academic requirements that the recipient can demonstrate are essential to the program of instruction being pursued by such student or to any directly related licensing requirement will not be regarded as discriminatory within the meaning of this section. Modifications may include changes in the length of time permitted for the completion of degree requirements, substitution of specific courses required for the completion of degree requirements, and adaptation of the manner in which specific courses are conducted.

(b) *Other rules.* A recipient to which this subpart applies may not impose upon handicapped students other rules, such as the prohibition of tape recorders in classrooms or of dog guides in campus buildings, that have the effect of limiting the participation of handicapped students in the recipient's education program or activity.

(c) *Course examinations.* In its course examinations or other procedures for evaluating students' academic achievement in its program, a recipient to which this subpart applies shall provide such methods for evaluating the achievement of students who have a handicap that impairs sensory, manual, or speaking skills as will best ensure that the results of the evaluation represent the student's achievement in the course, rather than reflecting the student's impaired sensory, manual, or speaking skills (except where such skills are the factors that the test purports to measure).

(d) *Auxiliary aids.*

(1) A recipient to which this subpart applies shall take such steps as are necessary to ensure that no handicapped student is denied the benefits of, excluded from participation in, or otherwise subjected to discrimination under the education program or activity operated by the recipient because of the absence of educational auxiliary aids for students with impaired sensory, manual, or speaking skills.

(2) Auxiliary aids may include taped texts, interpreters or other effective methods of making orally delivered materials available to students with hearing impairments, readers in libraries for students with visual impairments, classroom equipment adapted for use by students with manual impairments, and other similar services and actions. Recipients need not provide attendants, individually prescribed devices, readers for personal use or study, or other devices or services of a personal nature.

104.45 Housing.

(a) *Housing provided by the recipient.* A recipient that provides housing to its nonhandicapped students shall provide comparable, convenient, and accessible housing to handicapped students at the same cost as to others. At the end of the transition period provided for in Subpart C, such housing shall be available in sufficient quantity and variety so that the scope of handicapped students' choice of living accommodations is, as a whole, comparable to that of nonhandicapped students.

(b) *Other housing.* A recipient that assists any agency, organization, or person in making housing available to any of its students shall take such action as may be necessary to assure itself that such housing is, as a whole, made available in a manner that does not result in discrimination on the basis of handicap.

104.46 Financial and employment assistance to students.

(a) *Provision of financial assistance.*

(1) In providing financial assistance to qualified handicapped persons, a recipient to which this subpart applies may not (i) on the basis of handicap, provide less assistance than is provided to nonhandicapped persons, limit eligibility for assistance, or otherwise discriminate or (ii) assist any entity or person that provides assistance to any of the recipient's students in a manner that discriminates against qualified handicapped persons on the basis of handicap.

(2) A recipient may administer or assist in the administration of scholarships, fellowships, or other forms of financial assistance established under wills, trusts, bequests, or similar legal instruments that require awards to be made on the basis of factors that discriminate or have the effect of discriminating on the basis of handicap only if the overall effect of the award of scholarships, fellowships, and other forms of financial assistance is not discriminatory on the basis of handicap.

(b) *Assistance in making available outside employment.* A recipient that assists any agency, organization, or person in providing employment opportunities to any of its students shall assure itself that such employment opportunities, as a whole, are made available in a manner that would not violate Subpart B if they were provided by the recipient.

(c) *Employment of students by recipients.* A recipient that employs any of its students may not do so in a manner that violates Subpart B.

104.47 Nonacademic services.

(a) *Physical education and athletics.*

(1) In providing physical education courses and athletics and similar programs and activities to any of its students, a recipient to which this subpart applies may not discriminate on the basis of handicap. A recipient that offers physical education courses or that operates or sponsors intercollegiate, club, or intramural athletics shall provide to qualified handicapped students an equal opportunity for participation in these activities.

(2) A recipient may offer to handicapped students physical education and athletic activities that are separate or different only if separation or differentiation is consistent with the requirements of § 104.43(d) and only if no qualified handicapped student is denied the opportunity to compete for teams or to participate in courses that are not separate or different.

(b) *Counseling and placement services.* A recipient to which this subpart applies that provides personal, academic, or vocational counseling, guidance, or placement services to its students shall provide these services without discrimination on the basis of handicap. The recipient shall ensure that qualified handicapped students are not counseled toward more restrictive career objectives than are nonhandicapped students with similar interests and abilities. This requirement does not preclude a recipient from providing factual information about licensing and certification requirements that may present obstacles to handicapped persons in their pursuit of particular careers.

(c) *Social organizations.* A recipient that provides significant assistance to fraternities, sororities, or similar organizations shall assure itself that the membership practices of such organizations do not permit discrimination otherwise prohibited by this subpart.

Subpart F—Health, Welfare, and Social Services

104.51 Application of this subpart.

Subpart F applies to health, welfare, and other social service programs and activities that receive or benefit from Federal financial assistance and to recipients that operate, or that receive or benefit from Federal financial assistance for the operation of, such programs or activities.

104.52 Health, welfare, and other social services.

(a) *General.* In providing health, welfare, or other social services or benefits, a recipient may not, on the basis of handicap:

(1) Deny a qualified handicapped person these benefits or services;

(2) Afford a qualified handicapped person an opportunity to receive benefits or services that is not equal to that offered nonhandicapped persons;

(3) Provide a qualified handicapped person with benefits or services that are not as effective (as defined in § 104.4[b]) as the benefits or services provided to others;

(4) Provide benefits or services in a manner that limits or has the effect of limiting the participation of qualified handicapped persons; or

(5) Provide different or separate benefits or services to handicapped persons except where necessary to provide qualified handicapped persons with benefits and services that are as effective as those provided to others.

(b) *Notice.* A recipient that provides notice concerning benefits or services or written material concerning waivers of rights or consent to treatment shall take such steps as are necessary to ensure that qualified handicapped persons, including those with impaired sensory or speaking skills, are not denied effective notice because of their handicap.

(c) *Emergency treatment for the hearing impaired.* A recipient hospital that provides health services or benefits shall establish a procedure for effective communication with persons with impaired hearing for the purpose of providing emergency health care.

(d) *Auxiliary aids.*

(1) A recipient to which this subpart applies that employs 15 or more persons shall provide appropriate auxiliary aids to persons with impaired sensory, manual, or speaking skills, where necessary to afford such persons an equal opportunity to benefit from the service in question.

(2) The Assistant Secretary may require recipients with fewer than fifteen employees to provide auxiliary aids where the provision of aids would not significantly impair the ability of the recipient to provide its benefits or services.

(3) For the purpose of this paragraph, auxiliary aids may include brailled and taped materials, interpreters, and other aids for persons with impaired hearing or vision.

104.53 Drug and alcohol addicts.

A recipient to which this subpart applies that operates a general hospital or out-patient facility may not discriminate in admission or treatment against a drug or alcohol abuser or alcoholic who is suffering from a medical condition, because of the person's drug or alcohol abuse or alcoholism.

104.54 Education of institutionalized persons.

A recipient to which this subpart applies and that operates or supervises a program or activity for persons who are institutionalized because of handicap shall ensure that each qualified handicapped person, as defined in § 104.3(k)(2), in its program or activity is provided an appropriate education, as defined in § 104.33(b). Nothing in this section shall be interpreted as altering in any way the obligations of recipients under Subpart D.

Subpart G—Procedures

104.61 Procedures.

The procedural provisions applicable to title VI of the Civil Rights Act of 1964 apply to this part. These procedures are found in §§ 100.6–100.10 and Part 101 of this title.

Appendix D:
Sources of Information

Association on Higher Education and Disability (AHEAD)
P.O. Box 21192
Columbus, OH 43221-0192
614-488-4972

Higher Education and Adult Training for People with Handicaps (HEATH)
One Dupont Circle, NW, Suite 800
Washington, DC 20036-1193
202-939-9320

National Clearinghouse for Professions in Special Education
2021 K Street, NW, Suite 315
Washington, DC 20006
202-296-1800

National Information Center for Children and Youth with Disabilities
P.O. Box 1492
Washington, DC 20013
800-999-5599

National Organization on Legal Problems in Education
Southwest Plaza Building
3601 W. 29th Street, Suite 223
Topeka, KS 66614
913-273-3550

United States Department of Education
Office for Civil Rights
Policy and Enforcement Branch
Mary E. Switzer Building
330 C. Street, SW
Washington, DC 20202
202-732-1635

Notes

Introduction

1. "EHA" refers to the Education of the Handicapped Act, as amended Pub. L. 94-142, 20 U.S.C. 1401, *et seq.* I am aware that the EHA has been amended and is now referred to as IDEA. However, since the pertinent court decisions discussed concern the EHA, I will refer to Pub. L. 94-142 as the EHA in this text.

2. The Department of Education's Office for Civil Rights will hereinafter be referred to as the OCR.

3. Subparts F and G are not discussed because Subpart F is only marginally related to the educational arena, and Subpart G contains general procedural requirements not unique to Section 504. I have also not discussed issues that are purely related to litigation, such as whether individuals have a private right of action under Section 504.

Chapter 1

1. The Rehabilitation Act of 1973 prohibits discrimination against handicapped persons by government agencies, contractors, and recipients of federal financial assistance.

2. See *Rothschild v. Grottenthaler,* 907 F.2d 286 (2nd Cir. 1990); *Rogers v. Bennett,* 873 F.2d 1387 (11th Cir. 1989); *U.S. v. Board of Trustees of the University of Alabama,* 908 F.2d 740 (11th Cir. 1990); and *Wynne v. Tufts University School of Medicine,* F.2d 1990 WL 52715 (1st Cir. 1990) *rehearing en banc* No. 89-1670 (1st Cir. 1991).

3. Sections 104.11(a) and (b).

4. 660 F. Supp. 1418 (D. Conn. 1987).

5. Appendix A—Analysis of Final Regulation (hereinafter "Appendix A")—Code of Federal Regulations Vol. 34, Part 1 to 299 (Revised 7/1/88, p. 483).

6. *Nathanson v. Medical College of Pennsylvania,* 926 F.2d 1368, 1385 (3rd Cir. 1991). See also *Garrity v. Gallen, supra.*

7. *Alexander v. Choate,* 469 U.S. 287, 300, 83 L.Ed. 2d 661 (1985).

Chapter 2

1. Rehabilitation Act of 1973, § 504, 29 U.S.C.A. § 794.

2. *Southeastern Community College v. Davis* 442 U.S. 397, 406, 60 L.Ed.2d 980 (1979).

3. *Alexander v. Choate, supra,* at 299 n. 19. (For original citation, see the List of Cases cited appended to this work on p. 250.

4. See *School Board of Nassau County v. Arline,* 480 U.S. 273, 287 (1987), and *Alexander, supra* at 300.

5. *Davis, supra* at 400. This case involved a student with a serious hearing disability who sought to enroll in an associate degree nursing program. She was denied admission because she was dependent on her lipreading skills, and it was felt she could not participate safely in the clinical program. The Court also held that recipients were not required to make fundamental alterations of their programs or adopt measures which would impose undue financial and administrative burdens. *Id.* at 410, 412.

6. Representative Vanik's and Senators Humphrey's and Cranston's statements regarding the need for legislation to address the discrimination against the handicapped. 119 Cong. Rec. 5880, 5883 (1973); 118 Cong. Rec. 525–26 (1972), and 117 Cong. Rec. 45974 (1971).

7. *Dopico v. Goldschmidt,* 687 F.2d 644, 652 (2nd Cir. 1982); and Note, Accommodating the Handicapped: Rehabilitating Section 504 After Southeastern, 80 Colum. L. Rev. 171, 185–86 (1980).

8. *Americans Disabled for Accessible Public Transportation v. Skinner,* 881 F.2d 1184, 1192 (3rd Cir. 1989).

9. *School Board of Nassau County, supra* at 287.

10. *Rhone v. United States Department of Army,* 665 F. Supp. 734, 745, n. 19 (E.D. Mo. 1987). See also Chapter 6 for a detailed discussion of term "otherwise qualified."

11. *Alexander, supra* at 299 n. 19.

12. *Freeman v. Cavazas,* 923 F.2d 1434 (11th Cir. 1991); and *U.S. v. Board of Trustees of the University of Alabama, supra.* See also Chapter 19.

13. *Wynne v. Tufts University, supra;* and *Brennan v. Stewart,* 834 F.2d 1248 (5th Cir. 1988).

14. *Wynne v. Tufts University, supra.* See also, *Strathie v. Department of Transportation,* 716 F.2d 227 (3rd Cir. 1983); *Pushkin v. Regents of University of Colorado,* 658 F.2d 1372 (1981). See also Chapter 20.

15. *Davis, supra* at 410.

16. *Davis, supra* at 413.

17. *Consolidated Rail Corporation v. Darrone,* 465 U.S. 624, 634 (1984).

18. *Alexander, supra* at 304 n. 24.

19. No. 89-1670 (1st Cir. 1991).

20. 834 F.2d 1248 (5th Cir. 1988).

21. *Id.* at 1262. See also the opinion in *Doherty v. Southern College of Optometry,* 862 F.2d 570, 574–575 (6th Cir. 1988)—the question of "reasonable accommodation" may not be separated from the "otherwise qualified" issue.

22. See also Chapters 6 and 20.

23. *Regents of University of Michigan v. Ewing,* 474 U.S. 214 (1985). See also *Doherty v. Southern College of Optometry, supra; Doe v. New York University,* 666 F.2d 761 (2d Cir. 1981); and *Doe v. Region 13 Mental Health–Mental Retardation Comm'n,* 704 F2d 1402, 1410 (5th Cir. 1983).

24. "We certainly do not suggest that absolute deference is required. No rubber-stamp approval is suggested hereby. A sound, thorough record substantiating the expert's decision must be developed." *Doe v. Region 13, supra* at 1410. See also Chapter 20 for a complete discussion of this issue.

25. *Id.* at 287 n. 17.

26. *Strathie v. Department of Transportation, supra* at 231.

27. See *Colin K. by John K. v. Schmidt,* 715 F.2d, 1, 9 (1st Cir. 1983); *Turillo v. Tyson,* 535 F. Supp. 577; *Barnett v. Fairfax County School Board,* 927 F.2d 146 (4th Cir. 1991); *Eva N. v. Brock,* 741 F. Supp. 626 (E.D.Ky. 1990); *Doherty v. Southern College of Optometry, supra;* and *Americans Disabled for Accessible Public Transportation v. Skinner, supra.*

28. *Freeman v. Cavazas, supra; Department of Education v. Katherine,* 531 F. Supp. 517 (D. Haw. 1982); *David H. v. Spring Branch Independent School District,* 569 F. Supp. 1324 (S.D. Texas 1983); and *United States v. Board of Trustees of the University of Alabama, supra.*

Chapter 3

1. See *School Board of Nassau County v. Arline, supra* at 278 n. 2 ("Congress' decision to pattern § 504 after Title VI is evident in the language of the statute."). See also *Consolidated Rail Corporation v. Darrone, supra.*

2. *Anderson v. University of Wisconsin,* 841 F.2d 737, 740 (7th Cir. 1988).

3. See § 104.4(a), (b)(1).

4. *Garrity v. Gallen,* 522 F. Supp. 171, 206.

5. See § 104.4(b).

6. *Pushkin v. Regents of the University of Colorado, supra.*

7. *Davis, supra* at 406, and *Doe v. Region 13 Mental Health–Mental Retardation Comm'n, supra.*

8. *Doe v. New York University, supra* at 776.

9. See *U.S. v. Board of Trustees of the University of Alabama, supra.*

10. Section 104.4(b)(1)(iv).

11. 913 F.2d 1033, 1041 (2nd Cir. 1990).

12. *Alexander, supra* at 300.

13. Section 104.4(b)(2).

Chapter 4

1. The mandates of § 504 are applicable to "each recipient of federal financial assistance . . . and to each program or activity that receives or benefits from such assistance." (§ 104.2). Further, recipients are entities or persons "to which federal financial assistance is extended directly or through another recipient, including any successors, assignee or transferee of a recipient. . . ." (§ 104.3[f]). For our purposes, recipients are state and local education agencies and postsecondary institutions.

2. 465, U.S. 555, 79 L.Ed.2d 516 (1984)—Title IX, and 465 U.S. 624, 79 L.Ed.2d 568 (1984)—Section 504. The Court in *Grove City* held that since the only federal financial assistance the college received was BEOG (Basic Educational Opportunity Grant Program) funds, the student financial aid program—not the entire college—was the "program or activity" subject to the requirements of the regulations. In *Darrone* the Court relied on *Grove City* to apply the same program-specific limitations to Section 504.

3. See also *Niehaus v. Kansas Bar Association,* 793 F.2d 1159, 1162–63 (10th Cir. 1986).

4. *Gallagher v. Pontiac School District,* 807 F.2d 75, 79–81 (6th Cir. 1986).

5. Restoration Act § 4, 102 Stat. at 29 (29 U.S.C. § 794(b). See also *Leake v. Long Island Jewish Medical Center,* 869 F.2d 130, 131 (2nd Cir. 1989).

6. OCR, April 26, 1979, policy interpretation and 1988 University of Florida—Letter of Finding (LOF). See also § 104.4(b)(4).

7. *DeVargas v. Mason & Hanger-Silas Mason Co.,* 911 F.2d 1377 (10th Cir. 1990); *Leake v. Long Island Jewish Medical Center, supra; Ayers v. Allain,* 893 F.2d 732, *reh'g en banc granted,* 868 F.2d 1014 (5th Cir. 1990).

8. See *DeVargas, supra* at 1384–92, for an excellent discussion of the present state of the law regarding retroactive application, including seemingly irreconcilable Supreme Court rulings on the issue.

9. See *U.S. Department of Transportation v. Paralyzed Veterans of America,* 477 U.S. 597, 608, 91 L.Ed.2d 494 (1986); and *Grove City, supra* at 572 ("Most federal educational assistance has economic ripple effects").

10. *Darrone, supra* at 633 n. 13.

11. *Paralyzed Veterans, supra* at 606.

12. *Id.* at 603.

13. *Id.* at 606.

14. Para. 1, p. 482.

15. See *New Mexico Association for Retarded Citizens v. The State of New Mexico,* 678 F.2d 847 (10th Cir. 1982).

16. *Grove City, supra* at 564.

17. *Paralyzed Veterans, supra* at 606.

18. § 104.3(h). See also *Arline v. School Board of Nassau County, supra* (impact aid); and *Frazier v. Board of Trustees of Northwest Mississippi Regional Medical Center* 765 F.2d 1278 (5th Cir. 1985)—medicare/medicaid payments).

19. See *Jacobsen v. Delta Airlines,* 742 F.2d 1202, 1210 (9th Cir. 1984); and *DeVargas, supra* at 1382. See also *Cook v. Budget Rent-A-Car Corporation,* 502 F. Supp. 494 (D.C.N.Y. 1980)—receipt of federal funds under an automobile rental contract; *Bachman v. American Society of Clinical Pathologists,* 577 F. Supp. 1257 (D.C.N.J. 1983)—tax exempt status; and *Hingson v. Pacific Southwest Airlines,* 743 F.2d 1408 (9th Cir. 1984)—payments to the airline for carrying mail.

20. *Jacobsen, supra* at 1209.

21. *Id.* at 1210. See also *DeVargas, supra* at 1382.

22. § 104.5(a).

23. *Grove City, supra* at 533.

24. It is also important to note that § 104.5(c) provides that, with respect to real property, there will be "a covenant running with the land to assure nondiscrimination."

25. *United States v. Onslow County Board of Education,* 728 F.2d 628 (4th Cir. 1984).

Chapter 5

1. *Jasany v. U.S. Postal Service,* 755 F.2d 1244, 1248 (6th Cir. 1985)—"Jasany must satisfy the threshold requirement that he is a handicapped person." See also *Perez v. Philadelphia Housing Authority,* 677 F. Supp. 357, 359 (E.D.Pa. 1987) *aff'd* 841 F.2d 1120 (3rd Cir. 1988); and *Elstner v. Southwestern Bell Telephone Co.,* 659 F. Supp. 1328, 1341 (S.D. Tex. 1987).

2. "(i) 'Physical or mental impairment' means (A) any physiological disorder or condition, cosmetic disfigurement, or anatomical loss affecting one or more of the following body systems: neurological; musculoskeletal; special sense organs; respiratory, including speech organs; cardiovascular; reproductive, digestive, genito-urinary; hemic and lymphatic; skin; and endocrine; or (B) any mental or psychological disorder such as mental retardation, organic brain syndrome, emotional or mental illness, and specific learning disabilities."

3. Appendix A, para. 3, p. 483.

4. *Bowen v. American Hospital Association,* 476 U.S. 610 (1986); *Grube v. Bethlehem Area School District,* 550 F. Supp. 418 (E.D. Penn. 1982); *Reynolds v. Block,* 815 F.2d 571 (9th Cir. 1987); and *Arline, supra.*

5. Appendix A, para. 3, p. 483.

6. Appendix A, para. 3, p. 483. See also *Blackwell v. Department of Treasury,* 656 F. Supp. 713 (D.D.C. 1986).

7. 54 L.W. 2022, 37 Fed. Cases 1869.

8. *Blackwell, supra* at 715.

9. *De La Torresse v. Bolger,* 610 F. Supp. 593 (N.D. Texas 1985)—left-handed postal worker forced to use his right hand. The Court held that being left-handed was a "physiological condition" not a handicap; *Stevens v. Stubbs,* 576 F. Supp. 1409, 1414 (N.D. Ga. 1983)—Speculative or "transitory" condition; *Padilla v. City of Topeka,* 708 P. 2d 543 (Kansas, 1985)—The mere existence of a visual impairment does not render one "handicapped" within the meaning of Section 504; and *Tudyman v. United Airlines,* 608 F. Supp. 739 (C.D. Cal. 1984)—the fact that an individual's desire to be a body builder prevented him from meeting an airline's weight guidelines did not render him handicapped.

10. Union Beach Public School District, Education for the Handicapped Law Reporter (EHLR) 257:490 (1984).

11. Lowell Area School District, EHLR 352:574, 575 (1987).

12. 840 F.2d 701 (9th Cir. 1988).

13. October 6, 1988, Department of Justice policy statement.

14. 861 F.2d 1502 (11th Cir. 1988); on remand 711 F. Supp. 1066 (M.D. Fla. 1989). See also *Cain v. Hyatt,* 734 F. Supp. 671 (E.D. Pa. 1990); *Robertson by Robertson v. Granite City Community Unit School District No. 9,* 684 F. Supp. 1002 (S.D. Ill. 1988); and *Thomas v. Atascadero Unified School District,* 662 F. Supp. 376 (C.D. Cal. 1987).

15. See *Anderson v. University of Wisconsin,* 841 F.2d 737 (7th Cir. 1988); *Lemere v. Burnley,* 683 F. Supp. 275 (D.D.C. 1988); and *Wallace v. Veterans Administration,* 683 F. Supp. 758 (D. Kan. 1988).

16. Appendix A, para. 4, p. 484.

17. *Id.*

18. Section 512 of the Americans with Disabilities Act amends Section 504 as follows:

> The definition of handicapped individual does not include individuals who are "currently engaging in the illegal use of drugs" and "whose current use of alcohol prevents such individuals from performing the duties of the job in question or whose employment, by reason of such current alcohol abuse would constitute a direct threat."

See also *Burka v. New York City Transit Authority,* 680 F. Supp. 590, 597–601 (S.D.N.Y. 1988).

19. *Id.* at 483.

20. Appendix A, para. 3, p. 483.

21. Obesity must be viewed in the same fashion. The mere fact of being obese is not sufficient. It must also be determined that the excessive weight substantially limits one or more major life activities.

22. Appendix A, para. 3, p. 483.

23. *Diaz v. U.S. Postal Service,* 658 F. Supp. 484 (E.D. Cal. 1987).

24. *Perez v. Philadelphia Housing Authority, supra* at 360; *Jasany v. U.S. Postal Service, supra* at 1248; *Elstner v. Southwestern Bell Telephone Co., supra* at 1342; *E. E. Black, Ltd. v. Marshall,* 497 F. Supp. 1088, 1100 (S.D. Tex. 1987); *Forrisi v. Brown,* 794 F.2d 931, 933 (4th Cir. 1986); and *Trimble v. Carlin,* 633 F. Supp. 367 (E.D. Pa. 1987). See also Part I, Chapter 1 for a discussion of this issue.

25. § 104.3(j)(2)(ii).

26. Appendix A, para. 3, p. 483.

27. *Supra* at 360.

28. *E. E. Black, supra* at 1100.

29. *Id.* at 1099. See also *Trimble v. Carlin, supra;* and *Perez, supra* at 360.

30. *Forrisi, supra* at 933. See also *Elstner, supra* at 1342.

31. See Union Beach Public School District, EHLR 257:490 (1984); and School District of the City of Saginaw, EHLR 352:413 (1987).

32. School District of the City of Saginaw, at 352:414.

33. See *Jasany, supra* at 1248; *E. E. BLack, supra* at 1099–1100; and *Tudyman v. United Airlines, supra.*

34. *Perez v. Philadelphia Housing Authority, supra.*

35. *Carter v. Tisch,* 822 F.2d 465 (4th Cir. 1987).

36. *Harrison v. Marsh,* 691 F. Supp. 1223 (W.D. Mo. 1988).

37. *Shea v. Tisch,* 870 F.2d 786 (1st Cir. 1989).

38. *Franklin v. U.S. Postal Service,* 687 F. Supp. 1219 (S.D. Ohio 1988).

39. *Dexler v. Tisch,* 660 F. Supp. 1418 (D.C.D. Conn. 1987).

40. *Recanzone v. Washoe County School District,* 696 F. Supp. 1372 (D. Nev. 1988).

41. *Forrisi, supra* at 934; and *Jasany, supra* at 1250.

42. 104.3(j)(2)(iii) "'Has a record of such an impairment' means has a history of, or has been misclassified as having, a mental or physical impairment that substantially limits one or more major life activities. (iv) 'Is regarded as having an impairment' (A) has a physical or mental impairment that does not substantially limit major life activities, but that is treated by a recipient as constituting such a limitation; (B) has a physical or mental impairment that substantially limits major life activities only as a result of the attitudes of others toward such impairment; or (C) has none of the impairments defined in . . . (j)(2)(i) . . . but is treated by a recipient as having such an impairment."

43. *Arline, supra* at 282.

44. *Id.* at 282–83 ns. 9, 10.

45. *Davis, supra* 405–6 n. 5.

46. § 104.3(j)(2)(iv). See also *Pridemore v. Rural Legal Aid Society of West Central Ohio,* 625 F. Supp. 1180 (S.D. Ohio 1985).

47. Para. 3, p. 484.

48. 793 F.2d 969 (9th Cir. 1984).

Chapter 6

1. The regulations use the term "qualified handicapped person" instead of the statutory term "otherwise qualified handicapped persson" because it was felt that the latter was misleading if applied literally. See Appendix A, para. 5, p. 485.

2. *Rhone, supra* at 745, n. 19.

3. *Davis, supra* at 406.

4. *Alexander, supra* at 300–301.

5. See Chapter 2 for an in-depth discussion of the evolution of this compliance standard.

6. *Brennan v. Stewart*, 834 F.2d 1248, 1261–62 (5th Cir. 1988).

7. *Davis, supra* at 406. See also *Daubert v. United States Postal Service*, 733 F.2d 1367 (10th Cir. 1984); and *Dempsey By and Through Dempsey v. Ladd*, 840 F.2d 638 (9th Cir. 1987).

8. *Arline, supra* at 287.

9. *Doe v. Region 13 Mental Health–Mental Retardation Commission, supra.* See also *Pushkin v. Regents of the University of Colorado, supra; Fuqua v. Unisys*, 716 F. Supp. 1201 (D. Minn. 1989); *Jasany, supra*; and *Doe v. Syracuse School District*, 508 F. Supp. 333 (N.D. New York 1981).

10. *Doe v. Region 13, supra*; and *Pushkin v. Regents of the University of Colorado, supra.* See also *Lelsz v. Kavanagh*, 673 F. Supp. 828 (N.D. Tex. 1987); and *Bentivegna v. United States Dept. of Labor*, 694 F.2d 619, 621 (9th Cir. 1982).

11. 865 F.2d 592 (3rd Cir. 1989).

12. *Davis, supra* at 406; *Rothschild v. Grottenthaler*, 907 F.2d 286, 290 (2nd Cir. 1990); *Strathie, supra* at 230–31; *Arline, supra* at 287–88; *Brennan, supra* at 1262; *Bentivegna, supra* at 623; *Doe v. Region 13, supra* at 1410.

13. *Doe v. New York University*, 666 F.2d 781 (2nd Cir. 1981).

14. *Davis, supra* at 405, 410–12.

15. *Doe v. New York University, supra* at 776.

16. *Rothschild, supra* at 290.

17. *Rothschild, supra.*

18. *Pushkin, supra.*

19. *United States v. Board of Trustees of the University of Alabama, supra.*

20. *Fitzgerald v. Green Valley Area Education Agency*, 589 F. Supp. 1130 (S.D. Iowa 1984).

21. *Carter v. Casa Central*, 849 F.2d 1048 (7th Cir. 1988).

22. *Alexander, supra* at 300–301.

23. "The inquiry into reasonable accommodation is one aspect of the 'otherwise qualified' analysis." *Doherty v. Southern College of Optometry*, 862 F.2d 570 (6th Cir. 1988).

24. *Arline, supra* at 287.

25. See *Davis, supra* at 405–6, and *Alexander, supra* at 300–301.

26. *Strathie, supra* at 231.

27. 34CFR § 104.3(k)(1).

28. *Davis, supra* at 412–13.

29. *Rothschild, supra* at 293.

30. *U.S. v. Board of Trustees of the University of Alabama, supra* at 749.

31. *Carter v. Bennett*, 840 F.2d 63 (D.C. Cir. 1988).

32. *Eva N. v. Brock*, 741 F. Supp. 626 (E.D. Ky. 1990).

33. *Prewitt v. U.S. Postal Service*, 662 F.2d 292 (5th Cir. 1981).

34. Appendix A, para. 5, p. 485.

35. *Gwinn v. Bolger,* 598 F. Supp. 196 (D.D.C. 1984). See also *Fitzgerald v. Green Valley Education Agency, supra.*

36. *Hall v. U.S. Postal Service,* 857 F.2d 1073 (6th Cir. 1989); and *Smith v. St. Louis County,* 656 F.2d 316 (8th Cir. 1981).

37. *Wimbley v. Bolger,* 642 F. Supp. 481, 485 (W.D. Tenn. 1986). See also *Santiago v. Temple University,* 739 F. Supp. 974, 979 (E.D. Pa. 1990): the Court, in denying the claim of an X-ray attendant who challenged his termination for habitual absenteeism, held:

> To the contrary, while plaintiff agrees that all job tasks are performable by him when present, it is his mere presence at work in any predictable and reliable manner that is unobtainable. Due to the intermittent and unpredictable incidents of eye inflammation, plaintiff therefore claims that the University must tolerate the uncertainty and risk of plaintiff being allowed to sporadically appear at his job in the emergency room. An employee of any status, full or part-time, cannot be qualified for his position if he is unable to attend the work place to perform the required duties, because attendance is necessarily the fundamental prerequisite to job qualification.

See also *Stevens v. Stubbs,* 576 F. Supp. 1409, 1415 (N.D. Ga. 1983).

38. *Dancy v. Kline,* 639 F. Supp. 1076 (N.D. Ill. 1986).

39. Eligibility under the EHA is only one of the definitions of "qualified handicapped person." See Chapter 19 for a detailed discussion of this issue.

40. *Eva N. v. Brock,* 741 F. Supp. 626 (E.D. Ky. 1990).

41. *Riley v. Jefferson County Board of Education,* Case No. CV-89-P-0169-S (N.D. Ala. 1989).

42. EHLR 352:514 (1988). See also OCR's response to the Superintendent of Northwestern Local School District, EHLR 305:19 (1983).

43. Appendix A, para. 5, p. 485.

44. *Id.* at 291–92. See also OCR's LOF for Ramapo Central School District (1989), and OCR's Response to Mississippi School for the Deaf, EHLR 305:48 (1988).

45. *Anderson v. University of Wisconsin,* 841 F.2d 737 (7th Cir. 1988); and *McKelvey v. Turnage,* 485 U.S. 535, 99 L.Ed.2d 618 (1988).

46. *Burka v. New York City Transit Authority, supra.* See also § 512 of the Americans with Disabilities Act which amends Section 504 regarding the protection afforded alcoholism and drug addiction.

47. 840 F.2d 701 (9th Cir. 1988).

48. 662 F. Supp. 376 (C.D. Cal. 1987).

49. 861 F.2d 1502 (11th Cir. 1988).

50. 865 F.2d 930 (8th Cir. 1989).

Chapter 7

1. § 104.4(a) Discrimination Prohibited.

2. See § 104.4(b)(1).

3. See *Southeastern Community College v. Davis, supra; School Board of Nassau County v. Arline, supra; Alexander v. Choate, supra; Doe v. Region 13, supra; Doherty v. Southern College of Optometry, supra; Nathanson v. Medical College of Pennsylvania,* 926 F.2d 1368 (3rd Cir. 1991); and *Strathie v. Department of Transportation, supra.*

4. *Arline, supra* at 279.

5. § 104.4(b)(1).

6. See *Arline, supra* at 284–85; *Martinez v. School Board of Hillsborough County, supra; Rothschild v. Grottenthaler, supra; Carter v. Casa Central, supra; Pushkin v. Regents of University of Colorado; Riley v. Jefferson County Board of Education, supra;* and Special School District of St. Louis County, EHLR 352:156 (1986).

7. 927 F.2d 146 (4th Cir. 1991).

8. *Barnett, supra* at 151; see also *Rothschild, supra* at 293, to the effect that, requiring the school district to provide interpreters for hearing-impaired parents for extracurricular school functions was an undue financial and administrative burden.

9. See OCR Policy Interpretation: Western Illinois University, 8/25/82.

10. See *NAACP v. Wilmington Medical Center, Inc.,* 453 F. Supp. 330 (D. Del. 1978).

11. *Iron Arrow Honor Society v. Hufstedler,* 702 F.2d 549, 564 (5th Cir. 1983), *vacated as moot,* 464 U.S. 67, 78 L.Ed.2d 58 (1983). See also Appendix A, para. 6, p. 486: "This section would, for example, prohibit financial support by a recipient to a community recreational group or to a professional or social organization that discriminates."

12. *Niehaus v. Kansas State Bar Association, supra.* See also Appendix A, para. 6, p. 486.

13. § 104.4(b)(2).

14. Appendix A, para. 6, p. 486.

15. *P.C. v. McLaughlin,* 913 F.2d 1033, 1041 (2nd Cir. 1990):

> § 504 indicates that its central purpose is to assure that handicapped individuals receive 'evenhandedness treatment'. . . . The Act does not require all handicapped persons to be provided identical benefits.

See also *Doe v. Region 13, supra* at 1411.

16. *Fleming v. New York University,* 865 F.2d 478 (2nd Cir. 1989); and OCR Policy Memorandum, 6/30/81.

17. *Anderson v. University of Wisconsin, supra.*

18. OCR Policy Memorandum, 7/5/79.

19. OCR Policy Interpretation #3, Federal Register, 8/14/78.

20. Appendix A, para. 6, p. 486.

21. § 104.4(b)(3).

22. Appendix A, para. 6, p. 486.

23. § 104.4(b)(4).

24. See *G.C. by and Through W.S. v. Coler,* 673 F. Supp. 1093 (S.D. Fla. 1987). See also California State Department of Education, EHLR 352:549 (1987); and Seattle School District, EHLR 352:80 (1985).

25. § 104.4(b)(5).

26. Appendix A at 486.

Chapter 8

1. §§ 104.6–104.10.

2. § 104.6.

3. Appendix A, para. 10, p. 487; see also § 104.6(b).

4. *Burr v. Ambach,* 863 F.2d 1071 (2nd Cir. 1988).

5. Para. 9, p. 486. See also *Pendleton v. Jefferson Local School District,* 754 F. Supp. 570 (S.D. Ohio 1990)—an individual can recover back pay under Section 504.

6. *Burr v. Ambach, supra;* Chicago (IL) Board of Education, EHLR 257:568 (1984).

7. Appendix A, para. 9, p. 486. See also *Freeman v. Cavazos,* 923 F.2d 1434 (11th Cir. 1991)—federal funds were terminated because the district refused to permit the OCR to investigate complaints of violations of Section 504.

8. § 104.7(a). See Fontana (CA) Unified School District, EHLR 353:248 (1989).

9. § 104.7(b)—Grievance procedures need not be established regarding complaints from applicants for employment or for admission to postsecondary institutions. See also Fontana, *supra.*

10. § 104.8—Methods may include "the posting of notices, publication in newspapers and magazines, placement of notices in recipients' publication, and distribution of memoranda." See also Bristol-Plymouth (MA) Regional Vocational Technical School District, EHLR 353:241 (1989).

11. Appendix A, para. 12, p. 487.

12. See Hawaii State Department of Education, EHLR 311:52 (1985).

13. Arcadia Unified School District, EHLR 311:27 (1983), and the OCR's response to South Sioux City School District, EHLR 305:46 (1988). See also Jackson, EHLR 305:46 (1988).

14. OCR's 10/24/88 Policy Statement: Requirements for Nondiscrimination Notices.

15. § 104.10(a): "The obligation to comply . . . is not obviated or alleviated by the existence of any state or local law or other requirement that, on the basis of handicap, imposes prohibitions or limits upon the eligibility of qualified handicapped persons to receive services or to practice any occupation or profession."

16. Appendix A, para. 14, p. 488.

17. OCR's LOF, EHLR 305:40 (1987).

Chapter 9

1. § 104.21: "No qualified handicapped person shall, because a recipient's facilities are inaccessible to or unusable by handicapped persons, be denied the benefits of, be excluded from participation in . . . any program or activity." See also Appendix A, p. 490.

2. CV-867C-1779-S (N.D. Ala. 1989) *aff'd in part, rev'd in part* 908 F.2d 740 (11th Cir. 1990). See also May 11, 1990, press release regarding a settlement agreement involving Washington University. [The university agreed to make modifications to its facilities estimated to cost over two million dollars as a result of a complaint filed with the OCR and subsequent court action.]

3. *Id.,* at 20.

4. 908 F.2d 743, 751.

5. Appendix A, para. 20, pp. 490–91. See also Logan County (WV) School District, EHLR 353:286 (1989) and Johnson City (TN) School District, EHLR 312:107 (1988).

6. See Hindsdale (NY) Central School District, EHLR 401:349 (1989).

7. See *Lelsz v. Kavanagh,* 673 F. Supp. 828 (N.D. Tex. 1987); *Locascio v. City of St. Petersburg,* 731 F. Supp. 1522 (M.D. Fla. 1990); Hawaii State Department of

Education, EHLR 311:52 (1985); and Monroe Woodbury Central School District, EHLR 352:311 (1986).

8. § 104.23(a).

9. See Hawaii State Department of Education, *supra,* and OCR's Response to Inquiry, EHLR 305:24 (1985).

10. See Chapter 2 for a discussion of this issue.

11. See *Rothschild v. Grottenthaler,* 907 F.2d 286 (2nd Cir. 1990)—The District was required to provide interpreter services to hearing-impaired parents. See also Westwood Community School District, EHLR 352:470 (1987).

12. See *Rothschild, supra.*

13. Policy Interpretation No. 4, Federal Register, August 14, 1978, 43 FR 36035.

14. Duval County School District, EHLR 257:394 (1982). See also Fort Osage R-1 School District, EHLR 352:490 (1987); and Marion County Public Schools, EHLR 352:112 (1985).

15. Appendix A, para. 20, p. 491. See also Penna, EHLR 305:03 (1978).

16. § 104.22. Note: Subpart C required recipients to develop transition plans and make necessary modifications within three years of the effective date of the regulations. Since the time for complying with this requirement has long since passed, unless it is clear that the recipient never complied with § 104.22(d-e), these provisions of the regulations generally are not at issue. Further, § 104.22(f) requires that recipients implement procedures to ensure that "interested persons, including persons with impaired vision or hearing, can obtain information as to the existence and location of services, activities and facilities that are accessible."

17. Appendix A, para. 20, p. 490.

18. § 104.22(b).

19. See *Barnett v. Fairfax County School Board,* 927 F.2d 146 (4th Cir. 1991)—recipient is not required to provide accessible services to hearing-impaired students in their neighborhood schools.

20. Appendix A, para. 20, pp. 490–91.

21. *Board of Trustees of the University of Alabama, supra; Penna,* EHLR 305:03 (1978); and Marathon County Handicapped Children's Education Board, 305:24 (1985).

22. See OCR LOF, EHLR 305:40 (1985).

23. Para. 20, p. 490.

24. See Policy Interpretation No. 3, Federal Register, August 14, 1978, 43 FR 36034. The ADA, however, requires that you make modifications that are "readily achievable." Arguably, if one has fully complied with the mandates of Section 504, such modifications would have already been made. If you have not, you must keep in mind that the ADA, in some instances, may require structural modifications where Section 504 does not.

25. § 104.22(b).

26. OCR's Response to Inquiry, EHLR 305:21 (1984); See also Policy Interpretation No. 3, *supra.*

27. Policy Interpretation No. 4, Federal Register, August 14, 1978, 43 FR 36035, and *Gebhardt v. Ambach,* EHLR 554:341 (1982).

28. Policy Interpretation No. 4, *supra.*

29. § 104.23. Note: Previously, § 104.23(C) provided that American National Standards Institute accessibility standards or equivalent standards may be used to achieve compliance. Now recipients must utilize the Uniform Federal Accessibility Standards.

30. See Hawaii State Department of Education, *supra,* and OCR's Response to Inquiry, EHLR 305:24, *supra.*

31. Para. 21, p. 492; OCR's Response to Inquiry, EHLR 305:24, *supra.*
32. § 104.23(b); Appendix A, para. 21, p. 492.

Chapter 10

1. For purposes of this discussion, it will be assumed that all parties agree that the selected placement is the appropriate one.
2. *Black's Law Dictionary,* Sixth Edition, pp. 484, 1308–9.
3. Appendix A, para. 23, p. 493.
4. 743 F. Supp. 700 (D. Ariz. 1990). This case involved a child born in Arizona to parents who were Mexican citizens. She resided in Mexico until age 12 and then moved to Arizona to live with family friends who were granted legal guardianship. The Arizona Department of Education ruled that the child was not entitled to free services because she was not a resident. Department officials stated that residency was determined by the residency of the natural parents, who in this instance were Mexican citizens. The Court ruled against the state, holding that the child's presence, not the parents' residency, was the determining factor.
5. *Sonya C. By and Through Olivar v. Arizona Department of Education, supra* and *Rabinowitz v. New Jersey State Board of Education, supra.*
6. Meridian School District, EHLR 311:110 (1987); Coachella Valley Unified School District EHLR 311:42 (1985); Chicago Board of Education EHLR 257:568 (1984).
7. February 9, 1990, letter from Robert R. Davila, Asst. Secretary for the Office of Special Education and Rehabilitative Services, and William L. Smith, Acting Asst. Secretary for the Office for Civil Rights, to David Tatel. See also the March 5, 1990, letter from Messrs. Davila and Smith to Joe E. Lutjeharms, Commissioner of Education–Nebraska Department of Education.
8. Appendix A, para. 23, p. 493.
9. *Kerr Center Parents Association v. Charles,* 842 F.2d 1052 (9th Cir. 1988); see also Mitlelstedt, EHLR 305:15 (1982) and OSPR I/1/34, EHLR 133:04 (1979).
10. New Hampshire Department of Education, EHLR 352:197 (1986).
11. March 5, 1990, letter from Messrs. Davila and Smith to Joe E. Lutjeharms, Commissioner of Education–Nebraska Department of Education.
12. February 1989 Headquarters policy memorandum re Colorado School for the Deaf. See also, New Castle County School District LOF (6/81); Virginia Department of Correctional Education, EHLR 352:451 (1987); OSPR III/1/12 EHLR 133.12, and *Kerr Center Parents Association v. Charles,* 842 F.2d 1052 (9th Cir. 1988).
13. New Castle County School District—LOF (6/81), Virginia Department of Correctional Education, EHLR 352:451 (1987), and California Department of Youth Authority, EHLR 352:307 (1986).
14. Tuscaloosa City School District, EHLR 352:273 (1986).
15. Appendix A, para. 23, p. 493.
16. 104.3(f) "Recipient means any state or its political subdivision, any instrumentality of a state or its political subdivision, any public or private agency, institution, organization or other entity; or any person to which federal financial assistance is extended directly or through another recipient. . . ." 104.4(b)(4) "A recipient may not, directly or through contractual or other arrangements, utilize criteria or methods of administration (i) that have the effect of subjecting qualified handicapped persons to discrimination on the basis of handicap, (ii) that have the

purpose or effect of defeating or substantially impairing accomplishment of the objectives of the recipient's program with respect to handicapped persons, or (iii) that perpetuate the discrimination of another recipient if both recipients are subject to common administrative control or are agencies of the same state."

17. Texas Education Agency, EHLR 352:349 (1986); Illinois State Board of Education, EHLR 352:283 (1986); Mississippi State Department of Education, EHLR 257:545 (1984) and California State Department of Education, EHLR 352:549 (1987).

18. *New Mexico Association for Retarded Citizens v. The State of New Mexico,* 495 F. Supp. 391, 397 (D.N. Mex. 1980), rev'd on other grounds, 678 F.2d 847 (10th Cir. 1987).

19. *Hendricks v. Gilhool,* 709 F. Supp. 1362, 1368 (E.D. Pa. 1989).

20. California State Department of Education, EHLR 352:549 (1987).

21. 20 U.S.C. § 1414(d) – "Whenever a state educational agency determines that a local educational agency – (1) is unable or unwilling to establish and maintain programs of free appropriate public education . . . , (2) is unable or unwilling to be consolidated with other local educational agencies in order to establish and maintain such programs; or (3) has one or more handicapped children who can best be served by a regional or state center . . . , the state educational agency shall use the payments which would have been availabe to such local educational agency to provide special education and related services directly to handicapped children."

22. *Doe v. Maher,* 793 F.2d 1470, 1491–92 (9th Cir. 1986), aff'd sub. nom. *Honig v. Doe,* 484 U.S. 305, 98 L.Ed. 2d 686 (1988). See also *Eva N v. Brock,* 741 F. Supp. 616, 634 (E.D. Ky. 1990) and *GARC v. McDaniel,* 511 F. Supp. 1263, aff'd 716 F.2d 1565 (11th Cir. 1983), vacated on other grounds __U.S.__, 104 S.Ct. 3581, 82 L.Ed. 2d 880 (1984).

23. *Honig v. Doe, supra* at 329.

24. *Southeastern Community College v. Davis,* 442 U.S. 397, 411–12, 99 S.Ct. 2361, 2369–2370, 60 L.Ed. 2d 980 (1979); *Colin K. by John K. v. Schmidt,* 715 F.2d 1, 8–9 (1st Cir. 1983); and *Turillo v. Tyson,* 535 F. Supp. 577, 586–87 (D.R.I. 1982).

25. § 104.32 – " A recipient that operates a public elementary or secondary education program shall annually: (a) Undertake to identify and locate every qualified handicapped person residing in the recipient's jurisdiction who is not receiving a public education; and (b) take appropriate steps to notify handicapped persons and their parents or guardians of the recipient's duty under this subpart."

26. *David H. v. Spring Branch Independent School District,* 569 F. Supp. 1324, 1339 (S.D. Tex. 1983). See also York Community High School, EHLR 352:116 (1985) and Arcadia (CA) Unified School District, EHLR 311:27 (1983).

27. Capistrano (CA) Unified School District, EHLR 311:21 (1982); Red Oak (IA) Community School District, EHLR 311:24 (1982); Coachella Valley (CA) Unified School District, EHLR 311:42 (1985).

28. Luding (TX) Independent School District, EHLR 257:417 (1983).

29. § 104.32.

30. Ukiah Unified School District, EHLR 311:17 (1982), and Capistrano Unified School District, EHLR 311:21 (1982).

31. St. Clair R-XIII School District, EHLR 352:201 (1986) and Greater Johnstown (PA) School District, EHLR 352:104 (1985).

32. *David H. v. Spring Branch Independent School District, supra.*

33. New Castle County School District – LOF (6/81) and OSPR III/1/12, EHLR 133:12 (1981).

34. Sanger Unified School District, EHLR 257:02 (1978).

35. See Chapter 10 for an in-depth discussion of this concept.

36. § 104.3(k) "'Qualified handicapped person' means . . . (2). . .a handicapped person (i) of an age during which nonhandicapped persons are provided such services, (ii) of any age during which it is mandatory under state law to provide such services to handicapped persons, or (iii) to whom a state is required to provide a free appropriate public education under section 612 of the Education of the Handicapped Act."

37. *Riley v. Jefferson County Board of Education,* Case No. CV-89-P-0169-S (N.D. Ala. 1989). See also Milton Area Schools, EHLR 352:275 (1986).

38. December 12, 1979, letter from Bonnie Milstein, Deputy Asst. General Counsel to Steven Schatken.

39. Mesa Unified School District Number Four, 6/28/88 LOF. See also Chapter 19.

40. Williamson County (TN) School District, EHLR 352:514 (1988), and Iowa State Department of Public Instruction, EHLR 257:634 (1984).

41. *Eva N. v. Brock,* 741 F. Supp. 626, 632 (E.D. Ky. 1990).

42. December 12, 1979, letter from Bonnie Milstein, Deputy Asst. General Counsel, to Steven Schatken.

43. § 104.33(a).

44. *Honig v. Doe, supra.*

45. *Detsel v. Board of Education of Auburn,* 637 F. Supp. 1022 (N.D. N.Y., 1986); *Irving Independent School District v. Tatro,* 468 U.S. 883, 82 L.Ed.2d 664 (1984); *Department of Education, State of Hawaii v. Katherine D.,* 727 F.2d 809 (9th Cir. 1983).

46. *Timothy v. Rochester, New Hampshire School District,* 875 F.2d 954 (1st Cir. 1989), cert. denied, 107 L.Ed.2d 520 (1989).

47. *Martinez v. School Board of Hillsborough County,* 881 F.2d 1502 (11th Cir. 1988); on remand, 711 F. Supp. 1066 (M.D. Fla. 1989); *Thomas Atascadero Unified School District,* 662 F. Supp. 376 (C.D. Cal. 1987).

48. 20 U.S.C. § 1412(2)(C)—"[A]ll children residing in the state who are handicapped, regardless of the severity of their handicap, and who are in need of special education and related services are identified, located and evaluated."

49. 458 U.S. 176, 73 L.Ed.2d 690 (1982).

50. Appendix A, p. 492.

51. *Battle v. Pennsylvania,* 629 F.2d 269, 275 (3rd Cir. 1980), cert. denied, 452 U.S. 968, 69 L.Ed.2d 981 (1981); see also *Timothy W. v. Rochester, supra* at 970: "[E]ducation under the Act encompasses a wide spectrum of training, and that for the severely handicapped it may include, the most elemental of life skills." Further, the nature of some children's handicaps might require that they receive homebound services.

52. See Chapter 15 for a detailed discussion of disciplining handicapped students.

53. *Irving Independent School District v. Tatro,* 468 U.S. 883, 82 L.Ed. 2d 664, 673–4 (1984).

54. *Polk v. Central Susquehanna Intermediate Unit 16,* 853 F.2d 171 (3rd Cir. 1988), cert. denied 102 L.Ed.2d 970 (1989); *Detsel v. Board of Education of Auburn,* 637 F. Supp. 1022 (N.D. N.Y. 1986), and *Bevin v. Wright,* 666 F. Supp. 71 (W.D. Pa. 1987).

55. *Martinez v. School Board of Hillsborough County,* 861 F.2d 1502 (11th Cir. 1988), and *Arline v. School Board of Nassau County,* 480 U.S. 273, 94 L.Ed.2d 307 (1987).

Chapter 11

1. Appendix A, p. 493.
2. Sheffield (AL) City School, EHLR 352:242 (1986), Muscogee County (GA) School District, EHLR 352:323 (1986), and Special Education District of McHenry (IL) County, EHLR 258:125 (1985).
3. Tacoma (WA) School District No. 10, EHLR 257:420 (1983), Oklahoma State Department of Education, EHLR 257:622 (1984), and Vashon Island (WA) School District No. 402, EHLR 257:434 (1983).
4. Elgin (IL) School District U-46, EHLR 352:130 (1985), Seattle (WA) School District, EHLR 352:80 (1985), Ukiah (CA) Unified School District, EHLR 311:17 (1982).
5. Youngstown (OH) City School District, EHLR 257:580 (1984), Thornton Township (IL) High School District #205, EHLR 311:85 (1986); Eastern Upper Peninsula (MI) School District, EHLR 352:538 (1987), and New York City Board of Education, EHLR 352:638 (1988).
6. Pittsburgh (PA) School District, EHLR 257:443 (1983), Basin (ID) School District No. 72, EHLR 257:390 (1983), and Philadelphia (PA) School District, EHLR 257:377 (1983).
7. Kanawha County School District, EHLR 257:439 (1983), and Upper Peninsula (MI) School District, EHLR 352:538 (1987).
8. 569 F. Supp. 1324, 1331 (S.D. Tex. 1983). See also *Georgia Ass'n of Retarded Citizens v. McDaniel,* 511 F. Supp. 1263, 1280 (N.D. Ga. 1981):

> "...some special treatment may be necessary for handicapped children to benefit from [their education]. If a child needed a special service to gain equal benefit from his education, the denial of that service would constitute discrimination in violation of Section 504."

9. 414 U.S. 563 (1974), at 1333–4.
10. 458 U.S. 176, 73 L.Ed.2d 690, 102 S.Ct. 3034 (1982).
11. *Rowley, supra* at 200.
12. *Id., supra* at 199–201.
13. 862 F.2d 884, 886 (D.C. Cir. 1988).
14. *Kerkam v. McKenzie, supra* at 889.
15. 874 F.2d 1036, 1048 (5th Cir. 1989).
16. *Hendrick Hudson District Board of Education v. Rowley, supra* at 202.
17. *Id.,* at 204.
18. *Rowley, supra* at 203. See also *Daniel R.R. v. State Board of Education,* 874 F.2d 1036, 1044 (5th Cir. 1989).
19. *Lachman v. Illinois State Board of Education,* 852 F.2d 290 (7th Cir. 1988), cert. denied 102 L.Ed.2d 327 (1988).
20. Appendix A, pp. 492–3.
21. See Montgomery County, EHLR 353:111 (1988); Knox County, EHLR 353:158 (1988) and Illinois State Board of Education, EHLR 257:573 (1984).
22. See Intermediate Unit (PA) #22, EHLR 352:209 (1986); Thornton Township (IL) High School District #205, EHLR 311:85 (1986); Columbia County (GA) School District, EHLR 352:21 (1985); Lampasas (TX) Independent School District, EHLR 257:414 (1983), and Illinois Board of Education, EHLR 257:82 (1980).
23. *Daniel R.R. v. State Board of Education, supra* at 1048: "Congress left the choice of educational policies and methods where it properly belongs—in the hands of state and local school officials. Our task is not to second-guess state and local policy decisions; rather, it is a narrow one of determining whether state and local

school officials have complied with the Act." See also *Visco v. School District of Pittsburgh,* 684 F. Supp. 1310, 1313 (W.D. Pa. 1988), *Kerkam v. McKenzie, supra* at 887, *Vander Malle v. Ambach,* 667 F. Supp. 1015, 1040 (S.D. N.Y. 1987), and *Lachman v. Illinois State Board of Education,* 852 F.2d 290 (7th Cir. 1988), cert. denied 102 L.Ed.2d 327 (1988).

24. *Regents of University of Michigan v. Ewing,* 474 U.S. 214, 88 L.Ed.2d 523 (1985), and *Schuber v. University of Minnesota,* 788 F.2d 510 (8th Cir. 1986).

25. *Polk v. Central Susquehanna Intermediate Unit 16,* 853 F.2d 171 (3rd Cir. 1988), cert. denied, 102 L.Ed.2d 970 (1989)—That consultative services were insufficient for a child who needs direct physical therapy services. *Board of Education v. Diamond,* 808 F.2d 876 (3rd Cir. 1986)—The proposed educational program resulted in regression. *Daniel R.R. v. State Board of Education, supra* at 1048—"The Act does not permit states to make mere token gestures to accommodate handicapped students; its requirement for modifying and supplementing regular education is broad." *Vander Malle v. Ambach, supra* at 1041—". . . defendants cannot satisfy their obligation . . . to educate him simply by making available in another setting precisely the form of instruction which had failed him before." See also Fayette (MO) R-III School District, EHLR 257:25 (1978).

26. *Visco v. School District of Pittsburgh, supra* at 1314. See also *Daniel H. v. Spring Branch Independent School District, supra* at 1333: ". . . [Section 504] . . ., for practical purposes, places upon school districts and agencies which receive federal funds, such as the defendants, the duty of analyzing individually the needs of each handicapped student and devising a program which will enable each handicapped student to receive an appropriate, free public education." *Hendrick Hudson District Board of Education v. Rowley, supra* at 203: A state's duty is discharged "by providing *personalized instruction* with sufficient support services to permit the child to benefit" (emphasis added).

27. *Battle v. Pennsylvania,* 629 F.2d 269 (3rd Cir. 1980), cert. denied, 452 U.S. 968, 69 L.Ed.2d 981, 101 S.Ct. 3123 (1981); *Yarris v. Special School District of St. Louis County,* 558 F. Supp. 523 (D.E.D. Mo. 1983); *Garrity v. Gallen,* 522 F. Supp. 171 (D.N.H. 1981), and *Georgia Association of Retarded Citizens v. McDaniel,* 716 F.2d 902 (11th Cir. 1984), cert. denied, 469 U.S. 1228, 84 L.Ed.2d 365 (1985).

28. *Daniel R.R. v. State Board of Education, supra.* See also Brazosport (TX) Independent School District, EHLR 352:531 (1987).

29. See Wetzel County School District, EHLR 353:261 (1989); Greenville County School Board, EHLR 353:118 (1988), and Tucson (AZ) Unified School District, EHLR 352:547 (1987).

30. *Yaris v. Special School District of St. Louis, supra.* See also Dallas County Suburban Cooperative and Dallas County Schools, EHLR 352:360 (1987) [extended school-year services], Ukiah (CA) Unified School District, EHLR 311:17 (1982) [denial of speech therapy because of limited staff time], and New York City Board of Education, EHLR 352:638 (1988) [failure to implement IEPs].

31. Panhandle Community School District, EHLR 257:302 (1981).

32. Administrative Decision, Chicago Board of Education (8/19/88).

33. See Coffee County (GA) School District, EHLR 352:37 (1985), and Churchill County (NV) School District, EHLR 352:543 (1987).

34. *New Mexico Association for Retarded Citizens v. The State of New Mexico,* 678 F.2d 847, 854 (10th Cir. 1982): "The handicapped by definition demand vastly different learning programs."

35. Administrative Decision (Doc. No. 84-504-3, 4187), at page 5. See also Patrick County (VA) Schools, EHLR 257:210 (1980)—handicapped students only pro-

vided two and one-half hours of education per day; Muscogee County School District, EHLR 352:323 (1986)—failure to provide certified teachers; West Babylon Union Free School District, EHLR 352:305 (1986)—lack of instructional time; and Irving Independent School District, EHLR 257:278 (1981)—failure to provide trained teachers.

36. Appendix A, p. 493.

37. Muscogee County School District, *supra*. Wauwatosa (WI) Public School District, EHLR 257:357 (1982); and Canel, Aronson and Whitted (IL), EHLR 257:427 (1983).

38. Special Education District of McHenry (IL) County, EHLR 258:125 (1985); Coachella Valley (CA) Unified School District, EHLR 311:42 (1985); and Mobile County (AL) School District, EHLR 352:338 (1986).

39. Oak Park (MI) Public Schools, EHLR 352:292 (1986); Eastern Upper Peninsula (MI) School District, EHLR 352:538 (1987); and New York City Board of Education, EHLR 352:638 (1988).

40. Thornton Township (IL) High School District #205, EHLR 311:85 (1986); Columbia County (GA) School District, EHLR 352:21 (1985); and San Diego City (CA) Unified School District, EHLR 352:273 (1986).

41. Stafford Co. (VA) Public Schools, EHLR 352:449 (1987) and Walker County (AL) School District, EHLR 352:10 (1985).

42. Alabama State Department of Education, EHLR 352:41 (1985) and OSPR I/1/43, EHLR 133:05 (1979).

43. See Eastern Upper Peninsula School District and Oak Park Public Schools, *supra* n. 40.

44. Mississippi State Department of Education, EHLR 352:279 (1986)—State provided emergency certification to speech pathologists; and Massachusetts State Department of Education, EHLR 352:01 (1986)—State implements procedures to assure competency of teachers not having LD certification.

45. § 104.33(b)(2): "Implementation of an individualized education program developed in accordance with the Education of the Handicapped Act is one means of meeting the standard established in paragraph (b)(1)(i) of this section."

46. § 104.33(b)(1) defines an appropriate education as "the provision of regular or special education and *related aids and services*" (emphasis added).

47. Appendix A, p. 493.

48. Prescott Unified School District, EHLR 352:405 (1987).

49. *Detsel v. Board of Education of Auburn,* 637 F. Supp. 1022, 1025 (N.D. N.Y. 1986).

50. 468 U.S. 883, 82 L.Ed.2d 664, 672 (1984).

51. *Irving Independent School District v. Tatro, supra* at 673.

52. *Id.,* at 673–4; see also *Polk v. Central Susquehanna Intermediate Unit 16, supra;* and Clermont Northeastern Schools, EHLR 257:577 (1984).

53. *Detsel v. Board of Education of Auburn, supra* at 1026–7.

54. *Department of Education, State of Hawaii v. Katherine D., supra* at 813, 815.

55. *Bevin v. Wright,* 666 F. Supp. 71, 75 (W.D. Pa. 1987).

56. *Tokarcik v. Forest Hills School District,* 665 F.2d 443 (3rd Cir. 1981)—catheterization services are related aids and services.

57. *Bevin v. Wright, supra* at 75.

58. *Id.* See also *Granite School District v. Shannon M.* 787 F. Supp. 1020 (D. Utah 1992).

59. See Department of Public Instruction of the Commonwealth of Puerto Rico, EHLR 353:286 (1988); Eastern Upper Peninsula School District, EHLR 352:273

(1987); and San Diego City Unified School District, EHLR 352:273 (1986). See also *Granite, supra.*

60. *Tokarcik v. Forest Hills School District, supra.* See also Prescott Unified School District, EHLR 352:405 (1987), and Bethel (CT) Board of Education, EHLR 257:55 (1979)—Educational needs are not defined in purely academic or special education terms.

61. See Sumner County School District, EHLR 352:248 (1986); Sheffield City School, EHLR 352:242 (1986); Township High School District, EHLR 352:289 (1986); Fresno Unified School District, EHLR 257:248 (1980); and Columbia County School District, EHLR 352:21 (1985).

62. See Berlin Brothers Valley School District, EHLR 353:124 (1988)—District cannot condition provision of related aids and services (administering medication) on parents agreeing to sign a waiver of liability.

63. *B.G. v. Cranford,* 702 F. Supp. 1158 (D.N.J. 1988)—District is not responsible for psychological services that do not meet the educational needs of the student or provide some educational benefit.

64. See *Irving Independent School District v. Tatro, supra* at 675, and Oklahoma State Department of Education, EHLR 257:622 (1984).

65. For example, parents of students who receive physical therapy complain because the students primarily receive the services from a teacher or an aide instead of a licensed therapist. Unless the student needs direct services from a therapist, a school district will not be found in violation if an expert such as a speech therapist or physical therapist trains school personnel to provide necessary services. However, the specialist must provide necessary supervision to ensure that the services are being properly provided. If no supervision is provided, it will be considered a denial of a free appropriate education. Sumner County School District, EHLR 352:248 (1986), and Sheffield City School, EHLR 352:242 (1986).

Chapter 12

1. § 104.33(c)(1) "the provision of a free education is the provision of educational and related services without cost to the handicapped person or to his or her parents or guardian. It may consist either of the provision of free services or, if a recipient places a handicapped person in or refers such person to a program not operated by the recipient as a means of carrying out the requirements of this subpart, of payment for the costs of the program."

2. All pertinent provisions of subpart § 104.33(c) will be discussed in this chapter.

3. Salina (KS) USD #305, EHLR 352:204 (1986)—mental health evaluation necessary for provision of FAPE; Granite (UT) School District, EHLR 311:106 (1987); Bethel (CT) Board of Education, EHLR 257:55 (1979); Fresno (CA) Unified School District, EHLR 257:248 (1980) and Green Bay (WI) Area Public Schools, EHLR 257:471 (1983)—psychological services; and Colorado Department of Education, EHLR 352:373 (1987)—room and board.

4. New Trier (IL) School District #203, EHLR 257:409 (1982), and Illinois Board of Education, EHLR 257:82 (1980).

5. Clark County (NV) School District, EHLR 257:245 (1981), and Pennsylvania Department of Education, EHLR 257:106 (1980).

6. Salina (KS) USD #305, EHLR 352:204 (1986).

7. Wauwatosa (WI) Public School District, EHLR 257:357 (1982), and Board of Education of the City of New York (Case No. 02-88-1079) 12/6/89 LOF.

8. Case No. CV-89-P-0169-S (N.D. Ala. 1989). See also Oklahoma City (OK) Public Schools, EHLR 352:173 (1985).

9. Appendix A, para. 23, p. 493; § 104.33(c)(1) provides, in pertinent part: "Nothing in this section shall be construed to relieve an insurer or similar third party from an otherwise valid obligation to provide or pay for services provided to a handicapped person."

10. 614 F. Supp. 302, 306 (D.C. Tenn. 1985). See also School District No. 220 (IL), EHLR 257:200 (1981).

11. Illinois Board of Education, EHLR 257:82 (1980).

12. *Roncker v. Walters,* 700 F.2d 1058 (6th Cir. 1983), and *Age v. Bullitt County School District,* 673 F.2d 141, 145 (6th Cir. 1982). See also Hood River (OR) County School District, EHLR 352:482 (1987).

13. *Clevenger v. Oak Ridge School Board,* 744 F.2d 514, 517 (6th Cir. 1984).

14. § 104.33(c)(3): "If placement in a public or private residential placement is necessary to provide a free appropriate public education to a handicapped person because of his or her handicap, the program, including nonmedical care and room and board, shall be provided at no cost to the person or his or her parents or guardian."

15. Appendix A, para. 23, p. 493.

16. Colorado Department of Education, EHLR 352:373 (1987); New Trier (IL) School District #203, EHLR 257:409 (1982); Pennsylvania Department of Education, EHLR 257:106 (1980); and Clark County (NV) School District, EHLR 257:245 (1981).

17. *Colin K by John K v. Schmidt,* 715 F.2d 1 (1st Cir. 1983); *Turillo v. Tyson,* 535 F. Supp. 577 (D.R.I. 1982); and *Kruelle v. New Castle County School District,* 642 F.2d 687 (3rd Cir. 1981).

18. See Chapter 19: *Section 504 vs. the EHA* for a detailed discussion of the issue of whether Section 504 guarantees handicapped students a FAPE.

19. *Turillo, supra* at 586 and *Colin, supra* at 8–9.

20. *Department of Education v. Katherine D.,* 531 F. Supp. 517 (D. Haw. 1982).

21. The author was unable to uncover any evidence that the OCR has addressed the court findings that contest the validity of § 104.33(c)(3) on a national policy level.

22. 700 F. Supp. 1106 (N.D. Ga. 1987).

23. 742 F.2d 825 (4th Cir. 1984).

24. *Vander Malle v. Ambach,* 667 F. Supp. 1015 (S.D. N.Y. 1987).

25. Appendix A, para. 23, p. 493.

26. 733 F.2d 1397 (7th Cir. 1985), at 1404–5.

27. *Parks v. Pavkovic, supra* at 1406. See also *Vander Malle v. Ambach, supra* at 1040; *Kruelle v. New Castle County School District, supra* at 692, and *McKenzie v. Smith,* 771 F.2d 527, 534 (D.C. Cir. 1985).

28. Appendix A, para. 23, p. 493.

29. Maryland Department of Education, EHLR 257:97 (1980); Illinois Board of Education, EHLR 257:82 (1980), and New Trier School District, EHLR 257:409 (1982).

30. *Parks v. Pavkovic, supra* at 1404–5, and *Kruelle v. New Castle County School District, supra* at 692.

31. Appendix A, para. 23, p. 493.

32. *Maryland Department of Education, supra.*

33. § 104.33(c)(2): "If a recipient places a handicapped person in or refers such person to a program not operated by the recipient as its means of carrying out the requirement of this subpart, the recipient shall ensure that adequate transportation to and from the program is provided at no greater cost than would be incurred by

the person or his or her parents or guardian if the person were placed in a program operated by the recipient."

34. *McNair v. Oak Hills Local School District,* 872 F.2d 153 (6th Cir. 1989), and *Dubois v. Connecticut State Board of Education,* 727 F.2d 44 (2nd Cir. 1984). See also Wake County (NC) School District, EHLR 257:432 (1983).

35. San Antonio Independent School District, EHLR 311:40 (1984); Chicago (IL) Board of Education, EHLR 257:448 (1983); and Boone County School District, EHLR 257:103 (1980).

36. Richmond County School District, EHLR 352:240 (1986); and *Maryland Department of Education, supra.*

37. § 104.33(c)(4): "If a recipient has made available . . . a free appropriate public education to a handicapped person and the person's parents or guardian chooses to place the person in a private school, the recipient is not required to pay for the person's education in the private school." See also Lampasas (TX) Independent School District, EHLR 257:414 (1983).

38. *Parks v. Pavkovic, supra.* OSPR II/19, EHLR 133:11 (1980); Rankin County (MS) School District, EHLR 257:45 (1979).

39. "If the parent or guardian believes that his or her child cannot be suitably educated in the recipient's program, he or she may make use of the procedures established in § 104.36,"—Appendix A, para. 23, p. 493.

40. *Burlington School Committee v. Department of Education,* 471 U.S. 358, 370, 373–374, 105 S.Ct., 1996, 2003, 2005 (1985).

41. See also *Briggs v. Board of Education of the State of Connecticut,* 707 F. Supp. 623 (D. Conn. 1988).

42. *Tucker v. Bay Shore Union Free School District,* 873 F.2d 563, 568 (2nd Cir. 1989), and *Antkowiak v. Ambach,* 838 F.2d 635 (2nd Cir. 1988).

43. *Alamo Heights Independent School District v. State Board of Education,* 790 F.2d 1153, 1161 (5th Cir. 1986).

44. See *B.G. v. Cranford Board of Education,* 702 F. Supp. 1158 (D.N.J. 1988)—student placed without prior notice or discussion with school board; *Lenhoff v. Farmington Public Schools,* 680 F. Supp. 921 (E.D. Mich. 1988)—parents denied district the opportunity to evaluate the child; *Evans v. District No. 17 of Douglas County,* 841 F.2d 824 (8th Cir. 1988)—parents denied district the opportunity to try alternative placements.

45. Sumner (VA) School District, EHLR 352:565 (1987)—parents did not give the district enough time to implement an appropriate program; and Lake Washington School District, EHLR 257:611 (1985)—alternative placement was not proposed.

Chapter 13

1. § 104.34(a)—"A recipient to which this subpart applies shall educate, or shall provide for the education of, each qualified handicapped person in its jurisdiction with persons who are not handicapped to the maximum extent appropriate to the needs of the handicapped person. A recipient shall place a handicapped person in the regular educational environment . . . unless it is demonstrated by the recipient that the education of the person in the regular environment with the use of supplementary aids and services cannot be achieved satisfactorily."

2. The terms generally used to describe this mandate are "mainstreaming" or placement in the "least restrictive environment."

3. Appendix A, para. 24, p. 494.

4. See Chapter 3 for a detailed discussion of these principles.

5. See § 104.4(a)—"No qualified handicapped person shall, on the basis of handicap, be excluded from participation in, be denied the benefits of, or otherwise be subjected to discrimination under any program or activity."

6. § 104.4(b)—"Discriminatory actions prohibited (iv) Provide different or separate aid, benefits or services to handicapped persons or to any class of handicapped persons unless such action is necessary to provide qualified handicapped persons with aid, benefits or services that are as effective as those provided others." See also *Alexander v. Choate, supra.*

7. *Missouri State Department of Elementary and Secondary Education v. United States Department of Education* (Admin. Proceeding 4/87); Wyoming Public School District, EHLR 311:325 (1988); Special School District of St. Louis County, EHLR 352:156 (1986); Newark School District, EHLR 311:118 (1987); Thornton Township (IL) High School District #205, EHLR 311:85 (1986); and Elgin (IL) School District U-46, EHLR 352:130 (1985).

8. Marathon County (WI) Handicapped Children's Education Board, EHLR 352:47 (1985); Mobile County (AL) School District, EHLR 352:338 (1986); Special School District of St. Louis County, *supra.*

9. Wyoming (MI) Public School District, *supra;* Normal (IL) Community Unit School District, EHLR 352:434 (1987); and Brazosport (TX) Independent School District, EHLR 352:531 (1987).

10. See Chapter 2 for a detailed discussion of this issue.

11. 707 F. Supp. 623, 626 (D. Conn. 1988).

12. See Illinois School for the Deaf, EHLR 257:467 (1983); Carbon-Lehigh Intermediate Unit #21, EHLR 257:551 (1984); and Horry County School District LOF (6/6/89).

13. Spokane (WA) School District No. 81, EHLR 257:219 (1981); Carbon-Lehigh (PA) Intermediate Unit #21, *supra;* and Special School District of St. Louis County (MO), EHLR 257:322 (1981).

14. Hawaii State Department of Education, EHLR 311:52 (1985); Wake County (NC) School District, EHLR 257:432 (1983); and Lake Mills (WI) Area School District, EHLR 352:222 (1986). See Appendix A, para. 24, p. 494.

15. Brockton Public Schools, EHLR 257:452 (1983)—kindergarten orientation; Granite School District, EHLR 311:106 (1987); Van Buren (AR) Public School, EHLR 257:269 (1981)—transportation.

16. Appendix A, para. 24, p. 494. See also Ashwaubenon (WI) School District, EHLR 311:320 (1988); and New Mexico School for the Deaf, EHLR 257:386 (1982).

17. 874 F.2d 1036 (5th Cir. 1989).

18. *Lachman v. Illinois State Board of Education,* 852 F.2d 290, 295 (7th Cir. 1988), *cert. denied,* 102 L.Ed.2d 327 (1988). See also *Roncker v. Walters, supra* at 1063; *Daniel R.R. v. State Board of Education, supra* at 1044; and *A.W. v. Northwest R. 1 School District,* 813 F.2d 158, 163 (8th Cir. 1987).

19. Appendix A, para. 24, p. 494. See also *Daniel R.R. v. State Board of Education, supra* at 1049.

20. 709 F. Supp. 1362, 1366 (E.D. Pa. 1989). See also Carbon-Lehigh Intermediate Unit #21, *supra;* Alabama State Department of Education, EHLR 352:41 (1985); and *Students of California School for the Blind v. Honig,* 736 F.2d 538, *vacated,* 471 U.S. 148, *on remand* 760 F.2d 238 (1984).

21. Richmond (IN) Community School Corporation, EHLR 352:296 (1986); Bridgeport (CT) Board of Education, EHLR 257:508 (1984); and Fredericksburg (VA) City Public Schools, EHLR 257:205 (1981).

22. 927 F.2d 146 (4th Cir. 1991).

Chapter 14

1. See Chapter 19 for a detailed discussion of this issue.

2. Appendix A, para. 23, p. 493.

3. Rialto (CA) Unified School District, EHLR 353:201 (1989)—LEA failed to understand Section 504 definition of handicapped. Linden (CA) Unified School District, EHLR 352:617 (1988). See also School District of Pittsburgh, EHLR 257:492 (1984)—policy against evaluating and placing physically handicapped students not in the special education program; Mesa (AZ) School District, EHLR 352:562 (1987)—failure to develop program for a student with bowel/bladder problems; and Lake Washington (WA) School District No. 414, EHLR 257:611 (1985)—failure to evaluate a student with drug and alcohol addiction. The OCR also recognized that students diagnosed as having attention deficit disorders may also be considered "qualified handicapped persons" (see June 21, 1989, letter from Cathy Lewis, Acting Director, Policy and Enforcement Service, to Harvey Parker, Executive Director of Children with Attention Deficit Disorders).

4. Appendix A, para. 25, p. 494.

5. Wauwatosa (WI) Public School District, EHLR 257:357 (1982)—diagnostic placement; Bethel (CT) Board of Education, EHLR 257:55 (1979)—incomplete evaluation; and Humboldt (TN) City School District, EHLR 352:557 (1987)—incomplete evaluation.

6. Humboldt (TN) City School District, supra—change from private to public program; Columbia County (GA) School District, EHLR 352:21 (1985)—change in number of hours for occupational therapy; and Tacoma (WA) School District No. 1, EHLR 257:420 (1983)—eliminating all self-contained classes for learning disabled and behaviorally disabled students.

7. Salina (KS) USD #305, EHLR 352:204 (1986)—reassigning student from speech therapy to behavior disorders class; Clermont (OH) Northeastern Schools, EHLR 257:577 (1984)—terminating homebound instruction; St. Clair (MO) R-XIII School District, EHLR 352:201 (1986)—dismissal from special education; and Lampasas (TX) Independent School District, EHLR 257:414 (1983)—change from special education to regular education program.

8. Appendix A, para. 25, p. 494. See also Linden (CA) Unified School District, supra; Leslie Co. (KY) School District, EHLR 353:453 (1987); and Seattle (WA) School District No. 1, EHLR 257:424 (1983).

9. See Wilson v. Marana Unified School District, 735 F.2d 1178 (9th Cir. 1984); and Santee Unified School District, EHLR 353:210 (1989).

10. Baltimore County (MD) Public Schools, EHLR 352:352 (1987)—failure to evaluate student despite disruptive behavior and parents' request for evaluation; and Coachella Valley (CA) Unified School District, EHLR 311:42 (1985)—failure to accept referrals of students by teachers.

11. Portsmouth Public Schools, EHLR 257:346 (1982); and Carlinville Community Unit School District No. 1, EHLR 352:32 (1985).

12. DeLeon v. Susquehanna Community School District, 747 F.2d 149, 153 (3rd Cir. 1984).

13. Concerned Parents v. New York City Board of Education, 619 F.2d 751, 754 (2nd Cir. 1980).

14. Lunceford v. District of Columbia Board of Education, 745 F.2d 1577, 1582 (D.C. Cir. 1984). See also OCR's Response to Inquiry, EHLR 305:43 (1987).

15. See Lunceford v. District of Columbia Board of Education, supra at 1582; and Abner v. District of Columbia, 849 F.2d 1491 (D.C. Cir. 1988).

16. The OCR has held that the mandate of § 104.35(a), which requires that reevaluation occur prior to a significant change in placement, is akin to the EHA "stay put" doctrine. (March 29, 1988, Department memorandum analyzing the *Honig v. Doe* decision.) See also Chicago (IL) Board of Education, EHLR 257:515 (1984).

17. *Honig v. Doe*, 484 U.S.305, 323–24, 98 L.Ed.2d 686 (1988); *Burlington v. Massachusetts Department of Education*, 471 U.S. 358, 85 L.Ed.2d 385 (1985); and *Jackson v. Franklin County School Board*, 765 F.2d 535, 538 (5th Cir. 1985).

18. Anne Arundel County Public Schools, EHLR 257:639 (1985).

19. Logan County (WV) School District, EHLR 353:286 (1989); Community Unit School District #200, EHLR 311:94 (1986); and Vashon Island School District No. 402, EHLR 257:434 (1983).

20. *Foster v. District of Columbia Board of Education,* EHLR 553:520 (1982).

21. Chicago Board of Education and Illinois State Board of Education, March 28, 1986 LOF; School District of Philadelphia, EHLR 257:496 (1984).

22. Administrative Decision, Chicago Board of Education and Illinois State Board of Education (8/19/88).

23. Appendix A, para. 25, p. 494.

24. § 104.35(b) provides, in pertinent part: "A recipient . . . shall establish standards and procedures for evaluation and placement . . . which ensure that: 1) Tests and other evaluation materials have been validated for the specific purposes for which they are used and are administered by trained personnel. . . . 2) Tests and other evaluation materials include those tailored to assess specific areas of educational need and not merely those which are designed to provide a single general intelligence quotient; and 3) Tests are selected and administered so as best to ensure that, when a test is administered to a student with impaired sensory, manual, or speaking skills, the test results accurately reflect the student's aptitude or achievement level . . . rather than reflect the student's impaired sensory, manual, or speaking skills (except where those skills are the factors that the test purports to measure).

25. *Larry P. v. Riles*, 793 F.2d 969 (9th Cir. 1984)—It is improper to place students in special education classes using a single criterion—IQ tests. See also Rochester (NY) School District, EHLR 311:09 (1980)—placement based upon general intelligence testing; and San Francisco Unified School District, EHLR 352:362 (1986)—use of unvalidated assessment instrument.

26. *Larry P. v. Riles, supra* at 980. See also Northport–East Northport Union Free School District, EHLR 352:635 (1988)—use of an unvalidated test as placement criterion; and Winston County (AL) School District, EHLR 352:66 (1985)—district failed to implement evaluation procedures in compliance with § 104.35.

27. Perth Amboy School District, EHLR 352:65 (1985).

28. Butte (MT) School District #1, EHLR 311:70 (1986).

29. Winston County School District, EHLR 352:66 (1985).

30. *Brookhart v. Illinois State Board of Education*, 697 F.2d 179, 184 (7th Cir. 1983); and *Anderson v. Banks*, 520 F. Supp. 472 (S.D. Ga. 1981).

31. See Coachella Valley (CA) Unified School District, EHLR 311:42 (1985); Dysart (AZ) Unified School District #89, EHLR 311:32 (1983); and Special School District of St. Louis County (MO), EHLR 311:05 (1980). See also *Larry P. v. Riles, supra.*

32. § 104.35(c) "*Placement procedures* . . . A recipient shall (1) draw upon information from a variety of sources . . . , (2) establish procedures to ensure that information obtained from all such sources is documented and carefully considered, (3) ensure that the placement decision is made by a group of persons, including persons' knowledge about the child, the meaning of evaluation data, and the placement options and (4) ensure that the placement decision is made in conformity with § 104.34."

33. "It is not the intention of the Department, except in extraordinary circumstances, to review the result of individual placement and other educational decisions, so long as the school district complies with the 'process' requirements of this subpart." Appendix A, p. 492. See also The Greater Amsterdam (NY) School District, EHLR 257:436 (1983); and Special Education District of Lake County (IL), EHLR 257:34 (1979).

34. Hendrick Hudson District Board of Education v. Rowley, supra; see also Regents of University of Michigan v. Ewing, 474 U.S. 214 (1985), and Schuber v. University of Minnesota, 788 F.2d 510 (8th Cir. 1986).

35. Appendix A, para. 25, pp. 494–95. See Chapter 13 for a discussion of the duty to place the child in the most integrated setting appropriate.

36. Elmira City School District, EHLR 352:188 (1986)—no physical examination for student with a neurological impairment; St. Clair R-XIII School District, EHLR 352:201 (1986)—district failed to consider social or cultural background, adaptive behavior or achievement test information; Aldine Independent School District, EHLR 257:411 (1983)—failed to consider a psychologist's report; and Hoover Schrum School District No. 157, EHLR 257:136 (1980)—refused to permit staff to recommend extended school year services.

37. See Canel, Arenson and Whitted, EHLR 257:427 (1983).

38. Township High School District #211 (IL), EHLR 352:289 (1986).

39. Wauwatosa (WI) Public School District, EHLR 257:355 (1982).

40. See February 24, 1984, memorandum from the Assistant Secretary (OCR) regarding Muscogee County School District.

41. 669 F. Supp. 658 (N.D. Ill. 1988).

42. Riverview School District, EHLR 311:103 (1987); Chicago Board of Education, EHLR 257:308 (1981); and Special School District of St. Louis, EHLR 352:156 (1985).

43. S-1 v. Turlington, 635 F.2d 342, 347 (5th Cir. 1981); and Doe v. Maher, supra at 1488.

44. Hollenbeck v. Board of Education of Rochelle Township, supra at 668.

45. United States Department of Education v. Missouri State Department of Elementary and Secondary Education (Admin. Proceeding, 4/87); Brentwood Union Free School District, EHLR 311:50 (1985); and Hersey Public School District, EHLR 257:404 (1982). See also Chapter 13 for a detailed discussion of this issue.

46. 131 F.R.D. 654 (D. Conn. 1990). See also E.H. v. Tirozzi, 735 F. Supp. 57 (D. Conn. 1990). The Office of Special Education ruled in April 1988 that districts did not have authority under the EHA to prohibit tape recording (EHLR 213:127–28).

47. Harrison County School District, EHLR 353:120 (1988); and Houseman, EHLR 305:34 (1986).

Chapter 15

1. Lunceford v. District of Columbia Board of Education, 745 F.2d 1577 (D.C. Cir. 1984), supra at 1582.

2. The OCR has held that under some circumstances corporal punishment constitutes a change in placement. Portland (ME) School District, EHLR 352:492 (1987)—strapping a profoundly retarded student into a chair; see also Nash County (NC) School District, EHLR 352:37 (1985).

3. See Doe v. Maher, 793 F.2d 1470 (9th Cir. 1986), and S-1 v. Turlington, 682 F.2d 595 (6th Cir. 1982).

4. *Honig v. Doe, supra* at 325–26 n. 8.

5. See Muscogee County School District, 6/88 LOF; Chicago Board of Education, EHLR 257:369 (1982) and Chesterfield County Public Schools, EHLR 257:500 (1984). Short-term suspensions that do not represent an interruption of the delivery of services are not considered to be a change in placement. See Township (IL) School District #211, EHLR 257:364 (1982).

6. See OCR's Response to Inquiry, EHLR 305:26 (1985).

7. Arundel County (MD) Public Schools, EHLR 257:639 (1985).

8. *Honig v. Doe, supra* at 608. See also *Texas City Independent School District v. Jorstad,* 752 F. Supp. 231 (S.D. Tex. 1990)—a case in which the court applied this rule with respect to a student who physically attacked others, threatened to kill himself and others, and attempted to jump from a second-floor window.

9. See Assistant Secretary's Analysis of *Honig v. Doe* (1988).

10. *S-1 v. Turlington, supra* at 348, and *Kaelin v. Grubbs,* 682 F.2d 595, 602 (6th Cir. 1982).

11. See *Doe v. Maher, supra,* and the [OCR] Assistant Secretary's October 28, 1988, memorandum: "Long-term Suspension or Expulsion of Handicapped Students."

12. Note that, regarding infractions involving drugs and alcohol, Appendix A of the regulations provides that students who are alcoholics or drug addicts should be treated the same as nonhandicapped students with respect to the application of disciplinary rules prohibiting the use or possession of drugs or alcohol. Further, the Americans with Disabilities Act at § 512 amends Section 504 to provide: "Educational agencies may take the same disciplinary actions against handicapped students engaged in illegal use of drugs or the use of alcohol as are taken against nonhandicapped students."

Chapter 16

1. See *B.G. v. Cranford Board of Education, supra* at 1166—"[T]he cooperative efforts of parents and school authorities are inextricably intertwined with a handicapped child's inalienable right to a 'free appropriate public education'." See also *Burlington School Committee v. Department of Education, supra,* and *Alamo Heights Independent School District v. State Board of Education, supra* at 1161. The Supreme Court in *Honig v. Doe, supra* at 311–12, stated that procedural safeguards "guarantee parents both an opportunity for meaningful input into all decisions affecting their child's education and the right to seek review of any decisions they think inappropriate."

2. See Montgomery County Intermediate Unit #23, EHLR 353:111 (1988); San Diego City School District, EHLR 353:236 (1989); and Little Rock (AR) School District, EHLR 352:214 (1986).

3. Irving Unified School District, EHLR 353:192 (1989); and Augusta County (VA) School Division, EHLR 352:233 (1986).

4. See Hawaii State Department of Education, EHLR 353:144 (1988); and Township (IL) School District #211, EHLR 257:364 (1982). See also *Concerned Parents v. New York City Board of Education, supra,* and *DeLeon v. Susquehanna Community School District, supra.*

5. *Honig v. Doe, supra* at 708. See also Boston (MA) School District, EHLR 352:382 (1987).

6. Brockton (MA) Public Schools, EHLR 311:114 (1987); Missouri Department of Elementary and Secondary Education, EHLR 352:397 (1987); and Massachusetts Department of Education, EHLR 352:313 (1986).

7. Bristol-Plymouth Regional Vocational Technical School District, EHLR 353:241 (1989); and Edgerton School District, EHLR 353:219 (1989).

8. *Abney v. District of Columbia*, 849 F.2d 1491, 1494 (1988). See also Sachem (NY) Central School District, EHLR 352:462 (1987)—failure to obtain consent to evaluate a student and to destroy special education records; Powhattan (KS) Unified School District No. 150, EHLR 257:32 (1979)—failure to obtain consent to change placement; and Corinth (MS) Municipal Separate School District, EHLR 257:184 (1980)—failure to advise parents of right to file a due process hearing regarding the suspension of their child.

9. Hawaii State Department of Education, EHLR 311:52 (1985); Dawson (TX) Independent School District, EHLR 257:603 (1984); and Dysart (AZ) Unified School District #89, EHLR 311:32 (1983).

10. Mason City (IA) Community School District, EHLR 257:382 (1982).

11. Fredericksburg (VA) City Public Schools, EHLR 257:205 (1981).

12. Henry-Stark Counties (IL) Special Education District, EHLR 257:483 (1984).

13. Missouri School for the Deaf, EHLR 257:99 (1980).

14. School District of Philadelphia (PA), EHLR 257:496 (1984).

15. Elmira (NY) City School District, EHLR 352:188 (1986). See also Arcadia (CA) Unified School District, EHLR 311:27 (1983).

16. San Diego City (CA) School District, EHLR 353:236 (1989); Curwensville Area School District, EHLR 353:292 (1989); and Forest Park (MI) School District, EHLR 352:182 (1986).

17. § 104.4(b)(1)(iv). See also Tacoma (WA) School District, EHLR 257:383 (1983); and East Maine (IL) School District, EHLR 257:586 (1984).

18. Irvine Unified School District, EHLR 353:192 (1989); Montgomery County Intermediate Unit #23, EHLR 353:111 (1988); and East Shroudsburg Area School District, EHLR 353:108 (1988).

19. Irving Unified School District, *supra*, Augusta County (VA) School Division, *supra*, and Massachusetts Department of Education, *supra*. Further, recipients do not have the right to unilaterally judge the merits of the parents' case and determine that there is no issue in controversy and thus no need to proceed to due process. See Lewis Cass (MI) Intermediate School District, EHLR 352:211 (1986).

20. See *Honig v. Doe, supra* at 311–12, and *Burlington School Committee v. Department of Education, supra* at 2003, 2005.

21. Virginia Department of Education, EHLR 257:349 (1982).

22. *Honig v. Doe, supra* at 323–24. The Court was interpreting the language of 20 U.S.C. § 1415(e)(3) of the EHA. See also *Digre v. Roseville Schools Independent District*, 841 F.2d 245, 250 (1988).

23. March 29, 1988, memorandum from the Assistant Secretary analyzing the *Honig v. Doe* decision. See also Chicago (IL) Board of Education, EHLR 257:515 (1984); and Pennsylvania Department of Education, EHLR 257:534 (1984).

24. Montana State Office of Public Instruction, EHLR 352:372 (1987)—county superintendents permitted to act as hearing officers in their own counties; Illinois State Board of Education, EHLR 257:597 (1984)—hearing officer permitted to consult with state employees under circumstances where some of the state employees supervised the review officer; Missouri Department of Elementary and Secondary Education, EHLR 257:487 (1984); and Cobb County (GA) School System, EHLR 257:213 (1980)—withholding relevant information from the hearing officer.

25. The OCR's July 1987 letter for Ogden City School District and Utah State Office of Education. It is also permissible to use employees of state university systems that have no professional involvement in the delivery of educational services to students. See Wisconsin Department of Public Instruction, EHLR 352:357 (1986); and Mississippi Department of Education, EHLR 352:279 (1986).

26. *Kattan v. District of Columbia,* EHLR 441:207 (8/88).

27. Mingus Union High School District, EHLR 353:208 (1989). See also Brush Country (TX) Special Education Cooperative, EHLR 352:639 (1988).

28. Missouri Department of Elementary and Secondary Education, EHLR 257:487 (1984).

29. Pennsylvania Department of Education, EHLR 353:259 (1989); Massachusetts Department of Education, *supra;* North Kansas City (MO) School District, EHLR 257:04 (1978); Wisconsin Department of Public Instruction, EHLR 352:357 (1986); and St. Clair (MO) R-XIII School District, EHLR 352:201 (1986).

30. Georgia Department of Education, EHLR 257:77 (1979); Boulder Valley (CO) School District RE-2, EHLR 257:297 (1980); and Powhattan (KS) Unified School District No. 150, EHLR 257:32 (1979).

31. Orange County (CA) School District, EHLR 352:553 (1987); and California State Department of Education, EHLR 352:549 (1987).

32. Tacoma (WA) School District, *supra;* East Maine (IL) School District, *supra;* Northwestern Lehigh (PA) School District, EHLR 352:99 (1986); California School for the Deaf, EHLR 257:583 (1984); Missouri Department of Elementary and Secondary Education, EHLR 257:487 (1984); and Independent (MN) School District, EHLR 257:400 (1982).

Chapter 17

1. § 104.37(a).

2. Eldon (MO) R-1 School District, EHLR 352:144 (1986)—failure to advise of extracurricular activities and requiring parental permission for handicapped students, but not for nonhandicapped; Special School District of St. Louis County, EHLR 352:156 (1986)—denied students in self-contained special education classes the opportunity to participate in extracurricular activities; Elmira City (NY) School District, EHLR 352:188 (1986)—failed to provide physical education; and Brockton (MA) Public Schools, EHLR 257:452 (1983)—denied handicapped students the opportunity to participate in kindergarten orientation.

3. See Chapter 6 for a detailed discussion of this issue.

4. See the OCR's letter to Kevin McDowell, Indiana Department of Education, EHLR 305:39 (1987); and Fordland R-III School District, EHLR 353:127 (1988).

5. Appendix A, para. 26, p. 495.

6. See Freeman, EHLR 305:42 (1987); and Ogden City School District, EHLR 352:368 (1988).

7. Quaker Valley (PA) School District, EHLR 352:235 (1986); and Alpena (AR) Public School District, EHLR 257:565 (1984).

8. *Hollenbeck v. Board of Education of Rochelle Township,* 699 F. Supp. 658 (N.D. Ill. 1988); Dyzart Unified School District #89, EHLR 311:32 (1983); and Denver Public School District No. 1, EHLR 257:156 (1980).

9. 43 FR No. 157, pp. 36035–36.

10. See § 104.3(k).

11. Winston County (AL) School District, EHLR 352:66 (1985).

12. *Cavallaro v. Ambach,* 575 F. Supp. 171 (W.D. N.Y. 1983).

13. OCR 4/23/79 policy interpretation.

Chapter 18

1. Appendix A, p. 492.

2. "Adult Education" refers only to those educational programs and activities for adults that are operated by elementary and secondary schools. (Appendix A, p. 492).

3. Mississippi State Department of Education, EHLR 257:373 (1983).

4. Riverside (CA) Unified School District, EHLR 352:170 (1986).

5. The OCR policy interpretation, 1979 (OCR Digest, Vol. 1).

6. The regulations are applicable only to private education programs that are recipients. Private schools that do not receive federal financial assistance have no responsibility to comply with Section 504 and its implementing regulations. Private programs that are recipients cannot refuse to permit the OCR to conduct reviews of their programs. See Timothy School, EHLR 311:76 (1986).

7. Appendix A, para. 28, p. 495.

8. *Id.*

9. *Regents of University of Michigan v. Ewing, supra;* and *Schuber v. University of Minnesota, supra.* See also Peter's Child Development Center (PA), EHLR 352:479 (1987).

10. Life Christian School (WA), EHLR 352:523 (1987); and New Dimensions School, Inc. (CA), EHLR 257:127 (1979).

11. § 104.39(b).

12. 1988 memorandum from the Assistant Secretary for Civil Rights to Gilbert D. Roman, Regional Civil Rights Director.

Chapter 19

1. *Smith v. Robinson,* 468 U.S. 992, 1016–1020, 104 S.Ct. 3457, 82 L.Ed.2d 746 (1984); *Colin K. by John K. v. Schmidt,* 715 F.2d 1, 9 (CA 1/1983); and *Drew P. v. Clark County School District,* 676 F. Supp. 1559, 1566 (M.D. Ga. 1987).

2. Only states that receive financial assistance under Part B of the Education of the Handicapped Act must comply with the EHA and its regulations, while all entities that receive federal financial assistance from any source whatsoever must comply with Section 504.

3. See *Pennhurst State School v. Halderman,* 451 U.S. 1, 17, 67 L.Ed.2d 694 (1981)—". . . if Congress intends to place a condition on the grant of federal monies, it must do so unambiguously."

4. See Chapter 1 for a detailed discussion of compliance standards under civil rights statutes.

5. 873 F.2d 1387, 1390 n. 6 (11th Cir. 1989).

6. Appendix A, p. 492.

7. *Hendrick Hudson District Board of Education v. Rowley, supra* at 191–96.

8. Statements of Senator Hubert Humphrey, who introduced the bill. 118 Cong. Rec. 525 (1972).

9. *Smith v. Robinson, supra* at 1016–17.

10. *Southeastern Community College v. Davis, supra* at 410–11.

11. *Hendricks v. Gilhool,* 709 F. Supp. 1362, 1366 (E.D. Pa. 1989).

12. *Honig v. Doe, supra* at 597.

13. Appendix A, p. 492.

14. See *David H. v. Spring Branch Independent School District, supra* at 1334–36; *S-1 v. Turlington, supra* at 347; *Tatro v. State of Texas,* 625 F.2d 557, 565 (5th Cir. 1980); and *Georgia Association of Retarded Citizens v. McDaniel,* 511 F. Supp. 1263 (N.D. Ga. 1981).

15. In the Matter of: DeKalb County School District and Georgia Department of Education, April 26, 1990, administrative decision; *Southeastern Community College v. Davis, supra* at 412–13. See also *Alexander v. Choate, supra.*

16. § 104.33(c)(3). See also *Department of Education v. Katherine D.,* 531 F. Supp. 517 (D. Haw. 1982).

17. *Colin K. by John K. v. Schmidt, supra* at 8–9; *Turillo v. Tyson,* 535 F. Supp. 577, 586–87; *New Mexico Association for Retarded Citizens v. The State of New Mexico,* 678 F.2d 847 (10th Cir. 1982); and *Barnett v. Fairfax County School Board,* 927 F.2d 146 (4th Cir. 1991).

18. *David H. v. Spring Branch Independent School District, supra* at 1336.

19. In *Freeman v. Cavazos,* 923 F.2d 1434 (11th Cir. 1991), the court declined to accept the district's argument that the regulations implementing Section 504 were invalid because they require affirmative action. The court held that the line between what may be called affirmative action and what is illegal discrimination is not clear-cut. The court noted further that Supreme Court cases have not established "exactly how far the Secretary can go in requiring the modification of existing programs before he oversteps his authority." *Id.,* at 1438. See Chapter 2.

20. *Smith v. Robinson, supra* at 1018–19.

21. *Turillo, supra* at 587; and *Colin, supra* at 9. See also In the Matter of: DeKalb County School District, supra.

22. *Supra* at 1013.

23. Handicapped Children's Protection Act of 1986, Pub. L. No. 99-372, Section 3, 100 Stat. 796, Subsection 1415(f). See also *Digre v. Roseville School Independent District No. 623,* 841 F.2d 245 (8th Cir. 1988).

24. 832 F.2d 748, 756 (2d Cir. 1987). See also *Hayes v. Unified School District No. 377,* 877 F.2d 809, 812–13 (10th Cir. 1989).

25. *Rogers v. Bennett,* 873 F.2d 1387, 1396 (11th Cir. 1989).

26. *Eva N. v. Brock,* 741 F. Supp. 626 (E.D. Ky. 1990).

27. *Id.,* at 632.

28. *Southeastern Community College v. Davis, supra.*

29. *Eva N. v. Brock, supra* at 634.

30. The OCR has found that conditions such as Attention Deficit Disorder can be considered a handicap under Section 504. See the Department of Education's September 16, 1991, memorandum to the states regarding their responsibilities to students not eligible for special education pursuant to the IDEA, and the June 21, 1989, letter from Cathy H. Lewis, Acting Director, Policy and Enforcement Service, to Harvey Parker, Executive Director of Children with Attention Deficit Disorders.

31. See Mesa Unified School District Number Four, 6/28/88 LOF.

32. Appendix A, para. 23, p. 493.

33. Mesa Unified School District, *supra.* See also § 104.33(b)(2).

Part V Introduction

1. Appendix A, p. 495. See also § 104.41.
2. Civil Action No. 89-1670 (1st Cir. 1991); 908 F.2d 740 (11th Cir. 1990); and 926 F.2d 1368 (3rd Cir. 1991).

Chapter 20

1. See *Anderson v. University of Wisconsin,* 841 F.2d 737, 741 (7th Cir. 1988).
2. *University of Missouri v. Horowitz,* 435 U.S. 78, 92, 55 L.Ed. 2d 124 (1978).
3. *University of Michigan v. Ewing,* 474 U.S. 214, 220, 88 L.Ed.2d 523 (1985).
4. *Parate v. Isibor,* 868 F.2d 821, 827 (6th Cir. 1989).
5. *Doe v. New York University,* 666 F.2d 761, 776 (2nd Cir. 1981).
6. 442 U.S. 397 (1979).
7. 469 U.S. 287, 300 (1985).
8. *Alexander, supra* at 300–1 n. 20.
9. See *U.S. Board of Trustees of the University of Alabama, supra* at 748–49; *Wynne v. Tufts, supra;* and *Rogers v. Bennett,* 873 F.2d 1387 (11th Cir. 1989).
10. *Davis, supra* at 412–13.
11. The Supreme Court has articulated the following three-part test for discrimination cases:

> The plaintiff bears the initial burden of proving by a preponderance of evidence a *prima facie* case of discrimination. Once plaintiff has established a *prima facie* case, the burden shifts to the defendant to dispel this presumption of discrimination and articulate "some legitimate, nondiscriminatory reason for the employee's rejection." The ultimate burden of persuasion, which always rests with the plaintiff, may then be satisfied by proving by a preponderance of the evidence, that the allged reasons proffered by the defendant are pretextual.

See *Texas Dept. of Community Affairs v. Burdine,* 450 U.S. 248, 252–56, 67 L.Ed.2d 207 (1981).

12. *Wynne v. Tufts University, supra; Nathanson v. Medical College of Pennsylvania, supra; U.S. v. Board of Trustees of the University of Alabama, supra;* and *Pushkin v. Regents of the University of Colorado,* 658 F.2d 1372 (10th Cir. 1981).
13. *P.C. v. McLaughlin,* 913 F.2d 1033 (2nd Cir. 1990); *Villanueva v. Columbia University,* 746 F. Supp. 297 (S.D. N.Y. 1990); *Anderson v. University of Wisconsin, supra; Doe v. New York University, supra;* and *Doe v. Region 13 Mental Health–Mental Retardation Comm'n,* 704 F.2d 1402 (5th Cir. 1983).
14. *Wynne v. Tufts, supra* at 16.
15. *Id.,* at 18.
16. *Strathie v. Department of Transportation,* 716 F.2d 227, 231 (3d Cir. 1983). See also *Arline v. School Board of Nassau County,* 480 U.S. 273, 288 (1987).

Chapter 21

1. *Arline v. School Board of Nassau County, supra* at 277–80.
2. See § 104.4. See also Chapter 3.

3. *Southeastern Community College v. Davis, supra* at 405; *Doe v. Region 13 Mental Retardation Commission, supra; Pushkin v. Regents of the University of Colorado, supra;* and *Anderson v. University of Wisconsin, supra.*

4. *Alexander v. Choate, supra* at 301. See also *Kling v. County of Los Angeles,* 769 F.2d 532 (9th Cir. 1985).

5. Some evidence of actual discrimination must be shown to support a claim under the Act. See *Villanueva v. Columbia University, supra; P.C. v. McLaughlin, supra;* and *Fleming v. New York University,* 865 F.2d 478, 482 (2nd Cir. 1989).

6. See Chapter 6 for an in-depth discussion of the meaning of "otherwise qualified."

7. *Anderson v. University of Wisconsin, supra* at 740—"The Act forbids discrimination based on stereotypes," and *Arline, supra* at 287—"handicapped individuals must be protected from deprivation based on prejudice, stereotypes or unfounded fears."

8. *Davis, supra* at 406.

9. *Doe v. New York University, supra* at 776.

10. *Pushkin, supra* at 1391. See also *Kling v. County of Los Angeles,* 769 F.2d 532 (9th Cir. 1985).

11. *Anderson, supra* at 740. See also *Doe v. Washington* (E.D. Mo., October 2, 1991), a case in which the district court upheld a dental school's dismissal of a student who was HIV-positive "even though the risk of transmission . . . was not capable of precise measure."

12. *Davis, supra* at 406.

13. *Alexander, supra* at 299.

14. *Brennan v. Stewart,* 834 F.2d 1248 (5th Cir. 1988).

15. *Id.,* at 1262.

16. *Id.*

17. 862 F.2d 570 (6th Cir. 1988), *cert. denied,* 107 L.Ed.2d 22 (1989).

18. *Doherty, supra* at 575.

19. *Wynne v. Tufts, supra* at 16.

20. *Anderson, supra* at 741.

21. *Id.,* at 741. See also *Villanueva v. Columbia University, supra;* and *Fleming v. New York University, supra.*

22. 913 F.2d 1033, 1041 (2nd Cir. 1990).

23. The drafters of the regulation were conscious of the need to avoid major disruption of the established academic testing system. It was noted that proposed provision(s) of the regulations were revised based upon the concern of the professional testing services that the requirements would be too disruptive. See Appendix A, para. 29, p. 496.

24. See *Ability Testing of Handicapped People* (November 1981), National Academy Press.

25. OCR Policy Digest, Vol. 1, No. 2, p. 26; see also University of Washington, LOF-April 12, 1979.

26. Appendix A, para. 29, p. 496.

27. *Id.*

28. Connecticut State Department of Education, 3/13/1980 LOF.

29. See § 104.4(a).

30. *Doe v. Region 13, supra* at 1404.

31. *Southeastern Community College v. Davis, supra* at 405, 410–12.

32. *Doherty, supra* at 575.

33. See *Doe v. New York University, supra*—a case in which there was extensive

evidence that the student had a history of a mental disorder which resulted in her physically attacking others and injuring herself; *Anderson v. University of Wisconsin* — a student with a history of alcoholism who had harassed and threatened other students; and Tulsa Junior College-LOF 1985. See also Chapter 6.

34. See Maricopa County Community College LOF, 9/1978; and *Doe v. Syracuse School District*, 508 F. Supp. 333, 336–37 (N.D. N.Y. 1981).

35. Dolittle, EHLR 305:49 (1988).

36. See Memphis State University, 4/87 LOF.

37. Applicants self-identify; the information is provided in transcripts or letters of recommendation; flagging by testing services, etc.

38. *Horn v. Mitchell College*, 1984 LOF.

39. § 104.42(c).

Chapter 22

1. See Chapter 7 for a discussion of § 104.4.

2. Appendix A, paras. 30, 32, 34, pp. 496–98.

3. § 104.43(b).

4. See Dolan, EHLR 305:06 (1978).

5. Appendix A, para. 30, p. 496.

6. *Id.*

7. § 104.47(b).

8. Appendix A, para. 33, p. 497.

9. See *Fleming v. New York University*, 885 F.2d 478 (2nd Cir. 1989); and OCR's 6/30/81 Policy Memorandum.

10. Appendix A, para. 32, p. 497.

11. California State University System, LOF (1985).

12. Appendix A, para. 34, p. 498.

13. § 104.46(a)(2).

14. Appendix A states that this provision sets the same compliance standards as § 104.38 of Subpart D, and will be interpreted in a similar fashion. See Chapter 17 for a discussion of § 104.38.

15. 520 F. Supp. 489, 493 (E.D. Pa. 1981).

16. See 8/14/78 Dept. of HEW policy interpretations.

17. Whitworth College LOF (4/80).

18. 499 F. Supp. 496, *aff'd* 652 F.2d 445, *vacated on remand*, 458 U.S. 1102 702 F.2d 549 (5th Cir. 1983), *vacated as moot*, 464 U.S. 67, 78 L.Ed.2d 58 (1983), *on remand*, 722 F.2d 213.

19. *Id.*, at 504.

Chapter 23

1. § 104.44(a) — "Academic requirements. A recipient . . . shall make such modifications to its academic requirements as are necessary to ensure that such requirements do not discriminate or have the effect of discriminating, on the basis of handicap, against a qualified handicapped applicant or student . . . ," and (d) "Auxiliary aids (1) A recipient . . . shall take such steps as are necessary to ensure that no handicapped student is denied the benefits of, excluded from participation in, or

otherwise subjected to discrimination . . . because of the absence of educational auxiliary aids. . . ."

2. *U.S. v. Board of Trustees of the University of Alabama, supra* at 746–47.

3. *Nathanson, supra* at 1385. The court held that the student's need for a special chair to accommodate her back condition was the type of auxiliary aid contemplated under § 104.44(d).

4. *Tufts, supra* at 19–20.

5. *Id.* at 746–47. See also *Nathanson, supra* at 1386; and *Wynne v. Tufts, supra* at 10–16.

6. *Board of Trustees of the University of Alabama, supra* at 746.

7. *Tufts, supra* at 16.

8. See Chapters 3 and 20, *supra*. See also *Nathanson, supra* at 1386, *Tufts, supra* at 18, and *Board of Trustees of the University of Alabama, supra* at 750. Further, the regulations merely list examples of the types of modifications and auxiliary aids the recipient may be required to make or provide. [§§ 104.44(a) and (d)(2)]; it is *not* an exhaustive list.

9. § 104.44(a).

10. *Davis, supra* at 413.

11. *Doherty, supra* at 575.

12. *Nathanson, supra* at 1386.

13. § 104.44(a).

14. § 104.44(d)(2). It is important to note that the problem of faculty members not wishing to permit students to tape lectures is addressed in Appendix A. It is suggested that students be required "to sign agreements that they will not release the tape recording or transcription or otherwise hinder the professor's ability to obtain a copyright" (para. 31, p. 497). Therefore, it would not be permissible to deny a student the right to tape record solely on the basis of such an objection from a faculty member.

15. Appendix A, para. 31, p. 497.

16. See 1/28/81 letter from Mr. Burton Taylor, Postsecondary Division, OCR, to Mr. Darl Drumond, Affirmative Action Officer, Wisconsin Board of Vocational, Technical and Adult Education.

17. See *Board of Trustees of the University of Alabama, supra, Nathanson, supra; University of Texas v. Camenisch,* 616 F.2d 127 (5th Cir. 1980), *vacated as moot,* 451 U.S. 390, 68 L.Ed.2d (1981); and 1/28/81 letter from Burton Taylor (OCR) to Mr. Darl Drumond (Wisconsin Board of Vocational, Technical and Adult Education).

18. § 104.44(d)(2)—"Recipients need not provide attendants, individually prescribed devices, readers for personal use or study, or other devices or services of a personal nature." The OCR has defined the difference between services of a personal nature and auxiliary aids as being the difference between those things that are used by a student "primarily to cope with his or her disability" and those things used by a student "as a means of enjoying an educational opportunity equal to that enjoyed by nonhandicapped students." (See May 5, 1978, letter from the Assistant Attorney General [Mr. Hamlin] to Paul J. Forch.)

19. Para. 31, p. 497.

20. See *Wynne v. Tufts, supra; Davis, supra; Doherty, supra;* and University of Denver, LOF (11/23/78).

21. 402 N.W.2d 90 (Mich. Ct. App. 1986).

22. Lowell Area School District, EHLR 352:574, 575 (1987).

23. § 104.44(b)(4). See also *Nathanson, supra* at 1386.

24. *Nathanson, supra* at 1381.

25. *Id.*

26. See also *Salvador v. Bell,* 622 F. Supp. 438, 439, *aff'd* 800 F.2d 97 (7th Cir. 1986).

27. *Nathanson, supra* at 1386.

28. Appendix A, para. 31, p. 497.

29. *Id.* at 497. See also *Schornstein v. New Jersey Division of Vocational Rehabilitation Services,* 519 F. Supp. 773 (D. N.J. 1981); *Jones v. Illinois Department of Rehabilitation,* 689 F.2d 724 (7th Cir. 1982); and *Indiana Dept. of Human Services v. Firth* (Ind. App. No. 49 A02-9109-CV-413-4/15/92).

30. Cornell University, EHLR 257:02 (1978); and Louisiana Board of Elementary and Secondary Education, EHLR 352:218 (1986).

31. *University of Texas v. Camenisch, supra;* and *Barnes v. Converse College,* 436 F. Supp. 635 (D. S.C. 1977).

32. § 104.44(c). This section will be interpreted in the same way as § 104.42(b) which concerns admission tests.

33. See *Brennan v. Stewart, supra* at 1262; *Wynne v. Tufts, supra* at 16; and *Doherty v. Southern College of Optometry, supra.*

34. Brinckerhoff, L.C. "Establishing LD Support Services with Minimal Resources." *Journal of Postsecondary Education and Disability,* 8(2).

35. *Id.*

Chapter 24

1. See *Recanzone v. Washoe County School District,* 696 F. Supp. 1372, 1377 (D. Nev. 1988); and *Fitzgerald v. Green Valley Area Education Agency,* 589 F. Supp. 1130, 1136 (S.D. Iowa 1984)—"The prohibition of discrimination applies to job assignment and any other term or condition of employment."

2. *Consolidated Rail v. Darrone,* 465 U.S. 624 (1984); and *Meyerson v. State of Arizona,* 740 F.2d 684 (9th Cir. 1984). Therefore, a recipient may not challenge the applicability of Section 504 and its implementing regulations by asserting that the federal financial assistance provided to it was not for the specific purpose of providing employment.

3. *Davis, supra* at 405–6; *Alexander v. Choate, supra;* and *Arline, supra.*

4. Section 104.3(k)(1) defines a "qualified handicapped person" in the employment context as one "who, with reasonable accommodation, can perform the essential functions of the job in question." See Chapter 6 for a detailed discussion of this term. Remember that the denial of protection to a handicapped individual must be based upon a clear determination that he or she is not "qualified." It cannot be based upon "prejudice, stereotypes, or unfounded fear." *Arline, supra* at 287.

5. See Chapter 2 regarding the nondiscrimination mandate. See also *Alexander, supra* at 304; *Traynor v. Turnage,* 485 U.S. 535, 548, 99 L.Ed.2d 618 (1988); and *P.C. v. McLaughlin, supra* at 1041.

6. *Supra* at 405.

7. *Anderson v. University of Wisconsin,* 841 F.2d 737, 740 (7th Cir. 1988); and *Doe v. Region 13 Mental Health–Mental Retardation Commission,* 704 F.2d 1402 (5th Cir. 1983).

8. *Swann v. Walters,* 620 F. Supp. 741, 747 (D. D.C. 1984).

9. 551 F. Supp. 27 (D. D.C. 1982).

10. *Supra* at 31–32. See also *Crane v. Dole,* 617 F. Supp. 156, 158–9 (D.D.C. 1985).

11. *Supra* at 159. See also *Southeastern Community College v. Davis, supra* at 405: "Mere possession of a handicap is not a permissible ground for assuming an inability to function in a particular context."

12. *Dexler v. Tisch, supra.*

13. *Supra* at 1426.

14. *Supra* at 1427.

15. *Serrapica v. City of New York,* 708 F. Supp. 64 (D.D. N.Y. 1989).

16. *Jackson v. Maine,* 544 A.2d 291, 298 (Me. 1988).

17. See *Arline, supra* at 284–87; *Davis, supra* at 405; *Bentivegna v. United States Department of Labor,* 694 F.2d 619, 623 (9th Cir. 1982); *Crane v. Dole, supra; Fitzgerald v. Green Valley Education Agency, supra;* and *Carter v. Casa Central,* 849 F.2d 1048 (7th Cir. 1988).

18. Examples of relationships which are addressed under § 104.11(a)(4) include "employment and referral agencies, . . . labor unions, organizations providing or administering fringe benefits . . . and . . . organizations providing training and apprenticeship programs."

Regarding insurance plans, the OCR has held that it is not a violation to exclude treatment for particular conditions, such as alcoholism, from coverage under such plans. The OCR expressly stated that "to find otherwise would require the recipient to insure against every conceivable mental or physical condition that might require treatment." Section 504 does, however, "protect handicapped employees from being excluded or otherwise restricted in their eligibility for those fringe benefits that are available to nonhandicapped employees." (See OCR Policy Memorandum, 5/79.)

19. 733 F.2d 1367, 1369–70 (10th Cir. 1984). See also *Jasany v. United States Postal Service,* 755 F.2d 1244, 1251–52 (6th Cir. 1985); and *Shea v. Tisch,* 870 F.2d 786 (1st Cir. 1989).

20. A recipient that receives assistance under the Education of the Handicapped Act shall take positive steps to employ and advance in employment qualified handicapped persons in programs assisted under the Act. See also *Fitzgerald v. Green Valley Education Agency, supra* at 1136–37.

21. Appendix A, para. 15, p. 488.

22. Section 501 of the Rehabilitation Act requires federal agencies to take affirmative steps in hiring, placement and advancement of handicapped individuals. See *Southeastern Community College v. Davis, supra* at 410–11; *Rhone v. Department of Army,* 665 F. Supp. 734 (E.D. Mo. 1987); and *Dexler v. Tisch,* 660 F. Supp. 1418, 1425 (D. C.D. Conn. 1987).

Chapter 25

1. *Perez v. Philadelphia Housing Authority,* 677 F. Supp. 357 (E.D. Pa. 1987), aff'd 841 F.2d 1120 (3rd Cir. 1988).

2. *Davis, supra* at 412–13; and *Alexander, supra* at 300–303.

3. *Brennan v. Stewart, supra* at 1261–62; *Recanzone v. Washoe County School District, supra;* and *Crane v. Dole, supra.*

4. § 104.12(a).

5. *Dexler v. Tisch, supra* at 1426.

6. § 104.12(b) "(1) making facilities . . . readily accessible to and usable by handicapped persons, and (2) job restructuring, part-time or modified work

schedules, acquisition or modification of equipment or devices, the provision of readers or interpreters."

7. § 104.12(a).

8. *Alexander, supra* at 301 n. 21.

9. *Strathie v. Department of Transportation,* 716 F.2d 227, 231; and *Arline, supra* at 287 n. 17.

10. *Alexander, supra* at 300. See also Chapter 2 for a detailed discussion of the recipient's responsibility to provide reasonable accommodations.

11. § 104.12(c): "[F]actors to be considered include: (1) The overall size of the recipient's program; . . . number of employees, number and type of facilities, and size of budget; (2) The type of recipient's operation . . . and (3) The nature and cost of the accommodation." See also *Arline, supra* at 287 n. 17.

12. Appendix A, para. 16, p. 489.

13. *Carter v. Tisch,* 822 F.2d 465 (4th Cir. 1987); and *Jasany v. United States Postal Service, supra* at 1250. *Note:* Under the Americans with Disabilities Act, employers are required to consider reassigning employees to a vacant position as an accommodation.

14. *Treadwell v. Alexander,* 707 F.2d 473, 478 (11th Cir. 1983).

15. *Davis, supra* at 412–13.

16. While many of these cases involve the application of Section 501, which imposes an affirmative action obligation, they are still instructive regarding the interpretation of "undue hardship," despite the fact that a less stringent standard is applied under Section 504.

17. 567 F. Supp. 369 (E.D. Pa. 1983).

18. 691 F. Supp. 1223 (W.D. Mo. 1988).

19. 662 F. 2d 292 (5th Cir. 1981).

20. 696 F. Supp. 1372 (D. Nev. 1988).

21. 739 F. Supp. 974 (E.D. Pa. 1990).

22. 707 F.2d 473 (11th Cir. 1983).

23. 660 F. Supp. 1418 (D. C.D. Conn. 1987).

24. 696 F. Supp. 674 (D.C. 1987).

25. 840 F.2d 1139 (3rd Cir. 1988).

26. *Jasany v. United States Postal Service, supra* at 1250.

27. *Carter v. Casa Central, supra* at 1055–56. See also Chapter 6.

28. *Carter v. Bennett,* 840 F.2d 63 (D.C. Cir. 1988). See also Appendix A, para. 16, p. 488.

29. *Carter v. Bennett, supra* at 67–68.

30. 685 F. Supp. 153, 156 n.3 (E.D. Tex. 1988). See also *Butler v. Department of the Navy,* 595 F. Supp. 1063, 1066 (D.D. Maryland, 1984).

31. *Crane v. Lewis, supra.* See also Chapter 23, discussion of *Nathanson.*

32. *Shea v. Tisch,* 870 F.2d 786 (1st Cir. 1989); and *Franklin v. Postal Service,* 687 F. Supp. 1214 (S.D. Ohio 1988).

33. Appendix A, para. 16, p. 488.

Chapter 26

1. *Doe v. Region 13 Mental Health–Mental Retardation Commission, supra* at 1410–12.

2. *Davis, supra* at 406–8.

3. *Davis, supra* at 406–8; *Simon v. St. Louis County,* 735 F.2d 1082, 1084 (8th Cir. 1984); and *Treadwell v. Alexander, supra* at 475.
4. § 104.13(a)(2).
5. See Chapter 21.
6. 694 F.2d 666 (11th Cir. 1983).
7. *Stutts, supra* at 668.
8. Para. 17, p. 489.

Chapter 27

1. 508 F. Supp. 333 (N.D. N.Y. 1981).
2. § 104.14(a).
3. Appendix A, para. 18, p. 489.
4. *Id.*
5. *Doe v. Syracuse, supra* at 336–37.
6. *Burka v. New York City Transit Authority,* 680 F. Supp. 590, 597–601; and *Davis v. Bucher,* 451 F. Supp. 791 (E.D. Pa. 1978). See also Section 512 of the Americans with Disabilities Act which amends Section 504 with respect to alcoholism and drug addiction. It provides that current illegal drug users and those whose use of alcohol prevents them from performing the essential functions of the job are not entitled to protection under Section 504.
7. *Id.* at 601.
8. Appendix A, para. 18, p. 490. See also § 104.14(c).

Chapter 28

1. *Rothschild v. Grottenthaler,* 907 F.2d 286, 289–90 (2nd Cir. 1990). See also *Doherty v. Southern College of Optometry,* 862 F.2d 570, 573 (6th Cir. 1988); *Doe v. New York University,* 666 F.2d 761, 774–75 (2nd Cir. 1981); and *Pushkin v. Regents of University of Colorado,* 658 F.2d 1372, 1384 (10th Cir. 1981).
2. See Chapter 4 for a discussion of this issue.
3. *Arline, supra* at 279, 283–85.
4. *Doherty v. Southern College of Optometry, supra* at 573; *Doe v. New York University, supra* at 776–77; *Pushkin v. Regents of University of Colorado, supra* at 1386–87; and *Wynne v. Tufts University,* No. 89-1670 (1st Cir. 1991).
5. *Doe v. New York University, supra* at 776.
6. *Supra* at 776: "The burden then shifts to the institution or employer to rebut the inference that the handicap was improperly taken into account by going forward with evidence that the handicap is relevant to qualifications for the position sought."
7. *Supra* at 16–18; *Strathie v. Department,* 716 F.2d 227 (3rd Cir. 1983); and *Arline, supra* at 287–88. See also Chapters 3 and 20 regarding the recipient's responsibility to justify decisions that result in the denial of services, benefits, and opportunities to handicapped persons.
8. *Supra* at 299 n. 19.
9. See *P.C. v. McLaughlin,* 913 F.2d 1033, 1041–42 (2nd Cir. 1990); *Pendleton v. Jefferson Local School District,* 754 F. Supp. 570 (S.D. Ohio 1990); *Villanueva v. Columbia University,* 746 F. Supp. 297 (S.D. N.Y. 1990); and *Fleming v. New York University,* 865 F.2d 478, 482 (2nd Cir. 1989).
10. *Supra* at 292.

11. *Supra* at 295–97.

12. *Supra* at 1385. See also *Nathanson v. Medical College of Pennsylvania,* 926 F.2d 1368, 1384 (3rd Cir. 1991); and *New Mexico Assn. for Retarded Citizens v. New Mexico,* 678 F.2d 847, 854 (10th Cir. 1982).

Chapter 29

1. Appendix A, p. 492.

2. *Hendrick Hudson Central School District v. Rowley,* 458 U.S. 176, 206–7; and *University of Michigan v. Ewing,* 474 U.S. 214, 220, 88 L.Ed.2d 523 (1985).

3. See *Rowley, supra* at 206–7.

Chapter 30

1. See *Nathanson, supra* at 1385; and *Garrity v. Gallen,* 522 F. Supp. 171, 207 (D. New Hamp., 1981).

2. See *Doherty v. Southern College of Optometry, supra;* and *Barnett v. Fairfax County School Board,* 927 F.2d 146 (4th Cir. 1991).

3. See *The United States v. Board of Trustees of the University of Alabama, supra;* and *Freeman v. Cavazos,* 923 F.2d 1434 (11th Cir. 1991).

Index